CAMBRIDGE UNIVERSITY LIBRARY
GENIZAH SERIES 8

# Targumic Manuscripts in the
# Cambridge Genizah Collections

Cambridge University Library
Genizah Series
Edited by S. C. Reif

1. The Cambridge Genizah Collections: Their Contents and Significance, edited by Stefan C. Reif (2002)

2. Hebrew Bible Manuscripts in the Cambridge Genizah Collections
   Volume 1   Taylor-Schechter Old Series and other Genizah Collections in Cambridge University Library,
      by M. C. Davis, incorporating material compiled by H. Knopf (1978)
   Volume 2   Taylor-Schechter New Series, and Westminster College Cambridge Collection,
      by M. C. Davis (1980)
   Volume 3   Taylor-Schechter Additional Series 1-31, by M. C. Davis and Ben Outhwaite (2003)
   Volume 4   Taylor-Schechter Additional Series 32-225, with addenda to previous volumes,
      by M. C. Davis and Ben Outhwaite (2003)

3. Miscellany of Literary Pieces from the Cambridge Genizah Collections, by Simon Hopkins (1978)

4. Vocalised Talmudic Manuscripts in the Cambridge Genizah Collections
   Volume 1   Taylor-Schechter Old Series, by Shelomo Morag (1988)

5. A Hand-list of Rabbinic Manuscripts in the Cambridge Genizah Collections
   Volume 1   Taylor-Schechter New Series, by Robert Brody (1998)

6. Published Material from the Cambridge Genizah Collections: A Bibliography 1896-1980,
   edited by Stefan C. Reif (1988)

7. Palestinian Vocalised Piyyut Manuscripts in the Cambridge Genizah Collections, by J. Yahalom (1997)

8. Targumic Manuscripts in the Cambridge Genizah Collections, by Michael L. Klein (1992)

9. Karaite Bible Manuscripts from the Cairo Genizah, by Geoffrey Khan (1990)

10. Arabic Legal and Administrative Documents in the Cambridge Genizah Collections,
    by Geoffrey Khan (1993)

11. Medical and Para-medical Manuscripts in the Cambridge Genizah Collections,
    by Haskell D. Isaacs, with the assistance of Colin F. Baker (1994)

12. Arabic and Judaeo-Arabic Manuscripts in the Cambridge Genizah Collections, Arabic Old Series,
    by Colin F. Baker and Meira Polliack (2001)

13. Published Material from the Cambridge Genizah Collections: A Bibliography 1980-1997,
    compiled by Rebecca J. W. Jefferson and Erica C. D. Hunter (2004)

14. Arabic and Judaeo-Arabic Manuscripts in the Cambridge Genizah Collections, New Series,
    by Avihai Shivtiel and Friedrich Niessen (2006)

# TARGUMIC MANUSCRIPTS IN THE CAMBRIDGE GENIZAH COLLECTIONS

MICHAEL L. KLEIN

CAMBRIDGE
UNIVERSITY PRESS

This edition reprinted by Archaeopress by arrangement with
Cambridge University Press and Cambridge University Library

First published by Cambridge University Press 1992

© Cambridge University Library 2006

ISBN 1 905739 03 6

ARCHAEOPRESS PUBLISHING LTD
13-14 Market Square
Bicester
Oxfordshire
OX26 6AD
United Kingdom

info@archaeopress.com
www.archaeopress.com

To Shoshi,
Mattan, Elad,
Rachel and Ruth,
who all shared in the
wonderful Cambridge experience

## CONTENTS

| | |
|---|---|
| INTRODUCTION | *page* ix |
| SHORT TITLE INDEX | xv |
| DESCRIPTIONS OF MANUSCRIPTS | 1 |
| DECORATIONS IN MANUSCRIPTS | 121 |
| CANONICAL INDEX | 127 |
| GENERAL INDEX | 133 |
| PLATES | 137 |

# INTRODUCTION

One of the criteria for judging the usefulness of a manuscript collection is its accessibility to scholars for scientific research. That accessibility can be defined on several levels, the most elementary of which is permitting scholars to visit and study the collection *in situ*. An extension of this physical accessibility consists in making the manuscripts available in microform at other centres of learning throughout the world. And whereas in most cases of ancient or medieval manuscripts the microform copy cannot fully substitute for the original, it can facilitate much of the preliminary research. Indeed, it is now about ten years since the Cambridge Genizah Collections became fully available on microfilm, as is much of the manuscript collection of the Jewish Theological Seminary in New York.[1]

The highest level of accessibility entails providing users with an indexed, descriptive catalogue. This is especially important in the unparalleled case of the Cambridge Genizah Collections, where the mass of material is so great and of so many varied categories. The size of the collection – over 140,000 fragments – as well as the poor state of survival of many pieces, rendered the task almost impossible until recent times. It is only with the completion of a conservation project, under the direction of Dr Stefan C. Reif, that scholars can now conveniently scan the entire collection and systematically describe each of its manuscripts and printed fragments. And even here, the task is not a simple one. Each individual researcher or small team of scholars must review the *entire* collection in order to identify all of the fragments in any particular subject, since, for various historical reasons, not every example is to be found in the appropriately titled binder. In the present case, for instance, targum manuscripts were discovered in binders (originally boxes) listed as Bible, Bible translations, Massorah, Liturgy, Arabic, Talmud, Responsa, Magical texts and Documents.[2]

In the past, scholars spending periods of time at the Cambridge Genizah Unit tended to gravitate toward those binders that were likely to contain material in their respective fields of research. They did not usually have the time to scan the entire collection. There are two outstanding exceptions. Malcolm C. Davis spent several years in Cambridge preparing a 4-volume catalogue of the Bible manuscripts, two of which have already appeared and serve as a model for the entire series.[3] In all, Davis described some 25,000 fragments of biblical text. He provided an entry for *every* manuscript in the Bible binders, even if their subject was not Bible, and full listings for all Hebrew Bible manuscripts regardless of where they were found. However, he did not describe fragments of Bible in translation or multi-lingual texts containing the Hebrew version plus one or more translations, unless they had been mistakenly placed in a binder entitled "Bible". As a result, most of the 1,600 targum fragments described in the present volume fell outside the purview of Davis' catalogue.

The second scholar to go through the *entire* Cambridge Collection is Dr Robert Brody of the Hebrew University in Jerusalem. Coincidentally, he and I spent the 1987–88 academical year at the Genizah Research Unit. Although his particular interest lies in geonic writings, and his project for the year was to prepare a complete handlist of Rabbinica in the Cambridge Genizah Collections, he was extremely helpful in identifying a number of targumic pieces, particularly those that are to be found among the Arabic manuscripts.

Having been granted a sabbatical from Hebrew Union College in 1987–88, I was able to devote almost the entire year to documenting the targum manuscripts in Cambridge. The yield of this effort was very satisfying indeed – the identification of some 1,600 fragments of Targum of every known genre and form, as well as the discovery of text-types that had previously gone unnoticed.

As is to be expected, the collection includes over 1,000 fragments (=63%) of Onqelos, spanning the entire gamut from unilingual Aramaic texts with and without Hebrew lemmata, to

---

[1] Most recently, Hebrew Union College, with the assistance of a grant from the National Endowment for the Humanities, has undertaken a project to microfilm the entire Hebrew manuscript collection of the Jewish National and University Library in Jerusalem.

[2] See S. C. Reif (ed.), *Published Material from the Cambridge Genizah Collections. A Bibliography 1896-1980*. Cambridge: Cambridge University Press for Cambridge University Library, 1988. Introduction.

[3] M. C. Davis, *Hebrew Bible Manuscripts in the Cambridge Genizah Collections*, Cambridge: Cambridge University Press for Cambridge University Library, vol. 1, 1978; vol. 2, 1980.

bilingual fragments of Hebrew and Aramaic or Aramaic and Judaeo-Arabic, and to trilingual texts containing the Hebrew massoretic version, Targum Onqelos, and the Judaeo-Arabic translation of Saadya. Most of the multi-lingual texts are interlinear, giving the sequence of languages alternately, verse by verse. Some manuscripts, however, assign the various versions to parallel columns or even to opposite pages. There are abbreviated texts of Onqelos in which only the opening words of each verse, or the first letters of each word, are provided. These economical "shorthand" forms are commonly known for the Hebrew Bible, but were hitherto unattested for the targumim. Another newly discovered genre is the fragment-targum of Onqelos, in which only the non-standard words and phrases are preserved for each verse. This targum-type had previously been known only for the Palestinian targum to the Pentateuch. It is now recorded in several exemplars for Onqelos as well. One of the fragment-targums of Onqelos is a text that was already known and had been identified as a Massorah text "with hardly any massoretic notations".[4] We need no longer resort to such a description, now that additional examples of fragment-targum have made their appearance in the Genizah collection.

There are, of course, a number of fragments of Massorah to Onqelos, several of them newly identified, and at least one that belongs to a manuscript, fragments of which have already been published. Among the many other targum-types listed in the present catalogue are newly discovered fragments of Palestinian Targum and Palestinian Fragment-targum to the Pentateuch. Significant among them are additions to MSS D, E (Kahle-Klein) and H (Klein). We now have fragments of MS E to the Book of Exodus, in addition to the extensive portions from Genesis that have already been published. This increases the likelihood that this early manuscript of Palestinian Targum originally encompassed the entire Pentateuch. The discovery of an additional page of MS H has clarified its status as a fragment-targum. Finally, there is one fragment of Palestinian Targum with Judaeo-Arabic translation (T-S Ar.50.118).

Also noted in the present catalogue are targumic toseftot to the Pentateuch and the Prophets, either as insertions in running targum or as anthologies that had been collected in separate booklets. There are many newly discovered Aramaic poems in the collection. These include the extension of a poem in praise of the month of Nisan אליסון מה משבח הדין ירחא of which only three lines had been known; the only Genizah copy of a dirge on the death of Moses אזלת יוכבד; two copies of an Aramaic introductory poem to the targum of the haftarah, praising Jonathan ben Uzziel, the traditional author of the Targum to Prophets; and a lengthy new poem to the Scroll of Esther. Over 400 fragments (=25%) of targum to Prophets are represented, primarily in haftarah collections which are either unilingual or bilingual. Some of these manuscripts are of special importance because they preserve haftarah selections which are unattested in both the annual and triennial cycles. There are also trilingual manuscripts of the Prophets with Hebrew, Targum Jonathan and Judaeo-Arabic (e.g., T-S Ar.26.110). There are some fragments of targum which are likely to have come from complete books, or perhaps even from copies of the entire Prophets. The targums to Hagiographa are very sparse, most of the holdings belonging to Psalms, Proverbs, Song of Solomon and the Esther Scroll. Finally, the collection contains a few fragments with mediaeval commentaries, such as Rashi or Radaq, in addition to the Aramaic targum.

## Description of the Fragments

### 1. Classmarks:

The catalogue follows the order established by the editor for the catalogues of the Cambridge Collections, namely, Old Series, Bound Volumes, Arabic, Miscellaneous, New Series, Additional Series, Oriental and Westminster. The entries in each category are according to classmarks. In the case of fragments identified as part of the same original manuscript, a cross-reference is provided in parenthesis. For example: Or.1080 B18.1 (=T-S B13.4; NS 218.61). This indicates that the fragments from the Old Series and New Series belong to the same manuscript as the fragment from the Oriental collection that is being described in the entry. Such identifications were prompted by memory and checked by comparing the actual fragments. Since the catalogue was written over a period of almost a full year, many associations will not have been made, and

---

[4] Cf. I. Yeivin, "A Fragment of a Masoretic Treatise to the Pentateuch and Targum Onkelos", *Henoch Yalon Memorial Volume*, eds. E. Y. Kutscher, S. Lieberman and M. Z. Kaddari, Jerusalem, 1974, p. 158.

become the task of future scholars who study the texts in greater depth. The recording of these identifications is of special importance, in the light of the policy of the Genizah Research Unit not to alter classmarks nor physically to transfer fragments for reunification with others of the same manuscript, in order to avoid confusion in the location and citation of the material.

## 2. Canonical References:

The canonical reference in the Bible is provided for each text. Only in very few instances in the Additional Series, where identification was impossible due to the extremely poor state of preservation of the fragment, has the text been denoted as "unidentified". In the case of discontinuous text, the folio numbers are generally provided for each segment, and obvious haftarah selections are indicated as such. The definite identification of haftarot was not, however, always possible. Most frequently the fragments contain portions of several consecutive unrelated passages from Targum to Prophets or a heading at the beginning of a haftarah. Occasionally, the reading from Prophets follows directly after a pentateuchal passage, making certain the identification as an annual or triennial haftarah. There are, however, quite a number of examples of single passages from the Prophets, where probability favours their belonging to popular haftarah manuscripts (e.g., Judges 5; 2 Samuel 22; Ezekiel 37; Jonah; Habakkuk 3), but from which all identifying signs were absent. I was generally conservative in identifying these fragments merely as "Targum Jonathan to Prophets".

## 3. Language and Translation:

The languages of the texts are noted and the particular Aramaic targum identified. For targumic toseftot and poems the Aramaic dialect is also indicated. Hebrew is noted as a primary language, only if complete verses are given in Hebrew; otherwise, the presence of Hebrew lemmata is merely noted in parenthesis after the listing of the primary languages. As to Judaeo-Arabic, no attempt has been made to determine whether the translations diverge from the *Tafsir* of Saadya Gaon. Although as a rule the Judaeo-Arabic Bible translations may be assumed to be Saadya's, careful study by a specialist may eventually produce surprising results, just as traces of pre-Saadyan orthography have recently been discovered among the Genizah fragments.

## 4. Physical Description:

Each fragment is described according to the following features:

a. Material: paper or vellum. No distinction has been made between the various types of skin, all being termed "vellum" – except for a very thick brown skin which was called "leather". Likewise, no details are given of the various types of paper, except for the one watermark discerned in T-S B1.5, dating to the late fifteenth century.

b. Leaves: the number of leaves is given, with the number of conjoined leaves in parenthesis. Thus, if a fragment comprises 7 leaves, 4 of which are conjoined, the notation would be: 7 leaves (2 bifolia). Additional details might appear at the end of an entry, as in the case of a 2-column leaf that had been folded vertically along its centre margin, imparting the false impression of a bifolium (T-S NS 174.54).

c. State of Preservation: for the most part relates to mutilation of the vellum or paper and to the legibility of the script. The term "badly mutilated" has been used if the fragment is badly damaged and up to half the leaf destroyed; "very badly mutilated" implies that more than half of the leaf is missing. It may be noted in this regard that, in general, the relative condition of the fragments deteriorates progressively as one goes from pre-Schechterian manuscripts such as the Oriental Series to the Old Series, New Series, and finally to the smallest and most damaged fragments in the Additional Series. This, of course, reflects the history of the Cambridge Genizah Collection, in which the well-preserved and more readily decipherable material was catalogued first. And as will surely be retold by Dr Reif in his general introduction to the entire catalogue series, at one dormant stage in this history, someone at the University Library even suggested that all of the fragments in what was to become the Additional Series be classified as valueless.

Fortunately, this never transpired.

The physical description continues with the measurements of each fragment, height x width in centimetres. The dimensions provided are maximal, i.e., the largest measurements taken in either direction for a single leaf including margins. This can be deceptive. An L-shaped fragment of mostly empty margin but of large dimensions will be far less valuable than a smaller medial fragment that is full of text. The plus (+) sign has been used to indicate that a fragment is mutilated and that the full measurement in that direction is not available. In cases where a full measurement could be estimated, either by the reconstruction of missing lines in the text (for height) or by multiplying the width of a column and margin by the assumed number of columns (for width), the reconstructed dimensions are given in square brackets [ ]. The same has been done for the number of columns and lines that follow in each entry. Wherever reconstruction was not possible, the number of columns reflects only those actually preserved, although there may originally have been more. The number of columns is provided only if it is greater than one.

d. Script: the description of the script is given in terms of basic geographical origin, the main categories being Oriental, Spanish, Yemenite and Ashkenazi. There are a number of fragments that have tentatively been identified either as Persian(?), Italian/Spanish or North African, respectively. In general, however, no distinction has been made between North African, Palestinian and other Eastern Mediterranean scripts, which have all been denoted as "Oriental". Many of the geographical identifications are based upon comparisons with samples of similar scripts contained in the monumental work by C. Sirat and M. Beit Arié, *Manuscrits médiévaux en caractères hebraïques portant des indications de date jusqu'à 1540*, Vols. I-III, Paris-Jerusalem 1972, 1979, 1986.[5] The scripts have been further described as square, semi-cursive or cursive. Also, variations in the size of the script within a single fragment are noted under this rubric. However, no attempt has been made at dating the fragments.

e. Vocalisation: Vowels and accents have been noted according to the general categories of Tiberian, Babylonian, Palestinian or unpointed. Sub-divisions of simple or complicated systems within these categories have not been recorded. It may generally be assumed that the vocalisation is present throughout the fragment, unless specifically indicated as "sporadic". Manuscripts containing a mixture of systems are denoted as such, just as the presence of differently coloured inks is recorded. It is, in fact, quite common for the vocalisation to be in a different ink from that of the consonantal text, since it was often separately added by a special scribe (*naqdan*), or long after the manuscript had first been in use, by another hand.

f. Additional Information: This is a miscellaneous rubric which subsumes under one heading idiosyncratic details of the manuscripts and texts. In addition to the intrinsic value of these sundry details, many of the items may prove helpful in the dating of fragments, identifying their geographic origins, and in identifying fragments with one another, as belonging to a single manuscript. Some characteristics will no doubt be peculiar to an individual scribe or school of scribes.

We have consistently noted the form of representation of the divine name. Whereas in manuscripts of the Hebrew Bible the tetragrammaton, YHWH, is usually copied intact, in the context of targum texts it is most frequently transformed into the generic "Lord", 'DNY, or into abbreviations of one, two or three *yod*s with many variations. However, in very old scrolls[6] and in a few codices, the tetragrammaton appears in the targum as well.

Headings, colophons, and records of ownership are noted, and at least the essence of their texts is recorded.

The notation of parashot, sidrot, ciphers for the number of verses in a weekly synagogal lection are generally recorded, as well as majusculae that were employed by the scribes to denote the beginning of sections. Likewise, the use of illumination or other decorative script to indicate parashot, sidrot or catchwords at the end of quires has been noted by the sign ❂ in the respective

---

[5] I also had the benefit of personally consulting with Professor Malachi Beit Arié and Mrs Edna Engel, M.A., of the Hebrew Palaeography Project in Jerusalem, regarding the identification of a number of problematic fragments. I am grateful for their kind assistance.

[6] E.g., MS A (Kahle-Klein); cf M. Bregman, "An Early Fragment of *Avot de Rabbi Natan* from a Scroll", *Tarbiz* 52 (1983), pp. 205–6.

entries, and reproduced in plates at the end of the catalogue.

Scribal practices such as the special layout of pages for poetic passages, the use of "rabbinic bible" format of several columns of varied size and shape, abbreviations and unusual *custodes* to complete lines, and blank folios between books or sections of works have all been recorded. We have also noted under this miscellaneous rubric evidence of the participation of more than one scribe in the writing of a single manuscript, e.g., different handwritings or different colours of ink. This is especially important in the case of marginal and interlinear glosses, as well as in scribal errors that have been corrected in the manuscript.

Massoretic notes to Onqelos, calendrical and liturgical instructions, and rules regarding "forbidden targumim" that were not to be recited in the public, synagogal reading of the Torah and Targum are all carefully presented in their respective entries. We have also noted the repetitive sections of the Bible (e.g., Numbers 7), for which the scribe did not provide the full targum, out of considerations of economy.

Pen exercises are denoted as such, as are scribal errors that seem to have brought the scribe to abandon an entire folio. This should spare future scholars the chore of searching for the continuation of these fragments, which almost certainly never existed.

## 5. Bibliography:

A comprehensive bibliography of all references in scholarly publications to the Cambridge Genizah manuscripts has recently been produced by the Genizah Research Unit. The appearance of the first volume covering the literature up to 1980[7] and the continuation of this project for subsequent publications made redundant the inclusion of full bibliographical references in the present catalogue. It was, therefore, decided that the bibliographical section at the end of appropriate entries would include only references to *texts actually published* and not those merely mentioned in other publications.

## 6. Plates:

Twenty-four fragments have been reproduced in facsimile on plates at the end of the volume. They represent most of the major text-types and scribal variations in the collection. There is a reference note at the end of each entry in which the manuscript was selected for inclusion among the plates.

## Acknowledgements

From the time of Solomon Schechter in Cambridge until quite recently, scholars studying or cataloguing various boxes of manuscripts were wont to insert paper notes containing identifications or other observations that they happened to make in the process of their work. Many of the notes are anonymous; others are initialed or signed; still others may be identified by their handwriting. The information contained in these notes was generally accurate, and spared me much initial footwork. A relative "newcomer" to Genizah studies as myself must be grateful to the pioneers of past decades who laid much of the groundwork for those who followed.

More specific thanks go to Dr Geoffrey Khan[8] of the Genizah Research Unit and to Dr Robert Brody, sabbatical colleague, for their continuous friendship and kind assistance with every aspect of the manuscripts. To Professor Anthony Low, President of Clare Hall and Mr John Garrod, Bursar, I am grateful for the appointment as Visiting Fellow at Cambridge University and for the privilege of living at College. It was in that congenial and intellectually stimulating setting that the present work was produced. I am thankful to Dr Alfred Gottschalk, President of Hebrew Union College, who made the sabbatical year possible under such favourable conditions as to allow me to devote all of my time to the research for which the sabbatical was intended.

My deepest appreciation to Dr Stefan C. Reif for his warm hospitality and full confidence throughout the project. This found expression in the arrangements he made for my appointment as Visiting Research Associate at the Cambridge University Library with all the appertaining

---

[7] See note 2, above.

[8] The many interpretations of Arabic texts made by Dr Khan are noted throughout this catalogue by the bracketed initials "[GK]".

privileges, and for the inclusion of the present catalogue in the *Genizah Series* which he edits. He arranged for me to have full access to the University Library, in addition to the Genizah Collections, and provided ample working space within the Unit.

Mrs Shulie Reif computer-processed and sub-edited the several drafts of the volume with remarkable devotion and patience. To both Dr and Mrs Reif my heartfelt thanks for the personal friendship and professional co-operation that intensified during the course of the year.

Mrs Leticia Barda, of the Nelson Glueck School of Biblical Archaeology, Hebrew Union College, Jerusalem, produced the drawings of the illuminations and decorative script. I am thankful to her and to Dr Avraham Biran, Director of the School.

My sincere thanks to the University Librarian, Dr F. W. Ratcliffe, the University Library staff, and especially members of the Manuscripts Department, for their kind assistance in every matter.

Finally, my appreciation to Dr John Dawson of the Literary and Linguistic Computing Centre and Dr Douglas de Lacey for providing the specialised computer expertise.

# SHORT TITLE INDEX

C. M. Briquet = C. M. BRIQUET, *Briquet's Opuscula, monumenta Chertae Papyraceae Historiam Illustrantia* IV, Hilversum, 1955.

Davis, *HBMCGC* = M. C. DAVIS, *Hebrew Bible Manuscripts in the Cambridge Genizah Collections*, Cambridge, vol. I, 1978; vol. II, 1980.

Díez Macho, *Augustinianum* IX = A. DÍEZ MACHO, "Un nuevo fragmento del Targum Palestinense a Genesis", *Augustinianum* IX (1969), pp. 120–23.

Díez Macho, *EB* XVI = A. DÍEZ MACHO, "Nuevos manuscritos bíblicos babilonicos", *Estudios Biblicos* XVI (1957), pp. 235–77.

Díez Macho, *Manuscritos Hebreos y Arameos* = A. DÍEZ MACHO, *Manuscritos Hebreos y Arameos de la Biblia*, Rome, 1971.

Díez Macho, *Sefarad* XVI, = A. DÍEZ MACHO, "Nuevos Fragmentos de Tosefta Targumica", *Sefarad* XVI (1956), pp. 313–24; "Fragmento de una nueva recension del Targum Jonatan ben 'Uzziel a los Profetas", *Sefarad* XVI (1956), pp. 405–6.

Díez Macho, *Sefarad* XIX, = A. DÍEZ MACHO, "Un manuscrito babilonico de Onqelos en el que se confunden los timbres vocalicos *pataḥ* y *qameṣ*. *Sefarad* XIX (1959), pp. 273–82.

Fleischer, *Tarbiẓ* XXXVII = E. FLEISCHER, "The Great New Moon", *Tarbiẓ* XXXVII (1967–68), pp. 265–78.

Fuste Ara, *EB* XV = R. FUSTE ARA, "El fragmento targúmico T-S B3 de la Biblioteca Universitaria de Cambridge", *Estudios Biblicos* XV (1956), pp. 85–94.

Grelot, *REJ* XVI = P. GRELOT, "Une tosephta targoumique sur Genèse XXII dans un manuscrit liturgique de la Geniza du Caire", *Revue des Études Juives* N.S. XVI (1957), pp. 5–27.

Heinemann, *Hasifrut* IV = J. HEINEMANN, "Remnants of Ancient *Piyyutim* in the Palestinian Targum Tradition", *Hasifrut* IV (1973), pp. 362–75.

Kahle, *MdO* = P. KAHLE, *Masoreten des Ostens*, Leipzig, 1913.

Kahle, *MdW* II = P. KAHLE, *Masoreten des Westens* II, Stuttgart, 1930; reprinted Hildesheim, 1967.

Kasher, *HUCA* LX = R. KASHER, "A New Targum to the Ten Commandments According to a Genizah Manuscript", *Hebrew Union College Annual* LX (1989), pp. 1–17 [Hebrew].

Kasher and Klein, *HUCA* LXI = R. KASHER and M. L. KLEIN, "New Fragments of Targum to Esther from the Cairo Genizah", *Hebrew Union College Annual* LXI (1990), pp. 89–124.

Klein, *GMPT* I = M. L. KLEIN, *Genizah Manuscripts of Palestinian Targum to the Pentateuch*, Cincinnati, 1986.

Klein, *Sefarad* XLIX = M. L. KLEIN, "New Fragments of Palestinian Targum from the Cairo Genizah", *Sefarad* XLIX (1989), pp. 123–133.

Klein, *HUCA* XLIX = M. L. KLEIN, "A Genizah Fragment of Palestinian Targum to Genesis 15:1–4", *Hebrew Union College Annual* XLIX (1978), pp. 73–87.

Klein, *HUCA* L = M. L. KLEIN, "Nine Fragments of Palestinian Targum to the Pentateuch from the Cairo Genizah", *Hebrew Union College Annual* L (1979), pp. 149–64.

Rüger *VT* XIII = H. P. RÜGER, "Ein neues Genesis-Fragment mit komplizierter babylonischer Punktation aus der Kairo-Genizah", *Vetus Testamentum* XIII (1963), pp. 235–37.

Rüger *ZAW* LXXV (N.F. XXXIV) = H. P. RÜGER, "Ein neues Fragment des Richterbuches mit babylonischer Punktation", *Zeitschrift für die alttestamentliche Wissenschaft*", LXXV (N.F. XXXIV) (1963), pp. 223–25.

Sperber, *Bible in Aramaic* = A. SPERBER, *The Bible in Aramaic*, Leiden, 1959–68 (first 4 volumes).

Weil, *ALUOS* V = G. E. WEIL, "Fragment d'une Massorah alphabétique du Targum babylonien du Pentateuque", *Annual of Leeds University Oriental Society* V (1963–65), pp. 114–31.

Weil, *Textus* XI, = G. E. WEIL, "Nouveau fragment massorétique de la Massorah du Targum babylonien du Pentateuque et de la Massorah Magna tibérienne des Chroniques – Analyse méthodologique", *Textus* XI (1984), pp. 37–87.

Yeivin, *H. Yalon Mem. Vol.* = I. YEIVIN, "A Fragment of a Massoretic Treatise to the Pentateuch and Targum Onqelos", in *Henoch Yalon Memorial Volume*, eds. E. Y. Kutscher, S. Lieberman and M. Z. Kaddari, Jerusalem, 1974.

# DESCRIPTIONS OF MANUSCRIPTS

**T-S A2.3**   Exodus 32:25; 34:7, 13, 17, 21, 24
Hebrew; sporadic Aramaic glosses from Onqelos. Oriental square script; Tiberian vocalisation + accents; Massorah Magna and Parva; Targum glosses in semi-cursive script with Tiberian vocalisation.

Vellum; 3 leaves.   19.8 × 17.2;   19 lines.

Main Hebrew text: Exodus 32:21 – 34:26; variant (error?) תתרעון for תערעון.   [1]

**T-S A12.2.2(a)**   Proverbs 31:10
Hebrew; Aramaic glosses from Targum Proverbs. Oriental square script; Tiberian vocalisation + accents; Massorah Magna and Parva.

Vellum; 2 leaves; mutilated.   40.2⁺ × [39]; 1 col. (2 cols. for poem);   20 lines.

Main Hebrew text: Proverbs 29:20 – 31:30; gloss reads: אנתתא כשירתא מכיכה in contrast to printed Targum: אתתא כשירתא; this may be a title to the passage; cf. Davis, *HBMCGC* I, p.28.   [2]

**T-S A21.94**   Genesis 3:1–6; 5:10–16
Hebrew; Aramaic: Onqelos.   Oriental semi-cursive script; Targum with Tiberian vocalisation + accents; Hebrew unpointed.

Paper; 2 leaves (1 bifolium); mutilated.   14.8⁺ × 15.9; 9⁺ lines.

Divine name: Targum יי.   [3]

**T-S A21.145**   Genesis 31:34–40 (folio 1); 32:12–13 (folio 2)
Hebrew; Aramaic: Onqelos.   Oriental linear square script; Tiberian vocalisation.

Paper; 2 leaves (1 bifolium); mutilated.   16.1⁺ × 14.5; 12 lines.

Most of folio 2 is torn away, but seems originally to have been blank.   [4]

**T-S A24.12**   Exodus 20:12–15
Aramaic: Onqelos (+ Hebrew lemmata).   Oriental semi-cursive script; Tiberian vocalisation.

Paper; 1 leaf.   14.0 × 12.7;   12 lines.

Divine name: יי; *verso* blank.   [5]

**T-S A24.14**   Exodus 39:31–9
Hebrew; Aramaic: Onqelos.   Oriental semi-cursive script; Hebrew with Tiberian vocalisation + accents; Targum with Tiberian vocalisation.

Paper; 1 leaf.   14.9⁺ × 11.8;   16⁺ lines.

Divine name: Hebrew tetragrammaton; Targum ייי; illegible writing in margins of *recto*.   [6]

**T-S A24.96**   Exodus 3:8 – 4:1
Hebrew; Aramaic: Onqelos; Judaeo-Arabic. Oriental semi-cursive script; Hebrew with Tiberian vocalisation + accents; Targum with Tiberian vocalisation.

Paper; 4 leaves (2 bifolia); badly faded, barely legible. 17.0 × 12.5;   14–15 lines.

Divine name: Hebrew tetragrammaton; Targum יְיָ.   [7]

**T-S A24.112.4**   Exodus 15:18
Aramaic: Onqelos (insert).   Child's(?) square linear script; unpointed.

Paper; 4 leaves (2 bifolia).   16.2 × 12.3;   8 lines.

Divine name: יְיָ; main text Hebrew: Exodus 14:30 – 15:20; Onqelos to 15:18 is inserted after that verse (folio 4); *aleph* rotated 45° anti-clockwise. Selection of this verse is presumably under the influence of the daily morning service; cf. T-S A24.113.   [8]

**T-S A24.113**   Exodus 15:18
Aramaic: Onqelos (insert).   Oriental square script; Tiberian vocalisation (beginning 15:19).

Paper; 1 leaf.   18.7 × 14.0;   18 lines.

Divine name: יְי/יְיָ; main text Hebrew: Exodus 15:1–25; cf. T-S A24.112.4.   [9]

**T-S A28.36**   Numbers 5:11–15
Hebrew; Aramaic: Onqelos; Judaeo-Arabic. Oriental semi-cursive script; unpointed.

Paper; 1 leaf; mutilated.   12.4⁺ × 15.5;   9⁺ lines.

Divine name: Hebrew tetragrammaton; Targum יְיָ.   [10]

**T-S A28.112**   Numbers 21:16–24 (folio 1); 23:17–27 (folio 2)
Hebrew; Aramaic: Onqelos.   Spanish square script; Tiberian vocalisation + accents (Hebrew & Targum).

Paper; 2 leaves; mutilated.   20.2 × 14.2;   20 lines.

Divine name: Hebrew tetragrammaton; Targum יְיָ.   [11]

**T-S A39.4**   Joshua 6:27; 7:5, 7, 14(?), 21
Hebrew; sporadic Aramaic glosses from Targum Jonathan to Prophets.   Oriental square script; Babylonian vocalisation.

Vellum; 1 leaf.   25.3 × 20.2;   2 cols.;   28 lines.

Main Hebrew text: Joshua 6:25 – 8:4; marginal and interlinear glosses are in darker ink.   [12]

**T-S A39.7**   Genesis 22:1–5, 9–17
Hebrew; Aramaic: Onqelos.   Oriental square script; Babylonian vocalisation.

Vellum; 1 leaf; badly mutilated.   19.5⁺ × 13.0⁺; 2 cols.;   21⁺ lines.

Divine name: Hebrew tetragrammaton.

Kahle *MdO* pp.1–2.   [13]

**T-S A40.12**   Zechariah 14:10–13 (folio 1); 1 Kings 8:10–15 (folio 2); (*hafṭarot*)
Hebrew; Aramaic: Targum Jonathan to Prophets. Oriental square script; unpointed.

Paper; 2 leaves (1 bifolium).   13.4 × 11.0;   9 lines.

Divine name: יי; triennial *hafṭarot* to Deuteronomy 6:4; 10:1.   [14]

**T-S A40.25**   Genesis 6:4 – 7:5
Aramaic: Onqelos (+ Hebrew lemmata). Oriental semi-cursive script; Tiberian vocalisation.

Paper; 4 leaves (pasted together in pairs in incorrect order); badly faded.   17.4 × 12.6;   10 lines.

Divine name: ײַ; beginning of *parashat noah* noted in margin; ciphers for number of verses in *parashat bere'shit* קְמֹו, אמציה (=146) but also אקדם (=145!) added in darker ink; decorative פרש between the *parashot*. ❂.   [15]

**T-S A40.29**   Exodus 18:10–13 (folio 1); 18:20–22 (folio 2)
Hebrew; Aramaic: Onqelos.   Persian(?) square script; Tiberian vocalisation + accents (Hebrew & Targum).

Paper; 2 leaves (1 bifolium); mutilated.   16.7 × 16.3; 9 lines.

Divine name: Hebrew tetragrammaton; Targum יְיָ.   [16]

**T-S A40.30**   Genesis 41:7–11, 16–21
Hebrew; Aramaic: Onqelos; Judaeo-Arabic. Yemenite square script; Hebrew with Tiberian vocalisation + accents; Targum with Babylonian vocalisation.

Paper; 1 leaf; mutilated.   16.0⁺ × 20.7;   16⁺ lines.   [17]

**T-S A40.31**   Leviticus 18:1–30
Aramaic: Onqelos.   Oriental semi-cursive script; Tiberian vocalisation.

Paper; 1 leaf.   19.7 × 14.5;   19 lines.

Divine name: ךְ ; Judaeo-Arabic heading on *recto*: אלקול פי תצפית לחם אלחיואן לאן בתצפיתה יחל אכלה ודלך יטן אכלה which is not related to the present passage (and perhaps belongs to Leviticus 11); *verso* is inverted in relation to *recto*.   [18]

**T-S A40.32**   Exodus 22:15 – 23:16
Hebrew; Aramaic: Onqelos.   Yemenite square script; Hebrew with Tiberian vocalisation + accents; Targum with Babylonian vocalisation.

Paper; 1 leaf; mutilated.   24.6⁺ × 15.9⁺;   28⁺ lines.

Divine name: Hebrew tetragrammaton; Targum יוֹ(?).   [19]

**T-S A41.3**   Exodus 12:21–4
Aramaic: Onqelos (+ Hebrew lemmata). Oriental semi-cursive script; Tiberian vocalisation (part in darker ink).

Paper; 1 leaf; partially rubbed.   18.8 × 12.3;   15 lines.

Divine name יְ; heading in Judaeo-Arabic: בשׁם תרגום סידר אפסח [ אולה תרגום יום ראשון שלפסח. *Verso* contains only the following colophon and notes: תרגום כלמא יקרא פי [ כל פי ספר תורה ואו followed by a mnemonic device for calendrical calculation: כי נר מצוה ותורה אור   סימן מתי [מא] כאן מרחשון חסר... בדלך אן נר חנוכה יום מתן תורה אלדי הו אלמצוה ומתי מא כאן מרחשון מלא כאן ותורה אור יחיד יום מתן תורה ]ורו חנוכה חזו לילה אלתנאי.   [20]

**T-S A41.4**   Genesis 1:1–5
Aramaic: Onqelos (+ Hebrew lemmata).   Oriental square script; Tiberian vocalisation.

Paper; 1 leaf.   17.4 × 12.5;   11 lines.

Divine name: יְ; *verso* contains colophons: זה הכתב לר' אברהם המלמד החכם והנבון האלוהים יברוט אמן נֹאֹ(?) אנתקל בחכם אלשרי לעלי בר ישעיה הח נֹג and a similar note alongside the original colophon.   [21]

**T-S A41.9**   2 Kings 22:13 – 23:2 (folio 1); 25:24–30 (folio 2)
Aramaic: Targum Jonathan to Prophets (+ Hebrew lemmata).   Oriental semi-cursive script; unpointed.

Paper; 2 leaves (1 bifolium).   16.1 × 12.0;   17 lines.

Divine name: יְ; colophon: נשלמו ארבעה ספרים יהושע ושפטים ושמואל ומלכים בסיֹעֹ דשמייא בריך רחמנא דסייע בהדן: ברוך נותן ליעף כח ולאין אונים עצמה ירבה: ברוך הכותב וחזק הקורא אמן סלה.   [22]

**T-S A41.19**   Judges 5:30–31; (*hafṭarah*?)
Hebrew; Aramaic: Targum Jonathan to Prophets. Oriental square script; unpointed.

Vellum; 1 leaf; mutilated.   10.0⁺ × 14.6(?);   1 col.(?); 11⁺ lines.

Divine name: Hebrew & Targum יְ; colophon: חזק נשתלמה בעזרת הבורא לאבוסעיד ... בר נתנאל....   [23]

**T-S B1.1**   Numbers 15:13 – 17:2 (folios 1–10); 18:16–20 (folio 11)
Hebrew; Aramaic: Onqelos; Judaeo-Arabic. Oriental semi-cursive script; with Tiberian vocalisation (Hebrew & Aramaic).

Paper; 11 leaves (folio 10v rubbed).   15.0 × 11.0; 15–18 lines.

Divine name: יי. Notation marking end of *parashah* and number of verses in Judaeo-Arabic after Numbers 15:41 (folio 5r).   [24]

**T-S B1.2**   Numbers 4:43–47 (folio 1); 5:17–19 (folio 2)
Hebrew; Aramaic: Onqelos; Judaeo-Arabic. Oriental script; Hebrew square with Tiberian vocalisation + accents; Onqelos smaller, semi-cursive, unpointed.

Paper; 2 leaves (1 bifolium); rubbed.   15.5 × 12.0; 12 lines.

Divine name: Hebrew tetragrammaton; Aramaic יְ.   [25]

**T-S B1.3**   Genesis 5:14 – 7:2 (folios 1–8); 17:12–17 (folio 9); Exodus 4:1–6 (folio 10)
Hebrew; Aramaic: Onqelos; Judaeo-Arabic.
Oriental script; Hebrew square with Tiberian vocalisation + accents; Aramaic semi-cursive, with Tiberian vocalisation.
Paper; 10 leaves (3 bifolia); partially rubbed and mutilated.   16.5 × 12.8;   15–17 lines.
Possible notation at end of *parashah* on folio 5v. [26]

**T-S B1.4**   Genesis 1:20–23
Hebrew; Aramaic: Onqelos; Judaeo-Arabic.
Persian(?) script (large); unpointed.
Paper; 2 leaves; mutilated and rubbed.   20.6 × 14.3; 7 lines.
The order of the verses in all three languages is confused. [27]

**T-S B1.5**   Genesis 18:2–7 (folio 1); 18:33 – 19:4 (folio 2)
Hebrew; Aramaic: Onqelos; Judaeo-Arabic.
Oriental semi-cursive script; Tiberian vocalisation (only Onqelos).
Paper; 2 leaves (1 bifolium).   15.6 × 11.2;   11 lines.
Watermark, at foot of folio 1, has a flower emerging from middle finger of a hand. Bottom of watermark cut off. This dates the paper to 1480–1495; cf C. M. Briquet p. 198 and pl.xxxvii, items 303–7. [28]

**T-S B1.6**   Genesis 18:30–32 (folio 1); 19:9–12 (folio 2)
Hebrew; Aramaic: Onqelos; Judaeo-Arabic.
Oriental semi-cursive script; Hebrew with Tiberian vocalisation + accents; Onqelos with Tiberian vocalisation.
Paper; 2 leaves (1 bifolium).   15.6 × 10.8;   11 lines. [29]

**T-S B1.7**   Genesis 24:37 – 26:13
Hebrew; Aramaic: Onqelos; Judaeo-Arabic.
Oriental semi-cursive script; sporadic Tiberian vocalisation in Hebrew and Onqelos, fuller accents in Hebrew.
Paper; 10 leaves (5 bifolia).   18.4 × 12.7;   23–4 lines.
Divine Name: Hebrew & Onqelos (sometimes) tetragrammaton; notation marking *parashah* (*toledot*, Genesis 25:19) folio 7a. [30]

**T-S B1.8**   Genesis 31:44–52
Hebrew; Aramaic: Onqelos; Judaeo-Arabic.
Oriental script; Hebrew square with Tiberian vocalisation + accents; Onqelos smaller semi-cursive with Tiberian vocalisation.
Paper; 1 leaf.   19.1 × 14.3;   20 lines.
Divine name: Hebrew tetragrammaton; Onqelos אדני or יי. [31]

**T-S B1.9**   Genesis 37:36 – 38:6
Hebrew; Aramaic: Onqelos; Judaeo-Arabic.
Oriental square script; Hebrew with Tiberian vocalisation + accents; Onqelos smaller with Tiberian vocalisation.
Paper; 1 leaf.   17.3 × 13.2;   15 lines. [32]

**T-S B1.10**   Genesis 40:2–15
Hebrew; Aramaic: Onqelos; Judaeo-Arabic.
Oriental script; Hebrew square with Tiberian vocalisation + accents; Onqelos smaller, semi-cursive with Tiberian vocalisation.
Paper; 4 leaves (1 bifolium).   16.6 × 12.7;   12 lines.
See plate 6. [33]

**T-S B1.11**   Exodus 35:29–35 (folio 1); 36:3–12 (folios 2–3); 36:17–23 (folio 4)
Hebrew; Aramaic: Onqelos; Judaeo-Arabic.
Oriental script; Hebrew square with Tiberian vocalisation + accents; Onqelos smaller, semi-cursive with Tiberian vocalisation.
Paper; 4 leaves (2 bifolia).   17.8 × 13.5;   17–18 lines.
Divine name: Hebrew tetragrammaton; Onqelos יי. [34]

**T-S B1.12**   Leviticus 1:10–17 (folios 1–2); 4:31–35 (folio 3); 5:9–12 (folio 4)
Hebrew; Aramaic: Onqelos; Judaeo-Arabic.
Oriental square script; Hebrew with Tiberian vocalisation + accents; Onqelos with Tiberian vocalisation; Massorah Magna and Parva in margins.
Paper; 4 leaves (2 bifolia).   16.7 × 12.8;   14 lines.
Divine name: Hebrew tetragrammaton; Onqelos יי. [35]

**T-S B1.13**   Exodus 20:5/6–11
Hebrew; Aramaic: Onqelos; Judaeo-Arabic.
Oriental script; Hebrew square with Tiberian vocalisation + accents; Onqelos and Judaeo-Arabic in smaller semi-cursive script.
Paper; 1 leaf.   18.0 × 12.5;   14 lines.
Divine name: Hebrew tetragrammaton; Onqelos יי. [36]

**T-S B1.14**   Exodus 29:27–33 (folio 1); 30:25–35 (folio 2)
Hebrew; Aramaic: Onqelos; Judaeo-Arabic.
Oriental square script; Hebrew with Tiberian vocalisation + accents; sporadic vocalisation in Onqelos; Judaeo-Arabic in smaller square script with two lines in space of one.
Paper; 1 leaf.   19.5 × 14.5;   17 lines.
Divine name: Hebrew tetragrammaton; Onqelos ייי. [37]

**T-S B1.15**  Leviticus 25:28–46 (folios 1–3); 26:24–29 (folio 4)
Hebrew; Aramaic: Onqelos; Judaeo-Arabic. Oriental square script; Hebrew with Tiberian vocalisation + accents; Onqelos with Tiberian vocalisation.
Paper; 4 leaves (1 bifolium?).  18.0 × 12.7;  15 lines.
Divine name: Hebrew tetragrammaton; Onqelos ייֽ.  [38]

**T-S B1.16**  Exodus 10:12–14
Hebrew; Aramaic: Onqelos; Judaeo-Arabic. Oriental semi-cursive script; Hebrew and Onqelos with Tiberian vocalisation + accents.
Paper; 1 leaf.  19.2 × [13.2];  14 lines.
Divine name: Hebrew tetragrammaton; Onqelos יֽי.  [39]

**T-S B1.17**  Exodus 3:3–16 (folio 1); 4:10–18 (folio 2); 14:8 – 15:9 (folios 3–5); 39:21–37 (folio 6)
Hebrew; Aramaic: Onqelos; Judaeo-Arabic. Yemenite square script; Hebrew with Tiberian vocalisation + accents; Onqelos with Babylonian vocalisation + 'etnaḥta'.
Paper; 6 leaves.  28.0 × 19.0;  2 cols.;  26 lines.
Divine name: Hebrew tetragrammaton; Onqelos יְי. Entire column missing on folio 2. Blank line between Exodus 4:17 and 18 (folio 2v) indicates Palestinian triennial *sidra*. Most of line blank between Exodus 14:25 and 26 (folio 4r) with ה/ד(?) in margin. In order to preserve scribal layout of the 'Song of the Sea' (folio 4v–5r) the targum and Judaeo-Arabic of Exodus 14:28 – 15:26 follow the Hebrew version. Blank line between Exodus 39:21 and 22 with ד in margin and שֵׁשׁ inserted in the line by a later hand. Many abbreviations in text.  [40]

**T-S B1.18**  Exodus 1:1–7 (*verso*); colophon (*recto*)
Hebrew; Aramaic: Onqelos; Judaeo-Arabic. Oriental script; Hebrew square with Tiberian vocalisation + accents; Onqelos smaller, semi-cursive with Tiberian vocalisation.
Paper; 1 leaf.  27.4 × 19.4;  18 lines.
Text of colophon (in three lines): [קודש לה] אלהי ישראל
לכניסֽת מ/[מותו](?)  שהקדיש משה בר שלמה הלוי ידיעו
כראטין  אֽר[ו]ר מוכרֽו] או גונבו או ממשכנו וברוך הקורא בו .  [41]

**T-S B1.19**  Deuteronomy 21:19 – 22:24
Hebrew; Aramaic: Onqelos; Judaeo-Arabic. Oriental script; Hebrew square with Tiberian vocalisation + accents; Onqelos semi-cursive with Tiberian vocalisation.
Paper; 4 leaves (2 bifolia).  23.4 × 16.1;  22 lines.  [42]

**T-S B1.20**  Deuteronomy 25:8 – 26:3
Hebrew; Aramaic: Onqelos; Judaeo-Arabic. Oriental script; Hebrew square with Tiberian vocalisation + accents; Onqelos smaller square with Tiberian vocalisation.
Paper; 4 leaves (2 bifolia).  17.4 × 13.0;  13 lines.
Divine name: Hebrew tetragrammaton; Onqelos יֽי. Hebrew notation marking end of *parashah* (folio 3v) נשלמה פרשת כי תצא. The number of verses in the *parashah* is noted in Judaeo-Arabic; large פ at top of folio 4r.  [43]

**T-S B1.21**  Deuteronomy 31:24 – 32:8
Hebrew; Aramaic: Onqelos; Judaeo-Arabic. Oriental script; Hebrew square with Tiberian vocalisation + accents; Onqelos square with Tiberian vocalisation.
Paper; 2 leaves (1 bifolium).  17.9 × 13.6;  17 lines.
Divine name: Hebrew tetragrammaton; Onqelos ייֽ Phrase in Onqelos omitted: מסרבין הויתון קדם יוי (Deuteronomy 31:27, folio 1r). Marginal notation marking *parashah* at Deuteronomy 32:1 ✿; Deuteronomy 32 is written in two columns with only Hebrew and Onqelos.  [44]

**T-S B1.22**  Deuteronomy 34:10–12 (folio 1); Isaiah 51:12 (Hebrew only, folio 1v); Isaiah 61:11 (Hebrew only, folio 2)
Hebrew; Aramaic: Onqelos; Judaeo-Arabic. Oriental script; Hebrew square with Tiberian vocalisation + accents.
Paper; 2 leaves (1 bifolium).  14.4 × 11.4;  12 lines.
Divine name: Hebrew tetragrammaton; Onqelos יֽי. Notation marking end of Deuteronomy and end of Pentateuch (folio 1v): נשלם ספר אלה הדברים ומשלמה התורה כולה בעזרת שמים ברוך הנותן ליעף כח ולאין אונים עצמה ירבה; the Hebrew passages from Isaiah are the *hafṭarot* for *parashot shofṭim* to *niṣavim*.  [45]

**T-S B1.23**  Numbers 3:22 – 4:20 (folios 1–6v); Hosea 2:1–15 (*hafṭarah*, folios 7–8)
Hebrew; Aramaic: Onqelos; Judaeo-Arabic. *Hafṭarah*: Hebrew; Aramaic: Targum Jonathan to Prophets; Judaeo-Arabic. Oriental script; Hebrew square with Tiberian vocalisation + accents; Onqelos with Tiberian vocalisation.
Paper; 8 leaves (4 bifolia).  21.7 × 15.6;  23 lines.
Divine name: Hebrew tetragrammaton; Onqelos יֽי. Notation marking *parashah* ending in Hebrew נשלמה פרשת במדבר בעזרת תחלת כל דבר (folio 6v) and number of verses in Judaeo-Arabic.  [46]

**T-S B1.24**  Numbers 25:13–18 (folio 1 mutilated); 26:10–18 (folio 2)
Hebrew; Aramaic: Onqelos; Judaeo-Arabic. Spanish script; Hebrew largest, square with Tiberian vocalisation + accents; Onqelos smaller, with Tiberian vocalisation + accents; Judaeo-Arabic smallest.

[T-S B1.24, cont.]
Vellum; 2 leaves (1 bifolium); badly mutilated.
15.8 × 19.1; 10 lines.

Divine name: Onqelos יְיָ. [47]

**T-S B1.25** Genesis 38:14–20, 24–28 (unmarked folio bound with folio 5); 39:16 – 41:7 (folios 1–2); 41:12–26 (folio 3, fragmentary); 41:26 – 49:30 (folios 4–18)
Hebrew; Aramaic: Onqelos; Judaeo-Arabic.
Yemenite script; Hebrew square, with Tiberian vocalisation + accents; Onqelos with Babylonian vocalisation.

Paper; 19 leaves (2 badly mutilated; 7 bifolia).
28.6⁺ × 20.9; 30–31 lines.

Divine name: Onqelos יי. Blank line between 39:23 and 40:1 (Palestinian triennial *sidra*) (folio 1r). Notation marks *parashah* between 40:23 and 41:1 with numbers of verses in Hebrew cipher and sign in margin (folio 2v) ✿. Small design drawn in margin of folio 8r. Notation marks *parashah* between 44:17 and 18 with numbers of verses in Hebrew cipher and with design in margin (folio 10r). Half blank line between 46:27 and 28 (Palestinian triennial *sidra*). *Parashah* notation in margin at 47:28 (folio 15v) but no space. Blank line between 47:31 and 48:1 (Palestinian triennial *sidra*). Folio 17v divided into two columns in order to fit 49:8 at the top of a column. Explanatory note between the columns: תקון סופרים ב׳יה׳ שמ׳ .בראש הדף בראשית יהודה הבאים שמור מוצא ואעידה׃. Blank line between 49:13 and 14 (triennial *sidra*?) (folio 18r). [48]

**T-S B2.1** Numbers 9:6–14
Hebrew; Aramaic: Onqelos. Oriental square script; Babylonian vocalisation + accents.

Vellum; 1 leaf; mutilated. 18.3 × 16.2; 20 lines.

Divine name: Hebrew tetragrammaton; Onqelos יי. Probably part of same manuscript as T-S B2.3 although leaf is much shorter. [49]

**T-S B2.2** Ezekiel 40:14–48 (folio 1); Jeremiah 32:10 – 33:21 (folios 2–3); Jeremiah 47:6 – 48:30 (folio 4); (*haftarot*)
Hebrew; Aramaic: Targum Jonathan to Prophets.
Oriental square script; Babylonian vocalisation.

Vellum; 4 leaves; slightly mutilated and rubbed.
25.6 × 22.0; 28–34 lines.

Divine name: Hebrew tetragrammaton; Targum יי. Many abbreviations; Hebrew text *plene*. [50]

**T-S B2.3** Numbers 6:16 – 7:1
Hebrew; Aramaic: Onqelos. Oriental square script; Babylonian vocalisation + accents.

Vellum; 1 leaf; slightly mutilated. 19.0⁺ × 16.2; 20 lines.

Priestly blessing not translated (Numbers 6:24–26, *verso*) (cf. Mishnah *Megillah* 4:10). [51]

**T-S B2.4** 1 Kings 7:24–26 (folio 1); Ezekiel 43:23–27 (folio 2); (*haftarot*)
Hebrew; Aramaic: Targum Jonathan to Prophets.
Oriental square script; Babylonian vocalisation + accents.

Vellum; 2 leaves (1 bifolium); slightly mutilated.
14.4 × 11.7; 11 lines.

Divine name: Hebrew tetragrammaton = Targum יי; Hebrew אדני = Targum יי. (Notation for *haftarah* ואלה] פקדי ביחזקאל (bottom of folio 1v) implies that the preceding *haftarah* (1 Kings 7) was for *parashat wayaqhel*). [52]

**T-S B2.5** (? = T-S NS 115.71; West. Coll. Glass 36)
Deuteronomy 33:10 – 34:1
Aramaic: Onqelos (extract or condensation).
Oriental square script, ruled and suspended; sporadic Babylonian vocalisation (note long *waw*).

Vellum; 1 leaf. 19.7 × 14.8; 23 lines.

Phrases given in Hebrew and Aramaic followed by the word: תרג׃; massoretic style of note at 33:23 שבע קר ותרג. Yeivin *H. Yalon Mem. Vol.* pp. 158–60. See plate 15. [53]

**T-S B2.6** Numbers 11:35 – 13:18
Aramaic: Onqelos. Oriental square script; Babylonian vocalisation + accents.

Vellum; 1 leaf; mutilated. 21.5 × 14.4⁺; 26 lines.

Divine name: יי; personal names abbreviated. *Parashah* notation between 12:16 and 13:1 with cipher: קלו (=136) for number of verses in *parashat beha'alotekha*, and sign in margin (folio 1v) ✿. [54]

**T-S B2.7** Hosea 2:15–23; (*haftarah* for *parashat bamidbar* (but longer))
Hebrew; Aramaic: Targum Jonathan to Prophets.
Oriental square script; Babylonian vocalisation + accents.

Vellum; 1 leaf; slightly mutilated and rubbed.
19.8 × 14.6; 16 lines.

Divine name: Hebrew tetragrammaton; Targum יי. [55]

**T-S B2.8** Isaiah 60:21–22 (folio 1r); Isaiah 61:10 – 62:1 (folio 1r–v); (*haftarot*)
Hebrew; Aramaic: Targum Jonathan to Prophets.
Oriental script; mostly sporadic Babylonian vocalisation with one Tiberian sign (e.g. *recto*, line 9: יכֹּהֵן); these are *haftarot* for *parashot ki tavo'* and *niṣavim*.

Vellum; 1 leaf; mutilated. 16.2 × 12.7⁺; 14 lines.
[56]

**T-S B2.9**  Deuteronomy 34:5–11 (end of Pentateuch)
Hebrew; Aramaic: Onqelos.  Oriental square script; Hebrew with Tiberian accents; Onqelos with Babylonian vocalisation.
Vellum; 1 leaf; mutilated.  14.3⁺ × 22.4;  15⁺ lines.
Bottom of leaf containing last three lines destroyed. Targum of verse 11, and entire verse 12 missing; verso blank.  [57]

**T-S B2.10**  Exodus 17:6–16
Hebrew; Aramaic: Onqelos.  Oriental square script; Babylonian vocalisation.
Vellum; 1 leaf; badly mutilated.  17.0⁺ × 13.7⁺; 11⁺ lines.
Divine name: Hebrew tetragrammaton; Onqelos ײ.  [58]

**T-S B3.1**  Numbers 24:22 – 35:31 (folios 1–13); Deuteronomy 1:1 – 10:10 (folios 14–26)
Hebrew; Aramaic: Onqelos; Judaeo-Arabic. Yemenite square script; Hebrew with Babylonian vocalisation + Tiberian accents; Onqelos with Babylonian vocalisation.
Paper; 26 leaves (2 bifolia: folios 9–12).  30.1 × 20.5; 31 lines.
Divine name: Hebrew tetragrammaton; Onqelos ײי. Indication of *parashot* and some triennial *sidrot* by blank lines, majuscule פ decorated and framed in the margins, and ciphers for the number of verses in preceding *parashot* are found throughout the manuscript. A large decorative *waw* at Numbers 35:9 denotes a triennial *sidra* ✿. Massoretic marginal note at Deuteronomy 6:4 עין דשמע ודל׳ דאחד מאו׳ גדו׳ and a variant reading in Onqelos at Deuteronomy 9:8 תקיף רגזא for וההה רגז.
Fuste Ara *EB* XV, pp.90–94 (in part). See plate 2.  [59]

**T-S B4.1**  2 Samuel 23:3–8
Hebrew; Aramaic: Targum Jonathan to Prophets. Oriental square script; Babylonian vocalisation + accents.
Vellum; 1 leaf.  25.4 × 21.2;  2 cols.;  19 lines.
Divine name: Onqelos ײי.  [60]

**T-S B4.2**  Genesis 17:19 – 18:10
Hebrew; Aramaic: Onqelos.  Oriental square script; Babylonian vocalisation + accents.
Vellum; 1 leaf.  28.8 × 23.4;  2 cols.;  25–6 lines.
Divine name: Hebrew tetragrammaton; Onqelos ײי; cipher קט after 17:27 = number of verses in *parashat lekh lekha* (recto, column 2). Crown design at beginning of *parashat wayera'* (verso, col. 1). ✿.
Kahle *MdO* p.1 (in part).  [61]

**T-S B4.3**  Genesis 21:22–23, 26–29, 32–34, 22:2–3 (folio 1); Exodus 2:16–18, 21–23, 3:1–3, 6–7 (folio 2)
Hebrew; Aramaic: Onqelos.  Oriental square script; Babylonian vocalisation + accents; Massorah Magna and Parva (with Babylonian vocalisation).
Vellum; 2 leaves; badly mutilated.  23.0⁺ × 28.0; 2 cols.;  12⁺ lines.
Divine name: Hebrew tetragrammaton; Onqelos ײי.
Kahle *MdO* p.2 (in part).  [62]

**T-S B4.4**  Genesis 49:6–9, 12–30
Hebrew; Aramaic: Onqelos.  Oriental square script; Babylonian vocalisation.
Vellum; 1 leaf; badly mutilated.  23.0⁺ × [24.0]; 2 cols.;  29 lines.
Very similar to T-S B4.11.
Kahle *MdO* p.1 (in part).  [63]

**T-S B4.5**  Exodus 11:1 – 12:19 (folios 1–2); 15:1–23 (preceded by Hebrew for verses 15–19) (folio 3)
Hebrew; Aramaic: Onqelos.  Oriental script; Babylonian vocalisation + accents; Massorah Magna and Parva.
Vellum; 3 leaves (1 bifolium).  29.0 × 24.0;  2 cols.; 22 lines.
Divine name: Hebrew tetragrammaton; Onqelos ײי. Very similar to T-S B4.7.  [64]

**T-S B4.6**  Exodus 11:7 – 12:15
Hebrew; Aramaic: Onqelos.  Oriental square script; Babylonian vocalisation + accents; sporadic Tiberian vocalisation (e.g. 11:8).
Vellum; 1 leaf; badly mutilated.  19.7⁺ × [21.0]; 2 cols.;  22⁺ lines.
Divine name: Hebrew tetragrammaton; Onqelos ײי.  [65]

**T-S B4.7**  Exodus 12:35–37, 50–51; 13:1 (folio 1); 14:13–14, 25 (folio 2)
Hebrew; Aramaic: Onqelos.  Oriental square script; Babylonian vocalisation + accents.
Vellum; 2 leaves (1 bifolium); badly mutilated. 19.0⁺ × 22.8⁺;  2 cols.;  14⁺ lines.
Divine name: Hebrew tetragrammaton; Onqelos ײי. Very similar to T-S B4.5.  [66]

**T-S B4.8**  Exodus 34:32 – 35:21 (35:2–6 fragmented)
Hebrew; Aramaic: Onqelos.  Oriental square script; Babylonian vocalisation + accents.
Vellum; 1 leaf; badly mutilated.  28.5 × [22.0]; 2 cols.;  26–9 lines.
Divine name: Hebrew tetragrammaton; Onqelos ײי; cipher at end of *parashat ki tisa'* (34:35, recto): קלט.  [67]

**T-S B4.9**  Exodus 35:15–16, 19–21, 23–24, 27–28
Hebrew; Aramaic: Onqelos.  Oriental square script; Babylonian vocalisation + accents.
Vellum; 1 leaf; badly mutilated.  14.0⁺ × 24.3; 2 cols.; 9⁺ lines.  [68]

**T-S B4.10**  Exodus 32:35 – 34:3 (folio 1); 35:27 – 36:18 (folio 2)
Hebrew; Aramaic: Onqelos.  Oriental square script; sporadic Babylonian vocalisation + Tiberian accents (in later hand).
Vellum; 2 leaves.  28.7 × 25.4; 2 cols.; 29 lines.
Divine name: Hebrew tetragrammaton; Onqelos ץ/י.
Kahle *MdO* p. 5 (in part).  [69]

**T-S B4.11**  Exodus 37:13 – 38:14
Hebrew; Aramaic: Onqelos.  Oriental square script; sporadic Babylonian vocalisation.
Vellum; 1 leaf; mutilated.  27.8 × 24.6;  2 cols.; 29 lines.
Very similar to T-S B4.4.  [70]

**T-S B4.12**  Exodus 39:39 – 40:17
Hebrew; Aramaic: Onqelos.  Oriental square script; Babylonian vocalisation and Tiberian vocalisation + accents in dark ink (in later hand).
Vellum; 1 leaf; slightly torn.  34.5 × 29.0;  2 cols.; 24 lines.
Divine name; Hebrew tetragrammaton; Onqelos ייי.
Kahle *MdO* p. 6 (in part).  [71]

**T-S B4.13**  Leviticus 4:17 – 5:2
Hebrew; Aramaic: Onqelos.  Oriental square script; Babylonian vocalisation + accents.
Vellum; 1 leaf.  29.9 × 20.7;  2 cols.; 27 lines.
Divine name: Hebrew tetragrammaton; Onqelos ייי. Massorah to Onqelos in margins with Babylonian vocalisation and massoretic note on Hebrew at Leviticus 5:1 (לוא).
Kahle *MdO* p. 7 (in part).  [72]

**T-S B4.14**  Leviticus 5:10–19 (folio 1); 23:10–19 (folio 2); Deuteronomy 2:19–30 (folio 3); 5:2–9, 12 (folio 4)
Hebrew; Aramaic: Onqelos.  Oriental(?) square script; Babylonian vocalisation + accents; Massorah Magna and Parva in margins.
Vellum; 2 leaves; mutilated (folios 2, 4 very badly). 30.6 × 26.9;  2 cols.; 20 lines.
Divine name: Hebrew tetragrammaton; Onqelos ייי. Scribal deletion of end of Leviticus 5:10 (Hebrew); folio 2r overwritten (ink reinforced by a second hand).
Kahle *MdO* pp. 10–11 (in part).  [73]

**T-S B4.15**  Leviticus 14:24–57
Hebrew; Aramaic: Onqelos.  Oriental square script; sporadic Babylonian vocalisation + sporadic accents.
Vellum; 1 leaf.  27.6 × 24.4;  2 cols.; 29–30 lines.
Divine name: Hebrew tetragrammaton; Onqelos יי. Letter ס at 14:33 denotes Palestinian triennial *sidra*.
Díez Macho *EB* XVI, p. 268.  [74]

**T-S B4.16**  Leviticus 11:22–45
Hebrew; Aramaic: Onqelos.  Oriental square script; Babylonian vocalisation + accents.
Vellum; 1 leaf; badly mutilated.  22.0⁺ × [22.0]; 2 cols.; 22⁺ lines.
Marginal notes e.g. (11:42): וו הוא באמצע אותיות.
Kahle *MdO* p. 7 (in part).  [75]

**T-S B4.17**  Numbers 12:12 – 13:30
Hebrew; Aramaic: Onqelos.  Oriental square script; Babylonian vocalisation + accents.
Vellum; 1 leaf; badly mutilated.  28.7 × 22.0⁺; 2 cols.; 30 lines.
Hebrew tetragrammaton; cipher קלי for number of verses in *parashat beha'alotekha*. Some vocalisation on *verso* by second hand in darker ink.  [76]

**T-S B4.18**  Leviticus 26:13–33 (folio 1); Numbers 1:49 – 2:3, 6–17 (folio 2)
Hebrew; Aramaic: Onqelos.  Oriental square script; Babylonian vocalisation + accents.
Vellum; 2 leaves (1 bifolium); badly mutilated. 22.7⁺ × 24.0;  2 cols.; [28] lines.
Decorative letter ס in margin at Numbers 2:1 (folio 2r) denotes Palestinian triennial *sidra* ●.  [77]

**T-S B4.19**  Numbers 31:28–30, 33–7, 40–43, 48–50
Hebrew; Aramaic: Onqelos.  Oriental square script; Babylonian vocalisation; Tiberian vocalisation + accents.
Vellum; 1 leaf; badly mutilated.  16.5⁺ × 26.0; 2 cols.; 14⁺ lines.
Divine name: Hebrew tetragrammaton; Onqelos ייי.  [78]

**T-S B4.20**  Numbers 35:25–7, 30–31, 35:34 – 36:1, 3–4
Hebrew; Aramaic: Onqelos.  Oriental square script; Babylonian vocalisation + accents.
Vellum; 1 leaf; badly mutilated.  10.8⁺ × 20.8⁺; 2 cols.; 10⁺ lines.
Massoretic note at Numbers 35:30 (in Hebrew). Dittograph of verse 31 marked with supralinear dots for deletion.
Kahle *MdO* pp. 9–10.  [79]

**T-S B4.21** Deuteronomy 27:10–12, 15–18 (folio 1); 22–26, 28:2–7 (folio 2); 28:27–47 (folio 3); 28:49–63 (folio 4)
Hebrew; Aramaic: Onqelos. Oriental square script; Babylonian vocalisation; Massorah Magna in bottom margin.
Vellum; 4 leaves (2 bifolia); badly mutilated. 15.5⁺ × 20.4; 2 cols.; 15⁺ lines.
Divine name; Hebrew tetragrammaton; Onqelos ״׳; verses abbreviated in Targum for repetitive passages; massoretic note to Onqelos 28:28 ובשִׁגָּמֻוֹת לֹס ...וּבַמְשַׁגֻּמֻוּת לִי. [80]

**T-S B4.22** Deuteronomy 33:7 – 34:6
Hebrew; Aramaic: Onqelos. Oriental square script; Babylonian vocalisation + accents.
Vellum; 2 leaves. 34.2 × 28.8; 2 cols.; 21 lines.
Divine name: Hebrew tetragrammaton; Onqelos ״׳/״ס׳. [81]

**T-S B4.23** Joshua 22:22–30 (folio 1); Judges 1:24 – 2:1 (folio 2)
Hebrew; Aramaic: Targum Jonathan to Prophets. Oriental square script; Babylonian vocalisation + accents.
Vellum; 2 leaves (1 bifolium). 34.5 × 27.5; 2 cols.; 21 lines.
Divine name: Hebrew tetragrammaton; Targum ״׳.
Kahle *MdO* pp.19–22. [82]

**T-S B4.24** 2 Samuel 24:16 – 1 Kings 1:15 (folio 1); 1 Kings 3:5–28 (folio 2)
Hebrew; Aramaic: Targum Jonathan to Prophets. Oriental square script; Babylonian vocalisation + accents; Tiberian accents added in black ink at beginning of 1 Kings (folio 1r).
Vellum; 2 leaves (1 bifolium). 26.0 × 19.6; 2 cols.; 30 lines.
Divine name: Hebrew tetragrammaton; Targum ״׳.
Massoretic notes to Hebrew text in margins.
Kahle *MdO* pp.25–9 (in part). [83]

**T-S B4.25** Jeremiah 18:7–23 (folio 1); 23:27 – 24:2 (folio 2)
Hebrew; Aramaic: Targum Jonathan to Prophets. Oriental square script; Babylonian vocalisation + sporadic accents.
Vellum; 2 leaves; badly mutilated. 15.3⁺ × [20.0]; 2 cols.; 20⁺ lines.
Divine name: Hebrew tetragrammaton; Targum ״״׳.
Kahle *MdO* pp.38–40. [84]

**T-S B4.26** Jeremiah 5:22 – 6:10
Hebrew; Aramaic: Targum Jonathan to Prophets. Oriental(?) square script; Babylonian vocalisation + accents.
Vellum; 1 leaf; mutilated. 24.0⁺ × 20.0; 2 cols.; 26⁺ lines.
Divine name: Hebrew tetragrammaton; Targum ״׳.
Kahle *MdO* pp.41–3. [85]

**T-S B4.27** Numbers 29:15 – 30:9 (folio 1); 32:5–33 (folio 2)
Hebrew; Aramaic: Onqelos. Oriental square script; Babylonian vocalisation + accents.
Vellum; 2 leaves; mutilated (folio 2 torn into two parts, separately conserved). 28.5 × 26.0; 2 cols.; 31 lines.
Divine name: Hebrew tetragrammaton; Onqelos ö׳.
Massorah to Onqelos in bottom margin of folio 2. [86]

**T-S B4.28** Deuteronomy 4:23 – 9:18 (folios 1–7); 9:21–23 (folio 8r); 10:8–10 (folio 8v); 9:25–26, 10:1–3 (small fragment separately conserved); 13:16–19, 14:21–24 (folio 9); 14:28–29, 15:15–17 (folio 10)
Hebrew; Aramaic: Onqelos. Yemenite(?) square script; Babylonian vocalisation + accents; Babylonian Massorah Magna in bottom margin.
Vellum; 10 leaves (4 bifolia); mutilated (folios 8, 10 very badly). [31.0] × [24.0]; 2 cols.; [28] lines.
Divine name: Hebrew tetragrammaton; Onqelos ״׳; cipher: קמ׳(!) for number of verses in *parashat wa'ethanan* at Deuteronomy 7:11 (generally 118). [87]

**T-S B4.29** Deuteronomy 5:5 – 7:7
Hebrew; Aramaic: Onqelos. Oriental square script; sporadic Babylonian vocalisation; Tiberian vocalisation + accents.
Vellum; 2 leaves. 28.2 × 25.0; 2 cols.; 30 lines.
Divine name: Hebrew tetragrammaton; Onqelos ״׳/״.
Decorative *samekh* in margin at Deuteronomy 6:4 denotes Palestinian triennial *sidra* (folio 2r) ✿. [88]

**T-S B4.30** Deuteronomy 9:16 – 10:8 (folio 1); 11:31 – 12:18 (folio 2)
Hebrew; Aramaic: Onqelos. Oriental square script; Babylonian vocalisation + accents; Babylonian Massorah in margin.
Vellum; 2 leaves. 29.8 × 20.8; 2 cols.; 28 lines.
Divine name: Hebrew tetragrammaton; Onqelos ״׳. Sign ö at Deuteronomy 10:1 denotes Palestinian triennial *sidra* and massoretic notes to Onqelos at 9:24; 10:1, 6 and 12:14. [89]

**T-S B4.31** Deuteronomy 1:26–42
Hebrew; Aramaic: Onqelos. Oriental square script; Babylonian vocalisation + accents.
Vellum; 1 leaf; badly mutilated. 17.5⁺ × [22.0]; 2 cols.; 16⁺ lines. [90]

**T-S B4.32**   Deuteronomy 21:22 – 22:15 (folio 1); 26:10 – 27:3 (folio 2)
Hebrew; Aramaic: Onqelos.   Oriental square script; Babylonian vocalisation + sporadic accents.
Vellum; 2 leaves (1 bifolium); mutilated.   25.5 × 19.3; 2 cols.; 24 lines.
Divine name: Hebrew tetragrammaton; Onqelos ״׳. [91]

**T-S B4.33**   Deuteronomy 30:16 – 32:16
Hebrew; Aramaic: Onqelos.   Oriental square script; sporadic Babylonian vocalisation + accents.
Vellum; 2 leaves; mutilated.   28.4 × [24.0]; 2 cols.; 29 lines.
Divine name: Hebrew tetragrammaton; Onqelos ״׳. ס̇ in margin at 31:14 (folio 1v) denotes Palestinian triennial *sidra*. [92]

**T-S B4.34 (+ 1 leaf of T-S B4.35)**   Joshua 18:6–19 (folio 1); 19:27 – 20:2 (folio 2); Judges 8:5–23 (folio 3 see note); 8:24 – 9:6 (folio 4)
Hebrew; Aramaic: Targum Jonathan to Prophets. Yemenite square script; Babylonian vocalisation..
Vellum; 4 leaves; badly mutilated.   24.0⁺ × [22.0]; 2 cols.; [26] lines.
Folio 3 is now classified as part of T-S B4.35 (B4.34 and 35 are probably fragments of the same manuscript). [93]

**T-S B4.35**   Judges 6:3–19 (folio 1); 6:24–26, 39 (folio 2); 6:40 – 7:3, 12–13 (folio 3); 7:14–15, 7:25 – 8:2 (folio 4)
Hebrew; Aramaic: Targum Jonathan to Prophets. Yemenite square script; Babylonian vocalisation.
Vellum; 4 leaves (1 bifolium); badly mutilated. 17.0⁺ × 21.0; 2 cols.; 18⁺ lines.
Probably the same manuscript as B4.34. [94]

**T-S B4.36**   1 Samuel 13:22 – 20:12
Hebrew; Aramaic: Targum Jonathan to Prophets. Oriental square script; sporadic Babylonian vocalisation + accents; Tiberian vocalisation + accents (in paler ink for Hebrew text only); Massorah Magna and Parva in margins (in paler ink).
Vellum; 8 leaves; badly mutilated.   34.0 × [25.0]; 2 cols. (only 1 col. preserved on each side); 35–6 lines.
Divine name: Hebrew tetragrammaton; Targum ȯ׳. [95]

**T-S B4.37**   Jeremiah 8:22 – 9:18
Hebrew; Aramaic: Targum Jonathan to Prophets. Oriental square script; Babylonian vocalisation + accents.
Vellum; 1 leaf; badly mutilated.   26.5 × [19.6]; 2 cols.; 28 lines. [96]

**T-S B4.38**   Ezekiel 33:29 – 34:12 (folio 1); 36:18–29 (folio 2); 39:11–29 (folio 3); 40:16 – 41:5 (folios 4–5); 41:24 – 42:14 (folio 6)
Hebrew; Aramaic: Targum Jonathan to Prophets. Yemenite(?) square script; Babylonian vocalisation + sporadic accents.
Vellum; 6 leaves (2 bifolia); mutilated.   25.3 × 17.2 (folio 2: 19.5 × 16.5⁺); 2 cols.; 27–9 lines.
Divine name: Hebrew tetragrammaton; Targum ״׳. [97]

**T-S B4.39**   Jeremiah 1:10 – 2:6 (folio 1); 5:14 – 6:1 (folio 2)
Hebrew; Aramaic: Targum Jonathan to Prophets. Oriental square script; Babylonian vocalisation + accents.
Vellum; 2 leaves (1 bifolium); folio 1 badly mutilated. 28.3⁺ × 23.7; 2 cols.; 25 lines.
Divine name: Hebrew tetragrammaton; Targum ׳״׳. [98]

**T-S B4.40**   Nahum 2:13 – 3:17 (folio 1); Haggai 2:5–22 (folio 2)
Hebrew; Aramaic: Targum Jonathan to Prophets. Oriental square script; Babylonian vocalisation + accents.
Vellum; 2 leaves; mutilated (folio 2 torn into two parts, separately conserved).   32.0 × 25.8; 2 cols.; 22 lines.
Divine name: Hebrew tetragrammaton; Targum ׳״׳. [99]

**T-S B4.41**   Zechariah 3:7–47 (folio 1); 8:15 – 11:16 (folios 2–7)
Hebrew; Aramaic: Targum Jonathan to Prophets. Oriental square script; Babylonian vocalisation + accents (only folios 1–5r).
Vellum; 7 leaves (3 bifolia); partly mutilated. 16.0 × 20.0; 2 cols.; 13 lines.
Divine name: Hebrew tetragrammaton; Targum ׳״׳/׳״. [100]

**T-S B5.1**
There is no fragment at this classmark. [101]

**T-S B5.2**   Leviticus 16:5–15
Hebrew; Aramaic: Onqelos.   Oriental square script; unpointed.
Vellum; 1 leaf; slightly torn.   19.7 × 16.7; 19–20 lines.
Divine name: Hebrew tetragrammaton; Onqelos ״׳. Part of marginal drawing on stub of leaf originally conjoined. ❂. [102]

**T-S B5.3**   Isaiah 42:6–16
Hebrew; Aramaic: Targum Jonathan to Prophets. Oriental square script; sporadic Tiberian vocalisation (v.11).
Paper; 1 leaf; mutilated.   18.7 × 10.0⁺; 20 lines.
Divine name: Hebrew & Targum tetragrammaton ׳״. [103]

**T-S B5.4** Hosea 1:4 – 2:2 (folio 1); 5:9 – 6:4 (folio 2)

Hebrew; Aramaic: Targum Jonathan to Prophets. Oriental square script; unpointed.

Vellum; 2 leaves; badly mutilated.  16.0 × [20.0]; 2 cols.; 13 lines. [104]

**T-S B5.5** Genesis 1:6–14

Hebrew; Aramaic: Onqelos. Oriental script; Hebrew square; Onqelos smaller, semi-cursive; unpointed.

Paper; 1 leaf; slightly torn.  17.8 × 13.2; 17 lines.

Divine name: Hebrew אלהים; Onqelos ℅. [105]

**T-S B5.6** Genesis 21:9–18

Hebrew; Aramaic: Onqelos. Oriental square script; unpointed.

Vellum; 1 leaf; badly mutilated.  19.6 × 17.8; 17–19 lines. [106]

**T-S B5.7** Leviticus 23:25–39

Hebrew; Aramaic: Onqelos. Oriental square script; Tiberian vocalisation + accents.

Vellum; 1 leaf; badly mutilated.  16.5⁺ × [25.0]; 2 cols.; 11⁺ lines. [107]

**T-S B5.8 (a? There are two fragments with the same classmark of B5.8)**

Exodus 32:25 – 33:7

Hebrew; Aramaic: Onqelos. Oriental square script; Tiberian vocalisation (from 33:1 (*verso*)).

Vellum; 1 leaf; mutilated.  26.5 × 23.0; 2 cols.; 26 lines.

Divine name: Hebrew tetragrammaton; Onqelos ⁙. Targum of 32:35 was omitted in accordance with Mishnah *Megillah* 4:10, and added by a second hand in the margin and between the lines (*verso*); scribal error in 33:5: ארעה for אעשה. [108]

**T-S B5.8 (b?)** 1 Kings 6:1–6 (folio 1); Ezekiel 43:21–27 (folio 2); (*haftarot*)

Hebrew; Aramaic: Targum Jonathan to Prophets. Oriental square script; unpointed.

Vellum; 2 leaves (1 bifolium); badly mutilated. 11.8 × 11.8; 13 lines.

Divine name: Hebrew tetragrammaton; Targum ⁙. From the *haftarot* for *parashot terumah* and *teṣaweh*. [109]

**T-S B5.9** Deuteronomy 33:1 – 34:12 (end of Pentateuch)

Hebrew; Aramaic: Onqelos. North African script; Hebrew square, Onqelos semi-cursive; unpointed.

Paper; 7 leaves (3 bifolia); folios 1, 7 mutilated. 21.7 × 14.5; 13–15 lines.

Divine name: Hebrew & Onqelos ℅; *alephs* omitted, but also added as *matres lectionis*. Hebraism in Onqelos towards end (folio 6v). [110]

**T-S B5.10** Deuteronomy 17:11 – 18:1 (*recto*); 18:1–15(?) (*verso*)

Hebrew; Aramaic: Onqelos. Oriental square script; unpointed.

Vellum; 1 leaf; badly mutilated and very badly rubbed (*verso* almost entirely illegible). 27.8 × 23.8; 2 cols.; 26 lines.

Scribal error: תעשה for יעשה (Deuteronomy 17:12). [111]

**T-S B5.11** Zechariah 14:13–16 (folio 1); 1 Kings 8:7–10 (folio 2); (*haftarot*)

Hebrew; Aramaic: Targum Jonathan to Prophets. Oriental square script; unpointed.

Paper; 2 leaves (1 bifolium). 13.6 × 10.7; 9 lines.

These are the *haftarot* for first two days of Tabernacles. [112]

**T-S B5.12** Isaiah 42:10–16, 54:1; (*haftarot*)

Hebrew; Aramaic: Targum Jonathan to Prophets. Yemenite(?) square script; unpointed.

Vellum; 1 leaf. 23.0 × [20.5]; 2 cols.; 15 lines.

Divine name: Hebrew & Targum ⁙. *Haftarot* are for *parashot bere'shit* and *noah*. [113]

**T-S B5.13** Deuteronomy 21:15 – 22:8

Hebrew; Aramaic: Onqelos. Oriental square script; Tiberian vocalisation + accents; Massorah Parva in margin (21:22); and a Massorah Magna note in margin (*verso*, 22:2). Added accompanying note conserved at beginning of binder: "Ben Naftali – H.P.R. 9.10.59" [H. P. Rüger?].

Vellum; 1 leaf; slightly rubbed. 32.4 × 28.3; 2 cols.; 27 lines. [114]

**T-S B6.1** Deuteronomy 16:16 – 17:7

Hebrew; Aramaic: Onqelos. Oriental square script; Tiberian vocalisation + accents.

Vellum; 1 leaf; mutilated. 15.0⁺ × 22.0; 2 cols.; 14⁺ lines.

Divine name: Hebrew tetragrammaton; Onqelos ⁙. Small *aleph* for *custos*; extra words: על מימר in 17:6; cipher: קכד for number of verses in *parashat re'eh* (after 16:17). חֲצִי inserted in line between the *parashot* and ס in margin denotes *sidra* ●. [115]

**T-S B6.2** Numbers 23:4–27 (folio 1); Deuteronomy 9:4–21 (folio 2)

Hebrew; Aramaic: Onqelos. Oriental square script; Tiberian vocalisation + accents.

**[T-S B6.2, cont.]**
Vellum; 2 leaves; mutilated. 29.0 × 24.3; 2 cols.; 25 lines.

Divine name: Hebrew & Onqelos tetragrammaton (Numbers 23:8), but elsewhere, יֹ in Onqelos.. [116]

### T-S B6.3   Leviticus 23:41 – 26:25
Hebrew; Aramaic: Onqelos. Oriental square script; Tiberian vocalisation + accents; sporadic Massorah Parva in margin.

Vellum; 6 leaves (2 bifolia); very badly mutilated. 32.0 × [26.0]; 2 cols.; 26 lines.

Divine name: Hebrew tetragrammaton; Onqelos יֹ. [117]

### T-S B6.4   Leviticus 14:4–17
Hebrew; Aramaic: Onqelos. Oriental square script; Tiberian vocalisation + accents.

Vellum; 1 leaf; badly mutilated. 31.0 × 26.0; 2 cols.; 26 lines.

Faded and illegible at end. [118]

### T-S B6.5   Genesis 6:19 – 7:15 (folio 1); 18:23 – 19:6 (folio 2); 41:24–43 (folio 3); Exodus 31:3 – 32:1 (folio 4); 39:10–28 (folio 5); Leviticus 4:32 – 5:11 (folio 6); 7:32 – 8:12 (folio 7); 5:11–25 (folio 8 – direct continuation of folio 6v); 13:42–56 (folio 9)
Hebrew; Aramaic: Onqelos. Oriental square script; Tiberian vocalisation + accents.

Vellum; 9 leaves (1 bifolium); 5 leaves badly mutilated. 26.0 × 22.0; 2 cols.; 22 lines.

Divine name: Hebrew אלהים; Onqelos יײי (folio 1), יֹ (folios 2–9). Massorah Parva in margin (folios 2–9), Massorah Magna (folio 3r?). Vocalisation by two hands (black and brown ink); this classmark includes several distinct manuscripts. [119]

### T-S B6.6 (= T-S AS 11.176)   Exodus 39:23–38
Hebrew; Aramaic: Palestinian Targum. Oriental square script; Tiberian vocalisation + accents.

Vellum; 1 leaf; badly mutilated. 23.0+ × 28.0; 3 cols.; 19+ lines.

Divine name: Hebrew tetragrammaton; Targum אדני.
Klein *GMPT* I, pp.299–301. [120]

### T-S B6.7   Deuteronomy 32:10–21
Hebrew; Aramaic: Onqelos. Oriental square script; Hebrew with Tiberian vocalisation; Onqelos unpointed.

Vellum; 1 leaf. 20.1 × 15.6; 19 lines.

Divine name: Hebrew tetragrammaton; Onqelos יֹ; cipher: ײַ in upper corner of *recto* (pagination?). [121]

### T-S B6.8   2 Samuel 22:29–32 (folio 1); 22:43–51 (folios 2–4)
Hebrew; Aramaic: Targum Jonathan to Prophets. Oriental square script; Hebrew with Tiberian vocalisation + accents.

Vellum; 4 leaves (1 bifolium). 9.4 × 7.6; 9–12 lines.

Divine name: Hebrew tetragrammaton; Targum יֹ. Text ends on 2nd line of folio 4v, remainder of folio blank. [122]

### T-S B6.9   Deuteronomy 12:25 – 16:10
Hebrew; Aramaic: Onqelos. Oriental square script; Hebrew with Tiberian vocalisation + accents; Onqelos with sporadic vocalisation (folio 1).

Vellum; 8 leaves (4 bifolia); mutilated. 19.3 × 15.6; 22 lines.

Divine name: Hebrew tetragrammaton; Onqelos א. [123]

### T-S B6.10   2 Samuel 21:17 – 22:43
Hebrew; Aramaic: Targum Jonathan to Prophets. Oriental square script; sporadic Tiberian vocalisation.

Vellum; 6 leaves (3 bifolia); slightly torn. 10.5 × 11.8; 13 lines.

Divine name: Hebrew tetragrammaton; Targum יֹ/יֹיֹ. [124]

### T-S B6.11   1 Samuel 1:7–11 (folio 1); 2:1–3 (folio 2)
Hebrew; Aramaic: Targum Jonathan to Prophets. Persian(?) square script; Tiberian vocalisation + accents; Massorah Magna and Parva.

Vellum; 2 leaves (1 bifolium); mutilated. 18.8 × 14.5; 13 lines. [125]

### T-S B6.12   Isaiah 19:17–18, Judges 4:23 – 5:2, Isaiah 19:24–5 (bottom margin) (*recto*); Judges 5:8–12 (*verso*); (*haftarot*)
Hebrew; Aramaic: Targum Jonathan to Prophets. Oriental square script; Hebrew with Tiberian vocalisation + accents.

Vellum; 1 leaf (scrap). 20.5 × 8.2; 1+ col.; 23 lines (+ 4 added lines in bottom margin of *recto*).

The Isaiah passage indicates that the sheet was wider, and probably contained two columns. Note before Judges 4: ויהי בשלח בשפטי and Isaiah 19 is attested as the *haftarah* for *parashat bo'*. [126]

### T-S B6.13   Genesis 14:9 – 17:1
Hebrew; Aramaic: Onqelos. Spanish semi-cursive script; Tiberian vocalisation + accents.

Vellum; 4 leaves (2 bifolia). 18.3 × 12.9; 23 lines.

Divine name: Hebrew tetragrammaton; Onqelos יֹ. See plate 5. [127]

**T-S B6.14**  1 Samuel 22:26–45
Hebrew; Aramaic: Targum Jonathan to Prophets.
Oriental square script; Tiberian vocalisation +
accents.
Vellum; 1 leaf.  28.8 × 22.2;  1 col. (in poetic format);
25 lines.
Divine name: Hebrew & Targum tetragrammaton.  [128]

**T-S B6.15**  Jeremiah 2:11–18 (folio 1); 30:15–21
(folio 2)
Hebrew; Aramaic: Targum Jonathan to Prophets.
Oriental square script; Tiberian vocalisation.
Vellum; 2 leaves; mutilated.  19.5 × 16.0; 15 lines.
The word: דילוג and a small supralinear circle follow 2:11,
which might indicate that the reader of a *haftarah* is to
skip over a portion of the text. Miniature *alephs* and
apostrophes serve as *custodes* of left margin; scribal error
בעלי תודתא for מעלי תודתא (30:19).  [129]

**T-S B6.16**  Ezekiel 46:8–12 (*recto* and majority
of *verso*); 47:12 (last six lines of *verso*);
(*haftarah*)
Hebrew; Aramaic: Targum Jonathan to Prophets.
Oriental square script; Tiberian vocalisation +
accents.
Vellum; 1 leaf; mutilated and rubbed.  16.2 × 15.3;
15 lines.
Divine name: Hebrew tetragrammaton; Targum ייי. Gloss
in top margin of *verso*: מנחא with Babylonian
vocalisation. This is the *haftarah* for *parashat ha-hodesh*.
[130]

**T-S B6.17**  Genesis 2:9 – 3:22
Hebrew; Aramaic: Onqelos.  Oriental square
script; Onqelos with Tiberian vocalisation (in darker
ink).
Vellum; 2 leaves (1 bifolium); mutilated and rubbed.
24.0 × 19.7;  24 lines.
Divine name: Hebrew tetragrammaton; Onqelos ייי.
[131]

**T-S B6.18**  Genesis 36:43 – 37:23
Hebrew; Aramaic: Onqelos.  Oriental square
script; Tiberian vocalisation + accents (faint).
Vellum; 1 leaf; slightly torn.  28.2 × 24.2; 2 cols.;
25–6 lines.
Drawing at 37:1 to indicate *parashah* ✡; cipher in line
between 36:43 and 37:1 לס(?) perhaps לסוראי?.  [132]

**T-S B6.19**  Exodus 5:15 – 6:12
Hebrew; Aramaic: Onqelos.  Oriental square
script; Tiberian vocalisation + accents (some in pale
faded ink); Massorah Magna and Parva.
Vellum; 1 leaf.  25.6 × [23.0]; 2 cols.;  24 lines.
Divine name: Hebrew tetragrammaton and אלהים; Onqelos
ייי. ס in margin at 6:2 to indicate *parashat wa'era'* ✡;
cipher: קפב denotes number of verses in *parashat shemot*.
[133]

**T-S B6.20**  Exodus 2:23 – 3:8 (folio 1); 16:32 –
17:10 (folio 2)
Hebrew; Aramaic: Onqelos.  Oriental square
script; sporadic Tiberian vocalisation in dark ink;
(earlier full Tiberian vocalisation + accents faded).
Vellum; 2 leaves; leaf 1 badly mutilated.  25.4 × 25.0;
20–21 lines.
ס at 3:1 denotes Palestinian triennial *sidra* ✡. Arabic
scribblings and Judaeo-Arabic glosses in margins at 16:36
and 17:2; ס פ פ ס at 17:7/8; this is not attested as a
*sidra*, but as the reading for Purim.  [134]

**T-S B6.21**  Exodus 15:23–26 (folio 1); 16:12–15
(folio 2)
Hebrew; Aramaic: Onqelos.  Oriental square
script; Onqelos with Tiberian vocalisation + accents.
Vellum; 2 leaves (1 bifolium).  8.9 × 11.2;  7 lines.
Catchwords at bottom of folio 2v and ה perhaps to
indicate the number of the quire.  [135]

**T-S B6.22**  Exodus 30:10 – 32:1
Hebrew; Aramaic: Onqelos.  Oriental square
script; Hebrew with Tiberian vocalisation + accents.
Vellum; 2 leaves (1 bifolium); badly mutilated.
20.0⁺ × 20.0⁺; 18⁺ lines.
The words: כי תשא are written in large script to indicate
beginning of *parashah* (30:11).  [136]

**T-S B6.23**  Leviticus 14:17–32 (folio 1);
15:11–26 (folio 2)
Hebrew; Aramaic: Onqelos.  Spanish semi-cursive
script; Tiberian vocalisation + accents; Massorah
Parva.
Vellum; 2 leaves (1 bifolium); folio 2 partly mutilated and
rubbed.  26.2 × 24.3; 2 cols.; 21 lines.
Divine name: Hebrew & Onqelos tetragrammaton.  [137]

**T-S B6.24**  Genesis 16:15 – 17:5, 17:9–10,
15–21 (folio 1); 17:22–7, 18:5–18 (folio 2)
Hebrew; Aramaic: Onqelos.  Ashkenazi square
script; Tiberian vocalisation + accents.
Vellum; 2 leaves; mutilated.  38.4 × 25.8; 2 cols.;
29 lines.
Divine name: Hebrew tetragrammaton; Onqelos ייי. See
plate 3.  [138]

**T-S B7.1**  Isaiah 41:10–16
Hebrew; Aramaic: Targum Jonathan to Prophets.
Oriental semi-cursive script; Tiberian vocalisation +
accents.

**[T-S B7.1, cont.]**
Paper; 1 leaf.   16.8 × 12.9;   13 lines.
Divine name: Hebrew tetragrammaton; Targum יי׳.   [139]

### T-S B7.2   1 Samuel 17:13-18
Hebrew; Aramaic: Targum Jonathan to Prophets.
Oriental semi-cursive script; Tiberian vocalisation + accents.
Paper; 1 leaf; slightly rubbed.   16.9 × 13.0;   12 lines.   [140]

### T-S B7.3   Exodus 28:15-30 (folio 1); 28:42 – 29:13 (folio 2); 29:13-39 (folios 3-4 of this manuscript are found at classmark B7.4); 29:40 – 30:8 (folio 5); Ezekiel 43:17-27, Exodus 30:11-13 (folio 6); 1 Kings 18:39, Exodus 35:1-15 (folio 7); 36:3-15 (folio 8); Numbers 4:27-42 (folio 9); 7:80-9; Judges 13:2-5 (folio 10)
Hebrew; Aramaic: Onqelos, Targum Jonathan to Prophets.   Oriental semi-cursive script; Tiberian vocalisation + accents.
Paper; 10 leaves (4 bifolia); folios 2,5,7 mutilated. 24.9 × 17.0;   22 lines.
Divine name: Hebrew tetragrammaton; Targum (Onqelos & Targum Jonathan to Prophets) יי׳/יי׳. *Hafṭarah* for *parashat teṣaweh* (folio 6); notation פרשה פת and אפס בשפט (folios 5b, 10b); Arabic writing and pagination in upper corners, and an Arabic account with Coptic numerals on a strip pasted on to hold some of the folios together [GK]; sparse Massorah Parva; lower corner of folio 7 attached to folio 8.   [141]

### T-S B7.4   Exodus 32:10-19 (folio 1); 34:35 – 35:8 (folio 2); 36:19-30 (folio 3); 38:21-9 (folio 4) (2 additional folios, which are part of T-S B7.3, are described in the preceding entry)
Hebrew; Aramaic: Onqelos.   Spanish square script; Tiberian vocalisation + accents.
Paper; 4 leaves (2 bifolia); folio 2 mutilated. 21.1 × 15.2;   19-20 lines.
Divine name: Hebrew tetragrammaton; Onqelos ייֿ.   [142]

### T-S B7.5   Exodus 39:21-7
Hebrew; Aramaic: Onqelos.   Oriental semi-cursive script; Tiberian vocalisation + accents.
Paper; 1 leaf; slightly torn and rubbed.   17.4 × 12.2; 13 lines.
Divine name: Hebrew tetragrammaton; Onqelos יי׳; vocalisation reinforced on *verso*.   [143]

### T-S B7.6   Leviticus 27:20-26 (folio 1); 27:26-32 (folio 2)
Hebrew; Aramaic: Onqelos.   Oriental semi-cursive script; Tiberian vocalisation.
Paper; 2 leaves (1 bifolium); folio 1 badly mutilated. 16.4 × 13.2;   14 lines.
Divine name: Hebrew tetragrammaton; Onqelos יי׳.   [144]

### T-S B7.7   Exodus 37:16-18 (*recto*)
Hebrew; Aramaic: Onqelos.   Oriental square script; Tiberian vocalisation.
Paper; 1 leaf.   14.0⁺ × 12.0⁺;   10⁺ lines.
*Verso* (originally blank), contains scribal pen exercises.   [145]

### T-S B7.8   Numbers 1:27-34
Hebrew; Aramaic: Onqelos.   Oriental square script; Tiberian vocalisation (*recto* only).
Paper; 1 leaf.   20.2 × 17.4;   14-16 lines.   [146]

### T-S B7.9   Deuteronomy 31:3-17
Hebrew; Aramaic: Onqelos.   Oriental square script; Tiberian vocalisation (Hebrew & Onqelos) + accents (Hebrew).
Paper; 1 leaf.   25.4 × 20.6;   23 lines.
Divine name: Hebrew tetragrammaton; Onqelos יי׳.   [147]

### T-S B7.10   Exodus 14:26-8 (folio 1v); 20:3-9 (folio 2)
Hebrew; Aramaic: Onqelos.   Oriental semi-cursive script; Tiberian vocalisation.
Vellum; 2 leaves (1 bifolium?).   11.3 × 9.2; 12-13 lines.
Divine name: Hebrew and Onqelos יי׳. This is a booklet containing readings for the seventh day Passover and for Pentecost. Notation of ownership on folio 1r: תרגום ויושע עשרת הדברות and in untrained Oriental square majusculae: לייעיש בר יפת הלוי זהיה בישישים. Heading on folio 1v: תרגם ויושע. See plate 14.   [148]

### T-S B7.11   Genesis 42:36 – 43:7
Hebrew; Aramaic: Onqelos.   Oriental semi-cursive script; Tiberian vocalisation.
Paper; 1 leaf; slightly mutilated.   21.6 × 14.9;   18 lines.   [149]

### T-S B7.12   Genesis 1:1-4
Hebrew; Aramaic: Onqelos.   Oriental semi-cursive script; Tiberian vocalisation.
Paper; 1 leaf; mutilated.   15.0⁺ × 13.5;   18 lines.
Divine name: Hebrew אלהים; Onqelos יי׳; *verso* (originally blank) contains pen exercises.   [150]

### T-S B7.13   Genesis 41:5-12 (folio 1); 41:36-42 (folio 2)
Hebrew; Aramaic: Onqelos.   Oriental square script; Tiberian vocalisation.

**[T-S B7.13, cont.]**
Paper; 2 leaves (1 bifolium); rubbed. 19.0 × 14.3; 15–16 lines.
Divine name: Hebrew אלהים; Onqelos יי. [151]

**T-S B7.14** Genesis 42:15 – 43:7 (folios 1–4); 43:14–20 (folio 5)
Hebrew; Aramaic: Onqelos. Oriental square script; Tiberian vocalisation.
Paper; 5 leaves (2 bifolia); slightly rubbed. 20.5 × 15.2; 15–18 lines.
Divine name: Hebrew אלהים; Onqelos יי. [152]

**T-S B7.15** Deuteronomy 2:16–19
Hebrew; Aramaic: Onqelos. Oriental(?) square script; Hebrew with Tiberian vocalisation + accents; Onqelos in smaller script with Tiberian vocalisation.
Paper; 1 leaf. 14.5 × 10.6; 8 lines (Hebrew).
Two lines of Onqelos per line of Hebrew and across only part of the line. [153]

**T-S B7.16** Numbers 13:33 – 14:5 (folio 1); 14:14–18 (folio 2); 16:3–7 (2nd folio 1); 16:16–19 (2nd folio 2)
Hebrew; Aramaic: Onqelos. Oriental square script; Tiberian vocalisation + accents.
Paper; 4 leaves (2 bifolia); rubbed. 17.3 × 13.3; 11 lines.
Both bifolia are marked 1 & 2. [154]

**T-S B7.17** Numbers 24:16 – 25:11 (folios 1–2); 26:19–65 (folios 3–5)
Hebrew; Aramaic: Onqelos. Spanish square script; Tiberian vocalisation + accents.
Paper; 5 leaves (2 bifolia); mutilated and rubbed. 20.2 × 14.5; 20 lines.
Divine name: Hebrew tetragrammaton; Onqelos יי. [155]

**T-S B7.18** Deuteronomy 16:9–12
Hebrew; Aramaic: Onqelos. Oriental square script; Tiberian vocalisation (Onqelos).
Paper; 1 leaf; slightly torn. 14.3 × 10.2; 12–13 lines.
Divine name: Hebrew & Onqelos יי. [156]

**T-S B7.19** Genesis 43:7–13
Hebrew; Aramaic: Onqelos. Oriental square script; Tiberian vocalisation.
Paper; 1 leaf; mutilated and rubbed. 16.0⁺ × 15.2; 14⁺ lines. [157]

**T-S B8.1** Deuteronomy 5:19/22 – 26/29
Hebrew; Aramaic: Palestinian Targum. Oriental square script; Tiberian vocalisation + accents; Massorah Parva note to 5:26/29.
Vellum; 1 leaf; slightly torn. 31.3 × 29.0; 3 cols.; 19–24 lines.
Divine name: Hebrew tetragrammaton; Targum אדני.
Kahle *MdW* II, pp. 26–7; Klein *GMPT* I, pp. 335–37. [158]

**T-S B8.2** 2 Samuel 23:8–10,12
Aramaic: Targum Jonathan to Prophets (+ Hebrew lemmata). Oriental square script (untrained); unpointed.
Vellum; 2 leaves (1 bifolium); slightly torn. 13.2 × 7.5; 16 lines.
Textual variants: ספריא for סבייא (v.8); וסעיד לעותניא (v.8); and reversed word order; folio 2 is blank. [159]

**T-S B8.3** Genesis 36:8–9,24 (folio 1); 38:16–26 (folio 2)
Hebrew; Aramaic: Palestinian Targum. Oriental square script; Tiberian vocalisation + accents; Massorah Magna and Parva.
Vellum; 2 leaves (1 bifolium); folio 1 almost entirely missing, folio 2 slightly mutilated. 34.7 × 27.7; 3 cols.; 27 lines.
Kahle *MdW* II, pp. 18–19; Klein *GMPT* I, pp. 87–9. [160]

**T-S B8.4 (= T-S AS 68.144, 224)** Genesis 28:17 – 29:17 (folio 1); 31:15–34 (folio 2)
Aramaic: Palestinian Targum (+ Hebrew lemmata). Oriental square script; sporadic Palestinian and Tiberian vocalisation + accents (disjunctives).
Vellum; 2 leaves (1 bifolium); mutilated. 15.8 × 15.8; 18–20 lines.
Kahle *MdW* II, pp. 33–4, 41–2; Klein *GMPT* I, pp. 37–9, 57–9. [161]

**T-S B8.5 (= T-S AS 66.187)** Exodus 7:10–22 (folio 1); 9:21–34 (folio 2)
Hebrew; Aramaic: Palestinian Targum. Oriental square script; Tiberian vocalisation + accents; Massorah Magna and Parva.
Vellum; 2 leaves (1 bifolium); mutilated. 34.2 × 27.6; 3 cols.; 24 lines.
Divine name: Hebrew tetragrammaton; Targum יי; original script of folio 1r overwritten in black ink by a later hand.
Kahle *MdW* II, pp. 24–6; Klein *GMPT* I, pp. 179–85. [162]

**T-S B8.6** Genesis 43:7 – 44:23
Hebrew; Aramaic: Palestinian Targum. Oriental square script; Tiberian vocalisation + accents; Massorah Magna and Parva.

[T-S B8.6, cont.]
Vellum; 4 leaves (2 bifolia); badly mutilated.
24.8⁺ × 27.5; 3 cols.; 18⁺ lines.
Cipher at 44:18 denotes 40th Palestinian triennial *sidra* followed by Joshua 14:6 as *haftarah*.
Kahle *MdW* II, pp.19–22; Klein *GMPT* I, pp.127–33.
[163]

### T-S B8.7 (= T-S AS 64.27)   Genesis 48:11–21
Hebrew; Aramaic: Palestinian Targum. Oriental square script; Tiberian vocalisation + accents; Massorah Magna and Parva.
Vellum; 1 leaf; mutilated.   32.8 × 28.0;   3 cols.; 23 lines.
Kahle *MdW* II, pp.22–3; Klein *GMPT* I, pp.153–55.
[164]

### T-S B8.8 (= T-S NS 161.262)   Deuteronomy 26:18 – 27:12 (folio 1); 28:15–18 (folio 2r); 28:27–30 (folio 2v)
Hebrew; Aramaic: Palestinian Targum. Oriental square script; Tiberian vocalisation + accents; Massorah Parva.
Vellum; 2 leaves (1 bifolium); badly mutilated.
[37.0] × [27.5]; 3 cols.; 24 lines.
Divine name: Hebrew tetragrammaton; Targum ויי.
T-S NS 161.262 is an additional part of folio 2.
Kahle *MdW* II, pp.27–8; Klein *GMPT* I, pp.349–55.
[165]

### T-S B8.9 (folio 1) (= T-S NS 138.79; NS 271.183)   Genesis 22:5–9
Targumic *Tosefta*(?) (+ Hebrew lemmata).
North African(?) square script; sporadic Tiberian vocalisation.
Paper; 2 leaves (1 bifolium).   16.4 × 12.5;   11–13 lines.
Folio 2 contains a *seliḥah* poem from a New Year liturgy; and the targumic expansion (folio 1) is to the Torah reading for New Year.
Grelot *REJ* XVI, pp.5–27; Klein *GMPT* I, p.35.   [166]

### T-S B8.10 (= T-S AS 68.83)   Genesis 37:19–34
Hebrew; Aramaic: Palestinian Targum. Oriental square script; Tiberian vocalisation + accents; Massorah Parva; most of folio 1 missing; a midrashic passage on מדבר, באר and בארה של תורה in margin of folio 1.
Vellum; 2 leaves (1 bifolium); badly mutilated.
34.7 × 27.8; 3 cols.; 26 lines.
Kahle *MdW* II, pp.16–17 (mostly); Klein *GMPT* I, pp.79–81.
[167]

### T-S B8.11   Genesis 7:17 – 8:9
Hebrew; Aramaic: Palestinian Targum. Oriental square script; Tiberian vocalisation + accents.
Vellum; 1 leaf; slightly mutilated.   30.0 × 28.0; 3 cols.;   21 lines.
*Samekh* in margin at 8:1, denotes Palestinian triennial *sidra*.
Kahle *MdW* II, pp.15–16; Klein *GMPT* I, pp.21–3.
[168]

### T-S B8.12 (= T-S AS 64.239)
Exodus 5:20 – 6:11
Hebrew; Aramaic: Palestinian Targum. Oriental square script; Tiberian vocalisation + accents.
Vellum; 1 leaf; mutilated.   33.9 × 27.1;  3 cols.; 24 lines.
Divine name: Hebrew tetragrammaton; Targum ויי; fourth Palestinian triennial *sidra* denoted by *samekh* in margin at Exodus 6:2, also beginning of *haftarah* (Isaiah 42:8); outer margin has cipher פס ל for number of verses in *sidra*; and a cipher in the margin at 6:2 indicates number of verses in the *parashah* (קנד is error for קכד).
Kahle *MdW* II, pp.23–4; Klein *GMPT* I, pp.177–79.
[169]

### T-S B9.1   Deuteronomy 24:18 – 25:8
Aramaic: Onqelos.   Oriental semi-cursive script; Tiberian vocalisation.
Paper; 1 leaf; mutilated.   16.0⁺ × 13.3;   15 lines.
Divine name: יי; Hebrew or variant in 24:19 corrected in margin.   [170]

### T-S B9.2   Exodus 26:28 – 27:19 (folio 1); 32:25 – 33:13 (folio 2)
Aramaic: Onqelos.   Oriental square script; unpointed (except 27:7,14 Tiberian).
Paper; 2 leaves (1 bifolium); slightly mutilated.
17.3 × 12.9;   21 lines.
Divine name: יי.   [171]

### T-S B9.3   Isaiah 12:2–6
Aramaic: Targum Jonathan to Prophets.   Oriental square script; Tiberian vocalisation.
Paper; 1 leaf; mutilated and rubbed.   20.3 × 14.2; 13 lines.
Divine name: יי; *verso* blank.   [172]

### T-S B9.4   Joshua 5:10 – 6:1, 6:27; (*haftarah*)
Aramaic: Targum Jonathan to Prophets.   Oriental semi-cursive script (untrained); Tiberian vocalisation.
Paper; 2 leaves (1 bifolium); partly rubbed.   13.3 × 8.7; 17 lines.
Divine name: יי; attested as a *haftarah* for first day Passover; folio 2 blank.   [173]

### T-S B9.5 (= T-S B10.3)   Judges 5:26
Aramaic: Targum Jonathan to Prophets (including *tosefta*).   Oriental square script; Tiberian vocalisation.

[T-S B9.5 (= T-S B10.3), cont.]
Vellum; 1 leaf; slightly torn.   16.2 × 12.7;   9 lines (end of text).

Sign at end of text ✥; quotation of Onqelos to Deuteronomy 22:5; *verso* blank. [174]

## T-S B9.6   Genesis 21:12–23

Aramaic: Onqelos.   Oriental square script; Tiberian vocalisation.

Paper; 2 leaves (1 bifolium).   15.4 × 10.9;   10 lines.

Divine name: יי. [175]

## T-S B9.7   Genesis 24:27–66

Aramaic: Onqelos.   Oriental square script; Tiberian vocalisation.

Paper; 2 leaves (1 bifolium).   17.1 × 12.9;   18 lines.

Divine name: יי. [176]

## T-S B9.8   Exodus 12:33–42

Aramaic: Onqelos.   Oriental square script; Tiberian vocalisation (folio 1r, and only two words on folios 2–3).

Paper; 2 leaves (1 bifolium).   13.9 × 9.0;   11 lines.

Divine name: ייֽ; text ends abruptly on folio 2r, perhaps because of scribal omission that was added only in the margin (12:41); folio 2v blank. [177]

## T-S B9.9   Exodus 18:1 – 19:4

Aramaic: Onqelos (abridged).   Oriental square linear script (untrained); Tiberian vocalisation (until folio 2v).

Paper; 2 leaves (1 bifolium).   9.0 × 7.0;   8 lines.

Divine name: יי; each line contains only the first few words of a verse; the only lemma is on folio 2v line 4 (19:1): בחדש. [178]

## T-S B9.10 (= T-S NS 116.77, AS 68.42)
Exodus 25:20 – 28:7

Aramaic: Onqelos (extract).   Oriental square script; Tiberian vocalisation (faded).

Vellum; 2 leaves (1 bifolium); slightly torn and rubbed.   10.7 × 10.4;   14 lines.

Massorah to Onqelos in bottom margin; notation denotes *sidra* ואתה תצוה (27:20) in text and סדר occurs in margin ✥ (folio 2v); also Hebrew massoretic(?) note הָאַחַת/הָאֶחָת in text. See plate 16. [179]

## T-S B9.11   Genesis 15:11 – 16:14 (*recto*); Isaiah 61:9 – 62:9 (*verso*); (*haftarah*)

Aramaic: Palestinian Fragment-targum, Targum Jonathan to Prophets.   Oriental semi-cursive script; Tiberian vocalisation.

Paper; 1 leaf; mutilated and *recto* badly rubbed.   22.0 × 16.0;   21 lines.

Divine name: אדני; bottom quarter of *recto* blank, probably indicating end of *haftarah*; another folio of the same manuscript (HUC Genizah 1134) published by Klein in *HUCA* XLIX, pp. 73–87, and in *GMPT* I, pp. 28–9; II, pp. 10–11 and plate 100.

Klein *Sefarad* XLIX, pp. 123–133. [180]

## T-S B9.12   Genesis 21:1–10

Aramaic: Onqelos.   Oriental semi-cursive script; unpointed.

Paper; 1 leaf; slightly mutilated.   20.4 × 12.8⁺;   14 lines.

Divine name: יי; text ends abruptly, and bottom third of page left blank; *verso* blank except for large letters filled in with red ink: ...תרגום. [181]

## T-S B9.13   Genesis 22:17 – 23:13 (folio 1); 25:7–25 (folio 2); 28:5–21 (folio 3); 30:6–28 (folio 4)

Aramaic: Onqelos.   Oriental semi-cursive script; unpointed.

Paper; 4 leaves (2 bifolia); folios 2–3 badly mutilated.   22.9 × 14.0;   19 lines.

Divine name: יי; notation marks *parashah* in margin ✥ (folio 1r, 3r); Hebrew lemmata in text in majusculae; words completed in margin by original hand after space left to maintain justification. [182]

## T-S B9.14   Genesis 38:3–14 (folio 1); 38:25 – 40:14 (folio 2–5)

Aramaic: Onqelos.   Oriental semi-cursive script; Tiberian vocalisation.

Paper; 5 leaves (2 bifolia).   10.2 × 14.4;   10–11 lines.

Divine name: יי. [183]

## T-S B9.15   Genesis 49:3–17

Aramaic: Onqelos (+ sporadic Hebrew lemmata). Oriental square script; unpointed.

Paper; 1 leaf; badly mutilated.   14.2⁺ × 13.0;   17⁺ lines. [184]

## T-S B9.16   Exodus 16:31 – 17:1 (folio 1); 19:10–15 (folio 2)

Aramaic: Onqelos.   Oriental square script; Tiberian vocalisation.

Paper; 2 leaves; very badly mutilated.   11.0⁺ × 11.7⁺;   7⁺ lines.

Divine name: יי. [185]

## T-S B9.17   Leviticus 8:34 – 9:1; 9:21 – 10:1 (folio 1); 26:3–17; 26–39 (folio 2)

Aramaic: Onqelos.   Spanish semi-cursive script; Tiberian vocalisation + accents.

**[T-S B9.17, cont.]**
Vellum; 2 leaves (1 bifolium); very badly mutilated (folio 1 almost entirely missing). 19.0⁺ × 20.0; 17⁺ lines.

Divine name: ⟨ʾ⟩; *parashah* notation in majusculae (folio 2r). [186]

**T-S B9.18** Deuteronomy 28:50 – 29:8
Aramaic: Onqelos. Oriental square script; unpointed.

Vellum; 1 leaf; slightly mutilated. 20.0 × 18.5; 24–5 lines.

Divine name: יֹי; end of *parashah* notation at bottom of *verso*: סס in text, and [שׁ]פּ in bottom margin; בשם יי אלהי ישׂראל written in top margin of *verso*. [187]

**T-S B9.19** Habakkuk 3:16–19; Zephaniah 1:1 – 3:5 (folio 1); Zechariah 13:1 – 14:21; Malachi 1:1–6 (folio 2)
Aramaic: Targum Jonathan to Prophets. Oriental square script; sporadic Tiberian vocalisation + accents, and occasional Palestinian vocalisation.

Vellum; 2 leaves (1 bifolium – now separated); folio 2 mutilated. 21.8 × 24.9; 23 lines.

Divine name: ײ. [188]

**T-S B9.20** Exodus 19:13 – 20:19
Aramaic: Onqelos. Oriental semi-cursive script; partial Tiberian vocalisation.

Paper; 1 leaf. 31.0 × 12.5; 31 lines.

Psalms 119:165 and two Judaeo-Arabic notes כמל אלתרגום and הדא תמאם אל פראשה are inserted between 20:18/19 in Hebrew; *verso* is inverted in relation to *recto*, indicating that this is probably a complete single-sheet manuscript and not part of a larger work. [189]

**T-S B10.1** Exodus 2:19 – 3:17 (folio 1); 5:15 – 6:21 (folio 2)
Aramaic: Onqelos (+ Hebrew lemmata). Spanish square script; Tiberian vocalisation + accents.

Vellum; 2 leaves (1 bifolium). 23.8 × 19.3; 2 cols.; 21 lines.

Divine name: ײַ; *parashah* notation on folio 2r in margin (6:2). [190]

**T-S B10.2** Genesis 39:2 – 41:4
Aramaic: Onqelos (+ Hebrew lemmata). Spanish square script; unpointed.

Vellum; 1 leaf; mutilated. 24.5 × 19.0; 28 lines.

Divine name: ײַ; *parashah* notation on *verso* in majusculae on two lines in body of text (41:1). [191]

**T-S B10.3 (= T-S B9.5)** Judges 5:8, 11
Aramaic: Targum Jonathan to Prophets (*toseftot*). Oriental square script; Tiberian vocalisation.

Vellum; 2 leaves (1 bifolium); folio 2 mutilated. 16.2 × 13.7; 9–10 lines.

Quotation of Onqelos to Deuteronomy 32:17 in Judges 5:8; this seems to be a collection of targumic *Toseftot* to Judges 5:8, 11, 26...; folio 2 is blank. [192]

**T-S B10.4** Genesis 4:11–23 (folio 1); 6:21 – 7:14 (folio 2)
Aramaic: Onqelos (+ Hebrew lemmata). Oriental square script; unpointed (except for one word at 4:19).

Vellum; 2 leaves; mutilated. 14.2 × 12.3; 14–16 lines.

Divine name: ײ. [193]

**T-S B10.5** Genesis 3:16 – 7:8
Aramaic: Onqelos (+ Hebrew lemmata). Oriental square script; Babylonian vocalisation.

Vellum; 2 leaves; mutilated. 22.0⁺ × 20.7⁺; 26 lines.

Divine name: ײ.

Díez Macho *Sefarad* XIX, pp. 273–82. [194]

**T-S B10.6** Numbers 6:27 – 7:5 (folio 1); 7:86 – 8:2 (folio 2)
Aramaic: Onqelos (+ Hebrew lemmata). Oriental square script; Tiberian vocalisation (except folio 2r).

Vellum; 2 leaves; folio 1 badly mutilated. 15.4 × 10.3; 11 lines. [195]

**T-S B10.7** Numbers 18:24 – 19:14
Aramaic: Onqelos (+ Hebrew lemmata). Oriental square script; sporadic Tiberian vocalisation (by a second hand in black ink).

Vellum; 1 leaf; slightly mutilated. 20.0 × 15.3; 21 lines.

Divine name ײ; many abbreviations; 19:2 in Hebrew, Onqelos added in margin. [196]

**T-S B10.8** Genesis 9:27 – 10:32
Aramaic: Onqelos (+ Hebrew lemmata). Oriental square script; partial Tiberian vocalisation.

Vellum; 2 leaves (1 bifolium); slightly mutilated. 15.7 × 12.3; 12–13 lines. [197]

**T-S B10.9**

Not targum, rabbinic novellae. [198]

**T-S B10.10** Genesis 8:2–5 (folio 1); 8:12–16 (folio 2)
Aramaic: Onqelos (+ Hebrew lemmata). Oriental square script; Tiberian vocalisation.

Vellum; 2 leaves (1 bifolium); mutilated. 10.7 × 9.7; 7 lines.

Divine name: ײ. [199]

**T-S B10.11**  Genesis 1:1–13
Aramaic: Onqelos (+ Hebrew lemmata).  Oriental square script; unpointed.
Vellum; 1 leaf; mutilated.  18.5 × 17.0;  19 lines.
Divine name: ײ֔; *recto* is blank except for title (original): זו הּתורה תרגום and a pen exercise of the alphabet, in red ink.  [200]

**T-S B10.12**  Exodus 9:29–33 (folio 1r); Exodus 19:1 – 20:12 (folios 1v–5v)
Aramaic: Onqelos (+ Hebrew lemmata).  Oriental square script; Tiberian vocalisation + accents (except folio 1r).
Vellum; 5 leaves (1 bifolium); folio 1 badly mutilated.  12.5 × 11.3;  10–12 lines.
Folio 1r is in different hand and has different Divine name: Divine name (folio 1r): ײי; (folio 1v–5v): ײ֔; heading at top of folio 1v: [לחג] השבועות; Onqelos variants in margins, preceded by ג֔א.  [201]

**T-S B10.13**  Numbers 16:20 – 17:17 (folio 1); 19:16 – 20:25 (folio 2)
Aramaic: Onqelos (+ Hebrew lemmata).  Oriental square script; Tiberian vocalisation.
Vellum; 2 leaves (1 bifolium); rubbed.  24.5 × 19.6; 21–3 lines.
Divine name: ײ֔.  [202]

**T-S B10.14**  Exodus 26:5–32
Aramaic: Onqelos (+ Hebrew lemmata).  Spanish semi-cursive script; Tiberian vocalisation + accents.
Vellum; 1 leaf; mutilated, *verso* faded.  20.4⁺ × 18.7⁺; 21⁺ lines.  [203]

**T-S B10.15**  2 Samuel 22:25–45
Aramaic: Targum Jonathan to Prophets (+ Hebrew lemmata).  Oriental square script; unpointed.
Vellum; 1 leaf; badly mutilated.  16.0 × 14.5;  16 lines.
Divine name: ײי.  [204]

**T-S B10.16**  Isaiah 60:2–10
Aramaic: Targum Jonathan to Prophets (+ Hebrew lemmata).  Yemenite square script; sporadic Tiberian and Babylonian vocalisation.
Vellum; 1 leaf; (narrow scrap) mutilated.  20.5⁺ × 8.7; 34 lines.
This may be an isolated *haftarah* manuscript.  [205]

**T-S B11.1**  2 Samuel 22:8–17; (*haftarah*)
Aramaic: Targum Jonathan to Prophets (+ Hebrew lemmata).  Oriental semi-cursive script; Tiberian vocalisation.
Paper; 1 leaf.  16.3 × 12.5;  11 lines.
Divine name: ײ֔; Arabic instructional note "recite it" [*turattil bihi*] in margin of *recto* [GK]; *haftarah* for *parashat beshalah*.  [206]

**T-S B11.2**  Jeremiah 9:18–23; (*haftarah*)
Aramaic: Targum Jonathan to Prophets (+ Hebrew lemmata).  Oriental semi-cursive script; Tiberian vocalisation.
Paper; 1 leaf.  16.5 × 10.3;  14 lines.
Divine name: ײ֔; *verso* blank; end of *haftarah* for *parashat ṣaw*(?).  [207]

**T-S B11.3**  Ezekiel 28:24 – 29:10; (*haftarah*?)
Aramaic: Targum Jonathan to Prophets (+ Hebrew lemmata).  Oriental script; sporadic Tiberian vocalisation.
Paper; 1 leaf; mutilated.  16.0 × 12.2;  16–17 lines.
Divine name: ײ֔.  [208]

**T-S B11.4**  Ezekiel 37:23–28; 16:1–6 (folio 1); 43:19–27; 36:16–21 (folio 2); (*haftarot*?)
Aramaic: Targum Jonathan to Prophets (+ Hebrew lemmata).  Oriental script; Tiberian vocalisation.
Paper; 2 leaves (1 bifolium); mutilated.  16.2 × 12.8; 17 lines.
Notes on folio 1r: אפ[טרא]...ויהי דבר and on folio 2v: שֹׁבֹת פְּלֹהֹ בֶּן אָדָם בֵּית יִשְׂרָאֵל יוֹשְׁבִים.  [209]

**T-S B11.5**  Genesis 1:3–6
Aramaic: Onqelos (+ Hebrew lemmata).  Oriental square script; Tiberian vocalisation.
Paper; 1 leaf; mutilated.  13.0⁺ × 13.8;  9⁺ lines.
Divine name: ײ֔. The targum was abandoned due to a scribal omission of the divine name in the last line of the *recto*, after an attempt to add it in the margin. *Verso* contains Judaeo-Arabic liturgical instruction in semi-cursive script: ...מן יום ד' מרחשון...ואל יום פסח ותן טל ומטר... but for Baghdad and other communities on rivers ...מן יום תקופת תשרי....  [210]

**T-S B11.6**  Numbers 15:31 – 16:1 (folio 1); 18:2–10 (folio 2)
Aramaic: Onqelos (+ Hebrew lemmata).  Persian(?) square script; unpointed.
Paper; 2 leaves (1 bifolium); mutilated and rubbed.  16.2 × 12.2;  14 lines.
Divine name: ײ֔. Heading of *parashah* קרח ויקח at bottom of folio 1.  [211]

**T-S B11.7**  Genesis 8:16 – 9:10 (folio 1); 10:23 – 11:10 (folio 2)
Aramaic: Onqelos (+ Hebrew lemmata).  Oriental semi-cursive script; unpointed (except עָלָיו in 8:20).
Paper; 2 leaves; slightly rubbed.  18.4 × 13.3;  17 lines.
Divine name: ײ֔.  [212]

**T-S B11.8**  Ezekiel 16:1–14, 60 (folios 1–2r); (*haftarah*)
Aramaic: Targum Jonathan to Prophets (+ Hebrew lemmata).  Oriental semi-cursive script; unpointed.

**[T-S B11.8, cont.]**
Paper; 2 leaves (1 bifolium). 16.4 × 12.3; 17–18 lines.
Divine name: יי. Folio 2v contains praise of a leader in Judaeo-Arabic and Hebrew: יברך...הסר והאדיר חכם דורו... This is a *hafṭarah* for *parashat shemot*, with the last verse taken from the end of the chapter. [213]

## T-S B11.9   Leviticus 2:8 – 3:5
Aramaic: Onqelos (+ Hebrew lemmata). Oriental semi-cursive script; Tiberian vocalisation.
Paper; 2 leaves (folio 2 cut in half). 17.2 × 12.6; 16 lines.
Divine name: יְ. Folio 2 was cut before being written upon, and text is complete. [214]

## T-S B11.10   Leviticus 23:18–22
Aramaic: Onqelos (+ Hebrew lemmata). Oriental semi-cursive script; Tiberian vocalisation.
Paper; 1 leaf. 14.4 × 9.2; 12 lines.
Divine name: יי. Closing note, תמת בחמד אללה תעאלי, in outlined Hebrew square letters and Arabic at bottom of verso [GK]. Note: last word is in Arabic script. [215]

## T-S B11.11   Leviticus 5:17 – 6:3
Aramaic: Onqelos (+ Hebrew lemmata). Oriental semi-cursive script; unpointed.
Paper; 1 leaf. 19.0 × 14.1; 14 lines.
Divine name: ⟨. *Verso* contains heading: וידבר יי צו את in square majusculae in the text, and פרש in margin at 6:1. ❀. [216]

## T-S B11.12   Genesis 27:38 – 28:2 (folio 1); 44:25 – 45:3 (folio 2)
Aramaic: Onqelos (+ Hebrew lemmata). Oriental semi-cursive script; Tiberian vocalisation.
Paper; 2 leaves; rubbed and slightly mutilated. 18.2 × 13.7; 14 lines. [217]

## T-S B11.13   Genesis 32:13–22
Aramaic: Onqelos (+ Hebrew lemmata). Oriental semi-cursive script; Tiberian vocalisation.
Paper; 1 leaf; mutilated. 18.0 × 13.6; 14 lines.
Divine name: יי. [218]

## T-S B11.14   Genesis 20:7 – 21:9
Aramaic: Onqelos (+ Hebrew lemmata). Oriental script; Tiberian vocalisation.
Paper; 1 leaf; rubbed. 18.2 × 13.3; 18 lines. [219]

## T-S B11.15   Jeremiah 3:1–16
Aramaic: Targum Jonathan to Prophets (+ Hebrew lemmata). Oriental semi-cursive script; Tiberian vocalisation.
Paper; 1 leaf; mutilated. 17.6+ × 13.8+; 20 lines.
Divine name: יי; decorative *samekh* in margin ❀. [220]

## T-S B11.16   Isaiah 9:5–6; (*hafṭarah*)
Aramaic: Targum Jonathan to Prophets (+ Hebrew lemmata). Oriental semi-cursive script; Tiberian vocalisation.
Paper; 1 leaf. 12.9 × 9.1; 11 lines.
Most of *verso* blank; ∴תמת indicates end of *hafṭarah* for *parashat yitro*. [221]

## T-S B11.17   Isaiah 5:30 – 6:5
Aramaic: Targum Jonathan to Prophets (+ Hebrew lemmata). Oriental semi-cursive script; Tiberian vocalisation.
Paper; 1 leaf. 12.8 × 9.1; 14–15 lines.
Introductory passage with a legend of Jonathan b. 'Uzziel, cf. B. *Shabbat* 134a, *Sukkah* 28a [דכר זה] לעי באוריתא כל ציפור גפא דהוה פרח עלוהי באויר רקיע שמיא זה מתוקד משלהוביה יקרא דשרי עלוהי ופריש יאות והכי קא־אמר... (cf. T-S AS 71.64). [222]

## T-S B11.18   Exodus 12:23–27 (folio 1); 14:1–5 (folio 2)
Aramaic: Onqelos (+ lengthy Hebrew lemmata). Oriental semi-cursive script (lemmata in smaller script on separate lines); partial Tiberian vocalisation.
Paper; 2 leaves (1 bifolium). 13.5 × 9.5; 10–11 lines.
Divine name: יְיָ̈. [223]

## T-S B11.19   Numbers 30:10 – 31:27
Aramaic: Onqelos (+ Hebrew lemmata). Oriental semi-cursive script; Tiberian vocalisation.
Paper; 2 leaves (1 bifolium); slightly rubbed. 18.4 × 13.3; 18 lines.
Divine name: יְיָ. [224]

## T-S B11.20   Deuteronomy 2:13–23
Aramaic: Onqelos (+ Hebrew lemmata). Oriental semi-cursive script; unpointed.
Paper; 1 leaf. 17.5 × 13.1; 12 lines.
Divine name: יי. [225]

## T-S B11.21   Numbers 11:21–30
Aramaic: Onqelos (+ Hebrew lemmata). Oriental semi-cursive script; Tiberian vocalisation.
Paper; 1 leaf; slightly mutilated. 16.6 × 13.2; 14 lines.
Divine name: יְיָ. [226]

## T-S B11.22   Leviticus 23:37–40
Aramaic: Onqelos (+ Hebrew lemmata). Oriental semi-cursive script; Tiberian vocalisation.
Paper; 1 leaf; slightly mutilated. 12.8 × 10.0; 11–12 lines.
Divine name: יְיָ. Marginal note on *recto* unrelated to the text proper: נתן [ ] בלילי תשעה באב. [227]

**T-S B11.23** Numbers 23:21 – 24:11
Aramaic: Onqelos (+ Hebrew lemmata). Oriental semi-cursive script; Tiberian vocalisation (faded).
Paper; 2 leaves (1 bifolium); slightly mutilated and rubbed. 17.0 × 12.5; 14–15 lines.
Divine name: יי׳. [228]

**T-S B11.24** Genesis 29:12–25 (folio 1); 31:14–26 (folio 2)
Aramaic: Onqelos (+ Hebrew lemmata). Oriental semi-cursive script; Tiberian vocalisation.
Paper; 2 leaves (1 bifolium); badly mutilated and rubbed. 17.5 × 13.5; 14 lines.
Divine name: יְיָ. [229]

**T-S B11.25** Numbers 11:30 – 13:14
Aramaic: Onqelos (+ Hebrew lemmata). Oriental script; Tiberian vocalisation.
Paper; 4 leaves (2 bifolia). 16.6 × 13.1; 13–14 lines.
Divine name: יְיָ. Folios 3v and 4r are blank, but text is continuous. Variants of *Neharda'ei* in margins. Notation marks end of *parashah* פרש and שלח לך in majusculae; also cipher for number of verses in *parashat beha'alotekha* (folio 3r). [230]

**T-S B11.26** Numbers 27:17 – 28:5
Aramaic: Onqelos (+ Hebrew lemmata). Oriental square script; Tiberian vocalisation + accents.
Paper; 1 leaf; badly mutilated. 13.0⁺ × 9.8⁺; 13 lines.
Divine name: יְיָ. [231]

**T-S B11.27** Leviticus 4:33 – 5:12
Aramaic: Onqelos (+ Hebrew lemmata). Oriental semi-cursive script (lemmata in slightly larger square script); unpointed.
Paper; 1 leaf; badly mutilated. 18.3⁺ × 10.8⁺; 12 lines.
Divine name: יי׳. *Verso* faded and difficult to read. [232]

**T-S B11.28** Exodus 3:19 – 4:18
Aramaic: Onqelos (+ Hebrew lemmata). Oriental semi-cursive script; sporadic Tiberian vocalisation.
Paper; 1 leaf. 17.4 × 12.5; 21 lines.
Divine name: יְיָ. Hebrew in middle of 4:10 כִּי כְבַד פֶּה. [233]

**T-S B11.29** Exodus 29:16 – 30:8
Aramaic: Onqelos (+ Hebrew lemmata). Oriental semi-cursive script; Tiberian vocalisation.
Paper; 6 leaves (3 bifolia); rubbed. 16.8 × 12.5; 13 lines.
Tetragrammaton in targum; two outer folios not legible. [234]

**T-S B11.30** Genesis 32:26 – 33:18 (folio 1); 36:38 – 37:17 (folio 2)
Aramaic: Onqelos (+ Hebrew lemmata). Oriental semi-cursive script; sporadic Tiberian vocalisation.
Paper; 2 leaves; slightly mutilated. 16.0 × 12.4; 21–2 lines.
*Parashah* notation at 37:1: פר״ש וישב יעקב ❃. [235]

**T-S B11.31** Deuteronomy 11:21 – 13:11
Aramaic: Onqelos (+ Hebrew lemmata). Oriental semi-cursive script; sporadic Tiberian vocalisation.
Paper; 9 leaves; slightly rubbed; folio 9 mutilated. 17.8 × 13.5; 1 col. (1 side only); 17 lines.
Divine name: יי׳; manuscript written on only one side of each leaf; all pages begin with new verse and end with completed verse; *parashah* notation on folio 1 (11:26) ❃. [236]

**T-S B11.32** Genesis 21:32 – 22:6
Aramaic: Onqelos (+ Hebrew lemmata). Oriental semi-cursive script; Tiberian vocalisation.
Paper; 1 leaf; badly mutilated. 10.7⁺ × 13.6; 9⁺ lines.
Divine name: יְיָ. [237]

**T-S B11.33** Exodus 1:7–14
Aramaic: Onqelos (+ Hebrew lemmata). Oriental semi-cursive script; Tiberian vocalisation.
Paper; 1 leaf. 18.5 × 13.2; 12 lines. [238]

**T-S B11.34** Leviticus 1:1–16
Aramaic: Onqelos (+ Hebrew lemmata). Oriental semi-cursive script; unpointed.
Paper; 1 leaf; rubbed. 19.3 × 13.8; 18 lines.
Divine name: יי׳; heading for beginning of book: ויקרא אל משה on first line. [239]

**T-S B11.35** Exodus 12:22–9
Aramaic: Onqelos (+ Hebrew lemmata). Oriental semi-cursive script; Tiberian vocalisation.
Paper; 1 leaf. 14.0 × 9.2; 13 lines.
Divine name: יְיָ/יְיָ. [240]

**T-S B11.36** Numbers 22:38 – 23:8 (folio 1); 23:29 – 24:10 (folio 2)
Aramaic: Onqelos (+ Hebrew lemmata). Oriental semi-cursive script; Tiberian vocalisation.
Paper; 2 leaves (1 bifolium); badly rubbed. 17.0 × 13.8; 13 lines.
Divine name: יְיָ. [241]

**T-S B11.37** Numbers 29:1–3 (folio 1v); 29:22 (or 25, 28, 34 or 38) (folio 2)
Aramaic: Onqelos (+ Hebrew lemmata). Oriental irregular square script; Tiberian vocalisation.

**[T-S B11.37, cont.]**
Paper; 2 leaves.   15.6 × 12.4;   9 lines.
Heading on folio 1v: תרגום ראש השנה; folios 1r and 2v are blank, implying that this is a *maftir* collection; 29:38 is the most probable identification of the *verso* of folio 2, as this is closest to the end of the Tabernacles *maftir* reading, as indicated by the notation: תם ושלום.   [242]

**T-S B11.38**   Genesis 35:27 – 36:7
Aramaic: Onqelos (+ Hebrew lemmata).   Oriental square script; Tiberian vocalisation.
Paper; 1 leaf.   15.3 × 10.7;   13 lines.   [243]

**T-S B11.39**   Deuteronomy 34:2–5
Aramaic: Onqelos (+ Hebrew lemmata).   Oriental linear square script; Tiberian vocalisation.
Paper; 1 leaf.   13.8 × 10.2;   7–8 lines.
Illegible Arabic note on *verso* (the paper was probably taken from a chancery document [GK]).   [244]

**T-S B11.40**   Genesis 5:25 – 6:5
Aramaic: Onqelos (+ Hebrew lemmata).   Oriental semi-cursive script; Tiberian vocalisation.
Paper; 1 leaf.   17.7 × 12.7;   13 lines.
Divine name: יְ; additional mark ˅ over Hebrew lemmata.   [245]

**T-S B11.41**   Exodus 4:9–20
Aramaic: Onqelos (+ Hebrew lemmata).   Oriental semi-cursive script; unpointed.
Paper; 1 leaf; slightly mutilated.   14.0⁺ × 10.3⁺;   14 lines.
Divine name: יּ; three dots over lemmata.   [246]

**T-S B11.42**   Genesis 21:1–3
Aramaic: Onqelos (+ Hebrew lemmata).   Oriental semi-cursive script; Tiberian vocalisation.
Paper; 1 leaf; slightly mutilated.   14.5 × 10.5;   1 col. (1 side);   9 lines.
Divine name: יְ.   [247]

**T-S B11.43**   Numbers 3:33 – 4:5
Aramaic: Onqelos (+ Hebrew lemmata).   Oriental semi-cursive script; Tiberian vocalisation.
Paper; 1 leaf; slightly mutilated and rubbed. 18.2⁺ × 12.4⁺;   17 lines.
Divine name: ייִ; Hebrew lemmata in larger script.   [248]

**T-S B11.44**   Genesis 13:18 – 14:16
Aramaic: Onqelos (+ Hebrew lemmata).   Oriental semi-cursive script; Tiberian vocalisation.
Paper; 1 leaf.   17.0 × 13.0;   18 lines.
Divine name: יי; Hebrew lemmata abbreviated and marked with supralinear line.   [249]

**T-S B11.45**   Deuteronomy 32:23–39
Aramaic: Onqelos (+ Hebrew lemmata).   Oriental semi-cursive script; unpointed.
Paper; 1 leaf; mutilated.   16.5⁺ × 13.8;   17⁺ lines.   [250]

**T-S B11.46**   Leviticus 2:10 – 5:10
Aramaic: Onqelos (+ Hebrew lemmata).   Oriental semi-cursive script; Tiberian vocalisation.
Paper; 4 leaves (2 bifolia); slightly mutilated. 21.7 × 14.0;   19 lines.
Divine name: ℓ̇; supralinear line over dittograph in 5:4.   [251]

**T-S B11.47**   Exodus 14:19–24 (folio 1); 15:20–21 (folio 2r-v); Deuteronomy 15:19–20 (folio 2v)
Aramaic: Onqelos (+ Hebrew lemmata).   Oriental semi-cursive script; Onqelos larger than lemmata; Tiberian vocalisation (Onqelos only).
Paper; 2 leaves (1 bifolium).   13.5 × 9.4;   10–11 lines.
Divine name: יּ̈; collection of readings for Passover; folio 2v has heading: ליום שיני כל הבכור אשר.   [252]

**T-S B11.48**   Genesis 48:10 – 49:10 (folio 1); Exodus 6:2–28 (folio 2)
Aramaic: Onqelos (+ sporadic Hebrew lemmata). Spanish semi-cursive script; unpointed.
Paper; 2 leaves; slightly mutilated.   19.7 × 15.3; 20 lines.
Divine name: ℓ̈; marginal glosses to Genesis 49:10 and to Exodus 6:6 replace otherwise unattested readings יתכנשון and ובחיוניי; beginning of *parashah* at Exodus 6:2 (folio 2r) noted by majusculae.   [253]

**T-S B11.49**   Genesis 1:1–11 (folio 1v); 5:22 – 6:9 (folio 2)
Aramaic: Onqelos (+ Hebrew lemmata).   Oriental semi-cursive script; Tiberian vocalisation.
Paper; 2 leaves; slightly mutilated.   22.3 × 15.0; 19 lines.
Divine name: ℓ̇; folio 1r blank; *parashah* notation at 6:9 ✿.   [254]

**T-S B11.50**   Genesis 15:1–13
Aramaic: Onqelos (+ Hebrew lemmata).   Oriental semi-cursive script; Tiberian vocalisation.
Paper; 1 leaf; slightly mutilated and rubbed. 18.2 × 13.6;   14 lines.
Divine name: ℓ̇.   [255]

**T-S B11.51**   Exodus 19:21 – 20:17 (folios 1v–2v)
Aramaic: Onqelos (+ Hebrew lemmata).   Oriental square script; Tiberian vocalisation.

**[T-S B11.51, cont.]**
Paper; 2 leaves.   17.7 × 13.0/14.3;   15 lines.
Divine name: יְיָ; folio 1r blank; first line of folio 1v has heading: בשמך רחמא (possibly the beginning of a reading for Pentecost (usually 19:1)). [256]

### T-S B11.52 (= T-S B12.21)   Esther 5:10 – 6:1 (folio 1); 6:11 – 7:5 (folio 2)
Aramaic: Targum Esther (+ Hebrew lemmata). Oriental square script; unpointed.
Paper; 2 leaves (1 bifolium); mutilated.   18.7 × 13.5; 20 lines.
Divine name: יי; Hebrew lemmata end with: וג; this text is very expansive, in part parallel to the known Targum Sheni, and in part totally different, with many quotes from other books of the Bible.
Kasher and Klein *HUCA* LXI, pp. 89–124. [257]

### T-S B11.53 (= T-S B11.59)   Exodus 2:5–10
Aramaic: Onqelos (+ Hebrew lemmata). Oriental semi-cursive script; Tiberian vocalisation.
Paper; 1 leaf; mutilated.   16.0⁺ × 12.4;   10⁺ lines.
Variant readings in margins under בֿ. [258]

### T-S B11.54   Genesis 19:21 – 20:6 (folio 1); 21:32 – 22:18 (folio 2)
Aramaic: Onqelos (+ Hebrew lemmata). Oriental semi-cursive script; sporadic Tiberian vocalisation.
Paper; 2 leaves; slightly rubbed.   20.0 × 14.2;   19 lines.
Divine name: יְיָ; 19:33 rewritten in margin with variant. [259]

### T-S B11.55   2 Kings 5:2–12
Hebrew; Aramaic: Targum Jonathan to Prophets. Oriental semi-cursive script; Tiberian vocalisation + accents.
Paper; 1 leaf; mutilated.   23.7 × 15.5;   22 lines.
Divine name: Hebrew tetragrammaton; Targum יְיָ. [260]

### T-S B11.56   2 Samuel 5:10 – 9:10
Aramaic: Targum Jonathan to Prophets (+ Hebrew lemmata). Oriental semi-cursive script; unpointed.
Paper; 8 leaves (4 bifolia); slightly mutilated and stained.   16.4 × 12.4;   17 lines.
Divine name: יי/ייי; variant additional phrase at 6:23: ברם ביום מותה הוה לה בר ושמיה יתרעם. [261]

### T-S B11.57   Genesis 11:11–31
Aramaic: Onqelos (+ Hebrew lemmata). Oriental semi-cursive script; unpointed.
Paper; 1 leaf; slightly mutilated.   18.7 × 13.3; 17–18 lines. [262]

### T-S B11.58   Genesis 18:5–15
Aramaic: Onqelos (+ Hebrew lemmata). Oriental linear square script; Tiberian vocalisation.
Paper; 1 leaf.   17.9 × 11.7⁺;   12 lines.
Divine name: Hebrew יי; Targum יי. [263]

### T-S B11.59 (= T-S B11.53)   Exodus 2:10–15
Aramaic: Onqelos (+ Hebrew lemmata). Oriental semi-cursive script; Tiberian vocalisation.
Paper; 1 leaf; mutilated.   13.9⁺ × 12.3;   10⁺ lines. [264]

### T-S B11.60   Genesis 5:11 – 6:6
Aramaic: Onqelos (+ Hebrew lemmata). Oriental semi-cursive script; Tiberian vocalisation.
Paper; 1 leaf; slightly mutilated.   19.9 × 14.1;   18 lines.
Divine name: יְיָ. [265]

### T-S B11.61   Genesis 1:1–7 (*verso*)
Aramaic: Onqelos (+ Hebrew lemmata). Oriental semi-cursive script; unpointed.
Paper; 1 leaf; rubbed.   17.8 × 12.4;   13 lines.
Divine name: יי; *recto* blank; mark over first word and abbreviation(?) at top of folio עֹמֹ עֹשֹ. [266]

### T-S B11.62   Numbers 29:7–11
Aramaic: Onqelos (+ Hebrew lemmata). Oriental square script; unpointed.
Paper; 1 leaf.   14.1 × 9.3;   12 lines.
Divine name: ⁶; abbreviation: וג after each lemma; error in order of phrases in 29:7 underlined for correction; *maftir* for Day of Atonement. [267]

### T-S B11.63   Genesis 21:12–23
Aramaic: Onqelos (+ Hebrew lemmata). Oriental square script; Tiberian vocalisation.
Paper; 1 leaf.   17.3 × 12.7;   13 lines.
Divine name: יְיָ. [268]

### T-S B11.64   Exodus 19:12 – 20:1
Aramaic: Onqelos (+ Hebrew lemmata). Oriental semi-cursive script; Tiberian vocalisation.
Paper; 1 leaf; slightly mutilated.   20.7 × 14.7;   14 lines.
Divine name: יי. [269]

### T-S B11.65   Genesis 21:2–8
Aramaic: Onqelos (+ Hebrew lemmata). Oriental semi-cursive script; Tiberian vocalisation.
Paper; 1 leaf.   14.5 × 10.5;   9–11 lines.
Divine name: יְיָ. [270]

### T-S B11.66   Jonah 1:8 – 3:2
Aramaic: Targum Jonathan to Prophets (+ Hebrew lemmata). Oriental square script; unpointed.
Paper; 1 leaf; mutilated.   20.7⁺ × 13.0⁺;   22⁺ lines.
Divine name: א. [271]

**T-S B11.67**  Genesis 23:6–17
Aramaic: Onqelos (+ Hebrew lemmata).  Oriental semi-cursive script; Tiberian vocalisation.
Paper; 1 leaf; badly mutilated.  18.2 × 8.3⁺;  14 lines.
[272]

**T-S B11.68**  Deuteronomy 30:11–16
Aramaic: Onqelos (+ Hebrew lemmata).  Oriental linear square script; Tiberian vocalisation.
Paper; 1 leaf.  18.1 × 13.4;  12 lines.
*Verso* originally blank, full of pen exercises.  [273]

**T-S B11.69**  Numbers 7:2 – 8:16 (folios 1–2); 8:17 – 9:1 (folio 3)
Aramaic: Onqelos (+ Hebrew lemmata).  Oriental semi-cursive script; unpointed.
Paper; 3 leaves (1 bifolium + half leaf).  20.1 × 14.2;  21 lines.
Divine name: יי; *parashah* notation at 8:1; in the bottom half of folio 3v two layers have been peeled apart revealing two additional texts written vertically: 1. Calendrical list with days of the week on which holidays and new moons fall; 2. List of triennial *sidrot*.
[274]

**T-S B11.70**  Genesis 6:14 – 7:11 (folio 1); 13:12 – 14:11 (folio 2)
Aramaic: Onqelos (+ sporadic Hebrew lemmata). Oriental semi-cursive script; unpointed.
Paper; 2 leaves (1 bifolium); slightly mutilated and rubbed.  21.8 × 14.2;  18–19 lines.
Divine name: יי.  [275]

**T-S B11.71**  Leviticus 23:9–18
Aramaic: Onqelos (+ Hebrew lemmata).  Oriental semi-cursive script; Tiberian vocalisation.
Paper; 1 leaf; slightly rubbed.  20.4 × 14.3;  15 lines.
Divine name: יי.  [276]

**T-S B11.72**  Deuteronomy 33:16–21
Aramaic: Onqelos (+ Hebrew lemmata).
Oriental(?) square script; Tiberian vocalisation.
Paper; 1 leaf.  21.2 × 15.0;  10 lines.
Large ב in upper corner of *recto*.  [277]

**T-S B11.73**  Leviticus 14:32–57
Aramaic: Onqelos (+ Hebrew lemmata).  Oriental semi-cursive script; Tiberian vocalisation.
Paper; 1 leaf; mutilated.  22.8 × 15.2;  19 lines.
Divine name: יי.  [278]

**T-S B11.74**  Deuteronomy 33:22 – 34:10
Aramaic: Onqelos (+ Hebrew lemmata).  Oriental semi-cursive script; unpointed.
Paper; 1 leaf.  21.5 × 14.6;  21 lines.
Divine name: יי.  [279]

**T-S B11.75**  Genesis 10:5 – 11:5
Aramaic: Onqelos (+ Hebrew lemmata).  Oriental semi-cursive script; unpointed.
Paper; 1 leaf.  23.0 × 15.6;  19 lines.
Divine name: יי; catchword at bottom of *verso*: ויאמר; pen exercises in margins.  [280]

**T-S B11.76**  Genesis 1:1–22
Aramaic: Onqelos (+ Hebrew lemmata).  Oriental square script; unpointed (except 1:3).
Paper; 1 leaf; mutilated.  24.0 × 16.2;  22 lines.
Divine name: יי; Hebrew and Arabic jottings around margins, perhaps entire page was a trial; unusual Tiberian vocalisation in 1:3 וזֹ וַיאֹמֶר.  [281]

**T-S B11.77**  Leviticus 20:7–22
Aramaic: Onqelos (+ Hebrew lemmata).  Oriental semi-cursive script; unpointed.
Paper; 1 leaf.  20.5 × 14.8;  18 lines.
Divine name: יי; three dots over lemmata; scribal error marked with supralinear line (20:21).  [282]

**T-S B11.78**  Leviticus 16:1–3 (*recto*)
Aramaic: Onqelos (+ Hebrew lemmata).  Oriental semi-cursive script; Tiberian vocalisation corrected by a second hand in red ink.
Paper; 1 leaf.  19.2 × 14.3;  12 lines.
Divine name: יי/אל; heading בשם רחם תרגום כיפור; *verso* blank.  [283]

**T-S B11.79**  Leviticus 15:2–12 (folio 1); 16:34 – 18:3 (folios 2–3)
Aramaic: Onqelos (+ Hebrew lemmata).  Oriental square script; Tiberian vocalisation.
Paper; 3 leaves; slightly rubbed.  16.8 × 12.5;  15 lines.
Divine name: יי.  [284]

**T-S B11.80**  Genesis 11:25 – 12:17
Aramaic: Onqelos (+ Hebrew lemmata).  Oriental semi-cursive script; unpointed.
Paper; 2 leaves (1 bifolium); slightly mutilated and rubbed.  18.8 × 14.2;  12–13 lines.
Divine name: יי; *parashah* notation at 12:1 ✿ and number of verses in cipher קנב for *parashat noah*; variant reading in 12:5 ואזלו.  [285]

**T-S B11.81**  Song of Solomon 2:7–16 (folio 1); 4:12 – 5:8 (folio 2)
Aramaic: Targum Shir ha-Shirim.  Oriental semi-cursive small script; unpointed (except 5:2).

**[T-S B11.81, cont.]**
Paper; 2 leaves (1 bifolium); slightly mutilated and rubbed. 17.6 × 13.2; 24–6 lines.
Vocalisation in 5:2 עֶזְרָא and archaic forms: עילויהם, להום and יתהום. [286]

**T-S B11.82**  Genesis 1:15–20
Aramaic: Onqelos (+ Hebrew lemmata). Oriental semi-cursive script (lemmata in larger square script); Tiberian vocalisation.
Paper; 1 leaf; rubbed. 17.1 × 12.3; 14 lines.
Divine name: יי. [287]

**T-S B11.83**  Genesis 20:6–12
Aramaic: Onqelos (+ Hebrew lemmata). Oriental linear square script; unpointed.
Paper; 1 leaf; mutilated. 14.3⁺ × 12.7; 12 lines.
Letter ס in upper corner of *recto*. [288]

**T-S B11.84**  Numbers 17:6–14, 16–17
Aramaic: Onqelos (+ Hebrew lemmata). Oriental linear square script; Tiberian vocalisation (to 17:16).
Paper; 1 leaf; slightly rubbed. 18.0 × 12.0; 13 lines.
Divine name: יי; 17:15 was omitted by the scribe, who stopped vocalising. [289]

**T-S B11.85**  Genesis 24:63 – 25:2
Aramaic: Onqelos (+ Hebrew lemmata). Oriental semi-cursive script; Tiberian vocalisation.
Paper; 1 leaf; mutilated. 18.0 × 13.5; 14 lines.
Many abbreviations of names. [290]

**T-S B11.86**  Genesis 2:4–22 (folio 1); 4:5–20 (folio 2)
Aramaic: Onqelos (+ Hebrew lemmata). Oriental semi-cursive script; Tiberian vocalisation.
Paper; 2 leaves (1 bifolium); slightly mutilated and rubbed. 17.0 × 12.3; 16–19 lines.
Divine name: יי; *custodes* ✓✓ to fill lines: catchword (folio 1v): די נסיב מן אדם; also possibly Syriac script(?) on last line. [291]

**T-S B11.87**  Genesis 9:11 – 10:22
Aramaic: Onqelos (+ Hebrew lemmata). Oriental semi-cursive script; unpointed except for one word, בְּעַמְמֵהוֹן, at 10:5.
Paper; 2 leaves (1 bifolium); mutilated. 18.3 × 13.5; 16–17 lines.
Divine name: יי. [292]

**T-S B11.88**  Exodus 10:8–17 (folio 1); 13:1–14 (folio 2)
Aramaic: Onqelos (+ Hebrew lemmata). Oriental semi-cursive script; unpointed.
Paper; 2 leaves (1 bifolium). 18.9 × 13.7; 15 lines.
Divine name: יי. [293]

**T-S B11.89**  Numbers 9:1–12
Aramaic: Onqelos (+ Hebrew lemmata). Oriental semi-cursive script; Tiberian vocalisation.
Paper; 1 leaf; slightly rubbed. 20.0 × 14.8; 14 lines.
Divine name: ℓיי. [294]

**T-S B11.90**  Genesis 21:10–21
Aramaic: Onqelos (+ Hebrew lemmata). Oriental semi-cursive script; Tiberian vocalisation.
Paper; 1 leaf; rubbed. 19.0 × 14.3; 15 lines.
Divine name: יי. [295]

**T-S B11.91**  Genesis 23:17 – 24:8
Aramaic: Onqelos (+ Hebrew lemmata). Oriental semi-cursive script; Tiberian vocalisation.
Paper; 1 leaf; slightly rubbed. 18.3 × 13.9; 14 lines.
Divine name: יי/ℓיי. [296]

**T-S B11.92**  Numbers 10:31 – 11:6
Aramaic: Onqelos (+ Hebrew lemmata). Oriental semi-cursive script; Tiberian vocalisation + accents.
Paper; 1 leaf; slightly rubbed. 18.0 × 14.2; 13 lines.
Divine name: יי. [297]

**T-S B11.93**  Numbers 29:38 – 30:1; Leviticus 22:26 – 23:4
Aramaic: Onqelos (+ Hebrew lemmata). Oriental semi-cursive script; Tiberian vocalisation.
Paper; 1 leaf. 16.2 × 12.7; 14 lines.
Divine name: יי; *mafṭir* for *Shemini 'Aṣeret* (Numbers); festival reading (Leviticus). [298]

**T-S B11.94**  Numbers 11:1–15
Aramaic: Onqelos (+ three-word Hebrew lemmata). Oriental linear square script; Tiberian vocalisation (Onqelos).
Paper; 1 leaf; mutilated. 19.2⁺ × 16.7⁺; 19 lines.
Divine name: יי/יי; variant readings. [299]

**T-S B11.95**  Genesis 24:52 – 25:23
Aramaic: Onqelos (+ Hebrew lemmata). Oriental square script; Tiberian vocalisation.
Paper; 1 leaf; mutilated and rubbed. 19.5⁺ × 16.0; 26⁺ lines.
Divine name: יי. [300]

**T-S B11.96**  Exodus 15:14 – 18:8 (folios 1–4); Numbers 1:1 – 5:15 (folios 5–12)
Aramaic: Onqelos (+ Hebrew lemmata). Oriental semi-cursive script; Tiberian vocalisation.

**[T-S B11.96, cont.]**
Paper; 12 leaves (6 bifolia).   17.6 × 13.5;   16 lines.
Divine name: ״ה; notation marks *parashat yitro* at 18:1 פּ֞שׁ֞ in body of text; converse translation in 17:11 מתנברין/מתברין; the Numbers text has the vocalisation overwritten in darker ink and with many corrections; folios of Numbers not correctly numbered.   [301]

**T-S B11.97**   Exodus 34:22–6 (folio 1r–v); 12:21–9 (folios 1v–2v)
Aramaic: Onqelos (+ Hebrew lemmata). Yemenite(?) semi-cursive script; Tiberian vocalisation.
Paper; 2 leaves (1 bifolium).   16.3 × 12.3;   11 lines.
Divine name: ײי; these are readings for the intermediate days of Passover.   [302]

**T-S B11.98**   Genesis 25:19 – 26:9
Aramaic: Onqelos (+ Hebrew lemmata). Oriental linear square script; unpointed (except in abbreviations).
Paper; 2 leaves (1 bifolium).   15.6 × 16.2;   14 lines.
Divine name: ״ה; *parashah* notation at 25:19 פרשה פת.   [303]

**T-S B11.99**   Exodus 20:19–23
Aramaic: Onqelos (+ Hebrew lemmata). Oriental semi-cursive script; Tiberian vocalisation.
Paper; 1 leaf.   17.0 × 12.7;   12–13 lines.
Divine name: ײי; lemmata in square majusculae; Judaeo-Arabic heading פצל at beginning; כמל רשת יכתם בה at end of 20:23, before poem; the second half of the *verso* contains a Hebrew poem רשת, for Pentecost: אהלל אל בשירי העדולים(?) אשר סיבב בחכמה המלכים אשר הקריב לעבדו עם ישרון ושם לבם בידאתו סמכים .. והשמיעם עשרת דבריותיו למען יהיו בדם תמוכים .. והוריחם עלי יד ציר אמונים סגולת הנביאים הנמעו(?) .. זכותו יעמיד לכם    ליום ישועתכם תהיו רואים חוכים .. וכל עם אל ישישים....   [304]

**T-S B11.100**   Genesis 14:17 – 15:14 (folio 1); 17:20 – 18:14 (folio 2)
Aramaic: Onqelos (+ Hebrew lemmata). Oriental semi-cursive script; Tiberian vocalisation (folios 1r(2)–v only).
Paper; 2 leaves; slightly mutilated.   15.5⁺ × 10.2⁺; 18–19 lines.
Divine name: ײי; cipher קנג (folio 2r) for verses in *parashat lekh lekha*; this is an error for 126 (*noah* has 153 verses); scribal error: *nun* for *kaf*.   [305]

**T-S B11.101**   Jeremiah 31:7–20 (folios 1r–v); Isaiah 55:6 (folio 1v); Isaiah 57:18 – 58:13 (folio 2); (*haftarot*)
Aramaic: Targum Jonathan to Prophets (+ Hebrew lemmata). Yemenite(?) square script; Tiberian vocalisation.
Paper; 2 leaves; badly mutilated.   19.8⁺ × 16.7; 23⁺ lines.
Divine name: ײי; heading on bottom of folio 1v in Judaeo-Arabic: [שבתא דבי... לצומא קארי מפטיר בן]שעיהו; *haftarot* for second day New Year, Day of Atonement and Fast of Gedaliah.   [306]

**T-S B11.102**   Exodus 20:16/19 – 23/26
Aramaic: Palestinian Targum (+ most Hebrew lemmata).  Oriental semi-cursive script; lemmata larger square script with Tiberian vocalisation.
Paper; 1 leaf.   20.0 × 14.5;   14 lines.
Divine name: ״ה; lemmata on separate lines; colophon: נשלם בעזרת הבורא וכתב שלמה ביר שמואל הלוי ינ״ה ר״ח. See plate 12.   [307]

**T-S B11.103**   Genesis 1:11 – 5:29
Aramaic: Onqelos (+ Hebrew lemmata). Oriental semi-cursive script; unpointed.
Paper; 6 leaves; very slightly mutilated (margins trimmed).   17.6⁺ × 14.5⁺;   19 lines.
Divine name: ײי.   [308]

**T-S B11.104**   1 Samuel 8:15 – 14:19
Aramaic: Targum Jonathan to Prophets (+ Hebrew lemmata). Oriental semi-cursive script; very sporadic Tiberian vocalisation.
Paper; 11 leaves (4 bifolia).   22.4 × 15.7;   19 lines.
Divine name: ״ה.   [309]

**T-S B11.105**   Genesis 1:11 – 2:2 (folio 1); 6:6 – 7:6 (folio 2)
Aramaic: Onqelos (+ Hebrew lemmata). Oriental semi-cursive script; Tiberian vocalisation.
Paper; 2 leaves (1 bifolium?).   20.2 × 14.0;   18 lines.
Divine name: ײי; notation marking *parashat noah* at 6:9; cipher קמ for number of verses in *bere'shit*; pages are incorrectly pasted together.   [310]

**T-S B11.106**   Genesis 1:21 – 2:9 (folio 1); 8:1 – 9:5 (folio 2)
Aramaic: Onqelos (+ Hebrew lemmata). Oriental semi-cursive script; unpointed.
Paper; 2 leaves (1 bifolium); slightly mutilated and rubbed.   23.7 × 15.8;   19 lines.
Divine name: ״ה.   [311]

**T-S B11.107**   Genesis 26:32 – 29:33
Aramaic: Onqelos (+ Hebrew lemmata). Oriental linear square script; unpointed.
Paper; 6 leaves (3 bifolia); rubbed.   22.2 × 14.7; 19 lines.
Divine name: ״ה; cipher קp after *parashat toledot* (folio 4r).   [312]

**T-S B11.108**  Leviticus 5:17 – 8:25
Aramaic: Onqelos (+ Hebrew lemmata).  Oriental semi-cursive script; unpointed.
Paper; 4 leaves (2 bifolia); rubbed.  24.9 × 18.0; 19 lines.
Divine name: ⟨⟩; cipher קיא after 5:26 for number of verses in *parashat wayiqra'*.  [313]

**T-S B11.109**  Genesis 32:19 – 34:23 (folios 1–2); Exodus 12:16 – 13:14 (folios 3–4)
Aramaic: Onqelos (+ Hebrew lemmata).  Oriental semi-cursive script; Tiberian vocalisation + *'etnaḥta'*.
Paper; 4 leaves (1 bifolium); very slightly mutilated and rubbed.  23.8 × 16.5;  22 lines.
Divine name: יי.  [314]

**T-S B11.110**  Genesis 32:24 – 40:5
Aramaic: Onqelos (+ Hebrew lemmata).  Oriental semi-cursive script; sporadic Tiberian vocalisation.
Paper; 8 leaves (4 bifolia); slightly mutilated.  19.6 × 14.2;  22–5 lines.
Divine name: יי; cipher קד after 36:43 at end of *parashat wayishlaḥ* and note פרש before 37:1; variant reading in 37:23.  [315]

**T-S B11.111**  Exodus 19:21 – 20:23
Aramaic: Onqelos (+ Hebrew lemmata).  Oriental semi-cursive script; sporadic Tiberian vocalisation.
Paper; 1 leaf; slightly mutilated and rubbed.  24.5 × 17.8;  1 col. (1 side);  30 lines + around the margins.
Divine name: יי/ ⟨⟩; Arabic pen exercises and lists(?) on *verso*, also rosette design.  [316]

**T-S B11.112**  Genesis 22:10–19
Aramaic: Onqelos (+ Hebrew lemmata).  Oriental linear square script; Tiberian vocalisation.
Paper; 1 leaf; mutilated.  22.2⁺ × 18.9;  20⁺ lines.
Divine name: יי; *verso* blank.  [317]

**T-S B11.113**  Genesis 35:1–10
Aramaic: Onqelos; Judaeo-Arabic (+ Hebrew lemmata).  Oriental semi-cursive script; unpointed (except for one word, אֵל).
Paper; 1 leaf.  24.8 × 16.6;  18 lines.
Divine name: יי.  [318]

**T-S B11.114**  Genesis 29:30 – 30:30; Exodus 2:2 – 3:18; 28:39 – 36:4; Leviticus 26:23–37; Numbers 1:6–27; 20:5 – 21:30; Isaiah 58:11–14; Zechariah 14:1–4; (*hafṭarot*)
Aramaic: Onqelos (+ Hebrew lemmata).  Spanish square script with some Oriental features; unpointed except Genesis 29, 30 and Exodus 35.
Paper; 32 leaves (11 bifolia); 6 leaves badly mutilated.  23.4 × 16.5;  15 lines.
Divine name: ⟨⟩; folios neither numbered nor in correct order. The single torn folio with Isaiah and Zechariah is from a different manuscript – a *hafṭarah* collection; the preserved passages are for Day of Atonement and first day Tabernacles; *parashot ki tisa'* and *wayaqhel* marked by פ in margin and lemma in majusculae; Judaeo-Arabic פצל to mark end of sections inserted between lines (e.g. Numbers 21:4, 17). See plate 4.  [319]

**T-S B11.115**  Leviticus 25:40 – 26:8
Aramaic: Onqelos (+ Hebrew lemmata).  Oriental square script; Tiberian vocalisation + accents.
Paper; 1 leaf.  20.3 × 17.5;  22 lines.
Divine name: יי; *parashat behuqotai* (26:3) marked by פרש in line.  [320]

**T-S B11.116**  Exodus 1:18 – 5:11; 6:2 – 8:11
Aramaic: Onqelos (+ sporadic Hebrew lemmata); + separate Judaeo-Arabic translation.  Oriental semi-cursive script; Tiberian vocalisation.
Paper; 6 leaves + 2 fragments which fit the leaves; 2 leaves badly mutilated.  23.7 × 15.4;  27–8 lines.
Divine name: ⟨⟩/יי; beginning of *parashat wa'era'* (6:2) marked by large script lemma in red ink; Judaeo-Arabic translation written between *parashot* (2.5 folios); one folio contains Hebrew midrashic exposition of Exodus 14; folios neither numbered nor in correct order.  [321]

**T-S B11.117**  Genesis 3:5 – 4:20
Aramaic: Onqelos (+ Hebrew lemmata).  Oriental semi-cursive script; unpointed.
Paper; 1 leaf; mutilated.  33.3⁺ × 19.5;  46 lines.
Divine name: יי; *verso* contains part of a Judaeo-Arabic and Hebrew letter to a Jewish dignitary, in nine widely spaced lines, between which a liturgical work with Judaeo-Arabic instructions was later inserted [GK]: ...
עמוד מסיים תורת משה... שמה בקהל עדת מי מנה... שמחת בית השאיבה... לאלף ורבבה ורוח חין...  [322]

**T-S B11.118**  Genesis 1:1–6
Aramaic: Onqelos (+ Hebrew lemmata).  Persian(?) square script; unpointed.
Paper; 1 leaf; mutilated.  20.0⁺ × 17.4;  13⁺ lines.
Divine name: ⟨⟩/יי; *recto* originally blank, now contains Genesis 1:1 (Hebrew), and pen exercises.  [323]

**T-S B11.119**  Genesis 2:9 – 3:10
Aramaic: Onqelos (+ Hebrew lemmata).  Oriental semi-cursive script; Tiberian vocalisation.
Paper; 1 leaf; mutilated and rubbed.  25.4 × 17.3;  23 lines.
Divine name: ⟨⟩.  [324]

**T-S B11.120**   2 Samuel 22:2–7
Aramaic: Targum Jonathan to Prophets (+ Hebrew lemmata).   Oriental semi-cursive script; Tiberian vocalisation.
Paper; 1 leaf; slightly mutilated.   16.4 × 12.5;   11 lines.
Divine name: יְיָ.   [325]

**T-S B12.1**   1 Kings 2:3–8
Aramaic: Targum Jonathan to Prophets (+ Hebrew lemmata).   Oriental square script; unpointed.
Vellum; 1 leaf; slightly mutilated.   11.9 × 10.5;
14 lines.
Divine name: יי.
Díez Macho *Sefarad* XVI, pp. 405–6 (in part).   [326]

**T-S B12.2**   Genesis 44:18
Aramaic: Targum *Tosefta*.   Oriental square script; Tiberian vocalisation.
Paper; 1 leaf.   13.7 × 9.2;   12 lines.
Divine name: ייי /ייי (as in Onqelos manuscripts) also Onqelos morphology: אֲתִיבִינָהּ.
Díez Macho *Sefarad* XVI, p. 321; Klein *GMPT* I, p. 143.   [327]

**T-S B12.3**   Numbers 2:31 – 3:32
Aramaic: Onqelos (+ Hebrew lemmata).   Oriental semi-cursive script; Tiberian vocalisation.
Paper; 2 leaves; mutilated and badly rubbed.
18.4 × 12.9;   18 lines.
Divine name: יְיָ.   [328]

**T-S B12.4**   Exodus 12:31–6 (folio 1)
Aramaic: Onqelos.   Oriental semi-cursive script; unpointed.
Paper; 2 leaves (1 bifolium).   14.8 × 10.7;   10 lines.
Divine name: ייי; text ends abruptly in the middle of folio 1v in 12:36; remainder of folio 1v and folio 2v are blank; folio 1r contains a mystical text in rectangular frames: בשימות האילן א ע א ה מיע עמי .. הנה אל ישועתי... את בש
נר דק...   [329]

**T-S B12.5**   1 Kings 1:1
Aramaic: Targum *Tosefta* (Prophets).   Oriental square script; unpointed.
Vellum; 2 leaves (1 bifolium); slightly mutilated.
10.6 × 8.7;   1 col. (1 side);   15 lines.
Beginning of text = Targum Jonathan to Prophets apart from variant: ומכסין יתיה for ומכסן ליה; *tosefta* follows; folios 1v and 2 are blank.   [330]

**T-S B12.6**   1 Samuel 1:1–3
Aramaic: Targum Jonathan to Prophets.   Oriental semi-cursive script; sporadic Tiberian vocalisation.
Paper; 1 leaf; mutilated.   16.6 × 12.7;   13 lines.
Divine name: יְיָ; heading: בשם רחמנא; name: ופינחס rewritten in bottom margin(?).   [331]

**T-S B12.7**   Jeremiah 31:6–9 (folio 1r); 31:15–18 (folio 1v); Isaiah 55:7–11 (folio 2r); 56:3–7 (folio 2v); (*haftarot*)
Aramaic: Targum Jonathan to Prophets (+ Hebrew lemmata).   Oriental square script; Tiberian vocalisation.
Paper; 2 leaves (1 bifolium); very badly mutilated.
12.0⁺ × 7.0⁺;   13⁺ lines.
Divine name: יְיָ; this is from a *haftarah* collection; *haftarot* for New Year and Ninth of Av; variant in Jeremiah 31:16 אגר טב.   [332]

**T-S B12.8**   Jeremiah 34:8–9, 14–15
Aramaic: Targum Jonathan to Prophets (+ Hebrew lemmata).   Oriental semi-cursive script; Tiberian vocalisation.
Paper; 1 leaf (minute fragment).   6.0⁺ × 7.5⁺;   [1 col];
6⁺ lines.   [333]

**T-S B12.9**   2 Kings 4:27–8, 35–7
Aramaic: Targum Jonathan to Prophets.   Oriental square script; Tiberian vocalisation + accents.
Paper; 1 leaf (minute fragment).   10.7 × 5.5;   1 col.(?);
11⁺ lines.   [334]

**T-S B12.10**   Genesis 42:9–10, 14–15
Hebrew; Aramaic: Onqelos.   Oriental linear square script; Tiberian vocalisation.
Paper; 1 leaf; very badly mutilated and faded.
7.4⁺ × 14.5;   6⁺ lines.   [335]

**T-S B12.11**   Deuteronomy 3:6 – 4:4
Hebrew; Aramaic: Onqelos.   Oriental square script; Tiberian vocalisation (partly reinforced in darker ink).
Paper; 6 leaves (3 bifolia); slightly mutilated, very badly rubbed.   15.3 × 10.3;   12 lines.
Divine name: Hebrew tetragrammaton; Onqelos יְיָ.   [336]

**T-S B12.12**   Deuteronomy 32:7–13
Hebrew; Aramaic: Onqelos.   Oriental semi-cursive script; Tiberian vocalisation (Hebrew & Onqelos) + accents (Hebrew only).
Paper; 1 leaf; slightly rubbed.   17.1 × 12.1;   13 lines.
Divine name: Hebrew tetragrammaton; Onqelos יְיָ.   [337]

**T-S B12.13**   Exodus 12:8–10, 12–13 (folio 1); 13:2–3, 6–8 (folio 2)
Aramaic: Onqelos; Judaeo-Arabic (+ Hebrew lemmata).   Oriental semi-cursive script; unpointed.
Paper; 2 leaves (1 bifolium); very badly mutilated.
10.4⁺ × 17.0;   8⁺ lines.   [338]

**T-S B12.14**   Jeremiah 2:6–9; (*haftarah*)
Hebrew; Aramaic: Targum Jonathan to Prophets. Oriental script; Hebrew large square; Targum semi-cursive; Tiberian vocalisation.

Paper; 2 leaves (1 bifolium).   15.1 × 10.0;   11 lines.

Divine name: יּ; this is the *haftarah* for *parashat mas'ay*; folio 2 contains midrash on Deuteronomy 1:1 ודי זהב זה מעשה על תניא כל מקום שנאמרו דברים לשון תוכחה הן. במשה הוא אומ' וישמען ישורון ויבעא כיובא בו דברי עמוס... [339]

**T-S B12.15**   Exodus 20:1–11
Aramaic: Onqelos (+ Hebrew lemmata).   Oriental semi-cursive script; Tiberian vocalisation.

Paper; 1 leaf.   14.2 × 9.9;   13 lines.

Divine name: יָ.   [340]

**T-S B12.16**   Numbers 29:1–6
Aramaic: Onqelos.   Oriental linear square script; Tiberian vocalisation.

Paper; 1 leaf.   15.3 × 18.0;   8 lines.

Maftir for New Year; beginning of marriage(?) document on reverse: בע מן חדש אב שנת א תפד לשטרות באלקאהרה אלמחרוקה דסמיכה [ב]פסט[אם] מצרים דעל נילוס נהרא מותבה רשותיה דאדונינו נאונינו שר שלום שר שלום שלום הלוי. There are also pen exercises of mishnaic passages, which seem to be by heart and only approximate e.g. אין בין יום טוב ליום השבת אלא אוכל נפש בלבד.   [341]

**T-S B12.17**   Leviticus 1:2, 6–8, 11–13, 17
Hebrew; Aramaic: Onqelos.   Oriental square script; Babylonian vocalisation + accents.

Vellum; 1 leaf; very badly mutilated.   10.6⁺ × 10.6⁺; 2 cols.;   12⁺ lines.

Divine name: Hebrew tetragrammaton.   [342]

**T-S B12.18**   1 Kings 6:5–7, 10–13 (folio 1); 18:1–3, 5–7 (folio 2); (*haftarot*)
Hebrew; Aramaic: Targum Jonathan to Prophets. Oriental semi-cursive script; Tiberian vocalisation.

Paper; 2 leaves; very badly mutilated.   17.0⁺ × 10.2⁺; 16⁺ lines.

Folio 1v contains heading: י[חזק]אל and a trace of Ezekiel 43:10; these are *haftarot* for *parashot terumah, tesaweh* and *ki tisa'*.   [343]

**T-S B12.19**   Genesis 1:1–10 (*verso*)
Aramaic: Onqelos (+ Hebrew lemmata).   Oriental semi-cursive script; unpointed except for one word in v.9, כֵּן.

Paper; 1 leaf.   19.0 × 14.0;   17 lines.

Divine name: יי; heading: עלי תרגום ספר בראשית אלמתֿל; *recto* contains an introductory poem to the targum in Hebrew, headed: מקדמה עלי תרגום ספר בראשית   [344]

**T-S B12.20**   Numbers 16:1 – 18:27
Aramaic: Onqelos Fragment-targum + inserts of Sa'adya's Judaeo-Arabic translation.   Oriental semi-cursive script; unpointed.

Paper; 1 leaf.   18.2 × 13.0;   19 lines.

Verso blank.   [345]

**T-S B12.21 (= T-S B11.52)**   Esther 6:1 (folio 1); 6:10–11 (folio 2)
Aramaic: Targum Esther.   Oriental square script; unpointed.

Paper; 2 leaves (1 bifolium).   18.7 × 13.4;   20 lines.

The reference to a cross may reflect Jewish response to Christian pressure for conversion (folio 1v) לבושא דהוה לביש דמן רשיעא צירין עלוי צליבין חד מן קדמוי חד מן אחדוי ואן קמת וסגדת ליה משתכחת פלח לעבודה זרה. This version is far more expansive than the known Targum Sheni..

Kasher and Klein *HUCA* LXI, pp.89–124. See plate 13.   [346]

**T-S B12.22**   Isaiah 6:4 – 7:6
Aramaic: Targum Jonathan to Prophets (+ Hebrew lemmata).   Oriental square script; very sporadic Tiberian vocalisation.

Vellum; 2 leaves (1 bifolium).   14.6 × 9.7 / 5.0 × 9.7; 1 col. (vertical);   11/6 lines.

Divine name: יי; Judaeo-Arabic note at end of passages; text written vertically and *verso* is inverted in relation to *recto*.   [347]

**T-S B12.23**   Ezekiel 1:1 – 2:2 (folios 1r–2v); Habakkuk 2:20 – 3:19 (folios 2v–4r); (*haftarot*)
Aramaic: Targum Jonathan to Prophets (+ Hebrew lemmata).   Oriental square script; unpointed.

Paper; 4 leaves (2 bifolia); all folia torn in half vertically.   13.6 × 4.5⁺;   25–8 lines.

Divine name: יי; these are *haftarot* for the festival of Pentecost; folio 4v blank.   [348]

**T-S B12.24**   Poems to Exodus 12:1–2
Targumic poetry.   Oriental square script; Babylonian vocalisation.

Paper; 4 leaves; all folia vertically torn in half. 16.2 × 9.1⁺;   11–12 lines.

Cf. Klein, *GMPT* I, pp.187, 189.   [349]

**T-S B12.25**   Exodus 35:26 – 38:2 (folio 1); Leviticus 10:6 – 11:32 (folio 2)
Aramaic: Onqelos Fragment-targum or extract (+ Hebrew catchwords).   Oriental square script; sporadic Tiberian vocalisation.

Vellum; 2 leaves (1 bifolium); slightly rubbed. 12.7 × 15.3;   14–17 lines.

Divine name: יי (Leviticus 10:6, 11:1); massoretic note(?) in 37:18 סימן יצאים נפקין היוצאים דנפקן.   [350]

**T-S B12.26**   2 Samuel 22:32–7
Hebrew; Aramaic: Targum Jonathan to Prophets. Oriental square script; Tiberian vocalisation (Hebrew & Targum) + accents (Hebrew only).
Vellum; 1 leaf.   8.7 × 7.6;   11–12 lines.
Divine name: ʰ.   [351]

**T-S B12.27**   Judges 11:13–24 (folio 1); 1 Kings 19:4–11 (folio 2); (*haftarot*)
Aramaic: Targum Jonathan to Prophets (+ Hebrew lemmata).   Oriental linear square script; sporadic Tiberian vocalisation.
Paper; 2 leaves (1 bifolium).   17.3 × 13.5;   14–15 lines.
Divine name: Targum tetragrammaton; these are *haftarot* for *parashot ḥuqat* and *pinḥas*.   [352]

**T-S B12.28**   Genesis 15:8 – 16:4
Aramaic: Onqelos (+ Hebrew lemmata).   Oriental square script; partial Tiberian vocalisation.
Paper; 1 leaf; slightly mutilated.   17.5⁺ × 13.3⁺; [17] lines.
Divine name: ʾʾ.   [353]

**T-S B12.29**   Exodus 14:22–7
Hebrew; Aramaic: Onqelos.   Oriental script; Targum with Tiberian vocalisation.
Paper; 2 leaves (1 bifolium); mutilated and very badly rubbed.   12.7 × 8.4;   9–11 lines.
Text is barely legible.   [354]

**T-S B12.30**   Leviticus 1:10 – 2:10
Aramaic: Onqelos (+ Hebrew lemmata).   Oriental semi-cursive script; Tiberian vocalisation.
Paper; 2 leaves (1 bifolium); very badly mutilated, 1 leaf almost entirely missing.   20.6 × 10.2⁺;   19 lines.
Divine name: ʾʾ.   [355]

**T-S B12.31**   Jeremiah 30:13–17 (folio 1r); Obadiah 1:1–5 (folio 1v); Haggai 2:23; Isaiah 21:11–? (folio 2r); Isaiah 21:17 – 22:3 (folio 2v); Isaiah 22:4; 24:15; 46:3 (folio 3); (*haftarot*)
Hebrew; Aramaic: Targum Jonathan to Prophets. Oriental square script; sporadic Babylonian and Tiberian vocalisation.
Paper; 3 leaves; very badly mutilated.   15.0⁺ × 14.5⁺; 16⁺ lines.
Lectionary of triennial *haftarot* (end of folio 3); two of the folios display mirror writing; triennial *haftarot* to: Genesis 31 (Jeremiah); Genesis 32 (Obadiah); Exodus 12 (Isaiah 21); Exodus 13 (Isaiah 46).   [356]

**T-S B12.32**   1 Kings 10:18; 11:1 / or Esther 1:2
Aramaic: Targumic *Tosefta* to Targum Jonathan to Prophets or Targum Esther.   Oriental square script; unpointed.
Vellum; 1 leaf; mutilated.   14.3 × 14.5;   13–14 lines.
This version is significantly different from that of Sperber, *Bible in Aramaic*, II, pp. 239–40; IV, pp. 175–76.
Kasher and Klein *HUCA* LXI, pp. 89–124.   [357]

**T-S B12.33**   Exodus 12:41–7 (*recto*); Numbers 28:20–25 (*verso*)
Aramaic: Onqelos (+ Hebrew lemmata).   Oriental linear square script; Tiberian vocalisation.
Paper; 1 leaf; mutilated.   18.8 × 14.5;   13 lines.
Divine name: ʾʾ; two omitted verses in *recto* added in margin.   [358]

**T-S B12.34**   Genesis 49:4–15 (folio 1); Deuteronomy 32:17–19, 24–6 (folio 2); 33:1–12 (folio 3)
Aramaic: Onqelos (+ sporadic Hebrew lemmata). Linear square script (untrained); unpointed.
Paper; 3 leaves; very badly mutilated.   13.0⁺ × 12.5⁺; 12⁺ lines.
Extensive use of *aleph* for long *a* vowel (Arabic influence).   [359]

**T-S B12.35**   Ezekiel 23:49 – 24:2; 24:21–22 (folio 1); 32:24–5, 33:7–9 (folio 2)
Hebrew; Aramaic: Targum Jonathan to Prophets. Oriental square script; Babylonian vocalisation + accents.
Vellum; 2 leaves (1 bifolium); very badly mutilated. 8.8⁺ × 9.2⁺; 14⁺ lines.
Divine name: Hebrew tetragrammaton; Targum ʾʾ.   [360]

**T-S B12.36**   Numbers 6:22–7 (folio 1v); 8:2–4 (folio 2r)
Aramaic: Onqelos (+ Hebrew lemmata).   Oriental square script; Tiberian vocalisation and sporadic Babylonian vocalisation.
Vellum; 2 leaves (1 bifolium); folio 2 mutilated and rubbed.   15.6 × 11.3;   11 lines.
Divine name: ʾ/ʾʾ; folio 1r blank; folio 2r has only eight lines; folio 2v contains Hebrew liturgical poem.   [361]

**T-S B12.37**   Genesis 11:26–9
Hebrew; Aramaic: Onqelos.   Oriental linear square script; unpointed.
Paper; 1 leaf; rubbed.   20.3 × 12.0;   14 lines.
Pen exercises in margins; *verso* blank.   [362]

**T-S B12.38**   Exodus 14:25 – 16:4
Aramaic: Onqelos (+ Hebrew lemmata).   Spanish semi-cursive script; Tiberian vocalisation + accents.
Paper; 1 leaf; mutilated and badly rubbed.   23.3 × 20.5; 26⁺ lines.
Divine name: ʾʾ.   [363]

**T-S B12.39**   Isaiah 22:1–17

Aramaic: Targum Jonathan to Prophets (+ Hebrew lemmata).   Oriental semi-cursive script; unpointed (except for Divine name with Babylonian qameṣ).

Paper; 1 leaf; mutilated and rubbed.   23.3⁺ × 27.1; 19⁺ lines.

Divine name: יֳ; Arabic writing on reverse – petition formula [GK]; originally a longer vertical scroll of several sheets pasted together.   [364]

**T-S B13.1**   Leviticus 17.4 – 19.34 (folio 1); 26:5 – 27:34 (end of book, folio 2)

Massorah to Onqelos.   Oriental square script; Tiberian vocalisation (Hebrew only).

Vellum; 2 leaves (1 bifolium); folio 1 badly mutilated. 15.1 × 9.5;   22 lines.   [365]

**T-S B13.4 (= T-S NS 218.61; Or.1080 B18.1)**   Exodus 12:42, 21–34 (folio 1); Deuteronomy 26:2–14 (folio 2)

Aramaic: Palestinian Targum (+ Hebrew lemmata).   Oriental square script; sporadic Tiberian vocalisation.

Vellum; 2 leaves; badly mutilated and rubbed. 14.7 × 10.4⁺;   15⁺ lines.

Divine name: יֳי; heading in Judaeo-Arabic on folio 1r: תרגום אל פסח.

Klein *GMPT* I, pp.218–19.   [366]

**T-S B13.5**   Esther

Aramaic: Targumic poems to Esther.   Oriental square script; sporadic Tiberian vocalisation.

Vellum; 4 leaves (2 bifolia).   15.5 × 9.8;   18–21 lines.

Many Greek words in Galilean Aramaic.   [367]

**T-S B13.10**   Genesis 15:7–9; 16:2–3

Hebrew; Aramaic: Onqelos.   Oriental square script; Babylonian vocalisation.

Vellum; 1 leaf; very badly mutilated.   10.5⁺ × 10.5⁺; 2 cols.; 9⁺ lines.

Divine name: Hebrew tetragrammaton; Targum יי.   [368]

**T-S B13.12**   Joshua 5:2 – 6:1; (*hafṭarah*)

Aramaic: Introductory poem + expansive paraphrase.   Oriental square script; sporadic Tiberian vocalisation;.

Vellum; 5 leaves (2 bifolia); mutilated.   12.0 × 13.6; 13–14 lines.

Poem in alphabetic acrostic (partial) and Aramaic translation of blessings of *hafṭarah*; headings on both sides: תר[גום אל הפטרה בעת ההיא and ת[רגום בעת ההיא]; the paraphrase is not properly Targum or *Tosefta*, in that it lacks the literal translation of the Hebrew text.   [369]

**T-S B13.17**   Exodus 14:26 – 15:4

Aramaic: Onqelos (+ Hebrew lemmata).   Oriental linear square script; Tiberian vocalisation (lines 11–24, sporadic thereafter).

Paper; 1 leaf (vertical scroll); mutilated.   38.0⁺ × 14.8; 38⁺ lines.

Divine name: יֳ; lines 1–9 contain the end of a list of *parashot* with Judaeo-Arabic headings, line 19 heading: תרגום אל שירה.   [370]

**T-S B14.128**   Isaiah 11:16 – 12:4; Ezekiel 45:2–8; (*hafṭarot*)

Hebrew; Aramaic: Targum Jonathan to Prophets. Oriental square script; unpointed.

Paper; 1 leaf; badly rubbed.   22.0 × 19.0.

Triennial *hafṭarot* to Numbers 33:1 and 34:1; note on *recto*: זאת הארץ אשר תפל ביחזקאל (Numbers 34:2) חד... פסוק...אמר אל הכהנים (the triennial *hafṭarah* for 'emor (Leviticus 21:1) is indeed Ezekiel 44:25 – ) there may be 1 verse overlap which the scribe did not rewrite.   [371]

**T-S B14.131**   Joshua 5:14 – 6:1; 6:27; 2 Kings 22:1–7; 23:21–2; (*hafṭarot*)

Hebrew; Aramaic: Targum Jonathan to Prophets. Yemenite square script; Babylonian vocalisation.

Paper; 1 leaf.   27.4 × 18.6;   25 lines.

Divine name: Hebrew tetragrammaton; Targum יי; *hafṭarot* for first and second days Passover; Includes *toseftot* to Joshua 5:14 and 6:1; and headings: ליום שני במלכים , זה הזרגום תוספתא חה תוספתא.   [372]

**T-S B15.1**   Isaiah 61:10 – 62:9 (folio 1–2v); Hosea 14:2–3 (folio 2v); Isaiah 60:21–2 (margin folio 1r); Isaiah 63:7–16 (margins folio 2v); (*hafṭarot*)

Hebrew; Aramaic: Targum Jonathan to Prophets. Oriental square script; Babylonian vocalisation + accents.

Vellum; 2 leaves (1 bifolium).   34.6 × 26.0;   15 lines.

Divine name: Hebrew tetragrammaton; Targum יי; Judaeo-Arabic marginal note at end of passage (folio 1r): הדא תמאם קומי אורי.

Kahle *MdO* pp.36–8.   [373]

**T-S B15.2**   Isaiah 54:10 (folio 1r); 40:27 – 41:6 (folio 1r–v); 2 Kings 4:4–13 (folio 2); (*hafṭarot*)

Hebrew; Aramaic: Targum Jonathan to Prophets. Oriental square script; Tiberian vocalisation + accents; Babylonian vocalisation + accents added in lighter brown ink.

Vellum; 2 leaves (1 bifolium); slightly mutilated. 32.6 × 24.9;   16 lines.

Divine name: Hebrew tetragrammaton; Targum יי; *hafṭarot* for *parashot noaḥ, lekh lekha* and *wayera'*; Judaeo-Arabic note at top of folio 1r after Isaiah 54:10 תמאמה פי אפטארת רני עקרה.   [374]

**T-S B15.3**   Joshua 1:11; 1 Samuel 1–12 (folio 1); Jeremiah 31:14–20; Isaiah 57:14–18 (folio 2); (*hafṭarot*)

Hebrew; Aramaic: Targum Jonathan to Prophets. Oriental square script; Babylonian vocalisation + accents; sporadic Tiberian vocalisation + accents added (1 Samuel 1:12).

Vellum; 2 leaves (1 bifolium); badly mutilated. 21.5 × 21.5;  2 cols.;  19 lines.

Judaeo-Arabic notes on folio 2r: אלי הוא אלפטרה ויכתם הבן יקיר לי וג׳ and on folio 2v: דצפרא דיומא דכיפורי בישעיה. Kahle *MdO* pp.34–6 (in part). [375]

**T-S B15.4**   Judges 5:4–8, 13–17; 13:6–11; 1 Kings 3:22–8; 7:21–6; 2 Kings 4:25–9 (folio + small fragment); Isaiah 42:11–16, 54:1; Jeremiah 17:7–13; Ezekiel 22:15–16; 37:16–22; 34:4–10; (*hafṭarot*)

Hebrew; Aramaic: Targum Jonathan to Prophets. Oriental square script; Babylonian vocalisation + accents.

Vellum; 10 leaves; most leaves mutilated, not numbered. 22.2 × 17.5;  15 lines.

Divine name: Hebrew tetragrammaton; Targum ײַ; heading to Ezekiel 37:16 קדשים ביחזקאל. See plate 7. [376]

**T-S B15.5**   Malachi 2:7 – 3:4 (folios 1–2); Hosea 11:7 – 12:11 (folio 2); Obadiah 1:15–21; Amos 2:6–14 (folio 3); 1 Kings 3:23 – 4:1; Ezekiel 37:15–23 (folio 4r); Ezekiel 37:23–8; 1 Kings 2:1–8 (folio 4v); 1 Kings 2:9–12; Ezekiel 16:1–11 (folio 5); Ezekiel 29:6–21 (folio 6); 1 Kings 6:1–13; Ezekiel 43:10–12 (folio 7); Ezekiel 43:12–27 (folio 8); Ezekiel 22:1–14 (folio 9); Jeremiah 9:11–23; Isaiah 40:1 (folio 10); Isaiah 40:1–18 (folio 11); Isaiah 40:18–26; 41:17; 49:14–21 (folio 12); Joshua 5:2–14 (folio 13); 1 Samuel 1:22 – 2:5 (folio 14); (*hafṭarot*)

Hebrew; Aramaic: Targum Jonathan to Prophets. Yemenite square script; Babylonian vocalisation + Tiberian accents.

Paper; 15 leaves; folio 9 mutilated. 27.5 × 19.6; 25 lines.

Divine name: Hebrew tetragrammaton; Targum ײַ; these are *hafṭarot* for *parashot toledot* to *shemot, terumah, teṣaweh, 'aharei mot*, 9th of Av, *wa'ethanan, 'eqev*, first day Passover and first day New Year; in addition to standard headings for *hafṭarot*, note on folio 10: נהגו להפטיר בנחמות ישעיה מאחר תשעה באב עד ראש השנה הון שבע. [377]

**T-S B16.20**   1 Samuel 1:1–22

Hebrew; Aramaic: Targum Jonathan to Prophets. Oriental square script; unpointed.

Vellum; 1 sheet of scroll; first and 3rd cols. mutilated. 32.6 × 37.0⁺;  3⁺(?) cols.;  31 lines.

Divine name: Hebrew tetragrammaton; Targum ײַ / ײַ. [378]

**T-S B17.1**   Isaiah 65:17–25; 51:6 (folio 1v); Jeremiah 34:3–5, 12–13; Isaiah 33:17–24 (folio 2); (*hafṭarot*)

Aramaic: Targum Jonathan to Prophets (+ Hebrew lemmata). Oriental square script; Tiberian vocalisation.

Vellum; 2 leaves (1 bifolium).  16.7 × 16.7; 17–19 lines.

Divine name: ײַ/ײַ; triennial *hafṭarot* for Genesis 1:1 (Isaiah 65, heading: בראשית בישעיה); Genesis 2:4 (Isaiah 51, heading: אלה בישעיה); Genesis 16:1(?) (Jeremiah 34); Genesis 18:1 (Isaiah 33, heading: וירא אליו יוי בישעיה); folio 1r blank. [379]

**T-S B17.2**   Isaiah 51:8–16; Ezekiel 28:13–25; Isaiah 29:18–23; (*hafṭarot*)

Hebrew; Aramaic: Targum Jonathan to Prophets. Oriental square script; Hebrew with Tiberian vocalisation + accents (added in darker ink); Targum with sporadic Tiberian vocalisation.

Vellum; 1 leaf; slightly mutilated and rubbed. 30.6 × 25.8;  2 cols.;  31 lines.

Divine name: Hebrew tetragrammaton; Targum ײַ; triennial *hafṭarot* for Genesis 2:4 (Isaiah 51); Genesis 3:22 (Ezekiel 28, heading: הן האדם ביחזקאל); Genesis 5:1 (Isaiah 29, heading: זה ספר בישעיה); decorative *samekh* in margins to mark beginning of *hafṭarot*. [380]

**T-S B17.3** (= T-S B17.4, 7)   Isaiah 35:10; 1:19–27; 2:2–3; Judges 11:30–40; Hosea 2:16–17; (*hafṭarot*)

Hebrew; Aramaic: Targum Jonathan to Prophets. Oriental square script; Tiberian vocalisation (sporadic in Targum).

Vellum; 1 leaf; badly mutilated.  32.8 × [28.4]; 2 cols.;  31 lines.

Divine name: Hebrew tetragrammaton; Targum ײַ; decorative *samekh* in margins to mark beginning of *hafṭarot* ✿; triennial *hafṭarot* to Leviticus 25:35 (Isaiah 35); Leviticus 26:3 (Isaiah 1, 2, heading: אם בחקתי בישעיה); Leviticus 27:2 (Judges 11, heading: [איש כי יפליא]); Numbers 1:1 (Hosea 2, heading: וידבר בתרי עשר). [381]

**T-S B17.4** (= T-S B17.3, 7)   Isaiah 11:11–12; 51:1,6; Jeremiah 42:16–17 (folio 1); Isaiah 43:24–5; 44:4–5 (folio 2); Isaiah 48:13–19; Hosea 4:14; Isaiah 44:6–11, 23 (folio 3); Isaiah 7:23 – 8:4; 5:9–15 (folio 4); (*hafṭarot*)

Hebrew; Aramaic: Targum Jonathan to Prophets. Oriental square script; Hebrew with Tiberian vocalisation in darker ink; Targum with sporadic Tiberian vocalisation; some fragments with Tiberian accents and occasional Babylonian vocalisation.

**[T-S B17.4 (= T-S B17.3, 7), cont.]**
Vellum; 4 leaves; very badly mutilated.   31.5 × [28.0];
2 cols.;   31 lines.

Divine name: Hebrew tetragrammaton; Targum ״י;
decorative *samekh* in margin to mark beginning of
*haftarah* at Hosea 4 (bottom of folio 3) ✿; triennial
*haftarot* to Genesis 41:38 (Isaiah 11); Genesis 42:18
(Isaiah 51); Genesis 43:14 (Jeremiah 42); Genesis 49:1
(Isaiah 43, 44); Numbers 4:17 (Isaiah 48); Numbers 5:11
(Hosea 4, heading: [כי תש]מה); Genesis 49:1 (continuation)
(Isaiah 44); Leviticus 13:29 (Isaiah 7–8); Leviticus 14:33
(Isaiah 5). Perhaps not all the fragments at this classmark
belong to the same manuscript.   [382]

**T-S B17.5**   Jeremiah 31:21–3, 33; Zechariah 4:2,
8–10, 6:12; Isaiah 27:13–28; (*haftarot*)

Hebrew; Aramaic: Targum Jonathan to Prophets.
Oriental square script; sporadic Palestinian and
Tiberian vocalisation; Tiberian vocalisation added in
darker ink in Hebrew only.

Vellum; 1 leaf; badly mutilated.   22.0⁺ × [28.0];
2 cols.;   21⁺ lines.

Divine name: Hebrew tetragrammaton; Targum ״י;
triennial *haftarot* for Deuteronomy 4:25 (Jeremiah 31);
Numbers 8:1 (Zechariah 4, heading: בהעלותך בתרי עשר);
Numbers 10:1 (Isaiah 27, heading: [עשה לך ביש]עיה); note
irregular pentateuchal order!   [383]

**T-S B17.6**   Isaiah 56:11 – 57:5, 19; Hosea
10:2–12; Isaiah 11:1–6; (*haftarot*)

Hebrew; Aramaic: Targum Jonathan to Prophets.
Oriental square script; sporadic Tiberian
vocalisation.

Vellum; 1 leaf; very slightly mutilated.   33.0 × 29.2;
2 cols.;   31 lines.

Divine name: Hebrew tetragrammaton; Targum ״י;
triennial *haftarot* for Numbers 15:1 (Isaiah 56–7);
Numbers 16:1 (Hosea 10, heading: ויקח קרח בתרי עשר);
Numbers 17:16 (Isaiah 11, heading: [ו]קח מאתם בישעיה).
[384]

**T-S B17.7 (= T-S B17.3, 4)**   Isaiah 48:20 –
49:3; Ezekiel 18:4–17; Zechariah 5:3–11; 6:11–12;
Malachi 3:4 (folio 1); Isaiah 66:7–11; Jeremiah
10:2–10; Isaiah 4:3 – 5:2, 5–7, 16; Isaiah 65:22–3
(folio 2); (*haftarot*)

Hebrew; Aramaic: Targum Jonathan to Prophets.
Oriental square script; Hebrew with Tiberian
vocalisation + accents; Targum with sporadic
Tiberian vocalisation.

Vellum; 2 leaves (1 bifolium); mutilated and stained.
34.0 × 29.5;   2 cols.;   31 lines.

Divine name: Hebrew tetragrammaton; Targum ״י;
decorative *samekh* in margins to mark beginning of
*haftarot* ✿; triennial *haftarot* for Leviticus 1:1 (Isaiah
48–9 unattested); Leviticus 4:1 (Ezekiel 18, heading: נפש
כי תחטא ביחזקאל); Leviticus 5:1 (Zechariah 5, 6, heading:
תשמעה קול אלה בתרי עש׳); Leviticus 6:12 (Malachi 3,
heading: זה קרבן בתרי עש); Leviticus 17:1 (Isaiah 66);
Leviticus 18:1 (Jeremiah 10, heading: כמעשה ארץ בירמיה);
Leviticus 19:1 (Isaiah 4–5, heading: [קדשים] תהיו בישע[יה]);
Leviticus 19:23 (Isaiah 65, heading: ונטעתם בישעיה); Isaiah
48–9 may be the triennial *haftarah* for Exodus 22:24 or
Deuteronomy 30:11, but is not attested for the beginning
of Leviticus.   [385]

**T-S B17.8**   Genesis 46:28–34 (folios 6v–8v);
Isaiah 40:1–8, 31 (folios 1–6r); (*haftarah*)

Aramaic: Onqelos and Targum Jonathan to Prophets
(both + Hebrew lemmata).   Oriental semi-cursive
script; Tiberian vocalisation.

Paper; 8 leaves (4 bifolia); very slightly mutilated.
13.0 × 9.0;   10–11 lines (Onqelos);   7–8 lines (Targum
Jonathan to Prophets).

Isaiah 40:1 is not attested as a triennial *haftarah*; final
note: תשלום על ישר[אל] at end of folio 8v; folios 1r, 2v, 3v,
7v are all blank.   [386]

**T-S B17.9**   Jeremiah 34:2–5, 12–13; Isaiah
33:17–24; 35:10; Isaiah 17:14 – 18:4 (folio 1 pencil-
marked 4); Isaiah 51:10–11; Isaiah 13:3–4;
2 Samuel 5:18–19; 6:2; Isaiah 65:23 (folio 2 pencil-
marked 5); 1 Samuel 1:15–20; Jeremiah 30:10–18;
Obadiah 1:1–7 (folio 3 pencil-marked 6); (*haftarot*)

Hebrew; Aramaic: Targum Jonathan to Prophets.
Oriental square script; Hebrew with Tiberian
vocalisation.

Vellum; 3 leaves (1 bifolium); 2 leaves badly
mutilated.   32.7 × 29.0;   2 cols.;   31 lines.

Triennial *haftarot* for Genesis 16:1 (Jeremiah 34); Genesis
18:1 (Isaiah 33, 35, heading: [וירא אליו ב]ישעיה); Genesis
19:1 (Isaiah 17–18, heading: ויבאו שני המלאכים בישע׳);
Genesis 24:1 (Isaiah 51); Genesis 24:42 (Isaiah 13);
Genesis 25:1 (2 Samuel 5); Genesis 25:19 (Isaiah 65,
heading: תולדות יצחק בי[שעי]ה); Genesis 30:22 (1 Samuel 1);
Genesis 31:3 (Jeremiah 30, heading: שוב אל ארץ אבתיך
בירמיה); Genesis 32:4 (Obadiah, heading: וישלח יעקב בתרי
עש׳).   [387]

**T-S B17.34**   Habakkuk 3:9–13, 18–19; Isaiah
42:7–9, 12–15; Isaiah 49:10–16 (folio 2); Isaiah
49:18–23; Zephaniah 3:9–10, 13–15, 20; Joshua
24:3–6 (folio 1); (*haftarot*)

Hebrew; Aramaic: Targum Jonathan to Prophets.
Oriental square script; Hebrew with Tiberian
vocalisation + accents in darker ink; Targum with
sporadic Tiberian vocalisation.

**[T-S B17.34, cont.]**
Vellum; 2 leaves (2 smaller fragments belong to these 2 leaves); badly mutilated. 28.5⁺ × [28.0]; 2 cols.; 30⁺ lines.

Triennial *haftarot* for Genesis 8:1 (Habakkuk 3); Genesis 8:15 (Isaiah 42, heading: צא מן התבה בישע[יה]); Genesis 9:18 (Isaiah 49); Genesis 11:1 (Zephaniah 3, heading: ויהי כל הארץ); Genesis 12:1 (Joshua 24, heading: לך לך ביהושע); decorative *samekh* in margins marks beginning of *haftarot*. [388]

**T-S B18.1** 2 Samuel 24:14–16, 24–5 (folio 1); 1 Kings 8:35–6 (folio 2r); Isaiah 60:10–11 (folio 2v); (*haftarot*)

Hebrew; Aramaic: Targum Jonathan to Prophets. Oriental square script; Babylonian vocalisation + accents.

Vellum; 2 leaves (1 bifolium); very badly mutilated. 16.0⁺ × [21.4]; 2 cols.; 14⁺ lines.

Divine name: Hebrew tetragrammaton; Targum ייי; unattested order of triennial(?) *haftarot*. [389]

**T-S B18.2** Ezekiel 36:20–30 (folio 1r); Ezekiel 45:9–25; 47:12 (folios 1v–2r); Joshua 3:5, 6; 5:2–9 (folio 2v); Isaiah 10:32 – 12:6 (folios 3r–4r); Ezekiel 36:37 – 37:14 (folios 4r–v); Ezekiel 1:1–28 (folio 4v–5v); Isaiah 55:9 – 56:9 (folios 6r–v); Isaiah 57:14–15 (folio 6v); (*haftarot*)

Aramaic: Targum Jonathan to Prophets (+ Hebrew lemmata). Oriental (Yemenite?) square script; Tiberian vocalisation.

Paper; 6 leaves (2 bifolia); mutilated, 1 leaf very badly. 25.4 × 17.0; 25–8 lines.

Festival *haftarot*, headings: שבת רביעיה החדש ביום (folio 1v); דיומא תיניי בישעיה (folio 2r); דיומא קמא דפסחא ביה׳ (folio 2v); אפטרתא קמיתא דמוס דכיפורי בישעיה (folio 6v). [390]

**T-S B18.3** Micah 6:2, 8; Hosea 12:13 – 13:4; 14:2–3; Isaiah 60:15–16; (*haftarot*)

Hebrew; Aramaic: Targum Jonathan to Prophets. Oriental square script; unpointed.

Vellum; 1 leaf; mutilated and stained. 19.5 × 18.5; 21 lines.

Divine name: Hebrew tetragrammaton; Targum ייי; triennial *haftarot* for Genesis 27:28 (Micah 6); Genesis 28:10 (Hosea 12, heading: ויצא יעקב); Isaiah 60 – alternate *haftarah*(?) for Genesis 28:10. [391]

**T-S B18.4** 1 Kings 2:9–12; Ezekiel 16:1–14; (*haftarot*)

Hebrew; Aramaic: Targum Jonathan to Prophets. Spanish square script; Hebrew with Tiberian vocalisation + accents; Targum with sporadic Tiberian vocalisation.

Vellum; 1 leaf. 20.9 × 18.5; 2 cols.; 23 lines.

Divine name: Hebrew tetragrammaton: Targum ייי; *haftarot* for *parashot wayehi* (1 Kings) and *shemot* (Ezekiel, heading ואלה שמת ביחזקאל). [392]

**T-S B18.5** Isaiah 10:32 – 11:10; 12:4–6; (*haftarah* + *tosefta*) + 2 Samuel 6:1–2 (Hebrew only)

Hebrew; Aramaic: Targum Jonathan to Prophets. Ashkenazi/Italian square script; Tiberian vocalisation; Massorah Parva.

Vellum; 1 leaf. 32.8 × 29.0; 2 cols.; 29 lines.

Divine name: יי; this is the *haftarah* for eighth day Passover; text is preceded by the Hebrew version of the Isaiah passage, and followed by 2 Samuel 6:1–2, in Hebrew, and the note: אילן פרשיתא דקרינא דציבורא(ל) ביומא דפיסחא משך תורא קדש בכספא פסל מדברא שלח בוכרא׳ סימן ויהי ביום השמיני ומפ׳ בשמואל (this note is in semi-cursive script). [393]

**T-S B18.6** Joshua 1:5–7, 9–10; 6:27; Isaiah 61:9 – 62:9; 63:16; (*haftarot*)

Hebrew; Aramaic: Targum Jonathan to Prophets. Oriental square script; Hebrew with Tiberian vocalisation + accents; Targum with sporadic Tiberian vocalisation.

Vellum; 1 leaf; badly mutilated. 20.5 × 21.0; 2 cols.; 34–5 lines.

Divine name: Hebrew tetragrammaton; Targum ייי; colophon: חסלת אפטראתא ברחמי שמיא יהי רצון יעבד יתיה קודש בר הוא סימן טוב ותכלית קץ לישועת עמו ישראל אמן׳ צדוק הלבלר בר יצחק יזכה. Fragment of poem in last column (torn): ויפרח וירבה ולא יכבה: וידגה ויגדל ולא ידל: עד עולמי עד. Joshua 1 and Isaiah 61 are not attested as consecutive *haftarot*. [394]

**T-S B18.7** 1 Samuel 15:32 – 16:1, 12–13; Ezekiel 36:16–30; 45:9–11 (folio 2); Jeremiah 31:8–19; Isaiah 55:6–11 (folio 1); (*haftarot*)

Hebrew; Aramaic: Targum Jonathan to Prophets. Oriental square script; Hebrew with Tiberian vocalisation + accents; 1 Samuel unpointed; Targum unpointed; Massorah Parva (folio 2 only).

Vellum; 2 leaves. 27.0 × 25.0; 24 lines.

Divine name: Hebrew tetragrammaton; Targum ייי; *haftarot*: for *parashat zakhor* (1 Samuel); heading: פרה אדומה ביחזקאל (Ezekiel 36); heading: מפטיר החדש הזה לכם ביחזקאל (Ezekiel 45); for second day New Year (Jeremiah 31); heading: שבתא דשובה דבין ריש שתה לצומא (Isaiah 55); error in 1 Samuel 15:32 שאול for שמואל. [395]

**T-S B18.8** 1 Kings 1:22–31, 47 (folio 1); Hosea 12:4–11 (folio 2); (*haftarot*)

Hebrew; Aramaic: Targum Jonathan to Prophets. Oriental square script; Tiberian vocalisation (Hebrew only on folio 2).

Vellum; 2 leaves; badly mutilated. 21.5 × 20.5; 2 cols.; 18 lines.

Divine name: Hebrew tetragrammaton; Targum ייי; *haftarot* for *parashot hayye sarah* and *wayese'* respectively. [396]

**T-S B18.9**  Jeremiah 16:19 – 17:8 (folio 1); Judges 13:9–19 (folio 2); (*haftarot*)
Hebrew; Aramaic: Targum Jonathan to Prophets. Oriental square script; Tiberian vocalisation (faded).
Paper; 2 leaves (1 bifolium).  24.3 × 17.2; 21 lines.
Divine name: Hebrew tetragrammaton; Targum ײַ; *haftarot* for *parashot behuqotai* and *naso'* respectively. [397]

**T-S B18.10**  Judges 5:2–8; Isaiah 6:13; 9:5–6; Jeremiah 34:8–10; (*haftarot*)
Aramaic: Targum Jonathan to Prophets (+ Hebrew lemmata). Oriental semi-cursive script; unpointed.
Paper; 2 leaves (1 bifolium).  16.6 × 13.7; 14–16 lines.
Divine name: Targum tetragrammaton; *haftarot* for *parashot beshalah*, *yitro* and *mishpatim*; heading: ואלה המשפטים. [398]

**T-S B18.11**  Ezekiel 1:1 (*verso*); (*haftarah*)
Hebrew; Aramaic: Targum Jonathan to Prophets. Oriental square script; unpointed.
Paper; 1 leaf; slightly mutilated.  15.2 × 10.6; 12 lines.
Heading: בשׁמ׳ רחמ׳ אפטרתא דיומא קמא דעצרתא ברישא דיחזקאל; *recto* blank. [399]

**T-S B18.12**  Jonah 3:6 – 4:1; Micah 7:18–20; Zechariah 14:1–3; (*haftarot*)
Aramaic: Targum Jonathan to Prophets. Oriental square script; unpointed.
Paper; 1 leaf; mutilated.  19.3⁺ × 15.8; 21–23⁺ lines.
Divine name: א; *haftarot* for Day of Atonement (Jonah, Micah) and Tabernacles (Zechariah) headed: יומא קדמאה דסוכה בת׳ עש[ר]. [400]

**T-S B18.13**  Isaiah 5:30 – 6:13; 9:5–6 (in margin); (*haftarah*)
Aramaic: Targum Jonathan to Prophets (+ Hebrew lemmata). Oriental semi-cursive script; sporadic Tiberian vocalisation.
Paper; 1 leaf; mutilated.  25.3 × 17.8; 33 lines.
Divine name: ויֽ/יֽי; heading: תרגום אפטארה וישמע יתר׳ בישעיה; *verso* contains Palestinian Targum phrase: ית פרישׁ׳ מפתיא דיעבד מ [ ] לקבל (Deuteronomy 34:12?), and heading of commandments from Maimonides' Code, laws of ritual slaughter (pen exercises). [401]

**T-S B18.14**  Isaiah 60:21–2; 61:9, 6(!); 61:10 – 62:5; 63:16; 65:22–3; 66:7 (folios 1r–3v); Jonah 1:1–10 (folios 3v–5r); (*haftarot?*)
Hebrew; Aramaic: Targum Jonathan to Prophets. Oriental semi-cursive script; Tiberian vocalisation.
Vellum; 8 leaves; slightly mutilated.  10.0 × 7.5; 12–15 lines.
Divine name: ויֽי; note selection of verses from Isaiah 60–66; unattested as *haftarah*; Jonah 1 *haftarah* for Day of Atonement afternoon; top half of folio 1r, liturgical *zikhronot* from *'amidah* for High Holydays; folios 5v–8 blank. [402]

**T-S B18.15** (= T-S B18.16)  2 Kings 22:1–5; (*haftarah*)
Aramaic: Targum Jonathan to Prophets (+ Hebrew lemmata). Oriental square script; sporadic Tiberian vocalisation.
Vellum; 1 leaf; mutilated.  14.1 × 10.8; 16 lines.
Divine name: ײי; *haftarah* for second day Passover; heading: דיומא תנינא במלכי; *verso* contains blessings that follow *haftarah*. [403]

**T-S B18.16** (= T-S B18.15)  2 Kings 22:5–13 (folio 1); Ezekiel 37:8–14 (folio 2r); (*haftarot*)
Aramaic: Targum Jonathan to Prophets (+ Hebrew lemmata). Oriental square script; sporadic Tiberian vocalisation.
Vellum; 2 leaves (1 bifolium); slightly mutilated. 14.4 × 10.5; 14–17 lines.
*Haftarot* for second day Passover (2 Kings); intermediate Sabbath of Passover (Ezekiel); this is the direct continuation of B18.15; folio 2v blank. [404]

**T-S B18.17**  Isaiah 12:2–6; Ezekiel 1:1–3; (*haftarot*)
Aramaic: Targum Jonathan to Prophets (+ Hebrew lemmata). Oriental semi-cursive script; Tiberian vocalisation.
Paper; 1 leaf.  19.7 × 14.3; 14–15 lines.
Divine name: ײי; *haftarot* for eighth day Passover (Isaiah); Pentecost (Ezekiel); note at end of *recto*: נשלמו אפטריות שלפסח ביחזקאל and heading: חג שבעות בעזרת האל at top of *verso* with circles in red ink; variant in margin at Ezekiel 1:1 בְּעֶזְרָתָא לא בְעָזְרְתָא (for ). [405]

**T-S B18.18**  Ezekiel 43:23–7; 1 Kings 18:1–16 (folio 1); 1 Kings 7:21–2; 7:40–50; Isaiah 43:21 – 44:3 (folio 2); (*haftarot*)
Hebrew; Aramaic: Targum Jonathan to Prophets. Oriental square script; Tiberian vocalisation + accents (Hebrew only in lighter brown ink), Targum unpointed.
Vellum; 2 leaves (1 bifolium); badly mutilated. 18.5⁺ × 19.4;  2 cols.; 23⁺ lines.
Divine name: Hebrew tetragrammaton; Targum ײי; *haftarot* for *parashat tesaweh* (Ezekiel 43); heading: כי תשא במלכי (1 Kings 18); *parashat wayaqhel* (1 Kings 7:21–2); heading: הואלה פקודי במלכי (1 Kings 7:40–50); heading: דויקרא בישעיה (Isaiah 43). [406]

**T-S B18.19**   2 Kings 23:25 (folio 1r); Ezekiel 37:1–14 (folios 1r–2r); 1 Samuel 21:15 – 23:4 (folios 2r–6v); Zechariah 14:5–21 (folios 7r–8r); 1 Kings 7:51 – 8:15 (folios 8v–9v); (*haftarot*)
Aramaic: Targum Jonathan to Prophets (+ Hebrew lemmata).   Oriental square script; unpointed.

Paper; 9 leaves (3 bifolia); mutilated, some badly. 26.3 × 16.0;   20 lines.

Divine name: יי; *haftarot* for: second day Passover, intermediate Sabbath of Passover, seventh day Passover דכסא בשמואל(?), first day Tabernacles, second day Tabernacles.   [407]

## T-S B18.20

Not Targum, Hebrew Bible: 2 Kings 4:42 – 5:4; *haftarah tazri'a*.   [408]

**T-S B18.21**   Isaiah 42:4–7 (folio 1v); 1 Kings 1:1 (folio 2); 1 Samuel 12:17–20 (folio 3r); Judges 10:18 – 11:3 (folio 3v); (*haftarot*)
Aramaic: Targum Jonathan to Prophets (+ Hebrew lemmata).   Oriental square script; Tiberian vocalisation.

Paper; 3 leaves (1 bifolium); very badly mutilated. 14.0⁺ × 16.9;   10⁺ lines.

Divine name: יי; *haftarot* for *parashot bere'shit, hayye sarah, qorah* and *huqat*; folio 1r blank.   [409]

**T-S B18.22**   2 Kings 7:6–10 (folio 1); Ezekiel 20:8–13 (folio 2); (*haftarot*)
Hebrew; Aramaic: Targum Jonathan to Prophets. Oriental semi-cursive script; Tiberian vocalisation (incomplete in Targum).

Paper; 2 leaves (1 bifolium); one side badly rubbed. 17.3 × 12.8;   13 lines.

*Haftarot* for *parashot mesorah* and *qedoshim*.   [410]

**T-S B18.23**   Jeremiah 28:3–17 (folios 1r–2r); Malachi 2:17 – 3:10 (folio 2); (*haftarot*)
Hebrew; Aramaic: Targum Jonathan to Prophets. Oriental square script; Babylonian vocalisation + accents.

Vellum; 2 leaves (1 bifolium); very badly mutilated. 21.8 × 7.0⁺;   [2] cols.;   19 lines.

The Jeremiah text is unattested as a *haftarah*; Malachi text has heading: [ראה אנ]כי (Deuteronomy 11:26).   [411]

**T-S B18.24**   Isaiah 43:3–7 (folio 1); Isaiah 54:17–? (folio 1r); Isaiah 40:25, 26, 31, 27 (folio 2); (*haftarot*)
Aramaic: Targum Jonathan to Prophets (+ Hebrew lemmata).   Oriental semi-cursive script; Tiberian vocalisation.

Paper; 2 leaves (1 bifolium); mutilated and badly rubbed.   17.0⁺ × 10.5;   15⁺ lines.

Divine name: יְיָ; verses out of order in Isaiah 40; *haftarot* for *parashot bere'shit, noah* and *lekh lekha*.   [412]

**T-S B18.25**   1 Kings 8:1–8, 66 (folios 1r–2r); Joshua 1:1–8 (folio 2); (*haftarot*)
Hebrew; Aramaic: Targum Jonathan to Prophets. Oriental square script; unpointed.

Vellum; 2 leaves (1 bifolium); badly mutilated. 17.2⁺ × 16.6;   16⁺ lines.

Divine name: יי; *haftarot* for second day Tabernacles, *Simhat Torah* heading: אפטרתא דיום שמחת תורה.   [413]

**T-S B18.26**   1 Samuel 15:7–9, 31; Ezekiel 36:25–9; Numbers 19:1–2 (in upper margins); (*haftarot* + *maftir*)
Hebrew; Aramaic: Targum Jonathan to Prophets; Onqelos only for Numbers.   Oriental square script; Hebrew with Tiberian vocalisation + accents; Targum with Tiberian vocalisation.

Vellum; 1 leaf; mutilated and rubbed.   16.0 × 15.5; 17 lines.

Divine name: ייי; *haftarot* for *parashot zakhor* (1 Samuel) and *parah* (Ezekiel); *maftir* of *parashat parah* (Numbers).   [414]

**T-S B18.27**   2 Kings 4:27–37 (folio 1r); 1 Kings 1:1–31, 46–8 (folios 1r–2v); Malachi 1:1–8, 12–14; 2:1; 3:4 (folios 2v–3v); Hosea 11:7–8 (folio 3v); Obadiah 1:15–21 (folio 4a); Amos 2:6–7; 2:10 – 3:6 (folio 4r–v); Isaiah 19:11–25 (folio 5r); Judges 4:4–14; 5:26–31 (folios 5r–6r); Isaiah 6:1–13; 9:5–6 (folio 6); (*haftarot*)
Hebrew; Aramaic: Targum Jonathan to Prophets. Oriental square script; sporadic Tiberian vocalisation.

Vellum; 6 leaves (1 bifolium); badly mutilated. 25.8 × 18.8;   30 lines.

Divine name: Hebrew tetragrammaton; Targum ייי; headings to Malachi: ואלה תולדות יצחק בתרי עשר; to Amos: וישב יעקב בתרי עשר; to Isaiah 6: וישמע בישע'.   [415]

**T-S B18.28**   Isaiah 42:1–16 (folio 1r–v); Isaiah 54:1 – 55:5 (folios 1v–2v); Isaiah 41:12–17 (folio 3r); 2 Kings 4:1–37 (folios 3r–5v); 1 Kings 1:1–7 (folio 5v); (*haftarot*)
Hebrew; Aramaic: Targum Jonathan to Prophets. Yemenite square script; Hebrew with Tiberian vocalisation + accents; Targum with Tiberian vocalisation.

**[T-S B18.28, cont.]**
Paper; 5 leaves.   27.2 × 18.8;   23–6 lines.
Divine name: Hebrew tetragrammaton; Targum ʰ;
heading (folio 1r): בשם רחמן [א]תחיל לכתוב הפטריות כל השנה
[    ] שמפטי[רין] לתורה בעו[רת]. Title of each *haftarah* appears at beginning and in the upper margin of most folios (*bere'shit* to *hayye sarah*); error in title at top of folio 5r: וירא for לך לך.   [416]

## T-S B19.1   Isaiah 5:30 – 6:1 (*verso*); (*haftarah*)
Hebrew; Aramaic: Targum Jonathan to Prophets; Judaeo-Arabic.   Oriental semi-cursive script; Tiberian vocalisation (Hebrew & Targum).
Paper; 1 leaf; rubbed.   19.0 × 13.6;   16 lines.
Divine name: Hebrew & Targum tetragrammaton; contrast many other manuscripts with אדני in the Hebrew (6:1); heading: ישעיה יתרו בישעיה; *recto* blank.   [417]

## T-S B19.2   1 Kings 1:5, 11, 12–31, 46–8;
Malachi 1:1–9; Jeremiah 32:22–5, 36–44; (*haftarot*)
Hebrew; Aramaic: Targum Jonathan to Prophets; Judaeo-Arabic.   Oriental square script; Tiberian vocalisation (Hebrew & Targum).
Paper; 8 leaves (3 bifolia); some very badly mutilated. 20.3 × 21.6;   2 cols.;   16 lines.
Divine name: Hebrew tetragrammaton; Targum ʰ; heading to Malachi: ואלה תולדות יצחק ב[תרי] עשרה; folios not numbered and not in original order.   [418]

## T-S C7.112   Genesis 4:24 – 5:18
Aramaic: Onqelos (+ Rashi).   Ashkenazi (perhaps from northern Italy) square script (Onqelos); semi-cursive (Rashi); Tiberian vocalisation + 'etnaḥta'.
Vellum; 1 leaf; mutilated and rubbed.   15.7 × [14.0]; 2 cols.;   19–20 lines.
Divine name: ʰ; *verso*, col.2 (Rashi) blank. See plate 18.   [419]

## T-S C7.130
Commentary to Numbers 34:8 containing a citation of Palestinian Targum to Numbers 20:22; with scribal error דכבישתא for דכמען.   [420]

## T-S C7.132   Isaiah 24:5–11
Hebrew; Aramaic: Targum Jonathan to Prophets (+ Rashi and Radaq).   Spanish semi-cursive script; Hebrew with Tiberian vocalisation + accents; Targum with Tiberian vocalisation.
Paper; 1 leaf; mutilated.   15.7⁺ × 20.7;   19⁺ lines.
Hebrew, Targum, Rashi and Radaq follow in sequence, verse by verse in the same column, with headings: ת׳י, רש׳ and רד׳ק before the latter three. See plate 23.   [421]

## T-S D1.100   Exodus 22:14 – Deuteronomy 13:7⁺
Aramaic: Massorah to Onqelos.   Oriental semi-cursive script; sporadic Tiberian vocalisation.
Vellum; 2 leaves (1 bifolium); mutilated and rubbed. 23.8 × 18.9;   24 lines.
Sporadic Hebrew headings for beginnings of *parashot*; text contains many variants under אי and לנ (Nehardean), as well as total number of occurrences of particular translations; this Massorah is sparse.   [422]

## T-S E3.117   Isaiah 4:6 – 5:5 (*verso*); (*haftarah*)
Aramaic: Targum Jonathan to Prophets (+ Hebrew lemmata).   Oriental square script; Tiberian vocalisation + accents.
Vellum; 1 leaf; slightly mutilated and rubbed. 14.8 × 14.4⁺;   15 lines.
Heading: [אפטר]ה דיומא תנינא בישע[ה]; *haftarah* for the second day Tabernacles, *viz.* מטלת עני (4:6) (cf. Onqelos to Leviticus 23:43); *recto* contains Judaeo-Arabic translation of *Pirqei 'Avot*.   [423]

## T-S F8.81   Genesis 6:8 – 7:3
Aramaic: Onqelos (+ Hebrew lemmata).   Oriental semi-cursive script; unpointed.
Paper; 1 leaf; slightly mutilated and badly rubbed. 22.4 × 14.7;   19 lines.
Divine name: ʰ.   [424]

## T-S H2.24 (folios 2–4, 6–9r)   Leviticus
23:32–6, 40–44 (folios 2–3); Numbers 29:12–16 (folios 3–4); Deuteronomy 15:19 – 16:17 (folios 6–9r)
Aramaic: Onqelos (+ Hebrew lemmata).   Oriental semi-cursive script; Tiberian vocalisation (sporadic on some folios).
Paper; 10 leaves (4 bifolia).   12.7 × 9.0;   11–17 lines.
Divine name: יי/יי; folios are numbered 1–11 with folio 5 missing; one folio is missing between folios 2 and 3; folios 1, 9v, 10–11 contain Hebrew *piyyuṭim*. Judaeo-Arabic notes כמל, כמלת after Leviticus 23:44 (folio 3v) and Numbers 29:16 (folio 4v). Readings are for Day of Atonement and Tabernacles.   [425]

## T-S H2.97   Exodus 13:6–10; Numbers 28:16–20
Aramaic: Onqelos (+ Hebrew lemmata).   Oriental linear square script; Tiberian vocalisation.
Paper; 1 leaf.   19.0 × 14.5;   13 lines.
Divine name: יי; Judaeo-Arabic notes between the passages: כמל אלתרגום לליום אלאול מן אלפסח (*recto*, bottom) and תרגום מוסף אול אלפסח (*verso*, top).   [426]

## T-S H3.12 (folios 1–3v)   Exodus 19:12 – 20:18
Aramaic: Onqelos (+ Hebrew lemmata).   Oriental semi-cursive script; Tiberian vocalisation.
Paper; 4 leaves (2 bifolia).   19.1 × 10.2;   19 lines.
Divine name: ʰ; folios 3v–4v contain Hebrew poem on Ten Commandments.   [427]

**T-S H3.111** Exodus 19:1–3, 8–12 (folios 1v–2v)
Aramaic: Palestinian Targum (+ Hebrew lemmata). Oriental linear square script (untrained?); Tiberian vocalisation.
Paper; 2 leaves (1 bifolium). 15.5 × 11.2; 11–13 lines.
Divine name: ייי; folio 1r contains an Aramaic *reshut* to the Targum with the name: ישועה בר אברהם; text contains scribal errors and conflated versions, and the letters *dalet/resh* and *bet/kaf* are confused. [428]

**T-S H7.46** Jonah 4:11; Micah 7:18–20; Numbers 29:12–16; Zechariah 13:9 (*haftarot* and *maftir*)
Hebrew; Aramaic: Targum Jonathan to Prophets and Onqelos. Oriental square script; sporadic Tiberian vocalisation.
Vellum; 1 leaf. 20.5 × 17.4; 19 lines.
Divine name: Hebrew tetragrammaton; Targum ייי; headings: ואל פסוקי דהפטרה and עניין של סוכה שור או כשב וגו' (both before Numbers 29) and דהפטרתו של יום ראשון בנבואת זכריה בתרי עשר (before Zechariah 13). These are *haftarot* for Day of Atonement afternoon and *maftir* and *haftarah* for the first day Tabernacles. [429]

**T-S H10.29 (folio 2)**
Contains Aramaic poem in praise of God who created the world by ten utterances. [430]

**T-S H10.78** Exodus 12:2, Exodus 14; 2 poems (one alphabetic acrostic)
Aramaic: Targumic. Oriental linear square script; Tiberian vocalisation.
Vellum; 2 leaves (1 bifolium). 10.4 × 10.0; 10–11 lines.
Vocalisation very sporadic on folio 2; folio 1r blank.
Klein, *GMPT* I, pp. 191, 235. [431]

**T-S H10.109**
Two Aramaic poems, one leading up to Jeremiah 5:22, the other an alphabetic acrostic. [432]

**T-S H10.169** Habakkuk 3:1–19 (with *toseftot*); (*haftarah*)
Aramaic: Targum Jonathan to Prophets. Oriental semi-cursive script; sporadic Tiberian vocalisation.
Paper; 1 leaf (several sheets pasted together). 44.3 × 15.8; 50 lines.
Divine name: ייי; this is the *haftarah* for Pentecost; *verso* contains a Hebrew liturgical composition comprising a confessional and a song of praise. [433]

**T-S H11.51** Exodus 12:1–2; poems
Aramaic: Palestinian Targum + targumic poems. Oriental square script; Tiberian vocalisation (in darker ink).
Vellum; 7 leaves (1 bifolium). 10.8 × 10.5; 10–13 lines.
Divine name: ייי (folio 7v); many variants/corrections in margins; note of ownership [הכ ב סם ] קנה יוחיי ה[ נדבה לבו [והישר] בעיניו יעשה (folio 1r).
Klein, *GMPT* I, pp. 197–209. [434]

**T-S H12.8**
Aramaic poem with Hebrew refrain based upon Book of Daniel: איש חמדות חז חיוא תיינא. [435]

**T-S H12.9**
Aramaic poem (same as H12.8) with variants and much more preserved. [436]

**T-S H12.11 (folio 6r)**
Aramaic poem (זולת) on month on Nisan, related to Exodus 12:2; opening: בירחא קדמאה; alphabetic acrostic; see following entry for description of manuscript. [437]

**T-S H12.11 (folio 6v)** Exodus 12:2 poem (alphabetic acrostic)
Aramaic: Targumic. Oriental semi-cursive script; sporadic Tiberian vocalisation.
Paper; 6 leaves (3 bifolia). 26.3 × 17.7; 27 lines.
Divine name: ייי; only three lines of poem preserved, opening: אליסון מה משבח הדין ירדא; cf. T-S AS 116.453 for the same poem.
Fleischer *Tarbiz* XXXVII, p. 272; Heinemann *Hasifrut* IV, p. 365; Klein *GMPT* I, p. 191. [438]

**T-S H15.27**
Aramaic and Hebrew *reshut* to Targum Jonathan b. 'Uzziel. [439]

**T-S J2.80** Isaiah 51:9–11; 2 Samuel 5:20–21; 6:1–2; (*haftarot*)
Hebrew; Aramaic: Targum Jonathan to Prophets. Oriental square script; Hebrew with Tiberian vocalisation + accents; Targum unpointed.
Vellum; 1 leaf; very badly mutilated. 9.8⁺ × 8.9⁺; 13⁺ lines.
Divine name: Targum ייי; triennial *haftarot* for Genesis 24:1 and Genesis 25:1 respectively. [440]

**T-S K6.186** Exodus 19:1–4 (*verso*)
Aramaic: Onqelos (+ Hebrew lemmata, full Hebrew for 19:1). Oriental semi-cursive script; Tiberian vocalisation.
Paper; 1 leaf. 18.4 × 14.9; 13 lines.
Divine name: ייי; heading: בשם רחמן עניין עצרת, and note of ownership and scribe on *recto*: בשם רחמן סעדיה בר אלעזר ספ מה וכתב אלשיך אבו סער הלוי בשם יי. [441]

**T-S K22.23**  Genesis 1:1–14 (folio 1r); folios 1v–10v illegible and unidentified
Hebrew; Aramaic: Onqelos.  Oriental square script; unpointed.
Vellum; 10 leaves (1 bifolium); very badly shriveled and stained.  18.4 × 15.4;  2 cols. ? lines.
Divine name: Targum יֿי; only folio 1v remains legible.
[442]

**T-S K25.35**
Part of an Aramaic composition on symbolism of menorah, ending with Targum Jonathan to Zechariah 4:2 (folio 1v–2r); Aramaic composition of the 'four crowns bestowed by Heaven' summoning a bridegroom to the Torah (folio 2r); part of a Hebrew *piyyuṭ (maṣḥar)* and a *piyyuṭ* for mourners (folio 2v).  [443]

**T-S K25.129**  Genesis 3:24 – 4:2; 4:4–5, 7–12
Hebrew; Aramaic: Onqelos.  Oriental square script; Babylonian vocalisation + accents; Massorah Parva.
Vellum; 1 leaf; very badly mutilated.  17.8⁺ × 13.4⁺; 2 cols.; 17⁺ lines.
Divine name: Hebrew tetragrammaton: Onqelos ייי.
Rüger *VT* XIII, pp. 235–37.  [444]

**T-S K25.160**  Genesis 49:15, 22–4; Deuteronomy 32:7, 13–14, 16–17, 22–4, 27–36, 40–42; 33:7–8, 12–27
Aramaic: Onqelos.  Oriental semi-cursive script (untrained); unpointed.
Paper; 1 leaf + 5 fragments (separately conserved); rubbed.  15.4 × 12.6;  15 lines.
Divine name: יֿי; this may be a chidren's copying exercise, containing the Blessing of Jacob and the Song and Blessing of Moses.  [445]

**T-S K26.2**  Ezekiel 1:1–7 (folios 1–4); 1 Samuel 2:8–10 (folio 5); Jeremiah 31:2–11 (folios 6–8); Zechariah 14:8–9, 16–18 (folios 9–11r); 1 Kings 7:51 – 8:7 (folios 11v–13); (*hafṭarot*)
Hebrew; Aramaic: Targum Jonathan to Prophets. Oriental script; Hebrew large, square; Targum semi-cursive; unpointed.
Vellum; 13 leaves (2 bifolia); several mutilated, all very badly rubbed.  12.3 × 10.3;  12 lines.
Divine name: Hebrew & Targum יֿי; heading (folio 1r): ראשון [ד]עצרת(?) [   ]; these are *hafṭarot* for Pentecost (Ezekiel), first day New Year (1 Samuel), second day New Year (Jeremiah), first day Tabernacles (Zechariah) and second day Tabernacles (1 Kings).  [446]

**T-S K26.6**  Exodus 39:43; 40:5–6
Hebrew; Aramaic: Onqelos.  Oriental square script; Babylonian vocalisation and Tiberian vocalisation + accents added in darker ink to Hebrew only.
Vellum; 1 leaf; very badly mutilated, *verso* very badly rubbed.  7.0⁺ × 14.7⁺;  [2] cols.;  3⁺ lines.
Divine name: Hebrew tetragrammaton.  [447]

**T-S K26.14**  Isaiah 62:6–9
Aramaic: Targum Jonathan to Prophets (+ Hebrew lemmata).  Oriental semi-cursive script; sporadic Tiberian vocalisation (1 word with Babylonian vocalisation at beginning).
Paper; 1 leaf.  14.5 × 10.6;  16 lines.
Divine name: יֿי; the words על דא appear after verse 9.  [448]

**T-S K26.15**  Exodus 9:35(?) (folio 1r); 13:15 – 14:4 (folios 1v–2)
Aramaic: Onqelos (+ Hebrew lemmata).  Oriental semi-cursive script; unpointed.
Paper; 2 leaves (1 bifolium); folio 2 very badly mutilated and rubbed.  18.7 × 10.5⁺;  15 lines.
Divine name יֿיֿי; פֿסֿ and a cipher appear after 9:35 (folio 1r) and 13:22 (folio 2r).  [449]

**T-S K26.17**  Ezekiel 26:17–19; 26:20 – 27:3; 27:5–8, 10–14
Hebrew; Aramaic: Targum Jonathan to Prophets. Oriental square script; Babylonian vocalisation + accents.
Vellum; 1 or 2 leaves (three vertical strips, separately conserved); very badly mutilated and rubbed. 25.8⁺ × 11.2⁺ (largest);  [2] cols.;  19⁺ lines.
Very narrow strip unidentified.  [450]

**T-S K26.23** (= T-S K26.25, 27)  Deuteronomy 16:18 – 21:9
Aramaic: extract of Onqelos + Massorah.  Oriental square script; sporadic Babylonian vocalisation.
Vellum; 1 leaf; mutilated and rubbed.  24.2 × 15.2; 28–35 lines.
Divine name: ייי; heading: שפטים in red ink.
Yeivin *H. Yalon Mem. Vol.* pp. 123–28.  [451]

**T-S K26.24**  Exodus 13:17–20 (*recto*); 14:26 – 15:1 (*verso*)
Aramaic: Onqelos.  Oriental linear square script; Tiberian vocalisation.
Paper; 1 leaf.  25.0 × 17.0;  8–14 lines.
Divine name: ℤ; *verso* is inverted in relation to *recto*; Hebrew and Arabic jottings on *recto*, *verso* contains opening of Judaeo-Arabic responsum.  [452]

**T-S K26.25** (= T-S K26.23, 27)  Deuteronomy 31:21 – 32:52
Aramaic: extract of Onqelos + Massorah.
Vellum; 1 leaf.
See description of manuscript at K26.23, above.
Yeivin *H. Yalon Mem. Vol.* pp. 147–53.  [453]

**T-S K26.26**  Joshua 24:26, 28; 2 Samuel 21:15–17; (*hafṭarot*)
Hebrew; Aramaic: Targum Jonathan to Prophets. Oriental square script; unpointed.
Vellum; 1 leaf; badly mutilated.  9.2⁺ × 10.8;  12⁺ lines.
Divine name: Hebrew tetragrammaton; Targum ᵃ; variant ספר/סטר in Joshua 24:26; these are *hafṭarot* for *parashot niṣavim* and *ha'azinu*. [454]

**T-S K26.27** (= T-S K26.23, 25)  Deuteronomy 21:10 – 31:29 (folios 1–3); 33:1 – 34:12 + 33:26 (folio 4r–v)
Aramaic: extract of Onqelos + Massorah.
Vellum; 4 leaves (1 bifolium).
Folio 4v contains a Massorah to the Hebrew version of Joshua overwritten by a Judaeo-Arabic document; see description of manuscript at K26.23, above.
Yeivin *H. Yalon Mem. Vol.* pp.128–47, 153–57. [455]

**T-S K26.30**  Numbers 31:40 – 32:11
Aramaic: Onqelos (+ Hebrew lemmata).  Oriental square script; unpointed.
Vellum; 1 leaf; badly mutilated.  20.0 × 16.9;  21 lines.
Divine name: ᵃ. [456]

**T-S K26.31**  Exodus 36:36 – 37:12; 37:20 – 38:2
Aramaic: Onqelos (+ Hebrew lemmata).  Oriental square script; Tiberian vocalisation + accents.
Vellum; 1 leaf; badly mutilated and rubbed.
16.5⁺ × 20.2;  19⁺ lines. [457]

**T-S K26.36**  Ezekiel 29:9–12, 13 (in margin), 21 (folio 1); Isaiah 19:25; Judges 4:23 – 5:3 (folio 2); Judges 5:10–14 (folio 3); Jeremiah 34:8–13 (folio 4); 1 Kings 5:32 – 6:4 (folio 5); 1 Kings 6:4–12 (folios 6–7); 1 Kings 6:12; Ezekiel 43:10–12 (folio 8); Judges 11:7–11 (folio 9); Jeremiah 2:7–10 (folio 10); 1 Samuel 8:4–8 (folio 11); 1 Samuel 17:54; 18:14; Joshua 8:30–32 (folio 12); 1 Samuel 15:21–2, 31; Ezekiel 36:16–17 (folio 13, 2 fragments); Ezekiel 36:17–21 (folio 14); Ezekiel 36:34–6; 45:18–19 (folio 15); Ezekiel 45:19–23 (folio 16); Ezekiel 45:23 – 46:2 (folio 17); Isaiah 42:4–8 (folio 18); Jeremiah 31:2–12 (folios 19–20); Isaiah 54:5–10; 60:1; 62:1–5 (folios 21–2); (*hafṭarot*)
Hebrew; Aramaic: Targum Jonathan to Prophets. Oriental square script; Tiberian vocalisation; (folio 22 unpointed and folio 21 faint and partly reinforced in darker ink).
Vellum; 22 leaves (8 bifolia); several mutilated. 20.4 × 17.4 (largest);  13 lines (except folios 21–2, 12 lines).
Divine name: Hebrew tetragrammaton; Targum יי (folios 1–18), יי (folios 19–20), יי/יי (folios 21–2). This classmark includes three distinct manuscripts. The first (folios 1–18): *hafṭarot* for *parashot wa'era', bo', beshalaḥ, mishpaṭim, terumah, teṣaweh* (folios 1–8); *parashat ḥuqat* (folio 9); *parashot 'eqev, shofṭim, ki teṣe', ki tavo'* (folios 10–12); *parashot zakhor, parah, ha-ḥodesh* (folios 13–18). The second (folios 19–20): *hafṭarah* for second day New Year. The third (folios 21–22): *hafṭarot* for *ki teṣe', ki tavo'* and *niṣavim*, according to another tradition. Headings: ויהי בשלח במשפטים (folio 2r); ואתה תצוה ביחזקאל (folio 8r); והיה כי תבוא ביהושע; decorative פרש in margin ✸ (folio 12r); דפרה ביחזקאל (folio 13v); החדש ביחזקאל (folio 15v); קומי אורי ביש (folio 21v) and decorative קדש פרש in margin ✸ of folio 22v (not at beginning of *hafṭarah*!). Judaeo-Arabic note at bottom of folio 22v: תמת אלאפאטיר אלעניאנאת. [458]

**T-S 6H5.1**  Deuteronomy 31:16 (folio 1r); 2 Kings 2:1–12 (folios 1r–3r); Deuteronomy 32:1–3 (folio 3r); Isaiah 1:2–9, 18–19 (folios 3v–4v); Deuteronomy 33:1–3 (folios 4v–5r); Joshua 1:1–9 (folios 5r–6r); Exodus 30:11–16 (folios 6v–7r); Hosea 2:1–7, 21–2 (folios 7r–8r); Deuteronomy 25:17–19 (folio 8v); 1 Samuel 15:2–9, 31 (folios 8v–9v); Numbers 19:1–3 (folio 10r); Ezekiel 36:25–32; 37:14 (folios 10v–11v); Exodus 12:1–3 (folio 12r); Isaiah 41:27 – 42:9 (folios 12r–13r); Exodus 11:1–3 (folios 13v–14r); Haggai 2:6–8 (folio 14r–v); (*mafṭir* and *hafṭarah* readings)
Hebrew; Aramaic: Onqelos and Targum Jonathan to Prophets (some passages Aramaic only + Hebrew lemmata).  Oriental script; interspersed passages in square and untrained linear square (scribe and child?); Tiberian vocalisation (fuller in trained hand, very sporadic in the untrained passages).
Paper; 14 leaves.  13.8 × 8.9;  11–18 lines.
Divine name: ᵃ/ᵃᵃ/ᵃᵃ/ᵃ; these are parts of triennial *sidrot* and readings for four (or five) Sabbaths preceding Passover; the first few verses (usually three) of each reading are followed by the *hafṭarah*. The last two *sidrot* of Deuteronomy are numbered with cipher סֹר כֹה before Deuteronomy 32:1 (folio 3r) and סֹר כֹ and the word אפטארה precedes several *hafṭarot*. There are Arabic notations on folios 8r, 9v and 11v noting end of *hafṭarah*, and titles: עמלק (*parashat zakhor*, folio 8v), פרה אדמה (folio 10r), החדש הזה (folio 12r). The reading from Exodus 11 may be intended for Shabbat ha-Gadol(?); folio 14v (top) may contain a colophon: [ ] אם הבנים (?לה) מנחם. See plate 20. [459]

**T-S 8H16.24**  Isaiah 1:28 – 2:4 (folio 1v); 2 Samuel 22:1–15, 25–39 (folio 2); 2 Samuel 22:43–51 (folio 3r); Jeremiah 52:1–10, 14–20 (folio 4); Jeremiah 52:22–9, 31–4 (folio 5); 2 Samuel 23:1–3 (folio 5v); 2 Samuel 23:4–7 (folio 6r); Ezekiel 34:23:31 (folio 6v); (*hafṭarot*) Aramaic: Targum Jonathan to Prophets.   Oriental linear square script; sporadic Tiberian vocalisation.

Paper; 6 leaves; very badly mutilated.   15.7⁺ × 8.1⁺; 25⁺ lines.

Divine name: ײ; headings in Judaeo-Arabic: אלדי עאם מן [הפטארתא] (folio 1r, remainder of folio 1r blank); תמאם אפט [אפטארתא] (folio 1v); חזון ישעיהו (folio 1v); אלדי עאם מן אפטארתא (folio 5v); folio 3v blank; these are not attested as consecutive *hafṭarot*.  [460]

**T-S 8H18.19 (folio 1r)**   Genesis 49:18–24

Aramaic: Onqelos + *tosefta* 49:18 (+ Hebrew lemmata).   Oriental square script; unpointed.

Paper; 2 leaves (1 bifolium?); mutilated.   18.4⁺ × 13.5; 20⁺ lines.

Folio 2r contains *qiddush* for Sabbath eve with Hebrew and Judaeo-Arabic heading and instructions; folios 1v and 2v blank.  [461]

**T-S 13H3.11 (folio 1)**

Hebrew and Aramaic *piyyuṭ* woven about and including Targum Onqelos to Exodus 12:1–3.  [462]

**T-S 13J19.26**   2 Samuel 22:26–45 (*verso*)

Aramaic: Targum Jonathan to Prophets (+ Hebrew lemmata).   Oriental semi-cursive script; unpointed (except one word in 22:36, Tiberian).

Paper; 1 leaf (long sheet folded into 2 folios); mutilated and rubbed.   27.0⁺ × 17.1;  18 lines.

Divine name: ײ; *recto* contains Hebrew *piyyuṭ* written vertically in relation to text on *verso* as a single long sheet.  [463]

**T-S Ar.1a.15**   Genesis 3:12–18 (folio 1); 4:21–5 (folio 2)

Aramaic: Onqelos; Judaeo-Arabic (+ Hebrew lemmata).   Oriental semi-cursive script (lemmata in square script); Tiberian vocalisation.

Paper; 2 leaves (1 bifolium); slightly rubbed. 16.8 × 12.8;  13 lines.

Divine name: ײי; variants to Onqelos in margins.  [464]

**T-S Ar.1a.73**   Genesis 8:11–13, 16–19

Aramaic: Onqelos; Judaeo-Arabic (+ Hebrew lemmata).   Oriental semi-cursive script; unpointed.

Paper; 1 leaf; badly mutilated.   14.5⁺ × 16.4;  10⁺ lines.  [465]

**T-S Ar.1b.63**

Judaeo-Arabic commentary which quotes Targum Jonathan to Isaiah 21:12 and other shorter phrases.  [466]

**T-S Ar.8.32**   Zechariah 3:2, 9; 4:2 (*tosefta* to *hafṭarah*)

Aramaic: Targumic expansion.   Oriental linear square script (untrained); sporadic Tiberian vocalisation.

Paper; 1 leaf; slightly rubbed.   24.8⁺ × 16.4;  24⁺ lines.

Divine name: ײ; Zechariah 3 is *hafṭarah* for Sabbath Ḥanukkah.  [467]

**T-S Ar.21.8**   Exodus 29:7–14 (folio 1); 30:6–12 (folio 2)

Aramaic: Onqelos; Judaeo-Arabic (+ Hebrew lemmata).   Oriental semi-cursive script (lemmata in larger square script); unpointed.

Paper; 2 leaves (1 bifolium); mutilated and badly rubbed.   17.8 × 13.3;  13 lines.

Divine name: Hebrew tetragrammaton; Targum ײ; decorative חֻמָּ֫שׁ and cipher קֹ֫ק(!) for number of verses in *parashat teṣaweh* after 30:10.  [468]

**T-S Ar.21:53**   Deuteronomy 3:13–17; 3:28 – 4:2

Hebrew; Aramaic: Onqelos; Judaeo-Arabic. Oriental linear square script; unpointed.

Paper; 2 leaves (1 bifolium); rubbed.   17.9 × 13.4; 14 lines.

Divine name: Hebrew tetragrammaton; Targum ײ.  [469]

**T-S Ar.21.57**   Genesis 11:27 – 12:15 (folio 1); 12:16 – 13:16 (folio 2)

Aramaic: Onqelos (+ Hebrew lemmata).   Oriental semi-cursive script; unpointed (except Tiberian vocalisation in 12:13).

Paper; 2 leaves (1 bifolium).   20.5 × 14.2;  18 lines.

Divine name: ײ/ײ; cipher נֻצ for number of verses in *parashat noah* after 11:32; error in 13:16 ארעא for עפרא.  [470]

**T-S Ar.21.101**   Genesis 21:1–16

Aramaic: Onqelos (+ Hebrew lemmata).   Oriental semi-cursive script; unpointed.

Paper; 1 leaf; slightly rubbed.   17.1 × 12.4;  17 lines.

Divine name: ײ.  [471]

**T-S Ar.23.79, 80 (= T-S Ar.26.92)**   Genesis 26:20–29 (Ar.23.79); Exodus 12:10–15; 13:3–12 (Ar.23.80)

Aramaic: Onqelos; Judaeo-Arabic (+ Hebrew lemmata).   Oriental semi-cursive script (lemmata in square script); unpointed.

Paper; 3 leaves (1 bifolium); mutilated (Ar.23.80, badly rubbed).   24.6 × 16.8;  18 lines.

Divine name: ײ.  [472]

**T-S Ar.25.176**   Deuteronomy 4:18 – 5:24
(Targum begins at 4:24)
Aramaic: Onqelos; Judaeo-Arabic (on facing sides, each with Hebrew lemmata).   Oriental semi-cursive script; sporadic Tiberian vocalisation.
Paper; 7 leaves; slightly mutilated and rubbed (folio 1 very badly).   17.8 × 13.4;   17–19 lines.
Divine name: יְ/יְ.   [473]

**T-S Ar.26.92 (= T-S Ar.23.79, 80)**   Genesis 32:10–19
Aramaic: Onqelos; Judaeo-Arabic (+ Hebrew lemmata).   Oriental semi-cursive script; unpointed (except 1 word with Tiberian vocalisation in 32:18, added in lighter ink).
Paper; 1 leaf.   24.8 × 16.9;   18 lines.   [474]

**T-S Ar.26.110**   Jeremiah 32:17–22
Hebrew; Aramaic: Targum Jonathan to Prophets; Judaeo-Arabic.   Oriental square script; Tiberian vocalisation (very faint, lighter ink).
Paper; 1 leaf; mutilated and rubbed.   20.4 × 21.9; 2 cols.; 15 lines.
Divine name: יְ.   [475]

**T-S Ar.28.159**   Deuteronomy 19:14 – 20:11
Hebrew; Aramaic: Onqelos.   Oriental square script; unpointed.
Vellum; 1 leaf; mutilated, *recto* very badly rubbed. 23.8 × 20.2;   24–5 lines.
Divine name: Hebrew tetragrammaton; Targum ייי.   [476]

**T-S Ar.30.293**   Exodus 29:25–46
Aramaic: Onqelos.   Oriental linear square script (untrained); unpointed.
Paper; 1 leaf (long narrow strip).   27.2 × 8.9; 39, 30 lines.
Divine name: ייי; symbol ∅ as verse divider; *verso* written over an Arabic list with Arabic pen exercises at foot.   [477]

**T-S Ar.34.163**   Genesis 34:10–21
Aramaic: Onqelos (+ Hebrew lemmata).   Oriental semi-cursive script; unpointed (except one word with Tiberian vocalisation in 34:21).
Paper; 1 leaf; mutilated and rubbed.   14.9⁺ × 12.9; 14⁺ lines.   [478]

**T-S Ar.37.100**

Fragment of an Aramaic prayer for protection against enemies: [תפילום] תפילות לאליהו עליו הׁ[שלום] including Targum Onqelos to Genesis 1:1.   [479]

**T-S Ar.38.109**   Jeremiah 1:17–19 (*verso*)
Hebrew; Aramaic: Targum Jonathan to Prophets. Oriental semi-cursive script; sporadic Tiberian vocalisation.
Paper; 1 leaf (part of long vertical sheet); mutilated. 31.0⁺ × 18.5;   12⁺ lines.
Divine name: Hebrew & Targum גׄ; the word פחד is added after 1:19; lower half of *verso* blank; *recto* contains an Arabic letter to a dignitary [GK].   [480]

**T-S Ar.41.100**   Deuteronomy 3:18–22
Aramaic: Onqelos (+ Hebrew lemmata).   Oriental linear square script; unpointed (except several isolated words with Tiberian vocalisation).
Paper; 1 leaf (part of long sheet); mutilated and rubbed. 16.2 × 28.3;   9⁺ lines.
Divine name: ייי.   [481]

**T-S Ar.46.108 (folio 13)**   Numbers 9:1–14
Aramaic: Onqelos.   Oriental semi-cursive script; unpointed.
Paper; 13 leaves.   15.7 × 11.0;   21 lines.
Divine name: גׄ; folios 1–12 contain Judaeo-Arabic text relating to the Passover Haggadah; this is a reading for the intermediate days of Passover.   [482]

**T-S Ar.47.82**   Exodus 19:11–13; 19:25 – 20:6
Aramaic: Onqelos.   Oriental semi-cursive script; very sporadic Tiberian vocalisation; extensive use of *aleph* for vocalisational long ā;.
Paper; 1 leaf; slightly mutilated and rubbed. 13.7 × 10.7;   12, 13 lines.
Divine name: יׄ; 19:14–24 omitted by scribe *ex homoioarchon*; this is the reading for Pentecost.   [483]

**T-S Ar.48.34**

Aramaic *piyyuṭ* (זכות) with quotation of phrases from Onqelos to Genesis 22.   [484]

**T-S Ar.48.70**   Numbers 27:4–17
Hebrew; Aramaic: Onqelos; Judaeo-Arabic. Oriental semi-cursive script; sporadic Tiberian vocalisation.
Paper; 1 leaf; slightly mutilated and rubbed. 17.5 × 12.3;   21–2 lines.
Divine name: Hebrew & Targum יׄ.   [485]

**T-S Ar.48.104 (folio 2r)**   Genesis 1:11–12
Hebrew; Aramaic: Onqelos.   Oriental square script; unpointed.
Paper; 3 leaves.   19.5 × 14.6;   11 lines.
Divine name: יׄ; this text is written over an original Judaeo-Arabic text that is badly rubbed on folio 2r; remaining five folios contain only original Judaeo-Arabic text.   [486]

**T-S Ar.49.160**   Exodus 30:16 (*recto*); Deuteronomy 25:17–18 (*verso*)
Hebrew; Aramaic: Onqelos; Judaeo-Arabic. Oriental script; Hebrew square; Targum semi-cursive; unpointed.

Paper; 1 leaf; very badly rubbed.   20.3 × 14.4; 15 lines.

Divine name: Targum יְ; notes after Exodus 30: נשלם ענין [   ] + פרשת שקלים בעזרת האל + three illegible lines (*recto*) and [   ] השבת השנייה היא שקורין בה פרשת זכור (*verso*). [487]

**T-S Ar.50.118**   Exodus 20:13
Aramaic: Palestinian Targum; Judaeo-Arabic. Oriental semi-cursive script; unpointed.

Vellum; 1 leaf; slightly mutilated and very badly rubbed.   16.0 × 11.9; 15 lines. [488]

**T-S Misc.1.4**   Genesis 22:8–20
Aramaic: Onqelos (+ Hebrew lemmata).   Oriental semi-cursive script; Tiberian vocalisation.

Vellum; 2 leaves (1 bifolium).   14.5 × 12.3; 9–10 lines.

Divine name: יְ. [489]

**T-S Misc.1.66**   Genesis 31:19–24, 27–30
Aramaic: Onqelos; Judaeo-Arabic (+ Hebrew lemmata).   Oriental script; Tiberian vocalisation (Targum and lemmata).

Paper; 1 leaf; mutilated.   11.5⁺ × 10.5⁺; 12⁺ lines. [490]

**T-S Misc.1.71**   2 Kings 8:26; 9:2–7, 9–15, 18
Hebrew; Aramaic: Targum Jonathan to Prophets (added in margins).   Main text (Hebrew): Oriental square script; Tiberian vocalisation + accents; Targum: Oriental square linear script; Tiberian vocalisation; Massorah Parva.

Vellum; 1 leaf; mutilated.   17.5⁺ × 26.3⁺; 3 cols.; 19⁺ lines.

Divine name: Hebrew tetragrammaton; Targum יְיָ; main text continues to 2 Kings 9:19. [491]

**T-S Misc.1.114**   Leviticus 25:6–23
Hebrew; Aramaic: Onqelos.   Oriental square script; Tiberian vocalisation + accents (Hebrew & Targum).

Vellum; 1 leaf; badly mutilated.   25.1 × 22.2; 2 cols.; 22 lines.

Divine name: Hebrew tetragrammaton; Targum יְיָ. [492]

**T-S Misc.1.129**   Numbers 17:21–8; 18:9–15
Hebrew; Aramaic: Onqelos.   Oriental square script; unpointed.

Vellum; 1 leaf; badly mutilated.   27.0 × 11.7; [2] cols.; 27 lines.

Divine name: Hebrew & Targum tetragrammaton. [493]

**T-S Misc.3.81**   Numbers 31:10–15
Hebrew; Aramaic: Onqelos; Judaeo-Arabic. Oriental square script (Hebrew larger than Targum); unpointed.

Vellum; 1 leaf; badly mutilated and rubbed.   15.3 × 16.2; 9–10 lines. [494]

**T-S Misc.3.93**   Genesis 45:18 – 46:1 (folios 1–2); 46:30 – 47:1 (folio 3)
Hebrew; Aramaic: Onqelos; Judaeo-Arabic. Oriental square script; Tiberian vocalisation.

Paper; 3 leaves (1 bifolium); mutilated and badly rubbed.   23.0 × 15.3; 17–18 lines.

Most of text illegible with ink adhered from adjoining leaves producing mirror writing. [495]

**T-S Misc.3.94**   Isaiah 19:1–4 (*verso*); Hebrew introductory poem (*recto*); (triennial *haftarah*?)
Aramaic: Targum Jonathan to Prophets.   Oriental script; Tiberian vocalisation.

Paper; 1 leaf.   13.5 × 9.9; 10, 12 lines.

*Recto*: מרשות האל (האל) הגדול הגבור והנורא ומרשות התורה הקדושה והטהורה ....... על יד משיחו בן פרץ אשר בששה שמות נקרא ומר[שות] התורה הק[דושה] המ[הורה] ומר[שות] מו[לנו] אדו[ננו] כ׳ ג׳ חֲנַנְאֵל צפירת תפארה מרשות הקהלה הנקהלה [ה]ויקרא אפתח פי ואתרעם בתורה מרשות רבותינו. [496]

**T-S Misc.3.102**   Genesis 8:19–21; 9:8–12
Aramaic: Onqelos.   Ashkenazi square script; Tiberian vocalisation + accents.

Vellum; 1 leaf; badly mutilated and rubbed. 23.6⁺ × 11.0⁺; 1+ col.; 15⁺ lines.

The larger main column of Hebrew is entirely missing. In such manuscripts Onqelos occupies a narrow outer column; Rashi's commentary to Genesis 3 at foot. [497]

**T-S Misc.5.18**   Genesis 36:23–8
Hebrew; Aramaic: Onqelos; Judaeo-Arabic. Oriental script; Hebrew square with Tiberian vocalisation + accents; Targum semi-cursive, unpointed.

Paper; 1 leaf.   17.0 × 12.7; 12 lines. [498]

**T-S Misc.6.19**   Deuteronomy 17:14–17
Hebrew; Aramaic: Onqelos; Judaeo-Arabic. Oriental script; Hebrew square with Tiberian vocalisation + accents; Targum semi-cursive, unpointed.

Paper; 1 leaf; mutilated and rubbed.   13.7 × 11.8; 12 lines. [499]

**T-S Misc.6.29**   Numbers 29:1–5
Aramaic: Onqelos.   Oriental semi-cursive script; unpointed.

Paper; 1 leaf; mutilated.   13.7 × 9.4; 11 lines.

Divine name: יְיָ; heading: בש רח ותשע; *verso* contains part of a Hebrew poem in praise of a bridegroom. [500]

**T-S Misc.6.88**  Exodus 17:6–11
Aramaic: Onqelos.  Oriental semi-cursive script; unpointed.
Paper; 1 leaf; mutilated.  20.6 × 10.3⁺;  19 lines.
Divine name: יְ; *verso* blank.  [501]

**T-S Misc.6.141**  Genesis 1:10–14
Hebrew; Aramaic: Onqelos; Judaeo-Arabic.
Oriental script; Hebrew square; Targum semi-cursive; unpointed.
Paper; 1 leaf; rubbed.  19.0 × 14.3;  15–16 lines.
Divine name: יְ; pen exercises in margins.  [502]

**T-S Misc.7.28**
Judaeo-Arabic composition containing citations of Targum Onqelos to Genesis 19:28 or 26:8 and 31:49 on the root סכי.  [503]

**T-S Misc.7.66**  Isaiah 56:2–7; 57:19; 42:8–17; (*haftarot*)
Aramaic: Targum Jonathan to Prophets (+ Hebrew lemmata).  Oriental semi-cursive script; unpointed.
Paper; 1 leaf; slightly mutilated and badly rubbed. 14.1 × 9.7;  24–6 lines.
Divine name: יְ; heading at bottom of *recto*: ואראל; triennial *haftarot* for Exodus 4:18 (Isaiah 56, 57); Exodus 6:2 (Isaiah 42).  [504]

**T-S Misc.7.100**  Genesis 3:8–12
Hebrew; Aramaic: Onqelos; Judaeo-Arabic.
Oriental script; Hebrew larger, square; Targum semi-cursive, unpointed.
Paper; 1 leaf; torn and rubbed.  17.2⁺ × 13.2⁺; 18⁺ lines.
Divine name: Hebrew tetragrammaton; Targum יְ; *verso* contains halakhic text on ritual slaughter and jottings in Hebrew and Arabic.  [505]

**T-S Misc.7.134**  Genesis 16:1–5 (folio 1); 16:15 – 17:6 (folio 2)
Aramaic: Onqelos (+ Hebrew lemmata).
Oriental(?) square script; unpointed.
Paper; 2 leaves (1 bifolium); badly rubbed, folio 2 mutilated.  15.3 × 16.0;  9 lines.  [506]

**T-S Misc.9.6**  Numbers 18:30 – 19:8 (folio 1); 21:20–29 (folio 2)
Aramaic: Onqelos (+ Hebrew lemmata).  Oriental square script; unpointed.
Paper; 2 leaves (1 bifolium); badly stained and rubbed. 16.2 × 12.6;  14 lines.
Divine name: יְ; two lines mostly blank to mark *parashat ḥuqat* at 19:1.  [507]

**T-S Misc.9.11**  Jeremiah 9:11–21
Hebrew; Aramaic: Targum Jonathan to Prophets.
Oriental semi-cursive script; Hebrew with Tiberian vocalisation + accents; Targum with Tiberian vocalisation.
Paper; 2 leaves; mutilated.  13.0⁺ × 13.0;  10⁺ lines.  [508]

**T-S Misc.9.44**  Exodus 20:7–8
Aramaic: Palestinian Targum (expansive) + poems (+ Hebrew lemmata).  Oriental semi-cursive script; sporadic Tiberian vocalisation.
Paper; 1 leaf; torn and rubbed.  13.3 × 8.8;  14 lines.
Divine name: Ꝋ; *recto* contains poem with alphabetic acrostic.  [509]

**T-S Misc.10.72**  Numbers 28:26–30
Aramaic: Onqelos.  Oriental square script; unpointed.
Paper; 1 leaf; mutilated.  15.5 × 9.7⁺;  12 lines.
*Verso* contains pen exercises in Hebrew and Arabic.  [510]

**T-S Misc.10.121**  Exodus 27:16 – 28:3
Hebrew; Aramaic: Onqelos.  Oriental linear square script (untrained); Tiberian vocalisation.
Paper; 1 leaf; mutilated.  15.0⁺ × 10.7⁺;  2 cols.; 12⁺ lines.
Hebrew and Targum in parallel columns; most of Hebrew column missing.  [511]

**T-S Misc.10.161**  Joshua 1:14–18; 6:27; (*haftarah*)
Aramaic: Targum Jonathan to Prophets.  Oriental semi-cursive (untrained); sporadic Tiberian vocalisation.
Paper; 1 leaf.  17.9 × 12.5;  16 lines.
Divine name: Ꝋ; variant תעזרין for ותסעדון (1:14, Hebraism?); *verso* blank except for pen exercises.  [512]

**T-S Misc.10.192**  Numbers 6:72–87 (folio 1); 8:22 – 9:7 (folio 2)
Hebrew; Aramaic: Onqelos.  Oriental semi-cursive script; Hebrew with Tiberian vocalisation + accents; Targum with Tiberian vocalisation.
Paper; 2 leaves (1 bifolium); mutilated and badly rubbed.  17.0 × 12.8;  21 lines.  [513]

**T-S Misc.10.204**  Genesis 49:14–25
Aramaic: Onqelos (+ Hebrew lemmata).  Oriental linear square script; unpointed.
Paper; 1 leaf; *verso* badly rubbed.  16.1 × 10.5; 18 lines.  [514]

**T-S Misc.11.106** Zechariah 4:5–7 (folio 1r); (*hafṭarah*)

Aramaic: Targum Jonathan to Prophets (+ Hebrew lemmata). Oriental semi-cursive script; sporadic Tiberian vocalisation.

Paper; 2 leaves (1 bifolium); folio 1v badly rubbed. 14.0 × 9.0; 12–14 lines.

Folio 1v: the visible words, עליהון עממיא (line 11) seem to be targum; folio 2v contains a liturgical text. [515]

**T-S Misc.20.54** Genesis 7:8–23

Aramaic: Onqelos (+ Hebrew lemmata). Oriental semi-cursive script; unpointed.

Paper; 2 leaves; mutilated. 17.2 × 10.9; 13 lines. [516]

**T-S Misc.20.126** Exodus 4:1–6

Aramaic: Onqelos (+ Hebrew lemmata). Oriental semi-cursive script; Tiberian vocalisation.

Paper; 1 leaf; badly mutilated. 10.4⁺ × 9.8⁺; 7⁺ lines.

Divine name: יֽיֽ. [517]

**T-S Misc.20.192**

Fragment of unidentified Hebrew and Aramaic composition containing Hebrew and Onqelos to Genesis 2:3. [518]

**T-S Misc.20.223** Leviticus 9:9 – 13:11

Aramaic: Onqelos (+ Hebrew lemmata). Oriental semi-cursive script; Tiberian vocalisation.

Paper; 6 leaves (3 bifolia); mutilated and partially rubbed. 20.3 × 12.6; 17 lines.

Divine name: יֽ; upper portions of folios are illegible, including two or three verses before Leviticus 9:9. [519]

**T-S Misc.22.16** Exodus 20:17–23

Aramaic: Onqelos. Oriental semi-cursive script; unpointed.

Paper; 2 leaves (1 bifolium). 12.6 × 8.2; 16 lines.

Divine name: ∴ ; ending: שלם at bottom of folio 1r; folios 1v–2v blank except for some Arabic pen exercises on folio 2v. [520]

**T-S Misc.22.70** Genesis 21:15 – 22:14

Aramaic: Onqelos (+ Hebrew lemmata). Oriental semi-cursive script; sporadic Tiberian vocalisation.

Paper; 6 leaves (3 bifolia). 13.9 × 9.8; 10–12 lines.

Divine name: ῾; heading before 22:1 (folio 4r) עין יום שני to indicate reading for second day New Year. [521]

**T-S Misc.22.127** Exodus 12:7–10 (folio 1v); 14:2–6 (folio 2r)

Aramaic: Onqelos. Oriental square script; Tiberian vocalisation.

Paper; 2 leaves (1 bifolium); mutilated and badly rubbed. 17.3⁺ × 13.5; 11⁺ lines.

Folios 1r and 2v are illegible. [522]

**T-S Misc.22.243** Poem to Exodus 14:30 – 15:2

Aramaic: targumic. Oriental semi-cursive script; unpointed.

Paper; 1 leaf. 17.2 × 15.7; 16 lines.

In the dialect of Onqelos, but with vestigial phrases from Palestinian Targum גבורת ידא תקיפא (14:31); *verso* blank. [523]

**T-S Misc.22.272** Deuteronomy 34:10–12

Aramaic: Onqelos (+ Hebrew lemmata). Oriental semi-cursive script; unpointed.

Paper; 1 leaf. 21.5 × 14.6; [21 lines].

Divine name: יֽ; this is the last folio of a manuscript, with half of *recto* and entire *verso* blank; final note: שלים דין תרגום בריך רחמנא דסייען. [524]

**T-S Misc.24.136** Isaiah 10:33 – 11:9; (*hafṭarah*)

Aramaic: Targum Jonathan to Prophets (+ Hebrew lemmata). Oriental semi-cursive script; unpointed.

Paper; 1 leaf; mutilated. 13.2 × 8.6; 15–16 lines.

Divine name: ღ; *hafṭarah* for eighth day Passover. [525]

**T-S Misc.24.170** Exodus 13:17–19 (*verso*)

Aramaic: Onqelos. Oriental square script (untrained); unpointed.

Paper; 1 leaf. 19.1 × 14.5; 10 lines.

Divine name: ღ/ ღ; heading: בשלח (*verso*); *recto* blank except for title תרגום אלפסח יום רישון וכתב(?); and an Arabic note that the text was written on the 22 Safar 532(?) AH (= 9 November 1137 [GK]). [526]

**T-S Misc.24.183** Leviticus 4:21–4 (folio 1); 5:16–18 (folio 2)

Hebrew; Aramaic: Onqelos; Judaeo-Arabic. Oriental square script; Hebrew with Tiberian vocalisation + accents; Targum with Tiberian vocalisation; Massorah Parva.

Paper; 2 leaves (1 bifolium); mutilated and rubbed. 16.8⁺ × 13.1; 14⁺ lines.

Divine name: Hebrew tetragrammaton; Targum יֽיֽ. [527]

**T-S Misc.25.58** Genesis 6:4–7 (folio 1); 6:17–21 (folio 2)

Hebrew; Aramaic: Onqelos. Oriental script; Hebrew square; Targum smaller, semi-cursive; unpointed (except לָהֶן (6:4)).

Paper; 2 leaves (1 bifolium). 18.0 × 12.6; 11 lines.

Divine name: Hebrew tetragrammaton; Targum יֽ. [528]

**T-S Misc.25.114**  Genesis 37:25 – 38:12
Aramaic: Onqelos (+ Hebrew lemmata).
Oriental/Spanish semi-cursive script; Tiberian
vocalisation in darker ink.

Paper; 1 leaf.  20.9 × 14.5;  23 lines.

Variant readings introduced by נ׳א in margin.  [529]

**T-S Misc.25.125** (= T-S Misc.26.36)  Exodus 6:2 – 8:19
Aramaic: Onqelos (+ Hebrew lemmata).  Spanish square script; unpointed.

Paper; 6 leaves (3 bifolia); slightly rubbed.
23.4 × 17.0;  15 lines.

Divine name: י֗י; heading in larger script at beginning of *parashah*: וארא אל אברהם at 6:2 (top of folio 1r).  [530]

**T-S Misc.26.36** (= T-S Misc.25.125)  Exodus 5:13 – 6:1
Aramaic: Onqelos (+ Hebrew lemmata).  Spanish square script; unpointed.

Paper; 1 leaf; torn.  [23.4] × 17.2;  [15] lines.

Divine name: י֗י.  [531]

**T-S Misc.27.1.4**  Genesis 46:26 – 47:5 (folio 1); 47:29 – 48:10 (folio 2)
Hebrew; Aramaic: Palestinian Targum.  Oriental square script; Tiberian vocalisation + accents; Massorah Magna and Parva.

Vellum; 2 leaves (1 bifolium).  35.0 × 28.5;  3 cols.;
24 lines.

Divine name: Hebrew אלהים; Targum י׳י; triennial *sidrot* are marked in margins at 46:28 and 48:1.

Klein *GMPT* I, pp.145–51. See plate 9.  [532]

**T-S Misc.27.3.24**  Exodus 16:18–27
Hebrew; Aramaic: Onqelos; Judaeo-Arabic.
Yemenite square script; Babylonian vocalisation.

Vellum; 1 leaf.  31.5 × 20.9;  2 cols.;  23 lines.

Divine name: Hebrew tetragrammaton; Targum יי. See plate 1.  [533]

**T-S 12.770**  Genesis 1:30 – 2:22
Aramaic: Onqelos (+ Hebrew lemmata).  Spanish semi-cursive script; unpointed.

Paper; 1 leaf; slightly mutilated and rubbed.
25.0 × 16.9;  24 lines.

Divine name: י֗י; *verso* is inverted in relation to *recto* and ends in middle of page, followed by several pen exercises.  [534]

**T-S 12.868**  Deuteronomy 31:4–16
Hebrew; Aramaic: Onqelos.  Oriental square script; sporadic Babylonian vocalisation.

Vellum; 1 leaf; very badly mutilated.  25.3 × [19.1];
2 cols.;  24 lines.

Divine name: Hebrew tetragrammaton; Targum יי.  [535]

**T-S 20.155 (recto)** (= T-S NS 286.1;
AS 63.24, 51, 72, 85, 95, 96, 117, 129, 153;
AS 69.241)  Exodus 20:21/24 – 21:8;
21:13 – 23:3
Aramaic: Palestinian Targum (+ Hebrew lemmata).  Oriental square script; sporadic Palestinian vocalisation also sporadic Tiberian vocalisation + accents.

Vellum; scroll; badly mutilated.  [31.0] (height)
× 10.5/11.5 (width for column + margin);  6+ cols.;
35 lines.

Divine name: tetragrammaton in Targum; the ciphers ה׳ and י׳ are used to indicate the beginnings of the fifteenth and sixteenth *sidrot* in the Book of Exodus, according to the triennial cycle; *verso* originally blank, contains lectionary with Hebrew verses from *haftarot* written vertically in relation to text on *recto*.

Kahle *MdW* II, pp.1–5; Klein *GMPT* I, pp.283–97. See plate 8.  [536]

**T-S NS 6.9**  Exodus 2:6–10
Hebrew; Aramaic: Onqelos; Judaeo-Arabic.
Oriental semi-cursive script; Tiberian vocalisation + accents.

Paper; 1 leaf; badly mutilated.  15.5+ × 15.2;  13+ lines.  [537]

**T-S NS 10.17, 18**  Exodus 40:9–27
Hebrew; Aramaic: Palestinian Targum.  Oriental square script; Tiberian vocalisation + accents.

Vellum; 1 leaf; mutilated.  30.8+ × 29.1;  3 cols.;
22 lines.

Divine name: Hebrew tetragrammaton; Targum יי׳.

Klein *GMPT* I, pp.303–5.  [538]

**T-S NS 32.22**  Leviticus 4:28–31 (folio 1);
5:12–15 (folio 2)
Hebrew; Aramaic: Onqelos; Judaeo-Arabic.
Oriental square script; Hebrew with Tiberian vocalisation + accents; Onqelos with Tiberian vocalisation.

Paper; 2 leaves (1 bifolium); badly rubbed.
16.8 × 12.7;  14 lines.  [539]

**T-S NS 32.33**

Onqelos to Deuteronomy 1:1 followed by scattered verses of *haftarot* from the Hebrew version of Isaiah; *verso* contains Arabic and Judaeo-Arabic jottings.  [540]

**T-S NS 32.98**  1 Samuel 1:15–21 (folio 1);
Isaiah 42:5–11 (folio 2); (*haftarot*)
Aramaic: Targum Jonathan to Prophets (+ Hebrew lemmata).  Oriental semi-cursive script; Tiberian vocalisation.

[T-S NS 32.98, cont.]
Paper; 2 leaves (1 bifolium); slightly rubbed.
16.3 × 12.4; 10–11 lines.
Divine name: יֽ; these are *haftarot* for first day New Year and *parashat bere'shit*. [541]

**T-S NS 33.9**  1 Kings 7:51 – 8:1; (*haftarah*)
Aramaic: Targum Jonathan to Prophets (+ Hebrew lemmata). Oriental linear square script; Tiberian vocalisation.
Paper; 2 leaves (1 bifolium). 13.3 × 8.9; 13 lines.
Divine name: יֽ; heading: בשם יי אל עולם; text contains variants superior to printed edition; folios 1r, 2r–v blank. [542]

**T-S NS 33.16, 17**  Isaiah 60:2–19; 62:11; (*haftarah*)
Hebrew; Aramaic: Targum Jonathan to Prophets. Oriental semi-cursive script; Hebrew with Tiberian vocalisation + accents; Targum with Tiberian vocalisation.
Paper; 2 leaves; mutilated and rubbed. 17.3 × 13.0; 20–21 lines.
Divine name: Hebrew tetragrammaton; Targum יֽ. [543]

**T-S NS 33.22**  Leviticus 13:12–26 (folio 1); 14:54 – 15:12 (folio 2)
Aramaic: Onqelos (+ Hebrew lemmata). Oriental square script (Hebrew larger); unpointed.
Paper; 2 leaves (1 bifolium); mutilated and rubbed.
15.7⁺ × 13.6; 14⁺ lines.
Divine name: יֽ. [544]

**T-S NS 33.113**  Genesis 7:24 – 8:5
Hebrew; Aramaic: Onqelos; Judaeo-Arabic. Oriental script; Hebrew square with Tiberian vocalisation + accents; Onqelos semi-cursive with Tiberian vocalisation.
Paper; 2 leaves (1 bifolium). 15.6 × 11.0; 11 lines.
Divine name: יֽ. [545]

**T-S NS 33.117, 141**  Judges 11:24–36 (NS 33.117 (folio 1) + NS 33.141); Micah 6:5–8 (NS 33.117 folio 2r); 1 Kings 18:46 – 19:4 (folio 2v); (*haftarot*)
Aramaic: Targum Jonathan to Prophets (+ Hebrew lemmata). Oriental linear square script; sporadic Tiberian vocalisation.
Paper; 2 leaves (1 bifolium); torn apart in middle of folio 1. 17.2 × 13.0; 14–15 lines.
Divine name: tetragrammaton; these are the *haftarot* for *parashot ḥuqat, balaq* and *pinḥas*. [546]

**T-S NS 33.162**  Leviticus 5:3–10
Hebrew; Aramaic: Onqelos; Judaeo-Arabic. Oriental semi-cursive script; Hebrew with Tiberian vocalisation + accents; Onqelos with Tiberian vocalisation.
Paper; 2 leaves (1 bifolium); badly mutilated.
11.4⁺ × 5.7⁺; 10⁺ lines.
Divine name: Onqelos יֽ/יֽ. [547]

**T-S NS 34.252**  Leviticus 23:34–9
Hebrew; Aramaic: Onqelos. Spanish semi-cursive script; Tiberian vocalisation + accents.
Vellum; 1 leaf; very badly mutilated. 5.5⁺ × 9.0⁺; 1 col.(?); 10⁺ lines.
Divine name: Hebrew & Onqelos tetragrammaton. [548]

**T-S NS 37.38**  Genesis 38:16–23
Hebrew; Aramaic: Onqelos; Judaeo-Arabic. Oriental script; Hebrew square, large with Tiberian vocalisation + accents; Onqelos semi-cursive with Tiberian vocalisation.
Paper; 1 leaf; badly mutilated. 16.8⁺ × 18.0; 12⁺ lines. [549]

**T-S NS 38.7**  Isaiah 11:10–14; (*haftarah*)
Aramaic: Targum Jonathan to Prophets (+ Hebrew lemmata). Oriental linear square script; Tiberian vocalisation.
Paper; 1 leaf; very badly mutilated and rubbed.
14.3⁺ × 6.2⁺; 7⁺ lines.
Divine name: יֽ; this is the *haftarah* for eighth day Passover. [550]

**T-S NS 38.57**  Genesis 37:2–3
Hebrew; Aramaic: Onqelos. Oriental square script; unpointed.
Paper; 1 leaf; mutilated. 14.5 × 9.0⁺; 6 lines. [551]

**T-S NS 38.73, 100**  Genesis 21:10–15, 20–25
Aramaic: Onqelos (+ Hebrew lemmata). Oriental semi-cursive script; unpointed.
Paper; 1 leaf; badly mutilated. 12.0⁺ × 11.0⁺; 9⁺ lines.
Divine name: יֽ; these two fragments fit together. [552]

**T-S NS 38a.21**  Isaiah 57:14 – 58:14; 59:20–21; (*haftarah*)
Aramaic: Targum Jonathan to Prophets (+ Hebrew lemmata). Oriental semi-cursive script; Tiberian vocalisation.
Paper; 2 leaves; mutilated and rubbed. 27.3 × 9.2; 26–30 lines.
Divine name: יֽ; this is the *haftarah* for Day of Atonement. [553]

**T-S NS 44.37**  Judges 13:12–25; Zechariah 2:14 – 3:6; (*haftarot*)
Hebrew; Aramaic: Targum Jonathan to Prophets. Oriental square script; Hebrew with Tiberian vocalisation + accents; Targum unpointed.
Vellum; 1 leaf; mutilated and rubbed.  21.3 × 18.8; 2 cols.; 25 lines.
Divine name: Hebrew tetragrammaton; Targum ״/״׳; *haftarot* for *parashot naso'* and *beha'alotekha* respectively. [554]

**T-S NS 48.21**  Genesis 11:4–27
Hebrew; Aramaic: Onqelos. Oriental square script; Hebrew with Tiberian vocalisation + accents; Onqelos unpointed.
Vellum; 1 leaf; badly mutilated.  24.5 × 21.3; 2 cols.; 22 lines.
Divine name: Hebrew tetragrammaton; Targum ״׳. [555]

**T-S NS 49.1**  Leviticus 8:28 – 9:6
Hebrew; Aramaic: Onqelos. Oriental square script; Tiberian vocalisation + accents (Hebrew & Onqelos).
Vellum; 1 leaf; mutilated.  17.8⁺ × 22.0; 2 cols.; 16⁺ lines.
Divine name: Hebrew tetragrammaton; Onqelos ״. [556]

**T-S NS 49.46 (= T-S NS 49.51)**  Ezekiel 45:21–5; 47:12; 43:10–22; (*haftarot*)
Hebrew; Aramaic: Targum Jonathan to Prophets. Oriental square script; Hebrew with Tiberian vocalisation + accents; Targum unpointed.
Vellum; 1 leaf; mutilated.  22.0 × 18.3; 2 cols.; 25 lines.
Divine name: Hebrew tetragrammaton; Targum ״׳; *haftarot* for *parashot ha-ḥodesh* and *teṣaweh* respectively. [557]

**T-S NS 49.51 (= T-S NS 49.46)**  Isaiah 44:5–6; Jeremiah 7:21–9; 9:22–3; 2 Samuel 6:1–6; (*haftarot*)
Hebrew; Aramaic: Targum Jonathan to Prophets. Oriental square script; Hebrew with Tiberian vocalisation + accents; Targum unpointed.
Vellum; 1 leaf; badly mutilated.  20.5 × 19.7; 2 cols.; 21⁺ lines.
Divine name: Hebrew tetragrammaton; Targum ״׳/״; headings before Jeremiah: דצו בירמיה and before 2 Samuel: דויהי בשמואל; Isaiah is *haftarah* for *parashat wayiqra'*. [558]

**T-S NS 50.14**  2 Samuel 22:37–43
Hebrew; Aramaic: Targum Jonathan to Prophets. Oriental square script; Hebrew with Tiberian vocalisation + accents; Targum unpointed.
Vellum; 1 leaf.  9.2 × 7.9;  10–11 lines.
Divine name: Hebrew tetragrammaton; Targum ״. [559]

**T-S NS 52.16**  Genesis 1:2–5
Hebrew; Aramaic: Onqelos; Judaeo-Arabic. Oriental linear square script; Tiberian vocalisation.
Paper; 1 leaf; badly mutilated.  18.3 × 13.4;  10 lines.
Divine name: Targum ״׳. [560]

**T-S NS 52.50 (= T-S NS 53.14; NS 78.26)**
Genesis 1:8–11 (folio 1), 16–20 (folio 2)
Hebrew; Aramaic: Onqelos.  Oriental square script; unpointed.
Vellum; 2 leaves (1 bifolium).  8.9 × 8.9;  8 lines.
Divine name: Onqelos ה; marginal notation for closed paragraph, and the notation סדורה(?) at 1:20 (this is not an attested *sidra*); Onqelos variant in margin. [561]

**T-S NS 53.14 (= T-S NS 52.50; NS 78.26)**
Genesis 1:26–8 (folio 1); 2:12–15 (folio 2)
Hebrew; Aramaic: Onqelos.  Oriental square script; unpointed.
Vellum; 2 leaves (1 bifolium); mutilated.  8.5 × 9.2; 8 lines.
Divine name: Hebrew tetragrammaton; Onqelos ה; Onqelos variant in margin. [562]

**T-S NS 53.20**  Genesis 23:3 – 24:3 (folio 1); 24:30–48 (folio 2)
Aramaic: Onqelos (+ Hebrew lemmata).  Spanish square script; Tiberian vocalisation + accents.
Vellum; 2 leaves; folio 1 mutilated.  19.3 × 14.2;  20 lines.
Divine name: ה; some of the vocalisation overwritten in darker ink. [563]

**T-S NS 53.50**  1 Kings 8:58–62; (*haftarah*?)
Aramaic: Targum Jonathan to Prophets (+ Hebrew lemmata).  Oriental linear square script; unpointed.
Paper; 1 leaf; very badly mutilated.  9.3⁺ × 8.2⁺; 10⁺ lines.
Divine name: ה; this is the *haftarah* for *Shemini 'Aṣeret*; verso blank except for heading: וזאת הברכה. [564]

**T-S NS 53.66**  Numbers 10:27–9, 34–6
Aramaic: Onqelos.  Oriental semi-cursive script; Tiberian vocalisation (*verso* only).
Paper; 1 leaf (minute fragment).  6.0⁺ × 5.8⁺; 1 col.(?); 5⁺ lines.
Divine name: ײָ (supralinear addition). [565]

**T-S NS 54.1**  Genesis 3:8 – 5:15
Hebrew; Aramaic: Onqelos.  Ashkenazi square script; Tiberian vocalisation + accents.
Vellum; 2 leaves (1 bifolium).  38.0 × 31.2;  2 cols.; 31 lines.
Divine name: Hebrew tetragrammaton; Onqelos ה. [566]

**T-S NS 55.1**  Leviticus 14:12–15, 18, 23–30, 34–5, 38–43
Hebrew; Aramaic: Onqelos. Oriental square script; Tiberian vocalisation + accents.
Vellum; 2 leaves (1 bifolium); badly mutilated. 22.5⁺ × 15.0⁺; 2 cols.; 20⁺ lines.
Divine name: Hebrew tetragrammaton; Onqelos ״. [567]

**T-S NS 55.2**  Isaiah 32:6–13, 18; 66:12–23; 31:5 – 32:2; (haftarot)
Hebrew; Aramaic: Targum Jonathan to Prophets. Oriental square script; sporadic Tiberian vocalisation (Hebrew & Targum) + very sporadic Babylonian points (Targum only).
Vellum; 1 leaf; mutilated. 33.0 × 27.6; 2 cols.; 31 lines.
Divine name: Hebrew tetragrammaton; Targum ״׳; triennial *haftarot*; headings: כי תקרב [בש]עיה (Deuteronomy 20:10) before Isaiah 66 and כי יקרא (Deuteronomy 22:6) before Isaiah 31; Isaiah 32 is the *haftarah* for Deuteronomy 17:14. [568]

**T-S NS 55.26 (= T-S NS 56.61)**  Genesis 1:1–5
Aramaic: Onqelos (+ Hebrew lemmata). Oriental square script; Tiberian vocalisation.
Paper; 1 leaf; rubbed. 9.6 × 12.8; 8 lines.
Divine name: ״; large decorative rubric with letters framed in red ink בשם רחם בראשית; all lemmata are also in red ink; *verso* blank. [569]

**T-S NS 56.43**  Genesis 18:14 – 19:2
Aramaic: Onqelos (+ Hebrew lemmata). Oriental semi-cursive script; unpointed.
Paper; 1 leaf. 20.2 × 14.0; 19 lines.
Divine name: ״/׳. [570]

**T-S NS 56.52**  Genesis 47:24–6 (folio 1); 48:17–19 (folio 2)
Hebrew; Aramaic: Onqelos; Judaeo-Arabic. Oriental script; Hebrew large square with Tiberian vocalisation + accents; Onqelos semi-cursive with Tiberian vocalisation.
Paper; 2 leaves (1 bifolium); rubbed. 15.8 × 9.9; 12 lines. [571]

**T-S NS 56.61 (= T-S NS 55.26)**  Genesis 3:10–16
Aramaic: Onqelos (+ Hebrew lemmata). Oriental square script; Tiberian vocalisation.
Paper; 1 leaf; mutilated. 9.7 × 12.7; 8 lines.
Divine name: ״; Hebrew lemmata in red ink. [572]

**T-S NS 57.1**  Isaiah 19:10–18
Aramaic: Targum Jonathan to Prophets (+ Hebrew lemmata). Unusual Oriental square script (perhaps Persian); unpointed.
Vellum; 1 leaf. 10.1 × 16.6; 8–9 lines.
Divine name: ״. See plate 22. [573]

**T-S NS 57.5**  Deuteronomy 12:17–28
Hebrew; Aramaic: Onqelos. Oriental square script; Tiberian vocalisation + accents (Hebrew & Onqelos).
Vellum; 1 leaf; very badly mutilated. 16.6⁺ × 31.5; 3 cols.; 9⁺ lines.
Divine name: Hebrew tetragrammaton; Onqelos ״׳; Massorah Magna. [574]

**T-S NS 57.37**  Numbers 2:25–32
Hebrew; Aramaic: Onqelos; Judaeo-Arabic. Oriental semi-cursive script; Tiberian vocalisation (Hebrew & Onqelos).
Paper; 1 leaf; badly mutilated. 12.9⁺ × 10.5; 14⁺ lines. [575]

**T-S NS 60.14**  Numbers 21:7–30
Aramaic: Onqelos (+ Hebrew lemmata). Spanish square script; sporadic Tiberian vocalisation in darker ink.
Vellum; 1 leaf; very badly mutilated. 19.5 × 15.6; 21 lines.
Divine name: ״. [576]

**T-S NS 60.20**  1 Samuel 1:1, 4–5
Hebrew; Aramaic: Onqelos. Oriental square script; unpointed.
Vellum; 1 minute fragment. 6.5⁺ × 8.8; 1 col.(?); 6⁺ lines.
Divine name ״. [577]

**T-S NS 60.25**  Exodus 28:26–9, 32–6
Aramaic: Onqelos (+ Hebrew lemmata). Oriental square script; unpointed.
Paper; 1 leaf; badly mutilated. 13.3⁺ × 11.9⁺; 9⁺ lines. [578]

**T-S NS 60.26**  Exodus 37:14 – 38:12
Aramaic: Onqelos (+ Hebrew lemmata). Oriental square script; unpointed.
Paper; 1 leaf; slightly mutilated and rubbed. 21.0 × 14.7; 21–2 lines. [579]

**T-S NS 61.21**  Numbers 7:73 – 8:4
Aramaic: Onqelos (+ Hebrew lemmata). Oriental semi-cursive script; Tiberian vocalisation.

**[T-S NS 61.21, cont.]**

Paper; 1 leaf; badly mutilated. 13.7⁺ × 14.2; 14⁺ lines. Divine name: ד׳; majuscule cipher for number of verses in *parashat naso'*, and פר׳ש at 8:1; abbreviation of targum for repetitive verses in Numbers 7. [580]

### T-S NS 61.26   Exodus 37:6–12

Hebrew; Aramaic: Onqelos.   Oriental semi-cursive script; Tiberian vocalisation + accents.

Paper; 1 leaf; very badly mutilated. 15.5⁺ × 13.1; 12⁺ lines. [581]

### T-S NS 69.45, 48   Numbers 9:10–19

Hebrew; Aramaic: Onqelos.   Oriental square script; unpointed.

Vellum; 1 leaf; badly mutilated. 25.2⁺ × [23.2]; 2 cols.; 25⁺ lines.

Divine name: Targum יי; one column is almost entirely missing; the preserved column is torn into two parts, separately conserved. [582]

### T-S NS 69.50 (= T-S NS 34.252)   Leviticus 23:20–24, 26–9

Hebrew; Aramaic: Onqelos.   Spanish semi-cursive script; Tiberian vocalisation + accents.

Vellum; 1 leaf; very badly mutilated. 10.0⁺ × 9.5⁺; 1 col.(?) 15⁺ lines.

Divine name: Hebrew & Targum tetragrammaton. [583]

### T-S NS 71.101   Exodus 14:28 – 15:4

Aramaic: Onqelos.   Oriental semi-cursive script; unpointed.

Paper; 1 leaf; mutilated and rubbed. 24.7⁺ × 13.9; 22⁺ lines.

Divine name: ד׳; *verso* contains parts of two Hebrew compositions of condolence for death, the second introduced by the heading אחרת צדוק דין. [584]

### T-S NS 76.1   Genesis 41:32–42

Hebrew; Aramaic: Palestinian Targum.   Oriental square script; Tiberian vocalisation + accents; Massorah Parva.

Vellum; 1 leaf; very badly mutilated. 23.7 × 19.2; 3 cols.; 20⁺ lines.

Divine name: Targum ד׳; large ס in margin at 41:38 denotes triennial *sidra* and contains opening words of triennial *haftarah* (Isaiah 11:2).

Díez Macho *Augustinianum* IX, pp. 120–23; Díez Macho *Manuscritos Hebreos y Arameos*, pp. 217–20; Klein *GMPT* I, pp. 111–13. [585]

### T-S NS 78.26 (= T-S NS 52.50; NS 53.14)

Genesis 1:1–5 (folio 1); 22–6 (folio 2)

Hebrew; Aramaic: Onqelos.   Oriental square script; Tiberian vocalisation + accents (folio 1 only); Massorah Magna and Parva (folio 1 only).

Vellum; 2 leaves (1 bifolium); folio 1 mutilated and rubbed. 9.1 × 9.1; 8 lines.

Divine name: Hebrew אלהים; Targum יי. [586]

### T-S NS 81.70, 71, 72   Genesis 15:17 – 17:3

Aramaic: Onqelos (+ Hebrew lemmata).   Oriental semi-cursive script; Tiberian vocalisation.

Paper; 2 leaves (1 bifolium) (torn into three parts, separately preserved). [17.7] × 13.0; 14 lines.

Divine name: יי; variant readings of Onqelos in margins. [587]

### T-S NS 83.27   Isaiah 5:30 – 6:3

Aramaic: Targum Jonathan to Prophets (+ Hebrew lemmata).   Oriental semi-cursive script; unpointed.

Paper; 1 leaf. 12.0 × 9.3; 12 lines.

Divine name: יי; *verso* contains Judaeo-Arabic and Arabic jottings. [588]

### T-S NS 87.31   Genesis 9:15–18, 23–9 (folio 1); 12:11–14; 12:18 – 13:2 (folio 2)

Aramaic: Onqelos.   Oriental semi-cursive script; unpointed.

Paper; 2 leaves (1 bifolium); mutilated, upper halves of both leaves missing. 8.6⁺ × 12.7; 8⁺ lines. [589]

### T-S NS 89.36   Numbers 7:2–9 (folio 1); 7:78, 84 (abbreviated) (folio 2)

Aramaic: Onqelos.   Oriental semi-cursive script; Tiberian vocalisation.

Paper; 2 leaves (1 bifolium); folio 1 very badly mutilated. 12.7 × 8.5; 9⁺ lines.

Divine name: יי; only upper four lines of folio 2r contain targum, remainder of folio 2 contains liturgy for Ḥanukkah (Numbers 7 is the reading for Ḥanukkah). [590]

### T-S NS 91.76   1 Kings 21(end) – 22:23⁺

Aramaic: Targum Jonathan to Prophets (+ Hebrew lemmata).   Spanish semi-cursive script; Hebrew lemmata in square script; unpointed(?).

Paper; 1 leaf; very badly mutilated and rubbed. 14.3⁺ × 10.0⁺; 14⁺ lines.

Almost entirely illegible. [591]

### T-S NS 103.85

Part of an Aramaic poem with heading אפטרה לכדנייא, comprising an historical survey of events in the priestly lineage and in the life of Israel up to the story of the Exodus; not really targumic, perhaps an introductory poem (*reshut*). [592]

### T-S NS 105.20   2 Samuel 21:17 – 22:1

Aramaic: Targum Jonathan to Prophets (+ Hebrew lemmata).   Oriental semi-cursive script; Tiberian vocalisation.

**[T-S NS 105.20, cont.]**
Paper; 1 leaf. 16.0 × 12.5; 11 lines.
Divine name: יי̇. [593]

**T-S NS 105.39** Habakkuk 3:3–6 (folio 1); 15–17, 19 (folio 2); (*haftarah*)
Aramaic: Targum Jonathan to Prophets (+ Hebrew lemmata). Oriental semi-cursive script; sporadic Tiberian vocalisation.
Vellum; 2 leaves; mutilated. 10.6 × 8.5; 8–9 lines.
Divine name: יי; text ends with lemma of 3:19 followed by colophon: חזק לעמרם בר שמואל; there are traces of writing on the lower half on folio 2v; *haftarah* for second day Pentecost. [594]

**T-S NS 106.1(a)** Hosea 6:2–6, 10–11; 10:12; Ezekiel 16:9; (*haftarot*)
Hebrew; Aramaic: Targum Jonathan to Prophets. Oriental square script; very sporadic Babylonian and Tiberian vocalisation.
Paper; 1 leaf; mutilated and badly rubbed. 12.2⁺ × 19.2; 11⁺ lines.
These are triennial *haftarot* for Leviticus 15:1 and Leviticus 15:25; heading before Ezekiel: ואשה כי יוב זוב דם ביחזקאל. [595]

**T-S NS 106.53** Isaiah 55:7–9; Hosea 14:2–8; (*haftarot*)
Hebrew; Aramaic: Targum Jonathan to Prophets. Oriental square script; Hebrew with Tiberian vocalisation + accents; Targum with Tiberian vocalisation.
Paper; 1 leaf; mutilated. 14.5⁺ × 16.5; 13⁺ lines.
Divine name: Hebrew tetragrammaton; Targum יי; heading before Hosea: דתעניתא בתרי עשרה. [596]

**T-S NS 106.66** Genesis 34:12–21 (folio 1); 36:39 – 37:4 (folio 2)
Aramaic: Onqelos (+ Hebrew lemmata). Oriental semi-cursive script; unpointed.
Paper; 2 leaves (1 bifolium); mutilated and badly rubbed. 15.9 × 12.7; 11 lines.
Lemma to 37:1 (folio 2v) in majusculae to mark beginning of *parashah*. [597]

**T-S NS 106.82** Exodus 21:17–37 (folio 1); 26:6–24 (folio 2)
Aramaic: Onqelos (+ Hebrew lemmata). Oriental semi-cursive script; Tiberian vocalisation.
Paper; 2 leaves (1 bifolium); mutilated and folio 2 very badly rubbed. 17.3⁺ × 13.3; 16 lines. [598]

**T-S NS 106.85** Genesis 21:14–21
Aramaic: Onqelos (+ Hebrew lemmata). Oriental semi-cursive script; unpointed.
Paper; 1 leaf. 12.8 × 8.2; 14–15 lines.
Divine name: ייִ. [599]

**T-S NS 106.92** Exodus 6:8–12
Hebrew; Aramaic: Onqelos. Oriental square script; unpointed.
Paper; 1 leaf. 19.7 × 14.2; 16 lines.
Divine name: Hebrew tetragrammaton; Targum יי; *verso* blank. [600]

**T-S NS 106.99** Leviticus 19:20–34
Hebrew; Aramaic: Onqelos. Oriental square script.
Paper; 1 leaf. 25.7 × 16.1; 25 lines.
Divine name: Hebrew tetragrammaton; Targum יי. [601]

**T-S NS 106.116** Exodus 19:15–18
Hebrew; Aramaic: Onqelos; Judaeo-Arabic. Oriental script; Hebrew square with Tiberian vocalisation + accents; Onqelos smaller, semi-cursive with Tiberian vocalisation.
Paper; 1 leaf; mutilated and rubbed. 16.6 × 12.5; 13 lines.
Divine name: Hebrew tetragrammaton; Onqelos יי; catchword and signature number in lower left corner of *verso*. [602]

**T-S NS 106.118** Exodus 14:5–13
Aramaic: Onqelos (+ Hebrew lemmata). Oriental square script; Tiberian vocalisation.
Paper; 1 leaf; mutilated. 20.3 × 13.9; 15 lines.
Divine name: יִי̇. [603]

**T-S NS 106.122** Genesis 1:1–4, 1–5, 1, 1–3
Aramaic: Onqelos (+ separate Hebrew version). Oriental semi-cursive script; unpointed.
Paper; 1 leaf; large ink spill. 17.7 × 12.8; 18–19 lines.
Divine name: יִי; most of the text comprises pen exercises in Hebrew and Aramaic. [604]

**T-S NS 107.5(a)** Genesis 26:29 – 27:5
Aramaic: Onqelos (+ Hebrew lemmata). Oriental semi-cursive script; Tiberian vocalisation.
Paper; 1 leaf. 16.8 × 13.8; 14 lines.
Divine name: יִי. [605]

**T-S NS 107.42** Exodus 20:12–14, 16–18
Aramaic: Onqelos. Oriental linear square script; unpointed.
Paper; 1 leaf; mutilated. 13.0⁺ × 12.5; 9⁺ lines.
Divine name: ℔. [606]

**T-S NS 112.2** Numbers 29:1–6 (folio 1)
Hebrew; Aramaic: Onqelos. Oriental semi-cursive script; Tiberian vocalisation (Targum only).

**[T-S NS 112.2, cont.]**
Paper; 2 leaves (1 bifolium). 13.0 × 9.5; 16 lines.
Divine name: Hebrew & Targum יי; this is the *maftir* for New Year; folio 2 contains liturgical poems (*seliḥot*).
[607]

**T-S NS 114.30** Numbers 28:27–31
Aramaic: Onqelos. Oriental linear square script; Tiberian vocalisation.
Paper; 2 leaves (1 bifolium). 12.6 × 8.4; 9 lines.
Divine name: יי; folio 1v (foot) and folio 2 contain Hebrew poem on "the ages of man". [608]

**T-S NS 115.71 (= T-S B2.5(?); West. Coll. Glass 36)** Massorah to Onqelos (alphabetic, letter *lamed*)
Hebrew; Aramaic. Oriental square script; sporadic Babylonian vocalisation.
Vellum; 1 leaf; very badly mutilated. 11.0+ × 10.8+cm; 1 col. 15+ lines. [609]

**T-S NS 116.77 (= T-S B9.10; AS 68.42)** Exodus 34:18 – 35:12
Aramaic: Onqelos (extract). Oriental square script; Tiberian vocalisation.
Vellum; 1 leaf; badly mutilated. 10.5+ × 10.0; 14 lines.
Divine name: יי; decorative *sidra* notation in margin at 35:1. [610]

**T-S NS 116.90 (= T-S NS 118.50–53; NS 235.158)** Exodus 20:6–12(?)
Aramaic: Palestinian Targum (very expansive) (+ Hebrew lemmata). Oriental square script; Tiberian vocalisation.
Vellum; 1 leaf; badly mutilated. 13.0 × 8.7+; 14 lines.
Divine name: ייי;. [611]

**T-S NS 117.21** Exodus 20:2–3
Aramaic: Targumic poems. Oriental square script; unpointed.
Vellum; 1 leaf; mutilated. 15.8+ × 10.4; 24+ lines.
Poems (with alphabetic acrostic) for the first two of Ten Commandments, from pentateuchal reading for Pentecost; *verso* contains unrelated Hebrew poem on the Creation in a different hand. [612]

**T-S NS 118.50–53 (= T-S NS 116.90; NS 235.158)** Exodus 20:4–15/18
Aramaic: Palestinian Targum and poems (very expansive) (+ Hebrew lemmata). Oriental square script; Tiberian vocalisation.
Vellum; 6 leaves (2 bifolia); mutilated (some very badly). 13.5 × 10.4; 12–14 lines.
Folio 5 blank except for colophon(?) חזק משה קינש? and דייל? קינש and pen exercise (Exodus 20:18). [613]

**T-S NS 122.53** Exodus 9:14–22 (folio 1); 20:12–18/21; Numbers 28:26 (lemma only) (folio 2)
Aramaic: Onqelos (+ Hebrew lemmata). Oriental square script; unpointed (except sporadic Tiberian vocalisation in 9:21).
Vellum; 2 leaves (1 bifolium); slightly torn. 13.9 × 11.5; 11–12 lines.
Divine name: יי; heading before Numbers 28: מוסף חג השבועות; obvious scribal errors in text. [614]

**T-S NS 128.14** 1 Samuel 2:8–10; 2:11 (margin); 3:19–20
Aramaic: Targum Jonathan to Prophets (+ Hebrew lemmata). Oriental semi-cursive script; Tiberian vocalisation.
Paper; 1 leaf; mutilated and rubbed. 19.0 × 14.2; 15–16 lines.
Divine name: יי; Judaeo-Arabic heading in the middle of *verso* followed by an Aramaic liturgical composition. [615]

**T-S NS 128.37** Isaiah 40:15–16; 61:9 – 62:3; (*hafṭarot*)
Aramaic: Targum Jonathan to Prophets (+ Hebrew lemmata). Oriental semi-cursive script; Tiberian vocalisation.
Paper; 1 leaf. 17.0 × 13.3; 13 lines.
Divine name יי; heading on *verso* before Isaiah 61: כי היה תבוא crossed through and corrected to: אתם נצבים שוש אשיש. [616]

**T-S NS 134.38** Genesis 31:40–44
Hebrew; Aramaic: Onqelos. Oriental linear square script; Tiberian vocalisation.
Paper; 1 leaf; slightly mutilated and rubbed. 19.3 × 12.8; 12 lines. [617]

**T-S NS 134.50**
Part of an Aramaic ethical composition containing quotations of targum (Psalms 135:4) with variants. [618]

**T-S NS 136.2** Exodus 19:25 – 20:15/18 (folio 2)
Aramaic: Palestinian Targum (interspersed with Onqelos). Oriental semi-cursive script; unpointed.
Paper; 2 leaves (1 bifolium). 17.7 × 13.2; 21 lines.
Divine name: ייי; folio 1 contains a liturgical composition (*zulat*) for Pentecost. [619]

**T-S NS 136.7(b)**
*Recto* and top of *verso* contain part of an Aramaic poem with biblical allusions, not targum proper, perhaps a *reshut* for Pentecost; remainder of *verso* contains a Hebrew poem (*reshut*) for Tabernacles and *Shemini 'Aṣeret*. [620]

**T-S NS 138.79** (= T-S B8.9; NS 271.183)
Genesis 22
Aramaic: targumic *Tosefta*(?) (+ Hebrew lemmata with 'וגו). Oriental semi-cursive script; sporadic Tiberian vocalisation.
Paper; 1 leaf.   16.3 × 12.7;   13 lines.
Divine name: יי̇.   [621]

**T-S NS 141.56**   Genesis 1:9, 16, 21, 5 or 8
Aramaic: Onqelos (+ Hebrew lemmata).   Oriental square script; unpointed.
Paper; 1 leaf.   17.2 × 12.9;   8 lines.
Divine name: יי̇; lower half of *recto* blank; *verso* contains pen exercises from Genesis 1; entire *recto* may be a pen exercise, in view of confusion of verses.   [622]

**T-S NS 142.62**   Exodus 20:4–7 (folio 1r)
Aramaic: Onqelos.   Oriental semi-cursive script; unpointed.
Paper; 2 leaves (1 bifolium).   16.8 × 13.6;   6 lines.
Divine name: יי̇; lower half of folio 1r is blank and folios 1v–2v contain *piyyuṭim*.   [623]

**T-S NS 145.82**   Isaiah 34:1–5; 35:1–2; 48:15 – 49:3 (folio 1); Ezekiel 18:4–17 (folios 1v–2r); Zechariah 5:3–11+ (folio 2); (*hafṭarot*)
Aramaic: Targum Jonathan to Prophets (+ Hebrew lemmata).   Oriental square script; unpointed.
Paper; 2 leaves (1 bifolium); folio 2v badly rubbed.
14.1 × 9.4;   24–30 lines.
Divine name: יי̇; these are triennial *hafṭarot* for Exodus 39:33, followed by note in Judaeo-Arabic: ופרג אל ספר; Leviticus 1:1, heading: ויקרא בישע; Leviticus 4:1, heading: נפש כי תחטא ביחזקאל ושמעה קול אלה; Leviticus 5:1, heading: בתרי עשרה; there are also unclear headings at the top of folio 1r and bottom of folio 2v: [ דעצרתא דיומא ] and עד דיום טו מנהון.   [624]

**T-S NS 149.74**   Deuteronomy 6:22 – 7:2
Hebrew; Aramaic: Onqelos.
Oriental semi-cursive script; Hebrew with Tiberian vocalisation + accents; Onqelos with Tiberian vocalisation.
Paper; 1 leaf; very badly rubbed.   16.7 × 12.3;   13 lines.
Divine name: Hebrew tetragrammaton; Targum unclear.   [625]

**T-S NS 150.109**   Isaiah 1:29 – 2:3 (folio 1)
Aramaic: Targum Jonathan to Prophets (+ Hebrew lemmata).   Oriental semi-cursive script; Tiberian vocalisation.
Paper; 2 leaves (1 bifolium); mutilated and badly rubbed.   15.0 × 10.5;   12+ lines.
Divine name: ייי; folio 2 contains Hebrew list of *miṣwot*.   [626]

**T-S NS 151.51**   Leviticus 22:26–31
Aramaic: Onqelos.   Oriental linear square script (untrained?) Tiberian vocalisation.
Paper; 1 leaf; mutilated.   16.4 × 12.8;   11 lines.
Divine name: יְ̇.   [627]

**T-S NS 151.169**   Deuteronomy 29:5–9
Hebrew; Aramaic: Onqelos.   Oriental linear square script; Tiberian vocalisation (*recto* only).
Paper; 1 leaf; badly mutilated.   14.2+ × 13.0;   10+ lines.
Divine name: Hebrew tetragrammaton; Targum יְ̇; decorative *parashah* notation in margin at 29:9 פרש and cipher for number of verses in preceding *parashot* ✦.   [628]

**T-S NS 152.120 (folio 2)**   Numbers 29:13–16
Aramaic: Onqelos.   Oriental semi-cursive script; Tiberian vocalisation (folio 2v only).
Paper; 2 leaves (1 bifolium); slightly mutilated.
12.8 × 8.4;   11 lines.
Divine name: יְ̇; *mafṭir* for first day Tabernacles; folio 1 is inverted in relation to folio 2, contains Hebrew *piyyuṭ* (*seliḥah*).   [629]

**T-S NS 152.239**   1 Kings 1:11–18 (folio 1); Malachi 1:4–5 (folio 2); (*hafṭarot*)
Aramaic: Targum Jonathan to Prophets (+ Hebrew lemmata).   Oriental square script; Tiberian vocalisation.
Paper; 2 leaves (1 bifolium); slightly mutilated.
17.6 × 10.2;   15–16 lines.
Divine name יי'; these are *hafṭarot* for *parashot ḥayye sarah* and *toledot*; folio 2 contains another Hebrew text (poem?) written between the lines and in the margins.   [630]

**T-S NS 153.29**   Zechariah 14:1–5
Aramaic: Targum Jonathan to Prophets (+ Hebrew lemmata).   Oriental script; Hebrew larger, square; Targum semi-cursive; Tiberian vocalisation.
Paper; 1 leaf; rubbed.   13.6 × 9.4;   12–13 lines.
Divine name: יי̇.   [631]

**T-S NS 154.71**

Onqelos of Exodus 34:6–7 woven into the *seliḥot* prayers.   [632]

**T-S NS 154.87**   Jonah 1:5–8 (folio 1); Ezekiel 45:1–2; Joshua 10:14–17 (folio 2); (*hafṭarot*?)
Aramaic: Targum Jonathan to Prophets (+ Hebrew lemmata).   Oriental linear square script; unpointed.
Paper; 2 leaves (1 bifolium).   13.9 × 8.5;   14 lines.
Divine name: יי̇; top four lines of folio 2r contain Hebrew verse from Joshua.   [633]

## T-S NS 154.167

Onqelos to Numbers 29:6 in a fragment of New Year liturgy. [634]

## T-S NS 155.14  Exodus 33:12 – 34:3

Aramaic: Onqelos (+ Hebrew lemmata). Oriental semi-cursive script; Tiberian vocalisation.

Paper; 2 leaves (1 bifolium); slightly mutilated and rubbed. 17.1 × 12.5; 17 lines.

Divine name: יי; folio 2 blank except for 33:21 written on folio 2v (misplaced and crossed through in original text (folio 1v)); heading: שבת [חול ה]מועד חג המצות וחג הסוכות. [635]

## T-S NS 155.38  Deuteronomy 26:14 – 27:8

Aramaic: Onqelos (+ lengthy Hebrew lemmata). Oriental linear square script; Tiberian vocalisation (mostly faded).

Paper; 1 leaf. 19.9 × 16.2; 20 lines.

Divine name: יי/ יי/יי. [636]

## T-S NS 156.18  Genesis 1:26 – 2:12

Hebrew; Aramaic: Onqelos. Oriental square script; unpointed.

Paper; 2 leaves (1 bifolium); mutilated and very badly rubbed. 20.2 × 14.4; 17 lines.

Divine name: Hebrew אלהים; Targum tetragrammaton. [637]

## T-S NS 156.28  Leviticus 23:16–28

Aramaic: Onqelos (+ Hebrew lemmata). Oriental square script; sporadic Tiberian vocalisation.

Paper; 1 leaf. 16.0 × 12.7; 14 lines.

Divine name: יי. [638]

## T-S NS 157.83  Targum *Tosefta* to Genesis 44:18

Aramaic: Palestinian Targum. Oriental semi-cursive script; unpointed.

Paper; 1 leaf; rubbed. 16.5 × 13.6; 7–9 lines.

*Verso* contains Hebrew version of Song of Solomon 1:1–5, and the first line of the *recto* contains Song of Solomon 1:1 as a title; *tosefta* is added in blank space of *recto*. [639]

## T-S NS 157.132  Judges 5:1–8 (folio 1)

Aramaic: Targum Jonathan to Prophets (+ Hebrew lemmata). Oriental square script; unpointed.

Paper; 2 leaves (1 bifolium); slightly mutilated. 16.3 × 15.3; 18+ lines.

Divine name יי/יי; folio 2 contains part of a poetic Hebrew composition on the *miṣwot*. [640]

## T-S NS 159.116

Onqelos to Exodus 34:6 inserted into *seliḥot*. [641]

## T-S NS 161.17  Ezekiel 20:1–4, 8–9

Hebrew; Aramaic: Targum Jonathan to Prophets. Yemenite square script; Babylonian vocalisation + Tiberian accents.

Paper; 1 leaf; very badly mutilated. 12.0+ × 13.2+; 11+ lines.

Divine name: Hebrew tetragrammaton; Targum יי. [642]

## T-S NS 161.57  Genesis 21:1–15 (folio 1)

Aramaic: Onqelos. Oriental linear square script; Tiberian vocalisation.

Paper; 2 leaves (1 bifolium); slightly mutilated. 16.5 × 12.6; 15–17 lines.

Divine name: יי; folio 2 contains Hebrew version of Leviticus 11:33–40. [643]

## T-S NS 161.98  Genesis 3:3–8, 13–18

Aramaic: Onqelos (+ Hebrew lemmata). Oriental semi-cursive script; Tiberian vocalisation.

Paper; 1 leaf; badly mutilated and darkened. 12.2+ × 14.2; 11+ lines.

Divine name: יי. [644]

## T-S NS 161.104  Genesis 21:6–16

Aramaic: Palestinian Targum (+ Hebrew lemmata). Oriental linear square script; unpointed.

Paper; 1 leaf; slightly mutilated and rubbed. 14.5 × 10.5; 15 lines.

Klein *GMPT* I, p.31. [645]

## T-S NS 161.137  1 Samuel 17:3–4

Aramaic: Targum Jonathan to Prophets. Oriental square script; Tiberian vocalisation(?).

Vellum; 1 leaf (minute fragment). 5.0+ × 7.0+; 1 col.(?) 5+ lines.

*Verso* unidentified. [646]

## T-S NS 161.167  2 Samuel 21:15–17

Aramaic: Targum Jonathan to Prophets (+ Hebrew lemmata). Oriental semi-cursive script; Tiberian vocalisation.

Paper; 1 leaf; badly mutilated. 16.2 × 10.2; 11–12 lines.

*Verso* contains Hebrew version of 2 Samuel 22:25–30. [647]

## T-S NS 161.242  Exodus 13:9–17

Aramaic: Onqelos (+ Hebrew lemmata). Oriental square script; unpointed.

Paper; 2 leaves (1 bifolium). 17.3 × 12.5; 8 lines.

Divine name: יי. [648]

## T-S NS 161.246  Numbers 6:22 – 7:3

Hebrew; Aramaic: Onqelos. Oriental square script; Tiberian vocalisation.

**[T-S NS 161.246, cont.]**
Paper; 1 leaf; slightly rubbed.   15.7 × 12.1;   14 lines.
Divine name: Hebrew tetragrammaton; 6:23–5 are in Hebrew only (cf. Mishnah *Megillah* 4:10). [649]

**T-S NS 161.262 (= T-S B8.8)**   Deuteronomy 28:15–18, 21–3
Hebrew; Aramaic: Palestinian Targum.   Oriental square script; Tiberian vocalisation + accents.
Vellum; 1 leaf; very badly mutilated and rubbed. [37.0] × [27.5];   [3] cols.;   25 lines.
Divine name: Targum ᵒי.
Klein *GMPT* I, pp.353–55. [650]

**T-S NS 161.286**   1 Samuel 17:4–39
Hebrew; Aramaic: Targum Jonathan to Prophets. Oriental square script; Hebrew with Tiberian vocalisation + accents; Targum unpointed.
Vellum; 1 leaf; very badly mutilated.   20.4 × [18]; 2 cols.;   27 lines. [651]

**T-S NS 162.13 (= T-S AS 69.144)**   2 Samuel 17:29 – 18:23 (folios 1,5); 19:17 – 20:21 (folios 2,6,4,3)
Aramaic: Targum Jonathan to Prophets (+ Hebrew lemmata).   Oriental semi-cursive script; unpointed.
Paper; 6 leaves (3 bifolia); badly mutilated and rubbed. 16.5⁺ × 15.0;   16⁺ lines.
Folio numbers are not in correct order. [652]

**T-S NS 162.185**   Leviticus 9:20 – 11:36
Aramaic: Onqelos (+ Hebrew lemmata).   Oriental semi-cursive script; Tiberian vocalisation in darker ink.
Paper; 3 leaves (1 bifolium); very badly rubbed. 17.3 × 13.3;   16 lines.
Upper halves of leaves almost entirely illegible. [653]

**T-S NS 164.28**   Exodus 30:32 – 31:15 (folio 1)
Aramaic: Onqelos (+ Hebrew lemmata).   Oriental semi-cursive script; Tiberian vocalisation.
Paper; 2 leaves (1 bifolium); badly mutilated and badly rubbed (folio 2 almost entirely missing).   21.5 × 18.1; 15 lines.
Divine name: יי. [654]

**T-S NS 164.33**   Numbers 28:26–31
Aramaic: Onqelos.   Oriental linear square script; unpointed.
Paper; 1 leaf.   16.2 × 12.8;   15 lines.
Divine name: יֿ; *verso* and margin of *recto* contain the draft of an Arabic petition to a Faṭimid vizier [GK]. [655]

**T-S NS 164.77**   1 Samuel 1:17 – 2:10
Aramaic: Targum Jonathan to Prophets (+ sporadic Hebrew lemmata).   Oriental semi-cursive script; unpointed.
Paper; 2 leaves (1 bifolium); mutilated.   18.8⁺ × 14.4; [20] lines.
Divine name: יֿ. [656]

**T-S NS 167.34**
Unidentified; possibly part of the same manuscript as T-S NS 167.36. [657]

**T-S NS 167.36**   1 Samuel 2:4–7
Hebrew; Aramaic: Targum Jonathan to Prophets. Hebrew Oriental square script; Targum Oriental semi-cursive script; unpointed.
Vellum; 1 leaf; very badly rubbed.   12.0 × 10.4; 12–13 lines.
Divine name: יֿ. [658]

**T-S NS 169.19**   Leviticus 3:10 – 4:27
Aramaic: Onqelos.   Oriental semi-cursive script; Tiberian vocalisation.
Paper; 2 leaves (1 bifolium).   17.0 × 12.9;   17 lines.
Divine name: ייי; error in 4:22 כתנא רבא for רבא. [659]

**T-S NS 172.82**   Genesis 47:19 – 48:10
Aramaic: Onqelos.   Oriental semi-cursive script; Tiberian vocalisation.
Paper; 1 leaf; mutilated and rubbed.   20.6 × 14.7; 20–22 lines. [660]

**T-S NS 172.169**   Isaiah 46:6–13; 29:22 – 30:5; 30:18; 1:26 – 2:3; 32:1–5; (*hafṭarot*)
Hebrew; Aramaic: Targum Jonathan to Prophets. Yemenite(?) square script; Tiberian vocalisation (sporadic for Targum).
Vellum; 1 leaf; slightly mutilated.   32.5 × 28.3; 2 cols.;   31 lines.
Divine name: Hebrew tetragrammaton; Targum יי/יֿ; these are triennial *hafṭarot* for Deuteronomy 14:1; 15:7, heading: [כי] יהיה בך בישעיה; 16:18, heading: שפטים בישעיה; and 17:14, heading: אשימה עלי בישעיה. See plate 19. [661]

**T-S NS 173.2**   Leviticus 26:35–44
Hebrew; Aramaic: Onqelos.   Oriental square script; Babylonian vocalisation + accents.
Vellum; 1 leaf; very badly mutilated and *recto* very badly rubbed.   17.3⁺ × 19.5;   2 cols.;   17⁺ lines.
Variant of *Neharda'ei* to 26:43 בהשׁמה in margin. [662]

**T-S NS 173.59**   Genesis 1:1–2
Hebrew; Aramaic: Onqelos; Judaeo-Arabic. Oriental square script (of varying sizes); unpointed.

[**T-S NS 173.59, cont.**]
Vellum; scrap.   18.7 × 4.8;   17 lines.
*Verso* is inverted in relation to *recto*, apparently a pen exercise. [663]

**T-S NS 173.67**   Genesis 6:1–19
Hebrew; Aramaic: Onqelos.   Oriental square script; Tiberian vocalisation + accents (Hebrew & Onqelos).

Vellum; 1 leaf; mutilated.   23.2⁺ × 22.5;   22⁺ lines.

Divine name: Hebrew tetragrammaton; Onqelos ייי; decorative *parashah* notation in margin at 6:9 ✿ and cipher for number of verses in preceding *parashah*. [664]

**T-S NS 174.29**   Exodus 4:9–16
Hebrew; Aramaic: Onqelos.   Oriental semi-cursive script; Tiberian vocalisation.

Paper; 1 leaf; very badly mutilated.   13.0⁺ × 12.2; 12⁺ lines.

Divine name: Hebrew tetragrammaton; Onqelos יי. [665]

**T-S NS 174.54**   Numbers 32:35 – 33:13
Hebrew; Aramaic: Onqelos.   Oriental square script; unpointed.

Vellum; 1 leaf; very badly mutilated.   8.0⁺ × 18.0; 2 cols.;   11⁺ lines.

The leaf has been folded along the centre margin, and gives the false impression of being a bifolium. [666]

**T-S NS 174.81**   Ezekiel 1:25 – 2:2 (folio 1)
Aramaic: Targum Jonathan to Prophets.   Oriental square script; unpointed.

Vellum; 2 leaves (1 bifolium); very badly mutilated. 17.0 × 11.7;   14–15 lines.

Folio 2 contains a liturgical poem in mixed Hebrew and Aramaic (on repentance?). [667]

**T-S NS 179.2** (= T-S NS 179.31; NS 182.2, 69; NS 184.81)   *Toseftot* to Exodus 17:16; 20:23/26; 32:25 or 39:43; Leviticus 1:1
Aramaic: Palestinian targumic *toseftot* (+ Hebrew lemmata).   Oriental semi-cursive script; lemmata in larger square script; unpointed.

Paper; 1 leaf; very badly mutilated and faded. 12.8⁺ × 9.2⁺;   11⁺ lines.

This fragment is part of T-S NS 182.69 folio 4. [668]

**T-S NS 179.31** (= T-S NS 179.2; NS 182.2, 69; NS 184.81)   *Toseftot* to Leviticus 10:20; 22:27
Aramaic: Palestinian targumic *toseftot* (+ Hebrew lemmata).   Oriental semi-cursive script; unpointed.

Paper; 1 leaf; very badly mutilated and faded. 13.0⁺ × 8.4⁺;   11⁺ lines.

This fragment is part of T-S NS 182.69 folio 5. [669]

**T-S NS 182.1** (= T-S NS 182.49)   Genesis 1:2–11
Aramaic: Onqelos (+ Hebrew lemmata).   Spanish semi-cursive script; unpointed.

Paper; 1 leaf; very badly mutilated.   9.0⁺ × 10.9⁺; 12⁺ lines.

Divine name: ∴.. [670]

**T-S NS 182.2** (= T-S NS 179.2, 31; NS 182.69; NS 184.81)   *Toseftot* to Genesis 38:25, 26; 44:18 (folio 1)
Aramaic: Palestinian targumic *toseftot* (+ Hebrew lemmata).   Oriental semi-cursive script; lemmata in larger square script; Tiberian vocalisation.

Paper; 2 leaves (1 bifolium); folio 1 worm-eaten, folio 2 almost entirely missing, remainder badly faded and illegible.   17.2 × 12.9;   14 lines.

Divine name: ייִ.

Klein *GMPT* I, pp.93, 137. [671]

**T-S NS 182.10**   Numbers 26:50–59
Hebrew; Aramaic: Onqelos; Judaeo-Arabic. Oriental semi-cursive script; Tiberian vocalisation + *'etnaḥta'* (very faint).

Paper; 1 leaf; rubbed.   21.5⁺ × 16.1⁺;   18 lines. [672]

**T-S NS 182.12**   Genesis 28:18 – 29:2 (folio 1); 29:31 – 30:2 (folio 2)
Hebrew; Aramaic: Onqelos; Judaeo-Arabic. Oriental script; Hebrew linear, square; Onqelos and Judaeo-Arabic semi-cursive; Tiberian vocalisation.

Paper; 2 leaves (1 bifolium); slightly mutilated. 18.3 × 13.6;   17 lines.

Divine name: Hebrew tetragrammaton; Onqelos יִ. [673]

**T-S NS 182.14**   Genesis 4:20 – 5:26
Aramaic: Onqelos (+ Hebrew lemmata).   Oriental linear square script; unpointed.

Paper; 1 leaf; mutilated and rubbed.   19.0⁺ × 19.3; 27⁺ lines.

*Verso* contains Judaeo-Arabic document(?). [674]

**T-S NS 182.20**   Genesis 2:5–24
Aramaic: Onqelos (+ Hebrew lemmata).   Oriental semi-cursive script; Tiberian vocalisation.

Paper; 1 leaf; mutilated.   17.2 × 13.1;   15 lines.

Divine name: יִ. [675]

**T-S NS 182.33**   Exodus 30:22–38
Aramaic: Onqelos (+ Hebrew lemmata).   Oriental semi-cursive script; unpointed.

Paper; 1 leaf; badly mutilated.   15.0⁺ × 14.6;   13⁺ lines.

Divine name: ױיִ. [676]

**T-S NS 182.35**  Genesis 22:13–19
Aramaic: Onqelos (+ Hebrew lemmata). Oriental semi-cursive script; unpointed.
Paper; 2 leaves (1 bifolium).  12.8 × 7.9;  11–12 lines.
Divine name: ⟨⟩; scribe omitted 22:14, and then added it on folio 2r; folio 2v blank. [677]

**T-S NS 182.39**  Deuteronomy 17:5–8
Hebrew; Aramaic: Onqelos. Oriental square script; part with Tiberian vocalisation.
Paper; 1 leaf; mutilated.  19.6 × 12.2;  13 lines.
Scribal omission of Targum to 17:6. [678]

**T-S NS 182.41**  Genesis 25:21 – 26:2
Aramaic: Onqelos (+ Hebrew lemmata). Oriental semi-cursive script; Tiberian vocalisation.
Paper; 1 leaf; slightly mutilated.  17.2 × 12.0; 14–15 lines.
Divine name: ⟨⟩. [679]

**T-S NS 182.44**  Exodus 13:17 – 14:3
Aramaic: Onqelos (+ Hebrew lemmata). Oriental semi-cursive script; sporadic Tiberian vocalisation.
Paper; 1 leaf.  13.3 × 8.7;  13 lines.
Divine name: ⟨⟩. [680]

**T-S NS 182.49** (= T-S NS 182.1)  Genesis 1:12–21
Aramaic: Onqelos (+ Hebrew lemmata). Spanish semi-cursive script; unpointed.
Paper; 1 leaf; badly mutilated.  10.3⁺ × 11.3⁺;  14⁺ lines.
Divine name: ∴ verso contains Mishnah *'Avot* written vertically in relation to text on *recto*. [681]

**T-S NS 182.51** (= T-S NS 182.68, 82)  Isaiah 1:6–13 (folio 1); Jeremiah 1:9–16 (folio 2); (*haftarot?*)
Aramaic: Targum Jonathan to Prophets (+ Hebrew lemmata). Oriental semi-cursive script; Tiberian vocalisation.
Paper; 2 leaves (1 bifolium?); very badly mutilated and rubbed.  9.7⁺ × 10.1⁺;  8⁺ lines. [682]

**T-S NS 182.52**  Numbers 11:8–18 (folio 1); 12:5 – 13:2 (folio 2)
Aramaic: Onqelos (+ Hebrew lemmata). Oriental semi-cursive script; unpointed.
Paper; 2 leaves (1 bifolium); mutilated and badly rubbed.  18.5 × 13.9;  15–16 lines.
Divine name: ⟨⟩. [683]

**T-S NS 182.53**  Genesis 24:30–35, 46–50 (folio 1), 62–7 (folio 2r)
Aramaic: Onqelos (+ Hebrew lemmata). Spanish semi-cursive script; Tiberian vocalisation + accents.
Vellum; 2 leaves (1 bifolium); badly mutilated and stained.  10.2⁺ × 19.5;  9⁺ lines.
Divine name: ⟨⟩; marginal variant to 24:63 נמליא for נמלין; folio 2v very badly soiled, almost entirely illegible. [684]

**T-S NS 182.62**  Exodus 19:12–17
Hebrew; Aramaic: Onqelos. Oriental square script; Tiberian vocalisation (*recto* only).
Paper; 1 leaf; mutilated and rubbed.  14.1⁺ × 13.6; 10⁺ lines. [685]

**T-S NS 182.68** (= T-S NS 182.51, 82)
Jeremiah 1:1–2, 4–6; (*haftarot?*)
Aramaic: Targum Jonathan to Prophets (+ Hebrew lemmata). Oriental semi-cursive script; Tiberian vocalisation.
Paper; 1 leaf; very badly mutilated and rubbed. 8.8⁺ × 9.4⁺;  7 lines. [686]

**T-S NS 182.69** (= T-S NS 179.2, 31; NS 182.2; NS 184.81)  *Toseftot* to Genesis 44:18; 49:1, 18 (folio 2); Genesis 50:1, 16; Exodus 4:25–6; 12:42 (folio 3); Exodus 14:13–14 (folio 1); Exodus 15:1,3,12,18; 17:12 (folio 6); Exodus 17:16; Leviticus 1:1 (folio 4); Leviticus 10:19–20; 22:27 (folio 5)
Aramaic: Palestinian targumic *toseftot* (+ Hebrew lemmata). Oriental semi-cursive script; lemmata in larger square script; folios 2–3 with Tiberian vocalisation, remainder unpointed.
Paper; 6 leaves (3 bifolia); worm-eaten, badly mutilated and stained.  17.4 × 13.1;  14 lines.
The small fragment attached to folio 4 belongs to the inner margin of folio 5.
Klein *GMPT* I, pp.137, 163, 171, 173, 221, 223, 241, 255, 307, 311. See plate 11. [687]

**T-S NS 182.70**  Judges 5:5–10
Hebrew; Aramaic: Targum Jonathan to Prophets. Oriental square script; unpointed.
Vellum; 1 leaf; mutilated.  15.3 × 14.5;  [17] lines.
Divine name: ⟨⟩. [688]

**T-S NS 182.75**  Genesis 3:22 – 4:9
Aramaic: Onqelos (+ Hebrew lemmata). Spanish semi-cursive script; sporadic Tiberian vocalisation.
Paper; 1 leaf; very badly mutilated.  9.5⁺ × 11.0⁺; 14⁺ lines.
Probably belongs to the same manuscript as T-S NS 182.1, 49, although the script is smaller. [689]

### T-S NS 182.82 (= T-S NS 182.51, 68)
Jeremiah 1:18–19 (folio 2r); Isaiah 1:3–4 (folio 2v); Isaiah 1:15–18, 21–4 (folio 1); Isaiah 1:26–7; Jeremiah 6:16–18 (folio 4r); Jeremiah 6:20–22 (folio 4v); Jeremiah 7:6–8 (folio 3r); Jeremiah 8:16–18 (folio 3v); (*haftarot*?)
Aramaic: Targum Jonathan to Prophets (+ Hebrew lemmata). Oriental semi-cursive script; Tiberian vocalisation.

Paper; 4 leaves (2 bifolia); very badly mutilated and rubbed. 10.2⁺ × 10.4; 8⁺ lines.

Divine name: יי; *haftarah* notation between Isaiah and Jeremiah on folio 4r הפטרה איכה. [690]

### T-S NS 184.81 (= T-S NS 179.2, 31; NS 182.2, 69) *Toseftot* to Genesis 4:8; 38:25–6
Paper; 1 leaf.
Cf. description of T-S NS 182.2.
Klein *GMPT* I, pp. 11, 91. [691]

### T-S NS 185.17 Genesis 20:6–10; 20:15 – 21:3
Aramaic: Onqelos (+ Hebrew lemmata). Oriental semi-cursive script; unpointed.

Paper; 1 leaf; very badly mutilated. 11.9⁺ × 12.0⁺; 11⁺ lines.

Divine name: יי. [692]

### T-S NS 186.21 Targumic poems to Exodus 12:1–2, and Targum to Exodus 12:1
Galilean Aramaic. Oriental semi-cursive script; sporadic Tiberian vocalisation.

Paper; 1 irregular leaf. 22.1 × 8.0; 31 lines (*recto*), 9+18 lines (*verso*).

Second poem on *verso* is inverted in relation to *recto*.
Klein *GMPT* I, pp. 187–89. [693]

### T-S NS 188.27–29, 41 Numbers 14:33 – 15:10 (NS 188.27, folio 1 + NS 188.29, 41); Numbers 18:3–26 (NS 188.27, folio 2 + NS 188.28)
Aramaic: Onqelos (+ Hebrew lemmata). Oriental semi-cursive script; unpointed.

Paper; 2 leaves (1 bifolium, torn into 4 parts); mutilated. 16.5 × 14.0; 23 lines.

Divine name: יי. [694]

### T-S NS 189.24 Genesis 6:7–18
Aramaic: Onqelos (+ Hebrew lemmata). Oriental semi-cursive script; unpointed.

Paper; 1 leaf; slightly rubbed. 18.3 × 13.2; 13 lines.
Divine name: יי. [695]

### T-S NS 192.131 Exodus 18:12–13, 16, 22; 19:1–2
Aramaic: Onqelos. Ashkenazi square script; Tiberian vocalisation (very faint).

Vellum; 1 leaf; very badly mutilated. 4.7⁺ × 14.0; 2 cols.; 5⁺ lines.

Divine name: יי. [696]

### T-S NS 193.23 Targumic poem to Exodus 15 (folio 1)
Galilean Aramaic. Oriental linear square script; sporadic Tiberian vocalisation.

Paper; 2 leaves (1 bifolium); mutilated. 16.6 × 12.7; 16 lines.

Alphabetic acrostic is preserved from *nun* to *taw*; with instructions inserted in Judaeo-Arabic and Hebrew: ויזיר אללחן בחן [ ] הוא קול ראשון; folio 2 contains Hebrew poem on Nisan, first of the months. [697]

### T-S NS 197.76 Malachi 1:14 – 2:4; Isaiah 43:7–15; 2 Samuel 22:10–22; (*haftarot*)
Hebrew; Aramaic: Targum Jonathan to Prophets. Oriental square script; Hebrew with Tiberian vocalisation + accents; Targum with Tiberian vocalisation.

Vellum; 1 leaf; badly mutilated and rubbed. 20.8⁺ × 20.0⁺; 2 cols.; 21⁺ lines.

Divine name: Hebrew tetragrammaton; Targum יוי; these are triennial *haftarot* for Exodus 30:1; 31:1; 32:15 respectively; headings at Samuel: בשמואל [ ] and at Isaiah: [ ] לראה קראתי בן; part of vocalisation is in darker ink. [698]

### T-S NS 200.13, 19, 45 Genesis 19:17–21 (NS 200.19); 20:10–15 (NS 200.45); 47:15–19 (NS 200.13)
Hebrew; Aramaic: Onqelos. Ashkenazi square script; Hebrew with Tiberian vocalisation + accents; Onqelos with Tiberian vocalisation; Massorah Magna and Parva.

Vellum; 3 leaves; badly mutilated. 21.0⁺ × 14.0⁺; 13⁺ lines. [699]

### T-S NS 206.19 Exodus 20:2–7
Aramaic: Palestinian Targum (+ Hebrew lemmata). Oriental semi-cursive script; sporadic Tiberian vocalisation.

Paper; 1 leaf; rubbed. 18.1 × 12.3; 12 lines. [700]

### T-S NS 208.22 Judges 5:3; lemma of 5:8
Aramaic: Targum Jonathan to Prophets. Persian(?) square script; Targum with Tiberian vocalisation; lemmata with Tiberian vocalisation + accents.

Vellum; 1 leaf; mutilated. 16.5 × 14.2; 10 lines.
Divine name: יי/יוי. [701]

**T-S NS 209.6**  Deuteronomy 34:7, 10–12; + targumic poem
Aramaic: Onqelos abridged, and with variants. Oriental semi-cursive script; unpointed.
Paper; 1 leaf; badly mutilated and rubbed. 15.0⁺ × 17.5;  16 lines.
The poem is אזלת יוכבד. [702]

**T-S NS 216.16**  1 Samuel 1:24 – 2:8
Aramaic: Targum Jonathan to Prophets (+ Hebrew lemmata).  Oriental square script; unpointed.
Paper; 1 leaf; mutilated and badly rubbed. 19.5 × 14.6; 22(?) lines.
Divine name: יי. [703]

**T-S NS 218.54**  Leviticus 4:12–23
Aramaic: Onqelos (+ Hebrew lemmata).  Oriental semi-cursive script; unpointed.
Paper; 1 leaf; badly mutilated and rubbed. 14.7⁺ × 13.2;  14⁺ lines. [704]

**T-S NS 218.60**  Jeremiah 12:1–2; 15:15–16; Isaiah 61:6 – 62:5 (folio 1); Malachi 1:11 – 2:7; Isaiah 43:7–10 (folio 2); (*haftarot*)
Aramaic: Targum Jonathan to Prophets.  Oriental square script; very sporadic Tiberian vocalisation.
Paper; 2 leaves (1 bifolium); mutilated and rubbed. 14.1 × 9.3;  25 lines.
Divine name: יי; these are triennial *haftarot* for Exodus 27:20; 29:1 (heading: זה הדבר בישעיה); 30:1; 31:1 (heading: ראה קראתי בישעיה). [705]

**T-S NS 218.61** (= T-S B13.4; Or.1080 B18.1)  Exodus 12:40–45 (*recto*); Leviticus 22:27 (*verso*)
Aramaic: Palestinian Targum.  Oriental square script; unpointed.
Vellum; 1 leaf; very badly mutilated and rubbed. 7.2⁺ × 10.9⁺;  10⁺ lines.
Divine name: יי; this is part of a collection of readings for the festivals. [706]

**T-S NS 219.47**  Genesis 21:1–11
Aramaic: Onqelos (+ Hebrew lemmata).  Oriental semi-cursive script; Tiberian vocalisation.
Paper; 1 leaf; slightly mutilated. 21.3 × 14.3;  18 lines.
Divine name: יְיָ. [707]

**T-S NS 221.50**  Genesis 12:7–11
Hebrew; Aramaic: Onqelos; Judaeo-Arabic. Oriental semi-cursive script; Hebrew larger; Tiberian vocalisation (also for some Judaeo-Arabic).
Paper; 1 leaf; very badly mutilated. 17.5 × 10.3⁺; 14 lines.
Divine name: Hebrew tetragrammaton; Onqelos יְיָ. [708]

**T-S NS 221.68**  Genesis 50:17–26
Aramaic: Onqelos; Judaeo-Arabic (+ Hebrew lemmata).  Oriental semi-cursive script; unpointed.
Paper; 1 leaf; mutilated.  25.0 × 16.9;  18 lines.
Divine name: ייי; colophon: [ נג׳ ספר בראשית בעז]רת(?). [709]

**T-S NS 227.24**  Deuteronomy 33:13–17
Hebrew; Aramaic: Onqelos; Judaeo-Arabic. Hebrew in Oriental(?) square script; Aramaic & Judaeo-Arabic in semi-cursive script; unpointed.
Paper; 1 leaf; rubbed.  15.4 × 11.7;  14–15 lines. [710]

**T-S NS 235.158** (= T-S NS 116.90; NS 118.50–53)  Poem to Exodus 20:12 + Palestinian Targum
Aramaic.  Oriental square script; Tiberian vocalisation.
Vellum; 2 leaves (1 bifolium); mutilated and rubbed. 12.6 × 9.9;  12–13 lines.
Alphabetic acrostic preserved from *dalet* to *taw*, a direct continuation of T-S NS 116.90. [711]

**T-S NS 235.176** (folio 1v)
Contains Hebrew + Onqelos to Genesis 24:1–3 in prayers for bridegroom. [712]

**T-S NS 236.5**  Two targumic poems to Exodus 12:2 (folio 1)
Aramaic.  Oriental semi-cursive script; sporadic Tiberian vocalisation.
Paper; 2 leaves (1 bifolium); slightly rubbed. 12.3 × 8.4;  16–17 lines.
Folio 2 contains Hebrew liturgical poems. [713]

**T-S NS 245.13**  Genesis 1:6–12, 18–25
Aramaic: Onqelos.  Oriental square script; unpointed (except 1:21, Tiberian vocalisation).
Paper; 1 leaf; badly mutilated.  12.0⁺ × 16.1;  14⁺ lines.
Divine name: יְיָ. [714]

**T-S NS 245.98** (folio 1)
Liturgical work with extensive quotations from Onqelos (Leviticus 26:44); Targum Jonathan to Prophets (Isaiah 51:3); and a targumic *tosefta* to Ezekiel 1:1. [715]

**T-S NS 246.26.4(a)**  Zechariah 4:7–13; 5:3–4, 7–9 (folio 1)
Hebrew; Aramaic: Targum Jonathan to Prophets. Oriental square script; Babylonian vocalisation + accents (some in darker ink).
Vellum; 2 leaves (1 bifolium); very badly mutilated and rubbed.  11.2⁺ × [21.2];  2 cols.;  11⁺ lines.
Folio 2 almost entirely missing; unidentified. [716]

**T-S NS 246.26.4(b)**   Numbers 5:7–8, 13–14
Hebrew; Aramaic: Onqelos.   Oriental square script; Babylonian vocalisation + accents.
Vellum; 1 leaf (minute fragment); rubbed.
10.2⁺×7.5⁺;   1 col.(?);   7⁺ lines.   [717]

**T-S NS 246.26.5**   Jeremiah 41:9 – 42:4
Hebrew; Aramaic: Targum Jonathan to Prophets. Oriental square script; Babylonian vocalisation.
Vellum; 1 leaf; badly mutilated.   23.8×15.5⁺;   22 lines.
Divine name: Hebrew tetragrammaton; Targum ״׳.   [718]

**T-S NS 246.26.9**   Genesis 6:17 – 7:11
Hebrew; Aramaic: Onqelos.   Oriental square script; Babylonian vocalisation + accents.
Vellum; 1 leaf; badly mutilated.   17.3⁺×15.8⁺; 18⁺ lines.
Divine name: Targum ״׳.   [719]

**T-S NS 246.26.11(a&b), 13**   Genesis 7:13 – 8:11 (NS 246.26.11); 8:17 – 9:14 (NS 246.26.13)
Hebrew; Aramaic: Onqelos.   Oriental square script; Babylonian vocalisation + accents; variant to Onqelos (8:1).
Vellum; 2 leaves (in 3 fragments); very badly mutilated.   18.2⁺×[19.0];   2 cols.;   23⁺ lines.
Divine name: Hebrew tetragrammaton; Onqelos ״׳.   [720]

**T-S NS 246.26.15**   Malachi 3:1–7
Hebrew; Aramaic: Targum Jonathan to Prophets. Oriental square script; Babylonian vocalisation + accents.
Vellum; 1 leaf; very badly mutilated.   21.3×10.4⁺; 19 lines.
Divine name: Hebrew tetragrammaton; Targum ״׳.   [721]

**T-S NS 246.26.16**   Leviticus 11:26–8, 33–4, 39–40, 43–6
Hebrew; Aramaic: Onqelos.   Oriental square script; Babylonian vocalisation + accents.
Vellum; 1 leaf; very badly mutilated and rubbed.
19.7⁺×[21.0];   2 cols.;   17⁺ lines.
Babylonian massoretic note marking half the Pentateuch in letters, words and verses; and Onqelos variants in margins (11:44).   [722]

**T-S NS 246.26.17**   Jeremiah 8:20 – 9:11
Hebrew; Aramaic: Targum Jonathan to Prophets. Yemenite square script; Hebrew with Babylonian vocalisation + Tiberian accents; Targum with Babylonian vocalisation.
Paper; 1 leaf; mutilated.   27.1×19.2;   25 lines.
Divine name: Hebrew tetragrammaton; Targum ״׳.   [723]

**T-S NS 246.26.18(b)**   Jeremiah 30:9–11; 30:21 – 31:1
Hebrew; Aramaic: Targum Jonathan to Prophets. Oriental square script; Babylonian vocalisation.
Vellum 1 leaf (minute fragment).   8.2⁺×10.9⁺; 8⁺ lines.
Divine name: Hebrew tetragrammaton.   [724]

**T-S NS 247.2**   Genesis 24:23, 27–8, 30–32
Hebrew; Aramaic: Onqelos.   Oriental square script; Babylonian vocalisation + accents.
Vellum; 1 leaf; very badly mutilated and rubbed.
14.3⁺×10.8⁺;   2 cols.;   13⁺ lines.
Divine name: Targum ״׳.   [725]

**T-S NS 247.5**   Deuteronomy 14:11–17, 22–4, 26–9; 15:3–5
Hebrew; Aramaic: Onqelos.   Oriental square script; Babylonian vocalisation + accents.
Vellum; 1 leaf; badly mutilated.   15.8⁺×20.2; 2 cols.;   16⁺ lines.
Variants to Onqelos in margin (at 14:27) of *Neharda'ei*.   [726]

**T-S NS 247.6**   Deuteronomy 22:28–9; 23:24–5 (folio 1); 24:4–5; 25:3–6 (folio 2)
Hebrew; Aramaic: Onqelos.   Oriental square script; Babylonian vocalisation.
Vellum; 2 leaves (1 bifolium); very badly mutilated (4 full cols. missing) and rubbed.   12.0⁺×[24.8];   2 cols.; 11⁺ lines.   [727]

**T-S NS 247.7**   Deuteronomy 30:16–19; 31:14–16 (folio 1); 31:18–21; 32:9–13 (folio 2)
Hebrew; Aramaic: Onqelos.   Oriental square script; Babylonian vocalisation.
Vellum; 2 leaves (1 bifolium); very badly mutilated and rubbed.   20.5⁺×6.5⁺;   1 col.(?);   19⁺ lines.
Divine name: Hebrew tetragrammaton.   [728]

**T-S NS 247.8**   Deuteronomy 32:16 – 33:24
Hebrew; Aramaic: Onqelos.
Oriental square script; Hebrew unpointed; Targum with Babylonian vocalisation + accents (folio 1r full, folios 1v–2v sporadic); Massorah Parva.
Vellum; 2 leaves (1 bifolium); mutilated.
[28.0]×26.8;   2 cols.;   28 lines.
Divine name: Hebrew tetragrammaton; Onqelos ״׳.   [729]

**T-S NS 247.9**   Judges 7:16–17; 8:1–3
Hebrew; Aramaic: Targum Jonathan to Prophets. Oriental square script; Babylonian vocalisation.
Vellum; 1 leaf (minute fragment).   9.6⁺×6.4⁺; ? cols.;   11⁺ lines.
Rüger *ZAW* LXXV (N.F. XXXIV), pp.223–25.   [730]

**T-S NS 247.12**   Ezekiel 37:4–12
Hebrew; Aramaic: Targum Jonathan to Prophets. Oriental square script; Babylonian vocalisation + accents.
Vellum; 1 leaf.   25.9 × 21.0;   2 cols.;   19 lines.
Divine name: Hebrew tetragrammaton; Targum ״י.   [731]

**T-S NS 247.13**   Massorah to Onqelos (alphabetic)
Hebrew; Aramaic.   Oriental square script; sporadic Babylonian vocalisation.
Vellum; 1 leaf; badly mutilated.   17.8⁺ × 13.8; 25⁺ lines.   [732]

**T-S NS 251.48**   Deuteronomy 29:8–10, 13–15, 18–21
Hebrew; Aramaic: Onqelos.   Oriental square script; Babylonian vocalisation.
Vellum; 1 leaf; very badly mutilated.   16.0⁺ × [20.5]; 2 cols.;   15⁺ lines.
Divine name: Hebrew tetragrammaton.   [733]

**T-S NS 252.11**   Jeremiah 2:24, 28–9, 33–5; 3:1
Hebrew; Aramaic: Targum Jonathan to Prophets. Oriental square script; Babylonian vocalisation + accents.
Vellum; 1 leaf; very badly mutilated and rubbed. 16.4⁺ × 17.4⁺;   2 cols.;   14⁺ lines.   [734]

**T-S NS 252.12**   2 Kings 8:36; Isaiah 60:1–3, 5–6;   (*haftarot*)
Hebrew; Aramaic: Targum Jonathan to Prophets. Oriental square script; Babylonian vocalisation + sporadic accents.
Vellum; 1 leaf; very badly mutilated.   12.3⁺ × [22.5]; 2 cols.;   11⁺ lines.
Divine name: Hebrew tetragrammaton; Targum ״י.   [735]

**T-S NS 253.2**   Exodus 15:10–18
Aramaic: Palestinian Targum (+ Hebrew lemmata).   Oriental square script; unpointed.
Vellum; 1 leaf; rubbed.   14.3 × 12.7;   17 lines.
Divine name: Hebrew & Targum יְי.   [736]

**T-S NS 253.35**   Leviticus 23:27–37
Aramaic: Onqelos (+ Hebrew lemmata).   Oriental semi-cursive script; Tiberian vocalisation.
Paper; 2 leaves (1 bifolium).   14.5 × 10.0.   11–12 lines.
Divine name: יְי.   [737]

**T-S NS 253.40**   Jeremiah 31:8–20;   (*haftarah*)
Aramaic: Targum Jonathan to Prophets (+ Hebrew lemmata).   Oriental linear square script; unpointed.
Paper; 2 leaves (1 bifolium); slightly mutilated. 17.2 × 10.7;   31 lines.
Divine name: ״י; Targum written on alternate lines; other lines contain a liturgical composition for Day of Atonement; this is the *haftarah* for second day New Year.   [738]

**T-S NS 255.1(a)** (= T-S NS 255.24)   Genesis 7:11 – 9:24
Aramaic: Onqelos (+ Hebrew lemmata).   Oriental semi-cursive script; Tiberian vocalisation.
Paper; 4 leaves (2 bifolia); folio 1 rubbed.   17.8 × 13.2; 16 lines.
Divine name: יְי.   [739]

**T-S NS 255.1(b)**   Genesis 21:4–12 (folio 1); 21:23–31 (folio 2)
Aramaic: Onqelos.   Oriental square script; Tiberian vocalisation.
Paper; 2 leaves (1 bifolium); slightly rubbed. 15.1 × 11.0;   10 lines.
Divine name: יְי/יְי.   [740]

**T-S NS 255.1(c)**   Exodus 2:5–20
Aramaic: Onqelos (+ Hebrew lemmata).   Oriental square script; sporadic Tiberian vocalisation.
Paper; 1 leaf; slightly mutilated.   19.6 × 14.0;   16 lines.   [741]

**T-S NS 255.1(d)**   Genesis 1:1–8 (*verso*)
Aramaic: Onqelos (+ Hebrew lemmata to 1:1, 2). Oriental semi-cursive script; unpointed.
Paper; 1 leaf; mutilated and rubbed.   17.1⁺ × 14.0; 13⁺ lines.
Divine name יְי; heading: עְזְמֵ עַלֹ (= עזרי מעם י׳ עושה שמים וארץ, Psalms 121:2); *recto* blank.   [742]

**T-S NS 255.2(a&b)**
Leviticus 10:16 – 11:12 (b); 11:13–33 (a)
Hebrew; Aramaic: Onqelos.   Oriental square script; Tiberian vocalisation + accents.
Vellum; 2 leaves; badly mutilated.   18.1⁺ × 21.5; 2 cols.;   19⁺ lines.
Divine name: Hebrew tetragrammaton; Onqelos ״י; Massorah Parva; notation of triennial *sidra* with ס at 11:1 (b).   [743]

**T-S NS 255.3**   Genesis 2:13 – 4:6
Aramaic: Onqelos (+ Hebrew lemmata).   Spanish semi-cursive script; unpointed.
Paper; 2 leaves (1 bifolium); mutilated.   21.7 × 14.2; 19 lines.
Divine name: ײַ; deletion in 2:13.   [744]

**T-S NS 255.6**   Numbers 11:20–33
Aramaic: Onqelos (+ Hebrew lemmata).   Oriental semi-cursive script; Tiberian vocalisation + accents.
Paper; 2 leaves (1 bifolium); badly mutilated and rubbed.   13.0⁺ × 10.5;   10⁺ lines.   [745]

**T-S NS 255.9**   Genesis 27:13–20
Aramaic: Onqelos (+ Hebrew lemmata).   Oriental semi-cursive script; Tiberian vocalisation.
Paper; 1 leaf; mutilated and very badly rubbed. 18.5 × 13.7;   12 lines.
Divine name: ״׳.   [746]

**T-S NS 255.11**   Exodus 39:8–15
Hebrew; Aramaic: Onqelos.   Oriental semi-cursive script; Tiberian vocalisation + accents.
Paper; 1 leaf.   17.3 × 12.4;   13 lines.   [747]

**T-S NS 255.13**   Numbers 1:18–24 (folio 1); 2:9–19 (folio 2)
Hebrew; Aramaic: Onqelos.   Spanish square script; Tiberian vocalisation + accents.
Paper; 2 leaves (1 bifolium); badly mutilated and rubbed.   20.2 × 14.4;   20 lines.
Divine name: Hebrew tetragrammaton; Onqelos ׳ײ.   [748]

**T-S NS 255.15**   Exodus 21:37 – 22:4 (*recto*); 22:9–14 (*verso*)
Aramaic: Onqelos (+ Hebrew lemmata).   Oriental semi-cursive script; Tiberian vocalisation.
Paper; 1 leaf; very badly mutilated.   12.5⁺ × 12.7⁺; 10⁺ lines.   [749]

**T-S NS 255.16**   Exodus 19:5–7
Aramaic: Onqelos (+ Hebrew lemmata).   Oriental square script; Tiberian vocalisation.
Paper; 1 leaf; badly mutilated.   19.5⁺ × 14.4;   9⁺ lines.
*Verso* blank except for 2 words from 19:7.   [750]

**T-S NS 255.18**   Numbers 5:26–8 (folio 1); 6:8–11 (folio 2)
Hebrew; Aramaic: Onqelos; Judaeo-Arabic. Oriental semi-cursive script; Tiberian vocalisation.
Paper; 2 leaves (1 bifolium); slightly mutilated, folio 2v very badly rubbed and barely legible.   17.7 × 13.2; 11 lines.   [751]

**T-S NS 255.19**   Numbers 1:9–18
Hebrew; Aramaic: Onqelos; Judaeo-Arabic. Oriental square script; Tiberian vocalisation + accents.
Paper; 1 leaf; rubbed.   17.4 × 12.3;   14 lines.
Name lists in 1:9–15 are only in Hebrew; Massorah Parva in margin at 9:16.   [752]

**T-S NS 255.24 (= T-S NS 255.1(a))**   Genesis 6:20 – 7:11 (folio 1); 9:24 – 10:17 (folio 2)
Aramaic: Onqelos (+ Hebrew lemmata).   Oriental semi-cursive script; Tiberian vocalisation.
Paper; 2 leaves (1 bifolium); badly mutilated and very badly rubbed.   18.2 × 13.2;   16 lines.
Divine name: ײ; this the outer bifolium to T-S NS 255.1(a), (folios 1–2, 11–12).   [753]

**T-S NS 255.30**   Ezekiel 37:21–5
Hebrew; Targum Jonathan to Prophets.   Oriental semi-cursive script; sporadic Tiberian vocalisation.
Paper; 1 leaf; rubbed.   17.6 × 13.4;   16 lines.
Divine name: Targum tetragrammaton (37:21).   [754]

**T-S NS 255.35**   Deuteronomy 30:20 – 31:8 (folio 1); 32:47 – 33:4 (folio 2)
Aramaic: Onqelos (+ Hebrew lemmata).   Oriental semi-cursive script; sporadic Tiberian vocalisation.
Paper; 2 leaves (1 bifolium); slightly mutilated. 17.1 × 13.5;   14–16 lines.
Divine name: ײ.   [755]

**T-S NS 255.36**   Genesis 1:1–4
Aramaic: Onqelos (+ Hebrew lemmata).   Oriental square script; unpointed.
Paper; 1 leaf; slightly mutilated.   10.6 × 8.4;   10 lines.
Divine name: ײ; *verso* is blank except for several words from 1:4, heading: בשם ײ.   [756]

**T-S NS 255.36–39**   Jeremiah 6:26–9, 7:1–4 (NS 255.39); 8:20–21; 9:2–3 (NS 255.38); 9:7–9, 12–14 (NS 255.37)
Aramaic: Targum Jonathan to Prophets (+ Hebrew lemmata).   Oriental semi-cursive script; Tiberian vocalisation.
Paper; 3 leaves; very badly mutilated and faded. 10.2⁺ × 11.0⁺;   8⁺ lines.   [757]

**T-S NS 255.42**   Exodus 16:15–23; 16:35 – 17:9
Aramaic: Onqelos.   Oriental semi-cursive script; Tiberian vocalisation.
Paper; 1 leaf; very badly mutilated.   16.5⁺ × 12.8⁺; 18⁺ lines.
Divine name: ײ.   [758]

**T-S NS 255.43**   Numbers 6:17–18, 21–3
Aramaic: Onqelos (+ Hebrew lemmata).   Oriental semi-cursive script; unpointed.
Paper; 1 leaf; very badly mutilated.   8.9⁺ × 14.5; 6⁺ lines.
Divine name: ײ.   [759]

**T-S NS 255.45**   Genesis 1:10–18
Aramaic: Onqelos (+ Hebrew lemmata).   Oriental square script; Tiberian vocalisation.
Paper; 1 leaf; rubbed.   16.6 × 12.3;   12 lines.
Divine name: יְיָ.   [760]

**T-S NS 255.46**   Deuteronomy 32:27–38
Aramaic: Onqelos (+ Hebrew lemmata).   Oriental semi-cursive script; Tiberian vocalisation.
Paper; 1 leaf; badly mutilated.   17.7 × 13.4;   15 lines.
Divine name: יְיָ.   [761]

**T-S NS 255.48**   Genesis 41:23–45
Aramaic: Onqelos (+ Hebrew lemmata).   Oriental semi-cursive script; sporadic Tiberian vocalisation.
Paper; 1 leaf; mutilated.   15.9⁺ × 12.8;   21–3 lines.
Divine name: יי.   [762]

**T-S NS 255.49**   Numbers 1:21–8
Hebrew; Aramaic: Onqelos; Judaeo-Arabic. Oriental script; Hebrew square with Tiberian vocalisation + accents; Onqelos semi-cursive with Tiberian vocalisation.
Paper; 1 leaf; very badly mutilated.   16.5⁺ × 7.0⁺; 18⁺ lines.   [763]

**T-S NS 255.53**   Exodus 25:34 – 26:13
Aramaic: Onqelos (+ Hebrew lemmata).   Oriental semi-cursive script; Tiberian vocalisation.
Paper; 2 leaves (1 bifolium); badly mutilated. 15.5 × 12.2;   15 lines.   [764]

**T-S NS 255.55**   Exodus 9:10–16, 19–24
Aramaic: Onqelos (+ Hebrew lemmata).   Oriental semi-cursive script; Tiberian vocalisation.
Paper; 1 leaf; very badly mutilated.   14.0⁺ × 12.6⁺; 12⁺ lines.
Divine name: tetragrammaton; variant (9:15): אוּשְׁטַת; attested version added in margin.   [765]

**T-S NS 255.66**   Ezekiel 44:24–5; Jeremiah 17:7–8 (folio 1); Jeremiah 17:12–14; Ezekiel 34:1–2, 4–10, 23–7; Hosea 2:1–4 (folio 2); (haftarot)
Hebrew; Aramaic: Targum Jonathan to Prophets. Oriental square script; unpointed.
Vellum; 2 leaves (1 bifolium); very badly mutilated. 26.0⁺ × 23.0;   2 cols.;   26⁺ lines.
Divine name: Hebrew tetragrammaton; Targum ייי; these are haftarot for parashot 'emor, behar, behuqotai and bamidbar respectively; heading at Ezekiel 34:1 אם בחקתי (folio 2r).   [766]

**T-S NS 255.68**   Genesis 1:1–12, 15–21
Aramaic: Onqelos (+ Hebrew lemmata).   Oriental square script; Tiberian vocalisation.
Vellum; 1 leaf; badly mutilated and rubbed. 22.0 × 19.0;   2 cols.;   26 lines.
Divine name: יי; verso blank except for ink adhered from another manuscript producing mirror writing.   [767]

**T-S NS 255.70**   Ezekiel 44:29–31; Jeremiah 16:21 – 17:3; (haftarot)
Hebrew; Aramaic: Targum Jonathan to Prophets. Oriental square script; unpointed.
Vellum; 1 leaf; very badly mutilated.   14.5⁺ × [24.8]; [2] cols.;   15⁺ lines.
These are haftarot for parashot 'emor and behar; marginal variant to Hebrew with Babylonian vocalisation at Ezekiel 44:30 (recto).   [768]

**T-S NS 255.74**   Isaiah 54:2–9, 16–17; 55:1–2; 40:25–6; (haftarot)
Hebrew; Aramaic: Targum Jonathan to Prophets. Oriental square script; unpointed.
Vellum; 1 leaf; very badly mutilated.   15.5⁺ × 15.5⁺; 18⁺ lines.
Divine name: ייי; these are haftarot for parashot no'ah and lekh lekha; heading at Isaiah 40:25 לך לך בישעיה (verso).   [769]

**T-S NS 255.78**   2 Samuel 22:25–6; Malachi 2:5–6; (haftarot)
Hebrew; Aramaic: Targum Jonathan to Prophets. Oriental square script; Hebrew with Tiberian vocalisation + accents; Targum with Tiberian vocalisation.
Vellum; 1 leaf; very badly mutilated.   12.3⁺ × [26.5]; 2 cols.;   7⁺ lines.
These are not consecutive haftarot (ha'azinu and toledot), and the scripts are different on the recto and verso.   [770]

**T-S NS 255.79**   Jeremiah 35:17–19; 1 Kings 5:27 – 6:1 (folio 1); Judges 5:16–27 (folio 2); (haftarot)
Hebrew; Aramaic: Targum Jonathan to Prophets. Oriental square script; unpointed.
Vellum; 2 leaves (1 bifolium); very badly mutilated and rubbed.   21.7 × 18.6;   2 cols.;   20 lines.
Divine name: Hebrew tetragrammaton; Targum יי; these are not attested as consecutive haftarot; most of folio 2 reinforced in darker ink by a later hand.   [771]

**T-S NS 255.80**   Habakkuk 3:13, 18–19; Isaiah 42:10; 49:15–17; (haftarot)
Hebrew; Aramaic: Targum Jonathan to Prophets. Oriental square script; Hebrew with Tiberian vocalisation + accents; Targum with sporadic Tiberian vocalisation.

**[T-S NS 255.80, cont.]**
Vellum; 1 leaf; very badly mutilated. 14.3⁺ × 12.3⁺; 2 cols.; 11⁺ lines.

Divine name: Hebrew tetragrammaton; Targum ייי; these are triennial *haftarot* for Genesis 8:1, 8:15 and 9:18 respectively. [772]

**T-S NS 255.84** Numbers 26:38–42, 44–50
Aramaic: Onqelos (+ Hebrew lemmata). Oriental square script; unpointed.

Vellum; 1 leaf; badly mutilated. 21.5 × 14.4; 15⁺ lines. [773]

**T-S NS 255.87** 2 Kings 4:2–11
Hebrew; Aramaic: Targum Jonathan to Prophets. Oriental square script; Tiberian vocalisation + accents.

Vellum; 1 leaf; very badly mutilated. 15.5⁺ × 13.4⁺; 2 cols.; 13⁺ lines. [774]

**T-S NS 255.88** Exodus 7:28 – 8:2; 8:18–20
Hebrew; Aramaic: Onqelos. Oriental square script; unpointed.

Vellum; 1 leaf; very badly mutilated. 12.7⁺ × [19.2]; [2] cols.; 18⁺ lines.

Divine name: Hebrew tetragrammaton; Onqelos ייי. [775]

**T-S NS 255.90** Hosea 14:2–10; Joel 2:12–14; Isaiah 55:6 – 56:5; (*haftarot*)
Hebrew; Aramaic: Targum Jonathan to Prophets. Oriental square script; very sporadic Tiberian vocalisation.

Vellum; 1 leaf; mutilated. 26.1 × 19.1; 31 lines.

Divine name: Hebrew tetragrammaton; Targum ייי; these are *haftarot* for fast days including Ninth of Av; heading before Isaiah 55: בישעיה [    ]. [776]

**T-S NS 256.1** Ezekiel 34:10–14
Hebrew; Aramaic: Targum Jonathan to Prophets. Oriental square script; Babylonian vocalisation + sporadic accents.

Vellum; 1 leaf; badly mutilated. 12.3⁺ × 17.5; 12⁺ lines.

Divine name: Hebrew tetragrammaton; Targum ייי. [777]

**T-S NS 256.2(a)** Numbers 35:27 – 36:6
Hebrew; Aramaic: Onqelos. Oriental square script; Babylonian vocalisation.

Vellum; 1 leaf; badly mutilated and rubbed. 15.8⁺ × 21.4; 2 cols.; 15⁺ lines.

*Verso* partially overwritten in dark ink. [778]

**T-S NS 256.2(b)** Genesis 50:16–17, 21; Exodus 1:6–8
Hebrew; Aramaic: Onqelos. Oriental square script; Babylonian vocalisation + sporadic accents.

Vellum; 1 leaf; very badly mutilated. 9.3⁺ × [18.0]; 2 cols.; 10⁺ lines. [779]

**T-S NS 256.4** Exodus 4:5–6, 9–12, 14, 16
Hebrew; Aramaic: Onqelos. Oriental square script; Babylonian vocalisation + accents.

Vellum; 1 leaf; very badly mutilated. 10.3⁺ × 17.9; 2 cols.; 10⁺ lines.

Divine name: Hebrew tetragrammaton; Targum ייי. [780]

**T-S NS 256.5** Jeremiah 12:9–10, 14–17; 13:1, 4–7, 10–11
Hebrew; Aramaic: Targum Jonathan to Prophets. Oriental square script; Babylonian vocalisation + accents.

Vellum; 1 leaf; very badly mutilated. 18.3⁺ × [18.0]; 2 cols.; 27⁺ lines.

Divine name: Hebrew tetragrammaton; Targum ייי. [781]

**T-S NS 256.87** Leviticus 11:29, 40
Hebrew; Aramaic: Onqelos. Oriental square script; Tiberian vocalisation + accents.

Vellum; 1 leaf (minute fragment). 6.0 × 10.5; ? cols.; 3⁺ lines. [782]

**T-S NS 257.85** Ezekiel 44:23–4; Jeremiah 17:5–6; (*haftarot*)
Hebrew; Aramaic: Targum Jonathan to Prophets. Oriental square script; sporadic Tiberian vocalisation.

Vellum; 1 leaf (minute fragment). 8.5⁺ × 4.9⁺; ? cols.; 10⁺ lines.

These are *haftarot* for *parashot 'emor* and *behuqotai* respectively. [783]

**T-S NS 258.8, 9** Exodus 19:4 – 20:11
Aramaic: Onqelos (+ 1 Hebrew lemma (20:2)). Oriental semi-cursive script; Tiberian vocalisation.

Paper; 1 leaf (torn into two parts, separately preserved); mutilated. [21.5] × 12.5⁺; 25 lines.

Divine name: יי. [784]

**T-S NS 258.49** Leviticus 17:4–5, 8–9
Hebrew; Aramaic: Onqelos. Yemenite(?) square script; unpointed.

Paper; 1 leaf; very badly mutilated. 9.5⁺ × 8.9⁺; 8⁺ lines.

Divine name: Hebrew tetragrammaton; Onqelos יי. [785]

**T-S NS 258.80** Isaiah 44:10–11, 23
Aramaic: Targum Jonathan to Prophets. Oriental semi-cursive script; unpointed.

Paper; 1 leaf (minute fragment). 4.4⁺ × 7.5⁺; 7⁺ lines.

Divine name: יי; *verso* blank except for Hebrew blessing. [786]

## T-S NS 258.138 (= T-S NS 259.18, 135)
Exodus 16:25–35; 17:10–16
Aramaic: Onqelos.   Oriental semi-cursive script; Tiberian vocalisation.

Paper; 1 leaf; very badly mutilated.   8.8⁺ × 12.0⁺; 12⁺ lines.

Divine name: יי ; script smaller on *recto* than on *verso*.
[787]

## T-S NS 259.1   Numbers 5:15–21, 24–6, 28–31; 6:1–2
Hebrew; Aramaic: Onqelos.   Oriental square script; Babylonian vocalisation + accents; Massorah Magna and Parva.

Vellum; 1 leaf; very badly mutilated.   19.5⁺ × [22.0]; 2 cols.; 19⁺ lines.

Divine name: Hebrew tetragrammaton; Onqelos יי.
[788]

## T-S NS 259.18 (= T-S NS 258.138; NS 259.135)   Exodus 15:10–20, 21; 16:1–8
Aramaic: Onqelos.   Oriental semi-cursive script; Tiberian vocalisation.

Paper; 1 leaf; very badly mutilated.   14.5⁺ × 12.5⁺; 17⁺ lines.

Divine name: יי; T-S NS 259.135 is part of this leaf.
[789]

## T-S NS 259.73   Habakkuk 3:15–16, 19 (*recto*), 17–18 (*verso*)
Aramaic: Targum Jonathan to Prophets (+ Hebrew lemmata).   Oriental semi-cursive script; Tiberian vocalisation.

Paper; 1 leaf; mutilated and *verso* very badly rubbed. 13.8 × 9.3; 12 lines.

Colophon at bottom of *recto*: כמל הבן הנחמד יו[סף ברבי תנח[ום.
[790]

## T-S NS 259.135 (= T-S NS 258.138, NS 259.18)   Exodus 15:21–5; 16:8–13
Aramaic: Onqelos.   Oriental semi-cursive script; Tiberian vocalisation.

Paper; 1 leaf (minute fragment).   6.0⁺ × 6.8⁺; 8⁺ lines.

Divine name: יי/יי; this is part of the same leaf as T-S NS 259.18.
[791]

## T-S NS 259.166 (verso)
Lemmata to Song of Solomon 6:5, 8, 10; 7:1 with a few targumic words וארום (line 7) מי זאת מן דא (line 13); certainly not the known targum of Song of Solomon and probably not targum at all.
[792]

## T-S NS 263.20   Genesis 24:43–6 (folio 1), 58–61 (folio 2)
Hebrew; Aramaic: Onqelos; Judaeo-Arabic. Oriental script; Hebrew linear square with Tiberian vocalisation + accents; Onqelos semi-cursive with Tiberian vocalisation.

Paper; 2 leaves (1 bifolium); folio 2 badly mutilated. 10.7⁺ × 9.0⁺; 11 lines.

Divine name: Hebrew tetragrammaton; Onqelos יי.
[793]

## T-S NS 263.39   Genesis 27:28–9, 31–3
Hebrew; Aramaic: Onqelos; Judaeo-Arabic. Oriental square script; Hebrew larger with Tiberian vocalisation + accents; Onqelos with Tiberian vocalisation.

Paper; 1 leaf; badly mutilated.   13.7⁺ × 18.5; 10⁺ lines.

Divine name: Hebrew אלהים; Targum יי.
[794]

## T-S NS 263.121   Joshua 23:14–15; 24:17–18
Hebrew; Aramaic: Targum Jonathan to Prophets. Oriental square script; Tiberian vocalisation + accents; also Babylonian accents.

Vellum; 1 leaf (minute fragment).   8.9⁺ × 7.8⁺; 2 cols.; 11⁺ lines.

Divine name: Hebrew tetragrammaton.
[795]

## T-S NS 268.134, 135, 150   Numbers 5:26 – 6:3; 6:10–21
Aramaic: Onqelos (+ Hebrew lemmata).   Oriental semi-cursive script; unpointed.

Paper; 3 leaves (minute fragments separately preserved, all belonging to the same folio).   10.3⁺ × 8.4⁺ (largest); [23+] lines.

Divine name: יי.
[796]

## T-S NS 271.140   Genesis 49:13–25
Aramaic: Onqelos (+ Hebrew lemmata).   Oriental linear square script; Tiberian vocalisation.

Paper; 2 leaves (1 bifolium); mutilated.   14.7 × 10.3; 12 lines.
[797]

## T-S NS 271.183 (T-S B8.9, NS 138.79)
Targumic *tosefta*(?) to Genesis 22   Oriental semi-cursive script; sporadic Tiberian vocalisation.

Paper; 1 leaf.   16.3 × 12.8; 13 lines.
Divine name: ה.
[798]

## T-S NS 272.100, 101   Numbers 28:10–15 (NS 272.101, *recto*); 29:1–7 (NS 272.101, *verso*; NS 272.100, *recto*)
Hebrew; Aramaic: Onqelos.   Oriental square script; Tiberian vocalisation; 272.101, *recto* unpointed and in smaller script.

**[T-S NS 272.100, 101, cont.]**
Vellum; 2 leaves; 272.100 badly mutilated. 13.3 × 10.3 (NS 272.101 cut in irregular shape); 14–17 lines. Divine name: יי֞; headings at 29:1 מוסף ראש שנה and at 29:7 מוסף כפורים; 272.100, *verso* blank. [799]

**T-S NS 273.124** Numbers 28:26–7 (folio 1v)
Aramaic: Onqelos. Oriental linear square script; Tiberian vocalisation.

Paper; 2 leaves (1 bifolium); slightly mutilated. 12.6 × 8.3; 8 lines.

Divine name: יי֞; folios 1r and 2v blank; folio 2r contains part of a Hebrew poem on "the ages of man". [800]

**T-S NS 273.165** Targumic poem to Exodus 15:11
Aramaic (+ Hebrew lemmata). Oriental semi-cursive script; unpointed.

Paper; 1 leaf. 15.1 × 10.2; 18–19 lines.

Heading: גידהא מי כמכה; the preserved portion of the poem summarizes the events from Creation to Abraham. [801]

**T-S NS 274.88** Numbers 29:12–16 (folios 1r–2r)
Aramaic: Onqelos (+ Hebrew lemmata). Oriental semi-cursive script; unpointed.

Paper; 2 leaves (1 bifolium); slightly rubbed. 12.3 × 7.6; 10–12 lines.

Divine name יי֞; this is the *maftir* for first day Tabernacles followed by heading אליום אלתאני but text on folio 2v is a Hebrew *reshut* for the present passage and Deuteronomy 1:11. [802]

**T-S NS 274.124** Genesis 2:1–3
Hebrew; Aramaic: Onqelos. Oriental semi-cursive script; unpointed.

Paper; 1 leaf. 16.4 × 12.5; 9–10 lines.

Divine name: יי֞; verses are interspersed with stanzas of a Hebrew poem. [803]

**T-S NS 276.188** Exodus 20:11–13/16 (very expansive)
Aramaic (mixture of Palestinian Targum and Onqelos). Oriental semi-cursive script; unpointed (except one word in 20:12, with Tiberian *sere*).

Paper; 2 leaves (1 bifolium); mutilated. 16.0 × 11.2; 17–18 lines.

Kasher *HUCA* LX, pp. 1–17 (Hebrew section). [804]

**T-S NS 277.218** Leviticus 2:8–11 (*recto*)
Hebrew; Aramaic: Onqelos. Oriental linear square script; unpointed.

Paper; 1 leaf. 19.7 × 12.7; 9 lines.

Divine name: Hebrew tetragrammaton; Onqelos יי֞; word deleted in 2:10; bottom half of *recto* blank; *verso* contains part of a Hebrew composition on death, perhaps part of a eulogy. [805]

**T-S NS 280.32** 2 Kings 8:23–5, 28–9; 9:3, 8, 12–13, 16–17
Hebrew; Aramaic: Targum Jonathan to Prophets (in margins). Hebrew: Oriental square script with Tiberian vocalisation + accents; Aramaic: Oriental semi-cursive script with Tiberian vocalisation (in darker ink).

Vellum; 1 leaf; badly mutilated. 16.1⁺ × 28.0; 3 cols.; 10⁺ lines. [806]

**T-S NS 281.1** 1 Kings 6:3–8
Hebrew; Aramaic: Targum Jonathan to Prophets. Oriental square script; Babylonian vocalisation + accents (Hebrew & Targum); added Tiberian vocalisation (Hebrew only).

Vellum; 1 leaf; slightly mutilated and rubbed. 20.0 × 17.2; 15 lines.

Letter פ in margin at beginning of each verse. [807]

**T-S NS 281.3** Isaiah 23:9–17
Hebrew; Aramaic: Targum Jonathan to Prophets. Oriental square script; Babylonian vocalisation + accents; Massorah Parva.

Vellum; 1 leaf; very badly mutilated. 32.2⁺ × 10.4⁺; [2] cols.; 22⁺ lines.

Divine name: Hebrew tetragrammaton. [808]

**T-S NS 281.26** 1 Kings 19:13–14, 16–17, 19–21
Hebrew; Aramaic: Targum Jonathan to Prophets. Oriental square script; Tiberian vocalisation (Hebrew only).

Vellum; 1 leaf; very badly mutilated. 14.2⁺ × [19.0]; 2 cols.; 14⁺ lines.

Divine name: Hebrew tetragrammaton. [809]

**T-S NS 281.50**

Hebrew of Genesis 1, with pen exercise of Onqelos to Genesis 1:1 in margins. [810]

**T-S NS 283.1** Numbers 14:40 – 15:16
Hebrew; Aramaic: Onqelos. Oriental square script; Babylonian vocalisation + accents; Tiberian vocalisation added in darker ink (Hebrew only).

Vellum; 1 leaf; badly mutilated, *verso* very badly rubbed. 27.5⁺ × [25.0]; 2 cols.; 24⁺ lines.

Divine name: Hebrew tetragrammaton; Onqelos יי֞. [811]

**T-S NS 283.7, 8** Numbers 31:25–8, 30–31, 37–8, 44–8
Hebrew; Aramaic: Onqelos. Oriental square script; Babylonian vocalisation + accents.

**[T-S NS 283.7, 8, cont.]**
Vellum; 1 leaf; very badly mutilated (torn into two parts, separately conserved). 16.5⁺ × 6.0⁺; [2] cols.; 13⁺ lines.

Divine name: Onqelos יי. [812]

### T-S NS 283.14   Numbers 21:28–31 (*recto*); 21:34 – 22:2 (*verso*)

Hebrew; Aramaic: Onqelos. Oriental square script; Tiberian vocalisation + accents.

Vellum; 1 leaf; very badly mutilated. 14.0⁺ × 10.2⁺; [2] cols.; 15⁺ lines.

Divine name: Onqelos יי. [813]

### T-S NS 283.31   Deuteronomy 1:29–31, 43–4

Hebrew; Aramaic: Onqelos. Oriental square script; Babylonian vocalisation + accents.

Vellum; 1 leaf (minute fragment). 10.5⁺ × 11.0⁺; [2] cols.; 8⁺ lines.

Divine name: Hebrew tetragrammaton; Onqelos יי. [814]

### T-S NS 284.2   Deuteronomy 7:26 – 8:8; 8:13–15, 19–20; 9:1–3

Hebrew; Aramaic: Onqelos. Oriental square script; Tiberian vocalisation + accents.

Vellum; 1 leaf; very badly mutilated. 24.3⁺ × [24.0]; 2 cols.; 26⁺ lines.

Divine name: Hebrew tetragrammaton; Onqelos יי. [815]

### T-S NS 284.3   Leviticus 18:17–20, 24–7; 18:30 – 19:4; 19:9–12

Hebrew; Aramaic: Onqelos. Oriental square script; Babylonian vocalisation + accents.

Vellum; 1 leaf; very badly mutilated. 13.5⁺ × [18.2]; 2 cols.; 16⁺ lines.

Divine name: Hebrew tetragrammaton; variant readings under אד in margins. [816]

### T-S NS 284.10   Jeremiah 33:26 – 34:5; 34:12–13; Isaiah 33:17–18; (*haftarot*)

Hebrew; Aramaic: Targum Jonathan to Prophets. Spanish(?) square script; Hebrew with Tiberian vocalisation + accents; Targum with Tiberian vocalisation.

Vellum; 1 leaf; badly mutilated. 14.9⁺ × 16.8; 17⁺ lines.

Divine name: Hebrew tetragrammaton; Targum יי; heading to Isaiah: וירא אליו יי בישעיה; these are triennial *haftarot* for Genesis 17:1 and 18:1 respectively. [817]

### T-S NS 284.27

Manuscript of Exodus 7–9 (Hebrew) with two supralinear targumic massoretic (?) glosses at Exodus 9:3, כל מאדא מן קדם and כל מיתא תקיף; the latter is unattested. [818]

### T-S NS 284.52   1 Kings 8:59–65 (folio 1)

Hebrew; Aramaic: Targum Jonathan to Prophets. Hebrew: Oriental square script; Targum semi-cursive script; unpointed.

Vellum; 2 leaves (1 bifolium); very badly mutilated, folio 2 almost entirely missing. 14.5 × 12.2; 17 lines.

Divine name: Hebrew & Targum אל; folio 2 not identified. [819]

### T-S NS 285.17   Genesis 24:37–40 (folio 1), 64–7 (folio 2)

Hebrew; Aramaic: Onqelos; Judaeo-Arabic. Oriental script; Hebrew: linear square with Tiberian vocalisation + accents; Onqelos: semi-cursive with Tiberian vocalisation.

Paper; 2 leaves (1 bifolium); slightly mutilated. 15.8 × 11.0; 11 lines.

Divine name: Hebrew tetragrammaton; Onqelos יי. [820]

### T-S NS 285.19   Numbers 2:33 – 3:5

Hebrew; Aramaic: Onqelos; Judaeo-Arabic. Oriental semi-cursive script; Tiberian vocalisation (Hebrew & Onqelos).

Paper; 1 leaf; mutilated. 14.8 × 10.5; 15–17 lines.

Divine name: Hebrew and Onqelos יי. [821]

### T-S NS 285.22   1 Kings 1:10–17

Aramaic: Targum Jonathan to Prophets; Judaeo-Arabic; (+ Hebrew lemmata). Oriental semi-cursive script; Tiberian vocalisation (Targum).

Paper; 1 leaf. 16.5 × 12.3; 16 lines.

Divine name: יי. [822]

### T-S NS 285.113(b)   Exodus 1:10 – 2:1 (folio 1); 3:1–11 (folio 2)

Aramaic: Onqelos (+ Hebrew lemmata). Oriental semi-cursive script; Tiberian vocalisation (folio 1 only).

Paper; 2 leaves (1 bifolium); rubbed. 17.3 × 12.9; 15 lines.

Divine name: יי. [823]

### T-S NS 285.115 (= T-S NS 286.66)   Leviticus 3:13 – 4:8

Aramaic: Onqelos (+ Hebrew lemmata). Oriental semi-cursive script (lemmata in larger square script); unpointed.

Paper; 1 leaf; very badly mutilated and rubbed. 18.7 × 9.5⁺; 14 lines.

Divine name: יי. [824]

### T-S NS 285.124   Numbers 28:3–8

Hebrew; Aramaic: Onqelos; Judaeo-Arabic. Oriental script; Hebrew square; Onqelos semi-cursive; unpointed.

[T-S NS 285.124, cont.]
Paper; 1 leaf; mutilated and rubbed. 20.1 × 14.4; 17 lines.
Divine name יְ. [825]

**T-S NS 285.146** Leviticus 4:24–8
Hebrew; Aramaic: Onqelos; Judaeo-Arabic. Oriental square script; Hebrew with Tiberian vocalisation + accents; Onqelos with Tiberian vocalisation.
Paper; 1 leaf; very badly rubbed. 16.6 × 12.6; 14 lines.
Divine name: Hebrew tetragrammaton; Onqelos יְיָ. [826]

**T-S NS 286.1** (= T-S 20.155; AS 63.24, 51, 72, 85, 95, 96, 117, 129, 153; AS 69.241)
Exodus 23:8–14
Aramaic: Palestinian Targum (+ Hebrew lemmata). Oriental square script; very sporadic Tiberian vocalisation in original hand and ink.
Vellum; scroll (part of 1 column); badly mutilated. 14.6 × 6.8; 16+ lines.
Tiberian vocalisation in 23:12: דְּתְנוּ and in bottom margin: תְּשַׁבְּקוּן; verso contains a lectionary written vertically in relation to text on recto, in a later hand.
Klein GMPT I, p.297. [827]

**T-S NS 286.3** 2 Samuel 22:7–18
Aramaic: Targum Jonathan to Prophets (+ Hebrew lemmata). Oriental square script; Tiberian vocalisation.
Paper; 1 leaf; slightly mutilated and rubbed. 15.0 × 11.4; 13 lines.
Divine name: יְיָ. [828]

**T-S NS 286.13** Isaiah 42:1–4 (folio 1v); 2 Kings 4:1–12 (folio 2); (haftarot)
Hebrew; Aramaic: Targum Jonathan to Prophets. Oriental semi-cursive script; sporadic Tiberian vocalisation (folio 1); script on folio 1 larger than on folio 2.
Vellum; 2 leaves (1 bifolium). 16.2 × 12.4; 15 lines (folio 1), 20 lines (folio 2).
Divine name: Hebrew אלהים; Targum יְיָ; heading, folio 1v: אפטארה בראשית בישעיה; 2 Kings 4 is the haftarah for parashat wayera'; folio 1r blank. [829]

**T-S NS 286.14** Exodus 9:28 – 10:6
Aramaic: Onqelos (+ Hebrew lemmata). Oriental semi-cursive script (lemmata in larger square script); unpointed.
Paper; 1 leaf. 19.2 × 13.4; 17 lines.
Divine name: יְיָ; notation פרש after 9:35 (foot of recto). [830]

**T-S NS 286.15** Genesis 11:5–19 (folio 1); 13:15 – 14:8 (folio 2)
Aramaic: Onqelos. Oriental semi-cursive script; unpointed.
Paper; 2 leaves (1 bifolium). 17.8 × 12.9; 14 lines.
Divine name: יְיָ. [831]

**T-S NS 286.24** Genesis 21:12–18
Aramaic: Onqelos (+ Hebrew lemmata). Oriental semi-cursive script; Tiberian vocalisation.
Paper; 1 leaf. 16.4 × 12.3; 9–11 lines.
Divine name: יְיָ. [832]

**T-S NS 286.26** Deuteronomy 27:6 – 28:3 (folio 1); 31:27 – 32:14 (folio 2)
Aramaic: Onqelos (+ lengthy Hebrew lemmata). Oriental semi-cursive script; unpointed.
Paper; 2 leaves (1 bifolium); rubbed. 15.8 × 12.5; 24–5 lines.
Divine name: יְיָ; notation פרש at 32:1. [833]

**T-S NS 286.28** Deuteronomy 33:12–16
Hebrew; Aramaic: Onqelos. Spanish square script; Tiberian vocalisation (faded).
Paper; 1 leaf; slightly mutilated and stained. 21.5 × 14.4; 11 lines.
Divine name: Hebrew and Onqelos יְיָ. [834]

**T-S NS 286.32, 33** Ezekiel 29:5–12, 21; (haftarah)
Aramaic: Targum Jonathan to Prophets. Oriental semi-cursive script; unpointed.
Paper; 1 leaf (torn into two parts, separately conserved); badly mutilated. 9.5+ × 13.0; 9.0+ × 13.0; 20+ lines.
Divine name: יְיָ; haftarah for parashat wa'era'. [835]

**T-S NS 286.38** Ezekiel 1:8–14
Aramaic: Targum Jonathan to Prophets (+ Hebrew lemmata). Oriental semi-cursive script; sporadic Tiberian vocalisation.
Paper; 1 leaf; rubbed. 13.3 × 9.2; 15–16 lines. [836]

**T-S NS 286.41** Exodus 14:25–9; 15:3–10
Aramaic: Onqelos (+ Hebrew lemmata). Oriental semi-cursive script; Tiberian vocalisation.
Paper; 1 leaf; badly mutilated (top half of leaf cut away). 13.0+ × 15.3; 10+ lines.
Divine name: יְיָ. [837]

**T-S NS 286.57** Isaiah 54:10–11 and 54:10; (haftarah)
Aramaic: Targum Jonathan to Prophets (+ Hebrew lemmata). Oriental linear square script; Tiberian vocalisation (recto only), possibly a pen exercise.

[T-S NS 286.57, cont.]
Vellum; 1 leaf (small irregular shape). 6.3 × 7.0; 6 and 9 lines.
Divine name: יי; heading: והיה עקב תשמעון on both sides. [838]

### T-S NS 286.66 (= T-S NS 285.115)  Leviticus 4:10–19(?)
Aramaic: Onqelos (+ Hebrew lemmata). Oriental semi-cursive script (lemmata in larger square script); unpointed.
Paper; 1 leaf; very badly mutilated and rubbed. 18.8 × 10.3⁺; 14 lines.
Divine name: יֹ. [839]

### T-S NS 287.35 recto, lines 1–19  Genesis 37:4 – 49:7
Aramaic: Massorah to Onqelos. Oriental square script; sporadic Tiberian vocalisation.
Parchment; 1 leaf; slightly mutilated. 13.9 × 9.0; 24–28 lines.
*Recto*, lines 20–28 and entire *verso* contain Massorah Magna to I Chronicles 1:5 – 9:22.
Weil *Textus* XI, pp.37–87. [839a]

### T-S NS 288.183  Genesis 49:3–10
Aramaic: Onqelos (+ Hebrew lemmata). Oriental semi-cursive script; sporadic Tiberian vocalisation.
Paper; 1 leaf; mutilated. 12.9 × 8.9; 12–15 lines.
Variant in gloss to 49:10 ישתמעון/יתכנשון. [840]

### T-S NS 288.202
Aramaic poem on Esther with Hebrew phrases, but not targum. [841]

### T-S NS 289.120, 178, 187  Exodus 15:18–19
Aramaic: Palestinian Targum (+ Hebrew lemmata). Oriental semi-cursive script; Tiberian vocalisation.
Paper; 1 leaf; badly mutilated. 9.3⁺ × 8.3; 8⁺ lines.
Divine name: יֹ; Judaeo-Arabic note at end: כמלת אלזיאדה ירושלמי; *verso* blank. [842]

### T-S NS 289.135  *Tosefta* to Genesis 44:18
Aramaic. Oriental semi-cursive script; unpointed.
Paper; 1 leaf; very badly mutilated. 9.8⁺ × 14.5⁺; 11⁺ lines.
Variation to known versions towards end of fragment; *verso* contains part of a Hebrew liturgical poem in praise of a bridegroom. [843]

### T-S NS 289.178, 187
Minute fragments belonging to the same leaf as T-S NS 289.120; Palestinian Targum to Exodus 15:18–19. [844]

### T-S NS 290.81  Numbers 17:12–17
Hebrew; Aramaic: Onqelos; Judaeo-Arabic. Oriental script; Hebrew square with Tiberian vocalisation + accents; Onqelos smaller, semi-cursive with Tiberian vocalisation.
Paper; 1 leaf; mutilated and rubbed. 16.8 × 12.7; 14 lines.
Divine name: Hebrew tetragrammaton; Onqelos יי. [845]

### T-S NS 291.61  Jeremiah 31:10–17
Hebrew; Aramaic: Targum Jonathan to Prophets. Oriental semi-cursive script; unpointed.
Paper; 1 leaf. 16.7 × 12.7; 17–20 lines.
Divine name: Hebrew and Targum יי; variant + ירושלים in 31:16. [846]

### T-S NS 291.92  1 Kings 2:3–5
Aramaic: Targum Jonathan to Prophets (+ Hebrew lemmata). Oriental semi-cursive script; unpointed.
Vellum; 1 leaf. 8.7 × 7.2; 8 lines.
Divine name: יֹ. [847]

### T-S NS 298.74  Exodus 34:23–9
Hebrew; Aramaic: Onqelos. Oriental linear square script; Tiberian vocalisation (*recto* only).
Paper; 1 leaf; mutilated and rubbed. 20.1 × 10.0⁺; 15 lines.
Divine name: Hebrew tetragrammaton; Onqelos יֹי; *verso* ends with pen exercise. [848]

### T-S NS 303.52  Exodus 38:12 – 39:3
Aramaic: Onqelos (+ Hebrew lemmata). Oriental square script; unpointed.
Paper; 1 leaf; mutilated. 20.9 × 14.7; 21–2 lines. [849]

### T-S NS 303.85  Genesis 1:15–16
Hebrew; Aramaic: Onqelos; Judaeo-Arabic. Oriental script; Hebrew square; Onqelos smaller, semi-cursive; unpointed.
Paper; 1 leaf; mutilated. 14.6⁺ × 13.8; 4 lines.
Scribe abandoned text after first Hebrew word of 1:16; remainder of *recto* and all of *verso* blank and partly cut away. [850]

### T-S NS 312.3  Song of Solomon 5:8 – 6:2
Aramaic: Targum Song of Solomon (+ Hebrew lemmata). Oriental semi-cursive script; unpointed.
Paper; 1 leaf; badly mutilated and rubbed. 17.3 × 13.2; 22–3 lines. [851]

**T-S NS 318.36** Deuteronomy 21:13–19
Hebrew; Aramaic: Onqelos; Judaeo-Arabic.
Oriental script; Hebrew square with Tiberian vocalisation + accents; Onqelos semi-cursive, unpointed.
Paper; 1 leaf; slightly mutilated. 23.0 × 15.9; 22 lines.
[852]

**T-S NS 318.89** Exodus 18:22–6
Hebrew; Aramaic: Onqelos; Judaeo-Arabic.
Oriental script; Hebrew square with Tiberian vocalisation + accents; Onqelos semi-cursive with Tiberian vocalisation.
Paper; 1 leaf; mutilated. 17.4 × 13.4+; 13 lines.
Divine name: Hebrew אלהים; Onqelos יי.
[853]

**T-S NS 319.5** Isaiah 63:7–8, 11–13
Hebrew; Aramaic: Targum Jonathan to Prophets.
Oriental square script; unpointed.
Paper; 1 leaf; very badly mutilated. 9.5+ × 13.2; 5+ lines.
[854]

**T-S NS 319.21 (= T-S NS 319.44)** Exodus 17:10–11, 14–15
Aramaic: Onqelos (+ Hebrew lemmata). Oriental linear square script; Tiberian vocalisation.
Paper; 1 leaf (minute fragment). 4.0+ × 9.9; [11] lines.
[855]

**T-S NS 319.23** Numbers 7:8–12
Hebrew; Aramaic: Onqelos; Judaeo-Arabic.
Oriental script; Hebrew square with Tiberian vocalisation + accents; Onqelos semi-cursive with Tiberian vocalisation.
Paper; 1 leaf; mutilated. 17.0 × 13.2; 14 lines.
Divine name: Hebrew tetragrammaton; Onqelos ייי.
[856]

**T-S NS 319.35** Genesis 20:9–15; 20:18 – 21:10 (folio 1); 21:14–20, 25–32 (folio 2)
Aramaic: Onqelos (+ Hebrew lemmata). Oriental semi-cursive script; unpointed except 21:7 with Tiberian vocalisation (folio 1v).
Paper; 2 leaves (1 bifolium); badly mutilated. 13.5+ × 14.4; 12+ lines.
Divine name: יי.
[857]

**T-S NS 319.44 (= T-S NS 319.21)** Exodus 17:11–13, 15–16 (folio 1)
Aramaic: Onqelos (+ Hebrew lemmata). Oriental linear square script; Tiberian vocalisation.
Paper; 2 leaves (1 bifolium); badly mutilated. 12.5+ × 10.0; [11] lines.
Divine name: יי; word added at end ושלם; this is the reading for Purim; folio 2 blank.
[858]

**T-S NS 319.45** Genesis 15:18 – 16:2 (folio 1); 17:9–12 (folio 2)
Hebrew; Aramaic: Onqelos; Judaeo-Arabic.
Oriental script; Hebrew linear square with Tiberian vocalisation + accents; Onqelos semi-cursive with Tiberian vocalisation.
Paper; 2 leaves (1 bifolium); slightly rubbed. 15.9 × 10.9; 11 lines.
Divine name: Onqelos יי.
[859]

**T-S NS 319.59** Genesis 17:7–15 (folio 1); 18:13–21 (folio 2)
Aramaic: Onqelos (+ Hebrew lemmata). Oriental semi-cursive script; unpointed.
Paper; 2 leaves (1 bifolium); very badly mutilated. 16.7 × 13.4; 12 lines.
Divine name: יי.
[860]

**T-S NS 319.75** Exodus 15:11–21
Aramaic: Onqelos (+ Hebrew lemmata). Oriental linear square script; Tiberian vocalisation.
Paper; 1 leaf; slightly mutilated and rubbed. 18.3 × 10.4; 14 lines.
Divine name: יי.
[861]

**T-S NS 319.92** Genesis 49:12–28
Aramaic: Onqelos (+ Hebrew lemmata). Oriental semi-cursive script; sporadic Tiberian vocalisation.
Paper; 1 leaf; rubbed. 12.3 × 8.9; 20–22 lines.
Divine name: יי(?).
[862]

**T-S NS 319.94** 2 Kings 7:10–15
Hebrew; Aramaic: Targum Jonathan to Prophets.
Oriental script; Hebrew square with Tiberian vocalisation; Targum semi-cursive, unpointed.
Paper; 1 leaf. 17.3 × 12.8; 13 lines.
[863]

**T-S NS 319.104** Deuteronomy 16:17 – 17:2; 17:4–6, 8–10
Hebrew; Aramaic: Onqelos. Oriental square script; Hebrew with Tiberian vocalisation + accents; Onqelos with Tiberian vocalisation.
Vellum; 1 leaf; badly mutilated. 25.0+ × [26.0]; 2 cols.; 22+ lines.
Divine name: Hebrew tetragrammaton; Onqelos יי.
[864]

**T-S NS 323.26** Habakkuk 3:3–9, 13, 18–19 (*recto*), 10–12 (*verso*)
Aramaic: Targum Jonathan to Prophets (+ Hebrew lemmata). Oriental semi-cursive script; sporadic Tiberian vocalisation.
Paper; 1 leaf; slightly mutilated. 22.5 × 18.3; 24 lines.
Divine name: יי; *verso* is inverted in relation to *recto*, contains two lines in Judaeo-Arabic and the three verses of targum omitted on the *recto*.
[865]

**T-S NS 324.28**  Exodus 18:1–8 (*verso*)
Aramaic: Onqelos (+ Hebrew lemmata).  Oriental semi-cursive script; unpointed.
Paper; 1 leaf; slightly mutilated.  16.6 × 13.2;  13 lines.
Divine name: יֹ; *verso* contains title תרגום וישמע יתרו and *recto* contains colophon: שלמה בר יפתח נ״ע followed by
ללשיך אל אוּל אבו אען.  [866]

**T-S NS 325.81(b)**  Joshua 1:3–7 (*recto*)
Hebrew; Aramaic: Targum Jonathan to Prophets. Oriental square script; Hebrew with Tiberian vocalisation + accents; Targum unpointed.
Vellum; 1 leaf; badly mutilated.  9.9 × 10.5;  16⁺ lines.
Ownership note (*verso*): הדא אפטראתא מה דקנא שלמה בר איוב
בר שלמה בר שלמה בר [ש]מואל בר שאתון בדמו בֹ]  יפוט ויסני
למקרי בה [הוא חורע]יה חרע זרעיה ]  נצת סלה.
לימרהו:.  [867]

**T-S NS 334.126**  Genesis 1:5–8
Hebrew; Aramaic: Onqelos.  Oriental square script; unpointed; traces of decorative Massorah Magna at foot of *recto* and in margin.
Vellum; 1 leaf; badly mutilated.  8.3 × 7.5⁺;  8 lines.
[868]

**T-S NS 341.2**  Genesis 14:4–5, 9–10
Aramaic: Onqelos (+ Hebrew lemmata).  Oriental square script; unpointed.
Paper; 1 leaf (minute fragment).  4.7⁺ × 8.6⁺;  4⁺ lines.
[869]

**T-S NS 341.9**  Exodus 20:21/24–23/26 (*recto*); Numbers 28:28–30 (*verso*)
Hebrew (*verso*); Aramaic: Onqelos (+ Hebrew lemmata, *recto*).  Oriental semi-cursive script; Tiberian vocalisation (Onqelos only); these are reading and *maftir* for Pentecost.
Paper; 1 leaf (minute fragment).  6.4⁺ × 4.9⁺;  7⁺ lines.
[870]

**T-S NS 341.20**  Genesis 11:6–8, 25–6
Hebrew; Aramaic: Onqelos.  Oriental square script; Hebrew with Tiberian vocalisation + accents; Onqelos unpointed.
Vellum; 1 leaf (minute fragment).  7.0⁺ × 6.0⁺; ? cols.;  7⁺ lines.  [871]

**T-S NS 341.22**  Isaiah 6:6–13
Hebrew; Aramaic: Targum Jonathan to Prophets. Oriental semi-cursive script; unpointed.
Vellum; 1 leaf (minute fragment).  11.2⁺ × 4.4⁺; 16⁺ lines.  [872]

**T-S NS 341.23**  Genesis 1:20–22
Hebrew; Aramaic: Onqelos.  Oriental square script; unpointed.
Vellum; 1 leaf; very badly mutilated.  8.4⁺ × 8.4; 8⁺ lines.
Divine name: יֹ.  [873]

**T-S NS J525**  Deuteronomy 1:34 – 2:1 (folio 1); 4:5–16 (folio 2)
Hebrew; Aramaic: Onqelos.  Oriental square script; Hebrew with Tiberian vocalisation + accents; Onqelos with Tiberian vocalisation.
Vellum; 2 leaves (1 bifolium); mutilated.  19.5 × 15.2;  22 lines.
Divine name: Hebrew tetragrammaton; Onqelos יֹיֹ.  [874]

**T-S AS 1.123**  2 Samuel 22:11–12, 18–20
Hebrew; Aramaic: Targum Jonathan to Prophets. Spanish(?) square script; Tiberian vocalisation + accents.
Vellum; 1 leaf (minute fragment); very badly mutilated.  4.0⁺ × 6.1⁺;  1 col. (poetry format);  5⁺ lines.  [875]

**T-S AS 2.173**  Isaiah 55:12; 40:17–18; (*haftarot*)
Hebrew; Aramaic: Targum Jonathan to Prophets. Oriental square script; Hebrew with Tiberian vocalisation + accents (in darker ink); Targum with Tiberian vocalisation.
Vellum; 1 leaf (minute fragment); very badly mutilated.  7.5⁺ × 11.6⁺;  3⁺ lines.
These are *haftarot* for *parashot noaḥ* and *lekh lekha* respectively.  [876]

**T-S AS 3.27**  Genesis 42:8
Hebrew; Aramaic: Onqelos.  Oriental semi-cursive script; unpointed.
Vellum; 1 leaf; very badly mutilated.  14.8⁺ × 7.8⁺; 3 lines + 1 vertical line in the margin.
Hebrew and Targum alternate line by line (rather than the usual verse by verse); *verso* blank.  [877]

**T-S AS 3.190**  Ezekiel 43:11–13
Hebrew; Aramaic: Targum Jonathan to Prophets. Oriental square script; Tiberian vocalisation.
Vellum; 1 leaf; very badly mutilated.  8.3⁺ × 17.4⁺; 4⁺ lines.  [878]

**T-S AS 3.199**  Malachi 2:6–7; Isaiah 43:10–12; (*haftarot*)
Hebrew; Aramaic: Targum Jonathan to Prophets. Oriental square script; Tiberian vocalisation + accents (partly reinforced in darker ink).
Vellum; 1 leaf (minute fragment).  5.2⁺ × 4.9⁺;  5⁺ lines.
The text skips from the Hebrew of Isaiah 43:10 to the Targum of 43:12 (scribal deletion?); these are triennial *haftarot* for Exodus 30:1 (Malachi) and Exodus 31:1 (Isaiah).  [879]

**T-S AS 9.12, 13**  Leviticus 17:5,10 (AS 9.13); 18:10–11, 18 (AS 9.12)
Hebrew; Aramaic: Onqelos.  Oriental square script; unpointed.
Vellum; 2 leaves; very badly mutilated and rubbed. 7.8⁺ × 12.6⁺;  5⁺ lines.  [880]

**T-S AS 11.176 (= T-S B6.6)**  Exodus 34:32, 34, 35; 35:2
Hebrew; Aramaic: Palestinian Targum.  Oriental square script; Tiberian vocalisation + accents.
Vellum; 1 leaf; very badly mutilated.  6.1⁺ × 14.8⁺; [3] cols.; 3⁺ lines.  [881]

**T-S AS 12.85**  2 Kings 13:19; Isaiah 27:8–9; (*haftarot*)
Hebrew; Aramaic: Targum Jonathan to Prophets. Oriental square script; Tiberian vocalisation + accents.
Vellum; 1 leaf; very badly mutilated.  9.9⁺ × 6.6⁺; 11⁺ lines.
These are *haftarot* for *parashot wayeḥi* and *shemot* respectively.  [882]

**T-S AS 12.239**  Ezekiel 37:4–5, 8–9
Hebrew; Aramaic: Targum Jonathan to Prophets. Oriental square script; unpointed.
Vellum; 1 leaf (minute fragment).  4.7⁺ × 5.5⁺; 4⁺ lines.
Divine name: Targum יּ.  [883]

**T-S AS 14.21**
Partly identified as Job 5:18 (ימחץ) and Job 5:15 (חזק), possibly with targum; almost entirely illegible; verses in unusual order(?).  [884]

**T-S AS 14.22, 23**
Two unidentified Aramaic fragments, possibly targumic.  [885]

**T-S AS 16.76**  Deuteronomy 13:6 (*recto*)
Hebrew; Aramaic: Onqelos.  Oriental square script; Tiberian vocalisation (barely legible).
Vellum; 1 leaf (minute fragment).  5.1⁺ × 7.6⁺;  5⁺ lines.
*Verso* illegible.  [886]

**T-S AS 17.173**  Exodus 13:8–11, 15–16
Hebrew; Aramaic: Onqelos.  Yemenite square script; Babylonian vocalisation.
Vellum; 1 leaf; very badly mutilated.  10.1⁺ × 12.9⁺; 9⁺ lines.
Divine name: Hebrew tetragrammaton; Onqelos יי.  [887]

**T-S AS 17.201**  Malachi 2:14 – 3:5
Hebrew; Aramaic: Targum Jonathan to Prophets. Oriental square script; unpointed.
Vellum; 2 leaves (1 bifolium); very badly mutilated (folio 2 almost entirely missing).  17.0 × [20.2]; 2 cols.;  14 lines.
Divine name: Hebrew tetragrammaton; Targum ייי; and abbreviated י.  [888]

**T-S AS 18.42**  Numbers 33:47–9, 52–4
Hebrew; Aramaic: Onqelos.  Ashkenazi/Italian square script; Hebrew with Tiberian vocalisation + accents; Onqelos unpointed.
Vellum; 1 leaf; very badly mutilated.  9.5⁺ × 4.9⁺; 10⁺ lines.  [889]

**T-S AS 19.133, 138, 215 (= T-S AS 67.101, 179)**  2 Kings 8:27–8; 9:18–19 (AS 19.133); 8:29; 9:15 (AS 19.215); 16:1–2; 17:21 (AS 19.138); (+ additional verses in the Hebrew main text)
Hebrew (main text); Aramaic: Targum Jonathan to Prophets (added in margins).  Oriental script; Hebrew square with Tiberian vocalisation + accents; Targum linear square with sporadic Tiberian vocalisation; Massorah Parva.
Vellum; [2] leaves; very badly mutilated.  12.9⁺ × 7.8⁺; 8.8⁺ × 15.8⁺ (and minute fragment); [3] cols.; 6⁺ lines.
Divine name: ⓖ.  [890]

**T-S AS 20.49**  Joel 4:17; 1 Samuel 6:11–12(?); (*haftarot*)
Hebrew; Aramaic: Onqelos.  Oriental square script; Tiberian vocalisation + accents.
Vellum; 1 leaf; very badly mutilated.  11.0⁺ × 8.8⁺; 10⁺ lines.
*Qeri* in margin at 1 Samuel 6:11 and decorative *samekh* ✿ in margin after Joel 4:17 to indicate new *haftarah*; these are triennial *haftarot* for Exodus 7:8 (Joel) and Exodus 10:1 (1 Samuel).  [891]

**T-S AS 20.130**  Genesis 38:18–19, 21–2, 24–5, 28–9 (folio 1); 41:12–14, 16–17, 20–21, 24–5 (folio 2)
Hebrew; Aramaic: Onqelos.  Spanish square script; Tiberian vocalisation + accents.
Vellum; 2 leaves (mistakenly sewn together before being consigned to the genizah); very badly mutilated and rubbed.  7.2⁺ × 19.1⁺;  2 cols.;  8⁺ lines.
Each leaf has a portion of the margin of the original conjoined leaf still attached to it.  [892]

**T-S AS 21.193**  Jonah 1:2–7
Hebrew; Aramaic: Targum Jonathan to Prophets. Oriental square script; Tiberian vocalisation + accents.
Vellum; 1 leaf; very badly mutilated.  10.5⁺ × 4.6⁺; 10⁺ lines.  [893]

**T-S AS 21.248**   1 Samuel 17:32–8
Hebrew; Aramaic: Targum Jonathan to Prophets. Oriental square script; Hebrew with Tiberian vocalisation + accents; Targum with Tiberian vocalisation.

Vellum; 1 leaf; very badly mutilated.   12.7⁺ × 14.7⁺; 12⁺ lines.

Divine name: Hebrew tetragrammaton; Targum יי.   [894]

**T-S AS 22.183**   *Tosefta* to Genesis 44:18 (*recto*)
Aramaic (+ Hebrew lemma).   Oriental square script (very small); Tiberian vocalisation.

Vellum; 1 leaf (minute fragment).   4.9⁺ × 5.2⁺;   6⁺ lines.

Divine name: יי; *verso* contains an unrelated Hebrew text.   [895]

**T-S AS 23.99**   Isaiah 22:16, 18–19, 22–3; Isaiah 1:2; (*haftarot*)
Hebrew; Aramaic: Targum Jonathan to Prophets. Oriental square script; Tiberian vocalisation.

Vellum; 1 leaf; very badly mutilated.   7.1⁺ × 10.5⁺; 2 cols.;   9⁺ lines.

These are *haftarot* for *parashot mas'ei* and *devarim* respectively.   [896]

**T-S AS 23.111**   Genesis 8:17, 19
Hebrew; Aramaic: Onqelos.   Oriental square script; Tiberian vocalisation.

Vellum; 1 leaf (minute fragment).   4.3⁺ × 5.5⁺;   3⁺ lines.   [897]

**T-S AS 24:317**   Deuteronomy 15:12–13; 16:10–11
Hebrew; Aramaic: Onqelos.   Oriental square script; sporadic Babylonian and Tiberian vocalisation; sporadic Tiberian accents.

Vellum; 1 leaf (minute fragment).   3.5⁺ × 6.2⁺;   5⁺ lines.

*Recto* barely legible.   [898]

**T-S AS 25.39**   Leviticus 23:7–11, 14–18
Aramaic: Onqelos (+ lengthy Hebrew lemmata). Oriental linear square script; Tiberian vocalisation.

Paper; 1 leaf; very badly mutilated and stained. 10.9⁺ × 10.5⁺;   9⁺ lines.

Divine name: יי; variant in 23:17 פרישותא for ארמותא.   [899]

**T-S AS 26.184, 193**   1 Kings 6:9–13
Hebrew; Aramaic: Targum Jonathan to Prophets. Oriental square script; Tiberian vocalisation.

Vellum; 2 leaves (1 bifolium); very badly mutilated (1 leaf almost entirely missing).   19.8 × 15.5; [13] lines.

Divine name: Targum tetragrammaton (in margin); both fragments belong to the same leaf.   [900]

**T-S AS 27.1**   Joshua 5:7–8 (*recto*); (*haftarah*)
Hebrew; Aramaic: Targum Jonathan to Prophets. Oriental square script; unpointed.

Vellum; 1 leaf (minute fragment).   5.1⁺ × 5.9⁺;   4⁺ lines.

This is the *haftarah* for first day Passover; *verso* badly rubbed and unidentified.   [901]

**T-S AS 39.56**   Exodus 29:46 – 30:5 (folio 1)
Hebrew; Aramaic: Onqelos.   Oriental semi-cursive script; Hebrew with Tiberian vocalisation + accents (in darker ink); Onqelos with Tiberian vocalisation.

Paper; 2 leaves (1 bifolium); very badly mutilated and rubbed (folio 2 almost entirely missing).   8.0⁺ × 11.0; 8⁺ lines.   [902]

**T-S AS 39.269**   Numbers 10:36 – 11:11; 11:13–21
Aramaic: Onqelos (+ Hebrew lemmata).   Oriental semi-cursive script (very small); sporadic Tiberian vocalisation.

Paper; 1 leaf; very badly mutilated and worm-eaten. 13.7⁺ × 14.0⁺;   17⁺ lines.

Divine name: יי.   [903]

**T-S AS 40.141**   Exodus 27:14–19
Hebrew; Aramaic: Onqelos.   Oriental semi-cursive script; sporadic Tiberian vocalisation.

Paper; 1 leaf; very badly mutilated and rubbed (barely legible).   10.9⁺ × 9.6⁺;   9⁺ lines.   [904]

**T-S AS 40.164**   Exodus 32:23–4, 27–8, 30–32, 34–5
Hebrew; Aramaic: Onqelos; Judaeo-Arabic. Yemenite square script; Hebrew with Tiberian vocalisation + accents; Onqelos with Babylonian vocalisation.

Paper; 1 leaf; very badly mutilated.   12.2⁺ × [20.0]; 2 cols.;   11⁺ lines.

Divine name: Hebrew tetragrammaton; Onqelos יי.   [905]

**T-S AS 40.181**   Leviticus 1:1 (*recto*)
Aramaic: Onqelos (+ Hebrew lemmata).   Oriental semi-cursive script; unpointed.

Paper; 1 leaf; very badly mutilated.   5.8⁺ × 12.8; 3⁺ lines.

Divine name: unclear, perhaps omitted; margins of *recto* and entire *verso* contain Hebrew and Arabic jottings.   [906]

**T-S AS 40.198**   Numbers 15:40 – 16:3 (folio 1); 16:21–4 (folio 2r)
Hebrew; Aramaic: Onqelos.   Oriental semi-cursive script; Tiberian vocalisation + accents.

Paper; 2 leaves (1 bifolium); mutilated and very badly rubbed (folio 2r barely legible, 2v illegible). 17.3 × 13.4;   11 lines.   [907]

**T-S AS 41.2**  1 Samuel 1:14–17
Hebrew; Aramaic: Targum Jonathan to Prophets.
Oriental semi-cursive script; unpointed.
Paper; 1 leaf.  15.8 × 11.8;  10 lines.
Divine name: ײַ/ײ; error in 1:16 כען for כעת. [908]

**T-S AS 41.174**  Malachi 1:8; 3:4; (*haftarah*)
Hebrew(?); Aramaic: Targum Jonathan Proverbs.
Oriental square script; Tiberian vocalisation.
Paper; 1 leaf (minute fragment).  5.6⁺ × 7.6⁺;  6⁺ lines.
Divine name: Targum יי; this is *haftarah* for *parashat toledot*; heading after Malachi 3:4: ויצא יעקב [בת]רי עשרה. [909]

**T-S AS 43.1**  Genesis 25:11–22
Aramaic: Onqelos (+ Hebrew lemmata).  Oriental semi-cursive script; Tiberian vocalisation.
Paper; 1 leaf; badly mutilated and rubbed.  20.3 × 15.7; 13 lines.
Divine name: יי; marginal notation פרש at 25:19 (*verso*) and catchword במהא (25:22) in lower left corner of *verso*. [910]

**T-S AS 44.3** (= T-S AS 69.21, 60)
Deuteronomy 33:7–10
Hebrew; Aramaic: Onqelos; Judaeo-Arabic.
Oriental script; Hebrew large linear square; Onqelos semi-cursive; unpointed.
Paper; 1 leaf; stained.  15.2 × 11.0;  15–16 lines. [911]

**T-S AS 44.107**  Genesis 1:1–5 (folio 1); 2:18–24 (folio 2)
Hebrew; Aramaic: Onqelos; Judaeo-Arabic (1:1 only).  Oriental script; Hebrew square with Tiberian vocalisation + accents; Onqelos semi-cursive with Tiberian vocalisation.
Paper; 2 leaves (1 bifolium); folio 2 very badly mutilated.  18.7 × 14.0;  16 lines.
Divine name: Hebrew אלהים; Onqelos יי; folio 1r blank. [912]

**T-S AS 44.208**  Numbers 21:34 – 22:6
Hebrew; Aramaic: Onqelos.  Spanish square script; Tiberian vocalisation + accents.
Paper; 1 leaf; badly mutilated and very badly rubbed. 20.3 × 14.5;  [20] lines. [913]

**T-S AS 45.90**  Genesis 2:22–3; 3:2–3
Hebrew; Aramaic: Onqelos.  Oriental semi-cursive script; unpointed.
Paper; 1 leaf; very badly mutilated.  5.9⁺ × 10.6⁺; 4⁺ lines. [914]

**T-S AS 45.99**
Part of an unidentified Aramaic and Hebrew composition (probably not targum). [915]

**T-S AS 46.39**  Genesis 39:4–9
Hebrew; Aramaic: Onqelos; Judaeo-Arabic.
Oriental script; Hebrew large, square with Tiberian vocalisation + accents; Onqelos semi-cursive with Tiberian vocalisation.
Paper; 1 leaf; very badly mutilated.  12.5⁺ × 14.3⁺; 13⁺ lines.
Divine name: Hebrew tetragrammaton; Onqelos יי. [916]

**T-S AS 48.21**  Leviticus 24:8 – 25:4 (folio 1)
Aramaic: Onqelos (+ Hebrew lemmata).  Oriental semi-cursive script; Tiberian vocalisation.
Paper; 2 leaves (1 bifolium); very badly rubbed (folio 2 illegible except for vocalisation).  17.6 × 13.2;  16 lines. [917]

**T-S AS 48.81, 82**  Numbers 17:27 – 18:2 (AS 48.81); 18:3–5 (AS 48.82)
Hebrew; Aramaic: Onqelos; Judaeo-Arabic.
Oriental script; Hebrew large, square with Tiberian vocalisation + accents; Onqelos semi-cursive with Tiberian vocalisation.
Paper; 2 leaves (2 minute fragments).  5.5⁺ × 4.0⁺; 6⁺ lines. [918]

**T-S AS 51.153**  Leviticus 2:8–9, 12–13
Aramaic: Onqelos (+ Hebrew lemmata).  Oriental square script; Tiberian vocalisation + accents.
Paper; 1 leaf (minute fragment).  4.2⁺ × 6.3⁺;  4⁺ lines. [919]

**T-S AS 51.177**  Leviticus 23:8–9, 15–16
Aramaic: Onqelos (+ Hebrew lemmata).  Oriental semi-cursive script; Tiberian vocalisation.
Paper; 1 leaf (minute fragment).  4.9⁺ × 5.5⁺;  4⁺ lines.
Divine name: יי. [920]

**T-S AS 51.221**  Genesis 1:1–3 (*recto*)
Aramaic: Onqelos (+ Hebrew lemmata).
Persian(?) square script; Tiberian vocalisation.
Paper; 1 leaf; very badly mutilated.  9.3⁺ × 8.8⁺; 6⁺ lines.
*Verso* contains rabbinic quotations in a Judaeo-Arabic text. [921]

**T-S AS 51.222**  Leviticus 5:1 (*recto*)
Hebrew; Aramaic: Onqelos.  Oriental square script; Tiberian vocalisation.
Paper; 1 leaf (minute fragment).  6.2⁺ × 3.8⁺;  4⁺ lines.
Only three letters of Onqelos preserved; *verso* blank. [922]

**T-S AS 53.50**  2 Samuel 1:22–7 (folio 1); Isaiah 56:6–8; 61:9 (folio 2); (*hafṭarot*)
Hebrew; Aramaic: Targum Jonathan to Prophets. Oriental square script; Tiberian vocalisation.
Paper; 2 leaves (1 bifolium); slightly mutilated and rubbed.   15.8 × 11.4;   11 lines.
These are *hafṭarot* for mourning(?), public fast-day and Sabbath (after?) wedding respectively; heading before Isaiah 61: דבהלולא בישעיה and final note in Judaeo-Arabic: תמת בחמד אללה אלה אלחמד.   [923]

**T-S AS 53.72**  Leviticus 14:40–41, 43–4
Hebrew; Aramaic: Onqelos.   Oriental semi-cursive script; Tiberian vocalisation.
Paper; 1 leaf; very badly mutilated.   5.8⁺ × 7.6⁺; 5⁺ lines.   [924]

**T-S AS 54.30**  Exodus 17:8–9
Hebrew (only lemma for 17:9); Aramaic: Onqelos.   Oriental square script; Tiberian vocalisation for Hebrew 17:8; remainder unpointed.
Paper; 1 leaf; very badly mutilated.   16.9 × 12.8; 11 lines.
Divine name: ײַ; this is the pentateuchal reading for Purim.   [925]

**T-S AS 54.73**  Leviticus 4:24–7
Hebrew; Aramaic: Onqelos; Judaeo-Arabic. Oriental square script; Hebrew with Tiberian vocalisation + accents; Onqelos with Tiberian vocalisation.
Paper; 1 leaf; badly mutilated.   11.1⁺ × 9.5⁺;   11⁺ lines.   [926]

**T-S AS 54.108, 109, 111**
Genesis 38:29 – 39:1; 39:3–5, 8–12
Hebrew; Aramaic: Onqelos; Judaeo-Arabic. Yemenite square script; Hebrew with Tiberian vocalisation + accents; Onqelos with Babylonian vocalisation.
Paper; 1 leaf (torn into three parts, separately conserved); very badly mutilated.   7.4⁺ × 9.0⁺ (largest); 9⁺ lines.
Divine name: Hebrew tetragrammaton; Onqelos ײַ.   [927]

**T-S AS 54.172**  Ezekiel 20:1–3, 8–9; (*hafṭarah*)
Hebrew; Aramaic: Targum Jonathan to Prophets. Yemenite square script; Babylonian vocalisation.
Paper; 1 leaf; very badly mutilated.   7.3⁺ × 5.9⁺; 8⁺ lines.
Divine name: Hebrew tetragrammaton; this is *hafṭarah* for *parashat qedoshim*.   [928]

**T-S AS 54.268**  Genesis 19:26–7, 29–30
Hebrew; Aramaic: Onqelos.   Oriental linear square script; Tiberian vocalisation.
Paper; 1 leaf; very badly mutilated and rubbed. 13.0⁺ × 12.8⁺;   12⁺ lines.
Divine name: Hebrew tetragrammaton; Onqelos ײַ.   [929]

**T-S AS 55.199**  Isaiah 59:20–21; (*hafṭarah*)
Hebrew; Aramaic: Targum Jonathan to Prophets. Oriental square script; unpointed(?).
Paper; 1 leaf; very badly mutilated and rubbed. 7.2⁺ × 7.8⁺;   8⁺ lines.
This is an addition to *hafṭarah* for Day of Atonement; verso blank.   [930]

**T-S AS 55.342**  Numbers 21:20–21, 24–5
Hebrew; Aramaic: Onqelos.   Spanish square script; Tiberian vocalisation + accents (partially reinforced in darker ink).
Paper; 1 leaf; very badly mutilated and rubbed. 16.8⁺ × 13.8;   11⁺ lines.   [931]

**T-S AS 58.13**  Genesis 6:11–19 (folios 1–2); 7:18 – 8:4 (folios 3–4)
Hebrew; Aramaic: Onqelos.   Oriental semi-cursive script; Tiberian vocalisation + accents; Massorah Parva.
Paper; 4 leaves (2 bifolia); badly mutilated and rubbed. 15.8⁺ × 14.4;   12–13⁺ lines.
Decorative *samekh* in margin at 8:1 (folio 4r) denotes triennial *sidra* ❂.   [932]

**T-S AS 59.28**  Leviticus 22:22–3, 26–7
Hebrew; Aramaic: Onqelos.   Oriental semi-cursive script; Tiberian vocalisation.
Paper; 1 leaf; very badly mutilated.   6.6⁺ × 6.5⁺; 7⁺ lines.   [933]

**T-S AS 59.281**  Genesis 2:15–19
Hebrew; Aramaic: Onqelos.   Oriental square script; Tiberian vocalisation.
Paper; 1 leaf; very badly mutilated and rubbed. 7.8⁺ × 14.3⁺;   8⁺ lines.
Divine name: Hebrew tetragrammaton; Onqelos ײַ; variant of Onqelos in margin of *verso* בְּקִבְלָה (main text illegible).   [934]

**T-S AS 59.293, 294**  Genesis 14:16–21
Aramaic: Onqelos (+ Hebrew lemmata).   Oriental square script; unpointed.
Paper; 1 leaf (torn into two parts, separately conserved); badly mutilated and very badly rubbed.   [18.5] × 16.0; [10] lines.
Barely legible.   [935]

**T-S AS 59.348**  Leviticus 9:6–7
Hebrew; Aramaic: Onqelos; Judaeo-Arabic. Persian(?) square script; unpointed.

**[T-S AS 59.348, cont.]**
Paper; 1 leaf; slightly mutilated.  19.9 × 13.6;  7 lines.
Divine name: Hebrew tetragrammaton; Onqelos ״׳; error in Onqelos (9:7) which repeats 9:6 and probably caused the scribe to abandon this leaf. [936]

**T-S AS 60.1**  Genesis 43:10–11, 14
Hebrew; Aramaic: Onqelos.  Oriental semi-cursive script; Tiberian vocalisation.
Paper; 1 leaf; very badly mutilated and rubbed. 5.0⁺ × 12.8⁺;  2⁺ lines. [937]

**T-S AS 61.24**  Exodus 32:3–4, 8–9
Aramaic: Onqelos (+ Hebrew lemmata).  Oriental square script; unpointed.
Paper; 1 leaf; very badly mutilated and rubbed. 12.0⁺ × 7.2⁺;  8⁺ lines.
Divine name: Onqelos ײ. [938]

**T-S AS 61.110**  Genesis 23:5–13
Aramaic: Onqelos (+ Hebrew lemmata).  Oriental square script; Tiberian vocalisation.
Paper; 1 leaf; very badly mutilated.  17.3⁺ × 15.8; 13⁺ lines.
Barely legible. [939]

**T-S AS 61.112–114**  Numbers 3:23, 27 (AS 61.112); 3:31, 35 (AS 61.113); 3:38, 41, 44, 48 (AS 61.114)
Aramaic: Onqelos (+ Hebrew lemmata).  Oriental square script; sporadic Tiberian vocalisation.
Paper; 6 leaves (3 bifolia); very badly mutilated. 11.6⁺ × 13.2;  8⁺ lines. [940]

**T-S AS 62.50**  Massorah to Onqelos (Exodus 26⁺)
Hebrew and Aramaic.  Oriental semi-cursive script; mixed Tiberian and Babylonian vocalisation.
Paper; 1 leaf; very badly mutilated.  8.0⁺ × 7.5⁺; 14⁺ lines. [941]

**T-S AS 62.114**  Genesis 15:2,9
Hebrew; Aramaic: Onqelos.  Oriental square script; Babylonian vocalisation + accents.
Vellum; 1 leaf (minute fragment).  3.6⁺ × 3.0⁺;  3⁺ lines. [942]

**T-S AS 62.122**  1 Samuel 20:17–18
Hebrew; Aramaic: Targum Jonathan to Prophets. Oriental square script; unpointed.
Vellum; 1 leaf (minute fragment).  4.7⁺ × 3.3⁺;  6⁺ lines.
*Verso* rubbed and illegible. [943]

**T-S AS 62.129**  Deuteronomy 27:10–11, 15
Hebrew; Aramaic: Onqelos.  Oriental square script; Babylonian vocalisation.
Vellum; 1 leaf (minute fragment).  7.0⁺ × 5.8⁺;  4⁺ lines.
Divine name: Hebrew tetragrammaton. [944]

**T-S AS 62.130**  Genesis 15:18; 16:2–3
Hebrew; Aramaic: Onqelos.  Oriental square script; Babylonian vocalisation + accents.
Vellum; 1 leaf; very badly mutilated.  10.4⁺ × 6.5⁺; 4⁺ lines. [945]

**T-S AS 62.131**  Deuteronomy 34:12
Hebrew; Aramaic: Onqelos.  Oriental square script; Babylonian vocalisation.
Vellum; 1 leaf; very badly mutilated.  5.7⁺ × 10.7⁺; 3⁺ lines. [946]

**T-S AS 62.132**  Genesis 8:22 – 9:1; 9:10–11
Hebrew; Aramaic: Onqelos.  Oriental square script; Babylonian vocalisation + accents.
Vellum; 1 leaf; very badly mutilated.  10.1⁺ × 9.8⁺; 8⁺ lines. [947]

**T-S AS 62.136**
Unidentified minute vellum fragment, probably targum. [948]

**T-S AS 62.137**  Deuteronomy 31:26–31; 32:2–8
Hebrew; Aramaic: Onqelos.  Oriental square script; sporadic Babylonian vocalisation.
Vellum; 1 leaf; badly mutilated.  21.8⁺ × 9.5⁺; 20⁺ lines.
*Samekh* in margin at top of *verso* opposite assumed position of 32:1 (now missing). [949]

**T-S AS 62.138**  Leviticus 26:37–8
Hebrew; Aramaic: Onqelos.  Oriental square script; Babylonian vocalisation.
Vellum; 1 leaf (minute fragment).  5.8⁺ × 6.1⁺;  6⁺ lines.
*Verso* entirely rubbed and illegible. [950]

**T-S AS 62.139**  Numbers 10:11–12, 17–19
Hebrew; Aramaic: Onqelos.  Oriental square script; Babylonian vocalisation + accents.
Vellum; 1 leaf; very badly mutilated.  7.2⁺ × 9.3⁺; 6⁺ lines. [951]

**T-S AS 62.140**  Exodus 2:14; 3:3
Hebrew; Aramaic: Onqelos.  Oriental square script; Babylonian vocalisation + Tiberian accents.
Vellum; 1 leaf (minute fragment).  6.5⁺ × 6.6⁺;  4⁺ lines. [952]

**T-S AS 62.141**  Genesis 6:17; 7:4–6
Hebrew; Aramaic: Onqelos.  Oriental square script; Babylonian vocalisation + accents.
Vellum; 1 leaf (minute fragment).  6.3⁺ × 5.4⁺;  4⁺ lines. [953]

**T-S AS 62.145** (= T-S AS 62.160, 173, 320)
Joshua 17:3–4, 14–15
Hebrew; Aramaic: Targum Jonathan to Prophets. Oriental square script; Babylonian vocalisation + accents.
Vellum; 1 leaf (minute fragment). 8.0⁺ × 5.0⁺; 2 cols.; 5⁺ lines.
Divine name: Targum ׳׳׳; scribal omission of end of 17:3. [954]

**T-S AS 62.146** Genesis 18:28, 31–2
Hebrew; Aramaic: Onqelos. Oriental square script; Babylonian vocalisation + accents.
Vellum; 1 leaf; very badly mutilated. 10.0⁺ × 6.8⁺; 7⁺ lines.
Several fragments pasted together to form leaf, one incorrectly. [955]

**T-S AS 62.147** Deuteronomy 12:5–6, 11, 16–17, 22
Hebrew; Aramaic: Onqelos. Oriental square script; Babylonian vocalisation + accents.
Vellum; 1 leaf; very badly mutilated and rubbed. 7.3⁺ × 10.5⁺; 2 cols.; 6⁺ lines. [956]

**T-S AS 62.148** Deuteronomy 12:29; 13:13–14
Hebrew; Aramaic: Onqelos. Oriental square script; Babylonian vocalisation.
Vellum; 1 leaf (minute fragment). 4.4⁺ × 5.3⁺; 5⁺ lines. [957]

**T-S AS 62.149** Numbers 35:37, 31–2; 36:1,4
Hebrew; Aramaic: Onqelos. Oriental square script; Babylonian vocalisation.
Vellum; 1 leaf; very badly mutilated, *verso* very badly rubbed. 4.8⁺ × 9.4⁺; 2 cols.; 5⁺ lines. [958]

**T-S AS 62.150** Exodus 11:5, 10; 12:6, 11–12
Hebrew; Aramaic: Onqelos. Oriental square script; Babylonian vocalisation + accents.
Vellum; 1 leaf; very badly mutilated. 5.4⁺ × 6.5⁺; 2 cols.; 5⁺ lines.
Divine name: Hebrew tetragrammaton. [959]

**T-S AS 62.151** Numbers 10:12–17, 20–24
Hebrew; Aramaic: Onqelos. Oriental square script; Babylonian vocalisation + accents.
Vellum; 1 leaf; very badly mutilated and rubbed. 12.7⁺ × 11.7⁺; 14 lines.
Divine name: Hebrew tetragrammaton; Onqelos ׳׳׳. [960]

**T-S AS 62.153** Deuteronomy 13:17–18; 14:21–3
Hebrew; Aramaic: Onqelos. Oriental square script; Babylonian vocalisation + accents.
Vellum; 1 leaf; very badly mutilated. 7.7⁺ × 5.9⁺; 8⁺ lines.
Divine name: Hebrew tetragrammaton; Onqelos ׳׳׳. [961]

**T-S AS 62.154** Isaiah 23:13–14, 17–19
Hebrew; Aramaic: Targum Jonathan to Prophets. Oriental square script; Babylonian vocalisation + accents.
Vellum; 1 leaf; very badly mutilated and rubbed. 11.5⁺ × 9.6⁺; [2] cols.; 6⁺ lines. [962]

**T-S AS 62.160** (= T-S AS 62.145, 173, 320)
Joshua 17:4, 8, 11, 15–16
Hebrew; Aramaic: Targum Jonathan to Prophets. Oriental square script; Babylonian vocalisation + accents.
Vellum; 2 leaves (1 bifolium); very badly mutilated. 10.4⁺ × [23.4]; 2 cols.; 7⁺ lines.
Divine name: Targum ׳׳׳; variant in Hebrew text to 17:4, ביד משה for את משה! (scribal error?). [963]

**T-S AS 62.161** Joshua 24:5–7, 13–14
Hebrew; Aramaic: Targum Jonathan to Prophets. Oriental square script; Hebrew with Babylonian accents also Tiberian vocalisation + accents in lighter ink; Targum with Babylonian accents; Massorah Magna and Parva.
Vellum; 1 leaf; very badly mutilated. 10.7⁺ × 13.7⁺; 2 cols.; 9⁺ lines. [964]

**T-S AS 62.163** Genesis 24:44–5, 62–4
Hebrew; Aramaic: Onqelos. Oriental square script; Babylonian vocalisation + accents.
Vellum; 1 leaf; very badly mutilated. 7.3⁺ × 9.4⁺; [2] cols.; 7⁺ lines. [965]

**T-S AS 62.165** Leviticus 23:13, 15–18, 20–21
Hebrew; Aramaic: Onqelos. Oriental square script; Babylonian vocalisation + accents; Massorah Magna and Parva.
Vellum; 1 leaf; very badly mutilated. 14.7⁺ × 9.8⁺; 2 cols.; 9⁺ lines.
Divine name: Onqelos ׳׳׳. [966]

**T-S AS 62.169, 170, 171** Leviticus 26:32–3 (AS 62.169, 171(*recto*)); 26:36–7 (AS 62.170 (*recto*)); 26:41–2 (AS 62.170 (*verso*)); 26:44 (AS 62.169 (*verso*), 171 (*verso*))
Hebrew; Aramaic: Onqelos. Oriental square script; Babylonian vocalisation + sporadic accents.
Vellum; 1 leaf (torn into three parts, separately conserved); very badly mutilated. 6.9⁺ × 7.5⁺ (largest); [2] cols.; 4⁺, 6⁺ lines.
Divine name: Hebrew tetragrammaton. [967]

**T-S AS 62.173** (= T-S AS 62.145, 160, 320)
Joshua 17:2–3, 13–14
Hebrew; Aramaic: Targum Jonathan to Prophets.
Oriental square script; Babylonian vocalisation + accents.

Vellum; 1 leaf; very badly mutilated. 13.0⁺ × 7.7⁺;
[2] cols.; 12⁺ lines. [968]

**T-S AS 62.174** Exodus 29:9–10, 16, 21, 24–5
Hebrew; Aramaic: Onqelos. Oriental square script; Babylonian vocalisation + accents.

Vellum; 1 leaf; very badly mutilated. 7.8⁺ × 9.1⁺;
2 cols.; 6⁺ lines.

Divine name: Hebrew tetragrammaton; Onqelos ייי. [969]

**T-S AS 62.175** Numbers 14:45; 15:1–2, 6
Hebrew; Aramaic: Onqelos. Oriental square script; Babylonian vocalisation also Tiberian vocalisation + accents (in darker ink).

Vellum; 1 leaf; very badly mutilated and rubbed. 11.2⁺ × 8.5⁺; 9⁺ lines.

Verso almost entirely illegible. [970]

**T-S AS 62.187** Genesis 22:6–7, 10–12
Hebrew; Aramaic: Onqelos. Oriental square script; Babylonian vocalisation.

Vellum; 1 leaf; very badly mutilated. 10.0⁺ × 7.2⁺;
10⁺ lines.

Divine name: Hebrew tetragrammaton. [971]

**T-S AS 62.190** Leviticus 1:1–3; 2:5–9
Hebrew; Aramaic: Onqelos. Oriental square script; sporadic Babylonian vocalisation.

Vellum; 1 leaf; very badly mutilated. 10.7⁺ × 11.5⁺;
2 cols.; 12⁺ lines.

Divine name: Hebrew tetragrammaton; Onqelos י[ ]. [972]

**T-S AS 62.193** Hosea 10:1, 6–8, 11–13; 11:3–4
Hebrew; Aramaic: Targum Jonathan to Prophets.
Oriental square script; Babylonian vocalisation + accents.

Vellum; 1 leaf; very badly mutilated. 10.0⁺ × 12.5⁺;
2 cols.; 13⁺ lines.

Variant in 10:12 יורה צדק for ויורה צדק. [973]

**T-S AS 62.194** Deuteronomy 27:13–15, 20–21
Hebrew; Aramaic: Onqelos. Oriental square script; Babylonian vocalisation.

Vellum; 1 leaf; very badly mutilated. 7.2⁺ × 5.1⁺;
8⁺ lines.

Divine name: Hebrew tetragrammaton. [974]

**T-S AS 62.198** Zechariah 2:9–13; 2:17 – 3:1; 3:4–6
Hebrew; Aramaic: Targum Jonathan to Prophets.
Oriental square script; Babylonian vocalisation + accents.

Vellum; 1 leaf (+ margin of conjoined leaf); very badly mutilated. 16.8⁺ × 20.6; 2 cols.; 12⁺ lines.

Divine name: Targum ייי; variant in margin at 2:12 דמזק(?) for דמזיק. [975]

**T-S AS 62.199** Isaiah 6:13; 9:5; Jeremiah 34:8–11: (haftarot)
Hebrew; Aramaic: Targum Jonathan to Prophets.
Oriental square script; Hebrew with Babylonian vocalisation + accents also Tiberian vocalisation (in darker ink); Targum with Babylonian vocalisation + accents.

Vellum; 1 leaf; very badly mutilated. 16.5⁺ × 12.0⁺;
14⁺ lines.

Divine name: Hebrew tetragrammaton; Isaiah 9:5–6 Hebrew only added, mostly in margin and in darker ink; these are haftarot for parashot yitro and mishpatim; heading before Jeremiah: [ואלה] המשפטים בירמיה. [976]

**T-S AS 62.202** Ezekiel 26:20 – 27:3; 27:5–8
Hebrew; Aramaic: Targum Jonathan to Prophets.
Oriental square script; Babylonian vocalisation + accents also Tiberian vocalisation + accents (in very faint ink).

Vellum; 1 leaf; very badly mutilated. 18.3⁺ × 4.1⁺;
18⁺ lines. [977]

**T-S AS 62.208** Massorah to Hebrew and Onqelos to Leviticus 11–13; Numbers 3–6
Hebrew and Aramaic. Oriental square script; sporadic Tiberian vocalisation.

Vellum; 2 leaves (1 bifolium); very badly mutilated.
10.1⁺ × 7.5⁺; 15⁺ lines. [978]

**T-S AS 62.211, 213** Joshua 9:1–2; 10:12–14; 24:1–4 + 10:8–11 in margin (Hebrew only); (haftarot)
Hebrew; Aramaic: Targum Jonathan to Prophets.
Oriental square script; Babylonian vocalisation + accents.

Vellum; 1 leaf; very badly mutilated. 10.5⁺ × [23.9];
2 cols.; [20] lines.

Divine name: Hebrew tetragrammaton; Targum ייי;
10:8–11 in the margin of the verso are preceded by the heading: ומדלגין וקרינן and followed by תם יקרא אז ידבר (in a different hand); heading before Joshua 24: אתם נצבים ביהושע; Joshua 9–10 is not attested as a haftarah. [979]

**T-S AS 62.212** Jeremiah 32:31–44; 2:1–7; (*hafṭarot*)
Hebrew; Aramaic: Targum Jonathan to Prophets. Oriental square script; Hebrew with Tiberian vocalisation + accents; Targum with Babylonian vocalisation; no traces of vocalisation on *recto*.
Vellum; 1 leaf; badly mutilated and rubbed. 25.8 × 18.6⁺; 31 lines. [980]

**T-S AS 62.213**
See T-S AS 62.211. [981]

**T-S AS 62.214** (= T-S AS 62.248, 251)
Genesis 4:2–3, 6, 9, 11–13
Hebrew; Aramaic: Onqelos. Oriental square script; Babylonian vocalisation + accents.
Vellum; 1 leaf; very badly mutilated. 30.5 × 24.7; 2 cols.; 20 lines.
Divine name: Hebrew tetragrammaton; Onqelos ᵐ. [982]

**T-S AS 62.219** 1 Samuel 13:16–17 (*recto*)
Hebrew; Aramaic: Targum Jonathan to Prophets. Oriental square script; Babylonian accents.
Vellum; 1 leaf (minute fragment). 5.1⁺ × 3.2⁺; 6⁺ lines.
*Verso* illegible. [983]

**T-S AS 62.220** Deuteronomy 31:4–6, 13–14
Hebrew; Aramaic: Onqelos. Oriental square script; Babylonian vocalisation + accents; Massorah Magna.
Vellum; 1 leaf; very badly mutilated. 33.5 × 23.0; 2 cols.; 20 lines.
Divine name: Hebrew tetragrammaton; Onqelos ᵐ; pen exercise in margin of *verso*, Genesis 42:7–8. [984]

**T-S AS 62.221** Genesis 7:2–4, 11–14
Hebrew; Aramaic: Onqelos. Oriental square script; Babylonian vocalisation + accents; Massorah Magna.
Vellum; 1 leaf; very badly mutilated. 8.0⁺ × 16.7; 5⁺ lines. [985]

**T-S AS 62.222, 227** Genesis 5:21; 6:3,4
Hebrew; Aramaic: Onqelos. Oriental square script; Babylonian vocalisation + accents.
Vellum; 1 leaf (+ minute fragment); very badly mutilated. 6.8⁺ × 11.7⁺; 4⁺ lines.
Divine name: Onqelos ᵐ. [986]

**T-S AS 62.237** 1 Samuel 15:13–14, 18–19
Hebrew; Aramaic: Targum Jonathan to Prophets. Oriental square script; Babylonian vocalisation + accents.
Vellum; 1 leaf; very badly mutilated. 9.9⁺ × 7.0⁺; 7⁺ lines.
Divine name: Targum ᵐ. [987]

**T-S AS 62.242** Joshua 18:22 – 19:1; 19:7–9, 12–14, 17–23
Hebrew; Aramaic: Targum Jonathan to Prophets. Yemenite square script; Babylonian vocalisation.
Vellum; 1 leaf; very badly mutilated. 19.1⁺ × [24.0]; 2 cols.; 14⁺ lines.
*Qeri* in margin at 19:22. [988]

**T-S AS 62.244** Deuteronomy 12:28; 12:31 – 13:1; 13:5–6, 11
Hebrew; Aramaic: Onqelos. Oriental square script; Babylonian vocalisation + accents.
Vellum; 1 leaf; very badly mutilated. 7.5⁺ × 10.7⁺; 2 cols.; 9⁺ lines.
Divine name: Onqelos ᵐ. [989]

**T-S AS 62.245** Exodus 12:48 (folio 1v); 14:11, 16 (folio 2)
Hebrew; Aramaic: Onqelos. Oriental square script; Babylonian vocalisation + accents.
Vellum; 2 leaves (1 bifolium); very badly mutilated. 11.9⁺ × 12.9⁺; [2] cols.; 6⁺ lines. [990]

**T-S AS 62.247** Judges 5:16–17, 20–22, 25–7, 30–31
Hebrew; Aramaic: Targum Jonathan to Prophets. Yemenite square script; Babylonian vocalisation.
Vellum; 1 leaf; very badly mutilated. 10.3⁺ × [20.3]; 2 cols.; 9⁺ lines. [991]

**T-S AS 62.248, 251** (= T-S AS 62.214)
Genesis 3:24 – 4:2; 4:10–11
Hebrew; Aramaic: Onqelos. Oriental square script; Babylonian vocalisation + accents.
Vellum; 1 leaf (torn into two parts, separately conserved); very badly mutilated. [30.5] × [24.7]; 2 cols.; [20] lines. [992]

**T-S AS 62.249** Exodus 14:18, 21
Hebrew; Aramaic: Onqelos. Oriental square script; Babylonian vocalisation + accents.
Vellum; 1 leaf; very badly mutilated. 4.5⁺ × 9.7⁺; 4⁺ lines. [993]

**T-S AS 62.251**
See T-S AS 62.248. [994]

**T-S AS 62.253** (= T-S AS 62.268)
Deuteronomy 8:19; 9:6
Hebrew; Aramaic: Onqelos. Oriental square script; Babylonian vocalisation.

**[T-S AS 62.253 (= T-S AS 62.268), cont.]**
Vellum; 1 leaf (minute fragment). 4.3⁺ × 4.5⁺; 4⁺ lines.
Divine name: Hebrew tetragrammaton; Onqelos ״׳.
[995]

### T-S AS 62.268 (= T-S AS 62.253)
Deuteronomy 9:3, 7
Hebrew; Aramaic: Onqelos. Oriental square script; Babylonian vocalisation.
Vellum; 1 leaf (minute fragment). 3.8⁺ × 3.8⁺; 4⁺ lines.
[996]

### T-S AS 62.269    1 Samuel 20:15–16; 21:2(?)
Hebrew; Aramaic: Targum Jonathan to Prophets. Oriental square script; Babylonian vocalisation + accents and Tiberian vocalisation.
Vellum; 1 leaf (minute fragment). 4.1⁺ × 2.5⁺; 5⁺ lines.
[997]

### T-S AS 62.277    Jeremiah 28:16–17; Malachi 2:17 – 3:3; 3:5, 7–10; (*haftarot*)
Hebrew; Aramaic: Targum Jonathan to Prophets. Oriental square script; Babylonian vocalisation + accents.
Vellum; 1 leaf; very badly mutilated. 16.9⁺ × 7.8⁺; 2 cols.; 14⁺ lines.
Neither passage is elsewhere attested as a *haftarah*; heading before Malachi: בתרי] עמרה and design in margin ✿.
[998]

### T-S AS 62.287    Isaiah 62:6–9; (*haftarah*)
Hebrew; Aramaic: Targum Jonathan to Prophets. Oriental square script; Babylonian vocalisation + accents.
Vellum; 1 leaf; very badly mutilated; *verso* very badly rubbed. 14.9⁺ × 9.5⁺; 14⁺ lines.
Divine name: Targum ״׳; *verso* illegible; this is the *haftarah* for *parashat niṣavim*.
[999]

### T-S AS 62.290    Amos 3:8; Jeremiah 37:12, 19–20; (*haftarot*)
Hebrew; Aramaic: Targum Jonathan to Prophets. Oriental square script; Babylonian vocalisation + accents.
Vellum; 1 leaf; very badly mutilated. 21.5 × 7.3⁺; [2] cols.; [19–20] lines.
Heading before Jeremiah: [בירמיה וישב יעקב and decorative sign in margin ✿; but this may be mistaken since the Amos passage is attested for *parashat wayeshev*, and Jeremiah 37:12 is not attested at all.
[1000]

### T-S AS 62.292 (= T-S AS 62.299)    Exodus 12:35, 49
Hebrew; Aramaic: Onqelos. Oriental square script; Babylonian vocalisation + accents also Tiberian accents.
Vellum; 1 leaf (minute fragment). 2.5⁺ × 9.3⁺; 3⁺ lines.
[1001]

### T-S AS 62.293    Jeremiah 23:17–24
Hebrew; Aramaic: Targum Jonathan to Prophets. Oriental square script; Babylonian vocalisation + accents.
Vellum; 1 leaf; very badly mutilated. 21.8 × 9.9⁺; [2] cols.; 19 lines.
Divine name: Hebrew tetragrammaton; Targum ״׳.
[1002]

### T-S AS 62.294    Isaiah 37:27, 29, 30, 32
Hebrew; Aramaic: Targum Jonathan to Prophets. Oriental square script; Babylonian vocalisation + accents.
Vellum; 1 leaf; very badly mutilated. 18.7⁺ × 6.4⁺; 17⁺ lines.
[1003]

### T-S AS 62.299 (= T-S AS 62.292)    Exodus 12:40, 44
Hebrew; Aramaic: Onqelos. Oriental square script; Babylonian vocalisation + accents also Tiberian accents.
Vellum; 1 leaf; very badly mutilated. 6.5⁺ × 10.3⁺; 3⁺ lines.
[1004]

### T-S AS 62.304 (= T-S AS 62.318, 342)
Exodus 10:28 – 11:1; 11:5–7
Hebrew; Aramaic: Onqelos. Oriental square script; Babylonian vocalisation + Tiberian accents.
Vellum; 1 leaf; very badly mutilated. 10.1⁺ × 7.0⁺; [2] cols.; 10⁺ lines.
[1005]

### T-S AS 62.306, 307
Fragment of a Hebrew Bible with a single marginal gloss from Onqelos to Numbers 3:51, פריקא תרג.    [1006]

### T-S AS 62.309    Ezekiel 29:8–14 + 21 (Hebrew only in margin)
Hebrew; Aramaic: Targum Jonathan to Prophets. Oriental square script; Babylonian vocalisation + accents.
Vellum; 1 leaf; very badly mutilated. 21.2 × 6.4⁺; 19 lines.
[1007]

### T-S AS 62.310    1 Samuel 12:10–14; 13:8–13 (folio 1); 20:25–7; 21:5–6 (folio 2)
Hebrew; Aramaic: Targum Jonathan to Prophets. Oriental square script; Hebrew with Tiberian vocalisation + accents; Targum with Babylonian vocalisation + accents.
Vellum; 2 leaves (1 bifolium); very badly mutilated. 20.7⁺ × 9.0⁺; 25⁺ lines.
Divine name: Hebrew tetragrammaton; Targum ״׳.
[1008]

**T-S AS 62.311 (= T-S AS 62.463)** Exodus 40:7–10, 12–20

Hebrew; Aramaic: Onqelos. Oriental square script; Babylonian vocalisation + accents; Massorah Magna and Parva.

Vellum; 2 leaves (1 bifolium); mutilated (folio 2 almost entirely missing).   31.0×25.5;  2 cols.;  20 lines.
[1009]

**T-S AS 62.316** Deuteronomy 32:30–32, 36–9

Hebrew; Aramaic: Onqelos. Oriental square script; Babylonian vocalisation + accents (*recto*); script overwritten in darker ink and Tiberian vocalisation on *verso*.

Vellum; 1 leaf; very badly mutilated.  16.4⁺×13.4⁺; 2 cols. (poetic formation);  10⁺ lines.
[1010]

**T-S AS 62.318 (= T-S AS 62.304, 342)**
Exodus 10:20–21, 27–9; 11:5–6; 12:1–2

Hebrew; Aramaic: Onqelos. Oriental square script; Babylonian vocalisation + Tiberian accents.

Vellum; 1 leaf; very badly mutilated.  8.5⁺×12.6⁺; 2 cols.;  10⁺ lines.
[1011]

**T-S AS 62.320 (= T-S AS 62.145, 160, 173)**
Joshua 17:2–3, 6, 9, 13–14

Hebrew; Aramaic: Targum Jonathan to Prophets. Oriental square script; Babylonian vocalisation + accents.

Vellum; 1 leaf; very badly mutilated.  8.0⁺×8.5⁺; 2 cols.;  9⁺ lines.
[1012]

**T-S AS 62.324** Deuteronomy 19:13–14, 18–19

Hebrew; Aramaic: Onqelos. Oriental square script; Babylonian vocalisation.

Vellum; 1 leaf; very badly mutilated.  4.4⁺×8.3⁺; 2 cols.;  5⁺ lines.
[1013]

**T-S AS 62.335** Numbers 22:14–15, 19

Hebrew; Aramaic: Onqelos. Oriental square script; Hebrew with Babylonian vocalisation also Tiberian vocalisation + accents; Onqelos with Babylonian vocalisation; Massorah Magna.

Vellum; 1 leaf; very badly mutilated.  7.4⁺×9.7⁺; 4⁺ lines.

Divine name: Hebrew tetragrammaton; Onqelos ייי.
[1014]

**T-S AS 62.336** Exodus 6:29–30; 7:13–15

Hebrew; Aramaic: Onqelos. Oriental square script; Babylonian vocalisation + accents also Tiberian accents.

Vellum; 1 leaf; very badly mutilated.  13.2⁺×6.7⁺; 12⁺ lines.
[1015]

**T-S AS 62.342 (= T-S AS 62.304, 318)**
Exodus 10:21–3; 11:1, 7; 12:3–4

Hebrew; Aramaic: Onqelos. Oriental square script; Babylonian vocalisation + accents also Tiberian accents.

Vellum; 1 leaf; very badly mutilated.  8.2⁺×10.0⁺; 2 cols.;  10⁺ lines.
[1016]

**T-S AS 62.344** Genesis 17:8–11, 15–16, 20–21; 17:26 – 18:2

Hebrew; Aramaic: Onqelos. Oriental square script; Babylonian vocalisation + accents.

Vellum; 1 leaf; very badly mutilated.  10.5⁺×[19.4]; 2 cols.;  11⁺ lines.

Divine name: Hebrew tetragrammaton; Onqelos ייי; cipher קטו for number of verses in *parashat lekh lekha* after 17:27; Nehardean variant to Onqelos in margin at 17:27 לנ אתגזרו; quotation of midrash in margin at 18:1 מלמד שממרא ... עצה תחילה ... כך אברהם[...].
[1017]

**T-S AS 62.353** Exodus 2:14 (*recto*)

Hebrew; Aramaic: Onqelos. Oriental square script; Hebrew with Babylonian vocalisation also Tiberian vocalisation + accents; Onqelos with Babylonian vocalisation.

Vellum; 1 leaf (minute fragment); badly rubbed. 5.3⁺×5.3⁺;  3⁺ lines.

*Verso* entirely rubbed and illegible.
[1018]

**T-S AS 62.360** Exodus 13:11–12, 17

Hebrew; Aramaic: Onqelos. Oriental square script; Babylonian vocalisation.

Vellum; 1 leaf; very badly mutilated.  6.3⁺×8.6⁺; 4⁺ lines.
[1019]

**T-S AS 62.361** Numbers 8:11–22; 9:1–14

Aramaic: Onqelos (+ sporadic Hebrew lemmata). Oriental square script; sporadic Babylonian vocalisation.

Vellum; 1 leaf; badly mutilated and rubbed. 17.7⁺×12.5⁺;  22 lines.

Divine name: יי; 9:9 abbreviated: ומליל דב (perhaps for דבירא?).
[1020]

**T-S AS 62.362, 363 (= T-S AS 62.373)**
Exodus 14:11–13, 16, 23–4

Hebrew; Aramaic: Onqelos. Oriental square script; Hebrew with Babylonian vocalisation + accents also Tiberian vocalisation + accents; Onqelos with Babylonian vocalisation + accents.

Vellum; 1 leaf (torn into two parts, separately conserved); very badly mutilated and rubbed.  17.7⁺×13.5⁺; 2 cols.;  17⁺ lines.
[1021]

**T-S AS 62.365**  Ezekiel 34:6, 9–10
Hebrew; Aramaic: Targum Jonathan to Prophets. Oriental square script; Babylonian vocalisation and Tiberian vocalisation.

Vellum; 1 leaf (minute fragment). 3.3⁺ × 5.7⁺; 3⁺ lines. [1022]

**T-S AS 62.366**  Deuteronomy 14:26; 15:14
Hebrew; Aramaic: Onqelos. Oriental square script; Babylonian vocalisation + accents.

Vellum; 1 leaf (minute fragment). 5.3⁺ × 3.9⁺; 5⁺ lines. [1023]

**T-S AS 62.367**  Hosea 10:10–11, 14–15
Hebrew; Aramaic: Targum Jonathan to Prophets. Oriental square script; sporadic Babylonian vocalisation.

Vellum; 1 leaf; very badly mutilated. 5.3⁺ × 5.8⁺; 7⁺ lines.

Variant in Targum to 10:14 ביא for בין. [1024]

**T-S AS 62.370**  1 Samuel 20:24–5; 21:3–5
Hebrew; Aramaic: Targum Jonathan to Prophets. Oriental square script; Hebrew with Tiberian vocalisation + accents; Targum with Babylonian vocalisation + accents.

Vellum; 1 leaf; very badly mutilated. 7.6⁺ × 6.5⁺; 9⁺ lines. [1025]

**T-S AS 62.371**  1 Samuel 19:9–10 (*recto*)
Hebrew; Aramaic: Targum Jonathan to Prophets. Oriental square script; Babylonian vocalisation (?) + accents and traces of Tiberian vocalisation.

Vellum; 1 leaf; very badly mutilated and rubbed. 8.0⁺ × 5.4⁺; 4⁺ lines.

*Verso* entirely rubbed and illegible. [1026]

**T-S AS 62.373**  (= T-S AS 62.362, 363)
Exodus 14:13, 24

Minute fragment, 1.8⁺ × 5.6⁺; see description at T-S AS 62.362, 363 above. [1027]

**T-S AS 62.378**  (= T-S AS 62.382, 408)
Isaiah 62:6–7 (*recto*)
Hebrew; Aramaic: Targum Jonathan to Prophets. Oriental square script; Babylonian vocalisation + accents.

Vellum; 1 leaf (minute fragment). 6.8⁺ × 4.3⁺; [2] cols.; 3⁺ lines.
*Verso* illegible. [1028]

**T-S AS 62.381**  Jeremiah 5:27; 6:10
Hebrew; Aramaic: Targum Jonathan to Prophets. Oriental square script; Babylonian vocalisation; Massorah Magna.

Vellum; 1 leaf (minute fragment). 3.7⁺ × 8.7⁺; 1 line (+ 3 lines of Massorah). [1029]

**T-S AS 62.382**  (= T-S AS 62.378, 408)
Isaiah 62:9 (*recto*)

Vellum; 1 leaf; very badly mutilated. 5.5⁺ × 12.3⁺; 2 cols.; 3⁺ lines.
*Verso* illegible; see T-S AS 62.378 above. [1030]

**T-S AS 62.390**  Targum – unidentified
Hebrew; Aramaic. Oriental square script; Babylonian vocalisation + accents.

Vellum; 1 leaf (minute fragment). 3.7⁺ × 2.0⁺; 4⁺ lines. [1031]

**T-S AS 62.395**  Targum – unidentified
Hebrew; Aramaic. Oriental square script; Babylonian vocalisation.

Vellum; 1 leaf (minute fragment). 4.2⁺ × 3.5⁺; 4⁺ lines.
Only legible words: [הוֹצֵאתִי ... אפיקית. [1032]

**T-S AS 62.408**  (= T-S AS 62.378, 382)
Isaiah 62:5, 8–9 (*recto*)
Hebrew; Aramaic: Targum Jonathan to Prophets. Oriental square script; Babylonian vocalisation.

Vellum; 1 leaf; very badly mutilated and rubbed. 8.0⁺ × 6.8⁺; 2 cols.; 8⁺ lines.
*Verso* illegible. [1033]

**T-S AS 62.410**  Zechariah 2:4, 6–8
Hebrew; Aramaic: Targum Jonathan to Prophets. Oriental square script; sporadic Babylonian vocalisation.

Vellum; 1 leaf; very badly mutilated. 12.4⁺ × 3.5⁺; 13⁺ lines. [1034]

**T-S AS 62.414–416**  Deuteronomy 28:12, 15 (AS 62.416); 28:31, 36 (AS 62.414); 28:52, 56 (AS 62.415)
Hebrew; Aramaic: Onqelos. Oriental square script; Babylonian vocalisation.

Vellum; 1 leaf (torn into three minute parts, separately conserved). 3.3⁺ × 3.5⁺; 4⁺ lines. [1035]

**T-S AS 62.420**  Isaiah 30:29; 31:2
Aramaic: Targum Jonathan to Prophets. Oriental square script; Babylonian vocalisation.

Vellum; 1 leaf (minute fragment). 2.8⁺ × 4.3⁺; 2⁺ lines. [1036]

**T-S AS 62.425**  Genesis 42:33–4; 43:10–11
Hebrew; Aramaic: Onqelos. Oriental square script; Babylonian vocalisation + accents.

Vellum; 1 leaf; very badly mutilated. 7.5⁺ × 9.2⁺; 6⁺ lines. [1037]

**T-S AS 62.432**  Numbers 19:3–4, 9–10
Hebrew; Aramaic: Onqelos.   Oriental square script; Babylonian vocalisation + accents.
Vellum; 1 leaf; very badly mutilated.   6.5⁺ × 10.8⁺; 6⁺ lines.   [1038]

**T-S AS 62.433–435**  Deuteronomy 22:24–6; 23:19–22 (AS 62.435 (folio 1); AS 62.434); 23:26 – 24:3; 24:22 – 25:3 (AS 62.435 (folio 2); AS 62.433)
Hebrew; Aramaic: Onqelos.   Oriental square script; Babylonian vocalisation.
Vellum; 2 leaves (1 bifolium + 2 smaller fragments); very badly mutilated and rubbed.   [13.8⁺] × 8.5⁺;   [12⁺] lines.
Divine name: Hebrew tetragrammaton; Onqelos ״.   [1039]

**T-S AS 62.436**  Zechariah 1:1; 2:2–4
Hebrew; Aramaic: Targum Jonathan to Prophets. Oriental square script; Babylonian vocalisation + accents.
Vellum; 1 leaf; very badly mutilated.   9.9⁺ × 2.8⁺; 10⁺ lines.   [1040]

**T-S AS 62.440**  Exodus 11:6; 12:11–12
Hebrew; Aramaic: Onqelos.   Oriental square script; Babylonian vocalisation + accents.
Vellum; 1 leaf; very badly mutilated.   9.7⁺ × 9.0⁺; 8⁺ lines.
Variant readings in margin of *verso* בֹּיֹדְטֹן אוֹ (12:11) and midrashic quote אין לך כל אומה שהיא לוקה...  [1041]

**T-S AS 62.441**  Genesis 22:8, 12–13
Hebrew; Aramaic: Onqelos.   Oriental square script; Babylonian vocalisation.
Vellum; 1 leaf; very badly mutilated, barely legible. 9.2⁺ × 6.1⁺;   7⁺ lines.   [1042]

**T-S AS 62.458**  Deuteronomy 19:14, 19–20
Hebrew; Aramaic: Onqelos.   Oriental square script; Babylonian vocalisation.
Vellum; 1 leaf (minute fragment).   2.0⁺ × 5.6⁺;   2⁺ lines.   [1043]

**T-S AS 62.463 (= T-S AS 62.311)**  Exodus 40:10–12, 15–16
Hebrew; Aramaic: Onqelos.   Oriental square script; Babylonian vocalisation.
Vellum; 1 leaf; very badly mutilated, barely legible. 16.5⁺ × 7.3⁺;   12⁺ lines.
Massoretic note in margin at 40:13 or 14.   [1044]

**T-S AS 62.464**  Genesis 8:19–20; 9:2, 9–10, 16
Hebrew; Aramaic: Onqelos.   Oriental square script; Babylonian vocalisation + accents; Massorah Magna.
Vellum; 1 leaf; very badly mutilated.   7.5⁺ × 15.8⁺; 2 cols.;   5⁺ lines.
List of commandments to primevals and Patriarchs in bottom margin of *verso*: אדם הראשון נצטווה על ו׳ מצות נח על איבר מן החי אברהם על המילה יצחק חינכה(?) לח׳ יעקב על גיד הנשה [ ] יהודה על היבום אבל לא [ ]; also Massorah to Onqelos on *recto* (bottom margin); [ ] יהיה דמת (to 9:3 or 9:16).   [1045]

**T-S AS 62.465, 466, 476, 477**  1 Samuel 14:31–3, 39–40 (AS 62.466); 15:11–12, 20 (AS 62.477); 16:7–8 (AS 62.476, *recto*); 17:26–7 (AS 62.465, *recto*)
Hebrew; Aramaic: Targum Jonathan to Prophets. Oriental square script; Babylonian vocalisation + accents.
Vellum; torn into four small parts, separately conserved.   7.3⁺ × 4.3⁺;   9⁺ lines.   [1046]

**T-S AS 62.473**  Exodus 3:6, 9–10, 14, 18
Hebrew; Aramaic: Onqelos.   Oriental square script; Babylonian vocalisation + accents.
Vellum; 1 leaf; very badly mutilated and stained. 7.3⁺ × 10.3⁺;   2 cols.;   8⁺ lines.   [1047]

**T-S AS 62.476, 477**
See T-S AS 62.465 above.   [1048]

**T-S AS 62.484**  Leviticus 1:9–11; 1:16 – 2:1
Hebrew; Aramaic: Onqelos.   Oriental square script; sporadic Babylonian vocalisation + accents.
Vellum; 1 leaf; very badly mutilated.   7.3⁺ × 6.8⁺; 9⁺ lines.
Divine name: Hebrew tetragrammaton.   [1049]

**T-S AS 62.496**  Exodus 12:11–12; 12:29 (or 11:5)
Hebrew; Aramaic: Onqelos.   Oriental square script; sporadic Babylonian vocalisation + accents.
Vellum; 1 leaf (minute fragment).   5.1⁺ × 4.2⁺;   5⁺ lines.   [1050]

**T-S AS 62.503**  Joshua 24:7–12, 15
Hebrew; Aramaic: Targum Jonathan to Prophets. Oriental square script; Babylonian vocalisation + accents.
Vellum; 1 leaf; very badly mutilated.   17.0⁺ × 21.5; 2 cols.;   13⁺ lines.   [1051]

**T-S AS 62.506–509**  Exodus 40:22–4, 30–31
Hebrew; Aramaic: Onqelos.   Oriental square script; sporadic Babylonian vocalisation.
Vellum; 1 leaf; torn into four minute parts, separately conserved.   3.1⁺ × 2.7⁺;   3⁺ lines.
Divine name: Hebrew tetragrammaton; Onqelos ״׳.   [1052]

## T-S AS 62.511 (= T-S AS 62.512(?))

Numbers 31:51–4; 32:5–8, 14–16, 22(?)(*recto*)
Hebrew; Aramaic: Onqelos.    Oriental square script; Babylonian vocalisation; traces of Massorah Magna in bottom margin of column 2.

Leather scroll; badly mutilated.    15.5⁺ × 36.2⁺; 4 cols.;   (col. 4 almost entirely missing).

Divine name: Hebrew tetragrammaton; Onqelos יי; *verso* blank.    [1053]

## T-S AS 62.512 (= T-S AS 62.511(?))

Genesis 46:12–20, 29–31 (*recto*)
Hebrew; Aramaic: Onqelos.    Oriental square script; Babylonian vocalisation.

Leather scroll; very badly mutilated.   14.9⁺ × 23.3⁺; 3 cols. (col. 1 almost entirely missing, and col. 3 relatively narrow (6.1 )).

*Verso* blank.    [1054]

## T-S AS 62.514    Genesis 43:27–9

Hebrew; Aramaic: Onqelos.    Oriental square script; traces of Babylonian vocalisation.

Leather (scroll?); minute fragment.    5.4⁺ × 3.5⁺; 6⁺ lines.    [1055]

## T-S AS 62.529    Genesis 5:26, 30–31; 6:3(?)

Hebrew; Aramaic: Onqelos.    Oriental square script; Babylonian vocalisation + accents; Massorah Parva.

Vellum; 1 leaf; very badly mutilated.    7.7⁺ × 10.9⁺; 2 cols.;   6⁺ lines.    [1056]

## T-S AS 62.531    Genesis 47:13–15, 18–19, 24, 29–30

Hebrew; Aramaic: Onqelos.    Oriental square script; Babylonian vocalisation + accents.

Vellum; 1 leaf; very badly mutilated.    8.9⁺ × 9.5⁺; 2 cols.;   11⁺ lines.    [1057]

## T-S AS 62.535–537    Numbers 19:9–10, 12–13, 16–18; 19:22 – 20:1; 20:3–8

Hebrew; Aramaic: Onqelos.    Oriental square script; sporadic Babylonian vocalisation + accents..

Vellum; 1 leaf (torn into three parts, separately conserved); very badly mutilated.   10.8⁺ × 10.0⁺; 2 cols.;   12⁺ lines.

Divine name: Hebrew tetragrammaton; midrashic passage in margin (T-S AS 62.535, *verso*) at 20:1 מפני מה נסמכה מיתת מרים לפרה אדֹ לומר לך מה פרה [ ] סמוך למיתה קבורה. Hebrew and Aramaic variants in margin of *recto* of AS 62.535.    [1058]

## T-S AS 62.538, 539 (= T-S AS 62.542)

Genesis 18:8–9, 13–14 (AS 62.539); 24–5, 28–9, 32–3; 19:2–3 (AS 62.538)
Hebrew; Aramaic: Onqelos.    Oriental square script; Babylonian vocalisation + accents also Tiberian vocalisation.

Vellum; 1 leaf; very badly mutilated, barely legible. 10.4⁺ × 9.5⁺;   2 cols.;   12⁺ lines.

Massoretic note at 18:9: נקוד.    [1059]

## T-S AS 62.541 (= T-S AS 62.543–547)

1 Samuel 17:42–3; 18:6–10
Hebrew; Aramaic: Targum Jonathan to Prophets. Oriental square script; Babylonian vocalisation + accents and Tiberian vocalisation.

Vellum; 1 leaf; very badly mutilated and rubbed (*recto* almost illegible).    13.1⁺ × 5.6⁺;   16⁺ lines.    [1060]

## T-S AS 62.542 (= T-S AS 62.538, 539)

Genesis 16:11–12, 15–16; 17:6
Hebrew; Aramaic: Onqelos.    Oriental square script; Babylonian vocalisation + accents.

Vellum; 1 leaf; very badly mutilated.    9.9⁺ × 8.0⁺; 2 cols.;   11⁺ lines.

Decorative *samekh* in margin at 17:1 denotes triennial *sidra*. ✸.    [1061]

## T-S AS 62.543–547 (= T-S AS 62.541)

1 Samuel 13:16–18; 14:18–20 (AS 62.544); 14:26–7, 49–52 (AS 62.545); 15:6–8, 29 (AS 62.546); 16:1–2; 17:3–6, 11–12(?), 35–7 (AS 62.547); 19:10–11 (AS 62.543, *recto*)
Hebrew; Aramaic: Targum Jonathan to Prophets. Oriental square script; sporadic Babylonian vocalisation + accents also Tiberian vocalisation + accents (Hebrew only, in lighter ink).

Vellum; 6(?) leaves (1 bifolium); very badly mutilated and rubbed.    14.2⁺ × 5.7⁺;   15⁺ lines.

Divine name: Hebrew tetragrammaton.    [1062]

## T-S AS 62.552–921

Very minute scraps, some of which contain isolated words in Aramaic and may possibly be targumic; e.g., 584, 587, 589, 599, 601, 608, 610, 617, 643, 645, 772, 774.    [1063]

## T-S AS 63.5    Leviticus 4:28–34

Hebrew; Aramaic: Onqelos.    Oriental square script; Tiberian vocalisation; traces of Palestinian vocalisation.

Vellum; 1 leaf; very badly mutilated and rubbed. 15.7 × 10.5⁺;   12 lines.    [1064]

### T-S AS 63.24 (= T-S 20.155; NS 286.1; AS 63.51, 72, 85, 95, 96, 117, 129, 153; AS 69.241)   Exodus 22:19–21
Aramaic: Palestinian Targum (+ Hebrew lemmata).   Oriental square script; sporadic Palestinian vocalisation also sporadic Tiberian vocalisation + accents.

Vellum scroll; badly mutilated.   4.0⁺ × 9.0⁺; [6⁺] cols.; [35] lines.

*Verso* originally blank, contains lectionary with verses from *hafṭarot* written in a different hand vertically in relation to text on *recto*.

Klein *GMPT* I, pp.293–95; *HUCA* L, pp.149–64. See plate 8.   [1065]

### T-S AS 63.51 (= T-S 20.155 et al.)   Exodus 21:13–18, 34–5
Aramaic: Palestinian Targum (+ Hebrew lemmata).

Vellum scroll, 10.4⁺ × 8.3⁺; see description at T-S AS 63.24 above.

Klein *GMPT* I, p.287.   [1066]

### T-S AS 63.72, 85, 95 (= T-S 20.155 et al.)
Exodus 4:7–11

Aramaic: Palestinian Targum (+ Hebrew lemmata).

Vellum scroll, three small fragments: 4.6⁺ × 6.1⁺, 2.5⁺ × 2.8⁺, 5.0⁺ × 6.8⁺; all part of the same column; see description at T-S AS 63.24 above.

Klein *GMPT* I, p.173.   [1067]

### T-S AS 63.96 (= T-S 20.155 et al.)   Exodus 21:26–33
Aramaic: Palestinian Targum (+ Hebrew lemmata).

Vellum scroll, 11.2⁺ × 10.3⁺; see description at T-S AS 63.24 above.

Klein *GMPT* I, pp.285–87.   [1068]

### T-S AS 63.117, 129 (= T-S 20.155 et al.)
Exodus 22:17–19

Aramaic: Palestinian Targum (+ Hebrew lemmata).

Vellum scroll, two small fragments: 3.7⁺ × 4.5⁺, 2.4⁺ × 4.2⁺; see description at T-S AS 63.24 above.

Klein *GMPT* I, p.293. See plate 8.   [1069]

### T-S AS 63.153 (= T-S 20.155 et al.)   Exodus 21:30–36
Aramaic: Palestinian Targum (+ Hebrew lemmata).

Vellum scroll, 10.2⁺ × 10.5⁺; see description at T-S AS 63.24 above.

Klein *GMPT* I, p.287.   [1070]

### T-S AS 64.13 (= T-S AS 64.57, 218, 237)
Genesis 44:4–9, 12–15, 17–21 (including *tosefta* to 44:18)

Hebrew; Aramaic: Onqelos.   Ashkenazi/Italian square script; Hebrew with Tiberian vocalisation + accents; Onqelos unpointed.

Vellum; 1 leaf; badly mutilated and stained. 17.7⁺ × 20.3;   2 cols.;   20⁺ lines.

Klein *GMPT* I, p.143 (*tosefta* only).   [1071]

### T-S AS 64.17   Leviticus 14:31–3, 36–7
Hebrew; Aramaic: Onqelos.   Oriental square script; Tiberian vocalisation + accents.

Vellum; 1 leaf; very badly mutilated.   8.3⁺ × 8.5⁺; 8⁺ lines.   [1072]

### T-S AS 64.27 (= T-S B8.7)   Genesis 48:10–11, 20
Hebrew; Aramaic: Palestinian Targum.   Oriental square script; Tiberian vocalisation + accents; Massorah Magna and Parva.

Vellum; 1 leaf; badly mutilated.   10.6⁺ × 11.3⁺; [3] cols.;   [24] lines.

Klein *Sefarad* XLIX, pp.123–33.   [1073]

### T-S AS 64.34   Deuteronomy 26:10–11, 13–14; 26:19 – 27:1
Hebrew; Aramaic: Onqelos.   Oriental square script; Tiberian vocalisation + accents; Massorah Parva.

Vellum; 1 leaf; very badly mutilated.   12.8⁺ × 9.9⁺; 2 cols.;   14⁺ lines.

Divine name: Hebrew tetragrammaton; Onqelos ײ.   [1074]

### T-S AS 64.57 (= T-S AS 64.13, 218, 237)
Genesis 43:18–21; 43:34 – 44:3

Hebrew; Aramaic: Onqelos.   Ashkenazi/Italian square script; Hebrew with Tiberian vocalisation + accents; Onqelos unpointed.

Vellum; 1 leaf; very badly mutilated.   14.3⁺ × 8.0⁺; [2] cols.;   18⁺ lines.   [1075]

### T-S AS 64.59   Leviticus 26:26, 31–3, 36–7, 40
Hebrew; Aramaic: Onqelos.   Oriental square script; Tiberian vocalisation + accents.

Vellum; 1 leaf; very badly mutilated.   15.3⁺ × [24.8]; 2 cols.;   12⁺ lines.

Onqelos to 26:32 omitted.   [1076]

### T-S AS 64.66 (= T-S AS 66.124)   Exodus 30:6–9, 18–20
Hebrew; Aramaic: Onqelos.   Ashkenazi/Italian square script; Hebrew with Tiberian vocalisation + accents; Onqelos unpointed.

**[T-S AS 64.66 (= T-S AS 66.124), cont.]**
Vellum; 1 leaf; very badly mutilated. 7.0⁺ × 7.8⁺; 8⁺ lines.
Divine name: Hebrew tetragrammaton. [1077]

**T-S AS 64.109** Exodus 37:25–6; 37:29 – 38:1
Hebrew; Aramaic: Onqelos. Oriental square script; Tiberian vocalisation + accents.
Vellum; 1 leaf; very badly mutilated. 8.3⁺ × 8.3⁺; 7⁺ lines. [1078]

**T-S AS 64.123** Numbers 24:23–4; 25:18 – 26:1
Hebrew; Aramaic: Onqelos. Oriental square script; Tiberian vocalisation + accents.
Vellum; 1 leaf; very badly mutilated and rubbed. 5.4⁺ × 6.0⁺; 5⁺ lines. [1079]

**T-S AS 64.141, 143** Leviticus 5:1–2, 4–6 (AS 64.143); 5:11, 22–3 (AS 64.141)
Hebrew; Aramaic: Onqelos. Oriental square script; Tiberian vocalisation + accents.
Vellum; 1 leaf (torn into two parts, separately conserved); very badly mutilated. 10.7⁺ × [20] (larger); [2] cols.; 9⁺ lines. [1080]

**T-S AS 64.181** Exodus 36:29–30, 34–5
Hebrew; Aramaic: Onqelos. Oriental square script; Tiberian vocalisation + accents.
Vellum; 1 leaf; very badly mutilated. 9.4⁺ × 10.9⁺; [2] cols.; 8⁺ lines. [1081]

**T-S AS 64.202** Deuteronomy 31:26–7; 32:8–11, 17–20, 28–31
Hebrew; Aramaic: Onqelos. Oriental square script; Tiberian vocalisation + accents (very faint); Massorah Magna.
Vellum; 2 leaves (1 bifolium); very badly mutilated and rubbed. 9.3⁺ × [22.4]; 2 cols. (Deuteronomy 32 single column in poetry format); 7⁺ lines.
Divine name: Hebrew tetragrammaton; Onqelos ייי. [1082]

**T-S AS 64.218 (= T-S AS 64.13, 57, 237)**
Genesis 45:10–14, 17–19, 22–5; 45:27 – 46:2
Hebrew; Aramaic: Onqelos. Ashkenazi/Italian square script; Hebrew with Tiberian vocalisation + accents; Onqelos unpointed.
Vellum; 1 leaf; very badly mutilated and rubbed. 16.3⁺ × 18.4⁺; 2 cols.; 19⁺ lines. [1083]

**T-S AS 64.237 (= T-S AS 64.13, 57, 218)**
Genesis 44:21–6, 28–31; 44:34 – 45:8
Hebrew; Aramaic: Onqelos.
Vellum; 1 leaf; badly mutilated and rubbed. 19.0⁺ × 18.0⁺; 2 cols.; 20⁺ lines.
Divine name: Hebrew אלהים; Onqelos ייי; see T-S AS 64.218 above. [1084]

**T-S AS 64.239 (= T-S B8.12)** Exodus 5:6–7, 18–19
Hebrew; Aramaic: Palestinian Targum. Oriental square script; Tiberian vocalisation + accents.
Vellum; 1 leaf; very badly mutilated. 6.3⁺ × 8.5⁺; [3] cols.; 6⁺ lines.
Klein *Sefarad* XLIX, pp.123–133. [1085]

**T-S AS 65.19** Isaiah 48:18–19; Jeremiah 23:20; Isaiah 33:23; (*haftarot*)
Hebrew; Aramaic: Targum Jonathan to Prophets. Oriental square script; Tiberian vocalisation + accents (Hebrew only, partly overwritten in darker ink).
Vellum; 1 leaf; very badly mutilated. 6.9⁺ × 5.3⁺; 2 cols.; 6⁺ lines. [1086]

**T-S AS 65.68** Deuteronomy 32:44; 32:50 – 33:1; 33:6–9
Hebrew; Aramaic: Onqelos. Oriental linear square script; sporadic Tiberian vocalisation + accents; Massorah Parva.
Vellum; 1 leaf; very badly mutilated. 10.6⁺ × 9.1⁺; 2 cols.; 15⁺ lines.
Divine name: Onqelos יי. [1087]

**T-S AS 66.14 (= T-S AS 67.26)** Exodus 20:15–18
Aramaic: Onqelos (in shorthand). Oriental semi-cursive script; sporadic Tiberian vocalisation.
Paper; 1 leaf; mutilated. 16.6 × 6.8⁺; 16 lines.
Divine name: ℒ ; *verso* contains only four lines, remainder blank. [1088]

**T-S AS 66.23 (= T-S AS 66.32)** 2 Kings 4:2–5, 14–18; (*haftarah*)
Hebrew; Aramaic: Targum Jonathan to Prophets. Oriental square script; sporadic Tiberian vocalisation.
Vellum; 1 leaf; very badly mutilated. 7.5⁺ × 6.8⁺; 9⁺ lines.
This is the *haftarah* for *parashat wayera'*. [1089]

**T-S AS 66.32 (= T-S AS 66.23)** Malachi 1:7–10; 3:4; Hosea 11:7–9; (*haftarot*)
Hebrew; Aramaic: Targum Jonathan to Prophets. Oriental square script; sporadic Tiberian vocalisation.
Vellum; 1 leaf. 11.3⁺ × 6.5⁺; 12⁺ lines.
Divine name: Hebrew tetragrammaton; Targum ייי; these are the *haftarot* for *parashot toledot* and *wayese'* respectively. [1090]

**T-S AS 66.58**  Habakkuk 3:16–19; Jeremiah 6:16–17; 8:13 – 9:4; (*haftarot*)

Hebrew; Aramaic: Targum Jonathan to Prophets. Oriental square script; Hebrew with Tiberian vocalisation + accents (sporadic on *recto*); Targum unpointed; Massorah Parva.

Vellum; 1 leaf; mutilated and badly rubbed. 25.6 × 21.6⁺; 23–4 lines.

Divine name: Hebrew tetragrammaton; Targum ייי; Jeremiah 8:17 omitted; these are *haftarot* for second day Pentecost and Ninth of Av respectively; heading (*recto*, line 10); [ ] בירמיה [ ] באב ט [ ].  [1091]

**T-S AS 66.124** (= T-S AS 64.66)  Exodus 30:32–8; 31:9–13

Hebrew; Aramaic: Onqelos. Ashkenazi/Italian square script; Hebrew with Tiberian vocalisation + accents; Onqelos unpointed.

Vellum; 1 leaf; very badly mutilated. 10.9⁺ × 8.0⁺; 12⁺ lines.

Divine name: Hebrew tetragrammaton.  [1092]

**T-S AS 66.142**  Exodus 20:15/18–16/19; 21:11–13

Hebrew; Aramaic: Onqelos. Oriental square script; unpointed.

Vellum; 1 leaf; very badly mutilated and rubbed. 9.2⁺ × 10.2⁺; 2 cols.; 7⁺ lines.  [1093]

**T-S AS 66.146** (= T-S AS 66.184; AS 67.83)  2 Kings 4:26–31, 34–5; (*haftarah*)

Hebrew; Aramaic: Targum Jonathan to Prophets. Oriental square script; Hebrew with Tiberian vocalisation + accents; Targum with Tiberian vocalisation.

Vellum; 1 leaf; very badly mutilated. 17.8⁺ × 13.0⁺; 2 cols.; 16⁺ lines.

Divine name: Hebrew tetragrammaton; Targum ייי; this is the *haftarah* for *parashat wayera'*.  [1094]

**T-S AS 66.177**  Numbers 14:23–5

Hebrew; Aramaic: Onqelos. Oriental square script; Hebrew with Tiberian vocalisation + accents; Targum with Tiberian vocalisation.

Vellum; 1 leaf; mutilated. 13.9⁺ × 11.8; 12⁺ lines.

Variant in 14:24 ממרי in text, דחלתי in margin.  [1095]

**T-S AS 66.184** (= T-S AS 66.146; AS 67.83)  Isaiah 41:10–11, 14, 16–17; 2 Kings 4:1; (*haftarot*)

Hebrew; Aramaic: Targum Jonathan to Prophets. Oriental square script; Tiberian vocalisation + accents.

Vellum; 1 leaf; very badly mutilated. 9.0⁺ × 13.7⁺; 2 cols.; 7⁺ lines.

Divine name: Hebrew tetragrammaton; these are *haftarot* for *parashot lekh lekha* and *wayera'*.  [1096]

**T-S AS 66.187** (= T-S B8.5)  Exodus 7:15–17, 20

Hebrew; Aramaic: Palestinian Targum. Oriental square script; Tiberian vocalisation + accents.

Vellum; 1 leaf; very badly mutilated. 7.4⁺ × 9.7⁺; [3] cols.; 3⁺ lines.

Divine name: Hebrew tetragrammaton; *recto* overwritten in darker ink; this is part of col.2 of T-S B8.5.

Klein *Sefarad* XLIX, pp.123–133.  [1097]

**T-S AS 67.26** (= T-S AS 66.14)  Exodus 19:21 – 20:14/17

Aramaic: Onqelos (abbreviated in shorthand). Oriental semi-cursive script; sporadic Tiberian vocalisation.

Paper; 2 leaves (1 bifolium); slightly rubbed. 16.9 × 6.3; 17–18 lines.

Divine name: ל/ ו. See plate 17.  [1098]

**T-S AS 67.83** (= T-S AS 66.146, 184)  Isaiah 42:14–16; 54:1–2, 9–15; (*haftarot*)

Hebrew; Aramaic: Targum Jonathan to Prophets. Oriental square script; unpointed.

Vellum; 1 leaf; very badly mutilated. 11.8⁺ × 16.9⁺; 14⁺ lines.

Divine name: Hebrew tetragrammaton; Targum ייי; these are *haftarot* for *parashot bere'shit* and *noah*; heading: אלה תולדות {נח} בישעיה (*recto*, line 9).  [1099]

**T-S AS 67.101** (= T-S AS 19.133, 138, 215; AS 67.179)  2 Kings 17:15–18, 29–32

Hebrew (main text); Aramaic: Targum Jonathan to Prophets (added in margins). Oriental script; Hebrew square with Tiberian vocalisation + accents; Targum linear square with Tiberian vocalisation (in darker ink).

Vellum; 1 leaf; very badly mutilated. 10.5⁺ × 15.3⁺; [3] cols.; 7⁺ lines; (Hebrew).

Divine name: Hebrew tetragrammaton; Targum ייי.  [1100]

**T-S AS 67.115**  Numbers 14:34 – 15:15

Aramaic: Onqelos. Oriental square script; very sporadic Tiberian vocalisation (added in darker ink).

Vellum; 1 leaf; very badly mutilated and rubbed. 20.0 × 9.9⁺; 20 lines.

Divine name: יי.  [1101]

**T-S AS 67.179** (= T-S AS 19.133, 138, 215; AS 67.101)    2 Kings 17:18–20, 38–40

Hebrew (main text); Aramaic: Targum Jonathan to Prophets (added in margins).

One leaf (fragment, part of same leaf as T-S AS 67.101), 10.3⁺ × 8.1⁺; see description at T-S AS 67.101 above.

[1102]

**T-S AS 68.42** (= T-S B9.10; NS 116.77)

Exodus 35:18–29; 35:31 – 36:4

Aramaic: Onqelos (extract, Fragment-targum). Oriental square script; Tiberian vocalisation.

Vellum; 1 leaf; badly mutilated.    9.0⁺ × 9.3⁺;    13⁺ lines.
Divine name: יי.    [1103]

**T-S AS 68.83** (= T-S B8.10)    Genesis 37:8–11, 13–14, 16–17

Hebrew; Aramaic: Palestinian Targum. Oriental square script; Tiberian vocalisation + accents; Massorah Parva.

Vellum; 1 leaf; very badly mutilated, *recto* rubbed. 18.0⁺ × 19.0⁺;    3 cols.;    [25–6] lines.

Midrashic passage in bottom margin: אמר הקבה לראובן ...אתה.

Klein *Sefarad* XLIX, pp. 123–133.    [1104]

**T-S AS 68.110**    Exodus 19:19–20, 24; 20:4–5, 9–10

Hebrew; Aramaic: Onqelos. Oriental square script; Tiberian vocalisation + accents.

Vellum; 1 leaf; very badly mutilated. 5.8⁺ × [20.2]; 2 cols.;    4⁺ lines.

Divine name: Hebrew tetragrammaton; Onqelos יי/ייי.    [1105]

**T-S AS 68.144** (= T-S B8.4; AS 68.224)

Exodus 39:32–40, 40:2–12

Aramaic: Palestinian Targum (+ sporadic Hebrew lemmata). Oriental square script; sporadic Tiberian accents (disjunctives).

Vellum; 1 leaf; very badly mutilated.    14.6⁺ × 16.1; 15⁺ lines.

Vestige of decorative *samekh* in margin and beginning of line blank at 39:33 (*recto*, line 3) denotes triennial *sidra*.

Klein *Sefarad* XLIX, pp. 123–133.    [1106]

**T-S AS 68.224** (= T-S B8.4; AS 68.144)

Exodus 36:8–13, 22–9

Aramaic: Palestinian Targum. Oriental square script; sporadic Tiberian accents (disjunctives).

Vellum; 1 leaf (minute fragment).    8.0⁺ × 9.0⁺; 10⁺ lines.

Klein *Sefarad* XLIX, pp. 123–133.    [1107]

**T-S AS 68.234**    Deuteronomy 29:2, 5(?), 13–15

Hebrew; Aramaic: Palestinian Targum. Oriental square script; Tiberian vocalisation + accents.

Vellum; 1 leaf; very badly mutilated and rubbed. 12.3⁺ × 9.5⁺;    [3] cols.;    11⁺ lines.

Divine name: Hebrew tetragrammaton.

Klein *Sefarad* XLIX, pp. 123–133.    [1108]

**T-S AS 68.240**    Exodus 18:19, 22

Hebrew; Aramaic: Onqelos. Oriental square script; Tiberian vocalisation + accents (Hebrew reinforced in darker ink).

Vellum; 1 leaf; very badly mutilated.    5.9⁺ × 10.3⁺; 6⁺ lines.    [1109]

**T-S AS 69.4** (= T-S AS 69.75, 141)    Numbers 12:2 – 13:18

Aramaic: Onqelos (+ Hebrew lemmata). Byzantine(?) square script; unpointed.

Paper; 2 leaves (1 bifolium); very badly mutilated. 23.2 × 7.1⁺;    14 lines.

Divine name: יי; majusculae [ח]שלח at 13:1 to indicate beginning of *parashah*.    [1110]

**T-S AS 69.5**    Genesis 1:1–3

Aramaic: Onqelos (+ Hebrew lemmata). Oriental linear square script; unpointed.

Paper; 1 leaf (scrap).    15.0 × 6.9;    8 lines.

Divine name: יי; heading: בב; error in first word: בקמין.

[1111]

**T-S AS 69.8**    Deuteronomy 3:24–25 (*recto*)

Aramaic: Onqelos (+ Hebrew lemmata). Oriental semi-cursive script; Tiberian vocalisation.

Paper; 1 leaf (minute fragment).    7.7⁺ × 8.3⁺;    6⁺ lines.

*Verso* contains list of prophets (Zephaniah, Malachi) and kings (Darius); perhaps a *haftarah* lectionary.    [1112]

**T-S AS 69.9**    Genesis 13:3–14

Aramaic: Onqelos (+ Hebrew lemmata). Oriental semi-cursive script; Tiberian vocalisation.

Paper; 1 leaf; mutilated and rubbed.    16.8 × 13.1; 14 lines.

Divine name: יְ (Onqelos and Hebrew lemmata).    [1113]

**T-S AS 69.10**    Genesis 40:14 – 41:11

Aramaic: Onqelos. Oriental semi-cursive script; Tiberian vocalisation.

Paper; 1 leaf; mutilated.    10.4 × 10.1⁺;    10 lines.

*Parashah* notation is found in the margin at 41:1 פר׳. ●.    [1114]

**T-S AS 69.11**    *Toseftot*(?) to Genesis 17:11 (*recto*); 21:10 (*verso*)

Aramaic (with Hebrew quotations). Oriental semi-cursive script; Tiberian vocalisation.

**[T-S AS 69.11, cont.]**
Paper; 1 leaf; mutilated. 10.3⁺×9.8; 11⁺ lines.
This may be part of a liturgical composition for New Year.
Klein *GMPT* I, pp.31, 33. [1115]

### T-S AS 69.13  Exodus 17:9–16
Aramaic: Onqelos (+ Hebrew lemmata). Oriental semi-cursive script; Tiberian vocalisation.
Paper; 2 leaves (1 bifolium); badly mutilated. 12.7×8.4; 11–12 lines.
Divine name: יי; this is the pentateuchal reading for Purim; closing word (folio 2v): ונמר(?). [1116]

### T-S AS 69.15  Exodus 3:14 – 4:1
Aramaic: Onqelos (+ Hebrew lemmata). Oriental semi cursive script; unpointed.
Paper; 1 leaf; slightly mutilated and rubbed. 15.7⁺×13.5; 15 lines.
Divine name: יי. [1117]

### T-S AS 69.18  Genesis 6:1–2
Hebrew; Aramaic: Onqelos. Oriental semi-cursive script; unpointed.
Paper; 1 leaf (lower 2/3 cut away). 8.2⁺×15.9; 5 lines.
Scribe stopped after first word on line 5 and marked the text with a vertical line in right margin; *verso* blank. [1118]

### T-S AS 69.20  Leviticus 9:22 – 10:5
Aramaic: Onqelos (+ Hebrew of Leviticus 10:5–6 in separate column). Yemenite square script; unpointed.
Paper; 1 leaf; very badly mutilated. 10.0⁺×7.6⁺; 2 cols. (Hebrew & Onqelos); 19⁺ lines.
Divine name: יי. [1119]

### T-S AS 69.21 (= T-S AS 44.3; AS 69.60)
Deuteronomy 33:10–13
Hebrew; Aramaic: Onqelos; Judaeo-Arabic. Oriental(?) script: Hebrew square, Onqelos semi-cursive; unpointed.
Paper; 1 leaf; badly rubbed. 15.4×11.1; 15 lines.
Divine name: Hebrew and Onqelos יי. [1120]

### T-S AS 69.22 (= T-S AS 69.140)  Genesis 29:7–10
Hebrew; Aramaic: Onqelos. Oriental semi-cursive script; Tiberian vocalisation (Hebrew only).
Paper; 1 leaf; slightly mutilated. 8.5×13.1; 8 lines. [1121]

### T-S AS 69.24  Genesis 38:28 – 39:15
Hebrew; Aramaic: Onqelos; Judaeo-Arabic. Yemenite square script; Tiberian vocalisation + accents (Hebrew); Babylonian vocalisation (Onqelos).
Paper; 1 leaf; very badly mutilated. 25.5⁺×12.4⁺; 28⁺ lines.
Divine name: Hebrew tetragrammaton; Onqelos יי. [1122]

### T-S AS 69.25  Exodus 18:25 – 19:17
Aramaic: Onqelos (+ Hebrew lemmata). Oriental semi-cursive script; Tiberian vocalisation.
Paper; 1 leaf; slightly rubbed. 17.7×13.4; 16 lines.
Divine name: יי; indentation at 19:1. [1123]

### T-S AS 69.26 (= T-S AS 69.47, 153)  Exodus 28:33 – 29:9
Aramaic: Onqelos (+ Hebrew lemmata). Oriental semi-cursive script; sporadic Tiberian vocalisation.
Paper; 2 leaves (1 bifolium); very badly mutilated. 14.5⁺×9.9⁺; 15⁺ lines. [1124]

### T-S AS 69.27  Leviticus 19:20–21, 25–7
Hebrew; Aramaic: Onqelos. Oriental(?) square script; unpointed.
Paper; 1 leaf; very badly mutilated (upper half cut away). 9.3⁺×15.4; 7⁺ lines.
Divine name: יי. [1125]

### T-S AS 69.31  Leviticus 5:18–22
Hebrew; Aramaic: Onqelos; Judaeo-Arabic. Oriental square script; Tiberian vocalisation (Hebrew & Onqelos) + accents (Hebrew only).
Paper; 1 leaf; slightly rubbed. 17.3×12.8; 13 lines. [1126]

### T-S AS 69.32  Genesis 44:1–2, 4
Hebrew; Aramaic: Onqelos; Judaeo-Arabic. Oriental script; Hebrew square with Tiberian vocalisation + accents; Onqelos semi-cursive.
Paper; 1 leaf (minute fragment). 10.5⁺×5.7⁺; 6⁺ lines. [1127]

### T-S AS 69.33 (= T-S AS 69.54)  Genesis 12:11–15
Hebrew; Aramaic: Onqelos; Judaeo-Arabic. Oriental semi-cursive script (Hebrew with thicker point); Tiberian vocalisation (Hebrew sporadic, Onqelos full).
Paper; 1 leaf; mutilated. 17.8×13.9; 14 lines. [1128]

### T-S AS 69.37
Possibly targum, unidentified. [1129]

**T-S AS 69.40**  Genesis 25:30–31; 26:2–3
Aramaic: Onqelos (+ Hebrew lemmata).  Oriental semi-cursive script; Tiberian vocalisation.
Paper; 1 leaf (minute fragment).  7.3⁺ × 5.2⁺;  5⁺ lines.
[1130]

**T-S AS 69.41**  Exodus 12:27–28; Numbers 28:16–18 (folio 1); Exodus 13:19 – 14:1 (folio 2)
Aramaic: Onqelos (+ Hebrew lemmata).  Oriental semi-cursive script (lemmata smaller than Onqelos); Tiberian vocalisation (Onqelos only).
Paper; 2 leaves (1 bifolium); folio 2 badly mutilated. 13.3 × 9.4;  10 lines.
Divine name: יְיָ; readings and *mafṭir* for Passover.
[1131]

**T-S AS 69.43**  Isaiah 55:5; 40:25–6; 41:2–5; (*hafṭarot*)
Hebrew; Aramaic: Targum Jonathan to Prophets. Yemenite square script; Hebrew with Tiberian vocalisation + accents; Targum with Tiberian vocalisation.
Paper; 1 leaf; very badly mutilated.  9.0⁺ × 17.8; 8⁺ lines.
Divine name: Hebrew tetragrammaton; Targum יְיָ; heading before Isaiah 40: הפטרת לך לך בישעיה ס' מ' and heading at top of *verso*: הפטרת לך לך; Isaiah 55 is *hafṭarah* for *parashat noaḥ*.
[1132]

**T-S AS 69.44**  Genesis 11:5–11
Aramaic: Onqelos (+ Hebrew lemmata).  Spanish or Oriental script; lemmata large and square; Onqelos semi-cursive; unpointed.
Paper; 1 leaf; badly mutilated.  9.8⁺ × 13.6;  9⁺ lines.
Divine name: Hebrew tetragrammaton; Targum יי; *verso* contains several medical remedies in Judaeo-Arabic.
[1133]

**T-S AS 69.45** (= T-S AS 69.132)  Exodus 16:31–4; 17:6–9
Aramaic: Onqelos.  Oriental semi-cursive script; Tiberian vocalisation.
Paper; 1 leaf (minute fragment).  5.5⁺ × 8.0⁺;  6⁺ lines.
Divine name: יְיָ.
[1134]

**T-S AS 69.47** (= T-S AS 69.26, 153)  Exodus 28:34–7, 39–41
Aramaic: Onqelos (+ Hebrew lemmata).  Oriental semi-cursive script; unpointed.
Paper; 1 leaf (minute fragment).  7.5⁺ × 7.2⁺;  9⁺ lines.
Divine name: יי.
[1135]

**T-S AS 69.48**  Genesis 28:12–13
Hebrew; Aramaic: Onqelos; Judaeo-Arabic. Oriental square script; Tiberian vocalisation.
Paper; 1 leaf; very badly mutilated.  10.0⁺ × 9.5⁺; 8⁺ lines.
Divine name: Onqelos יְיָ.
[1136]

**T-S AS 69.50** (= T-S AS 69.67, 95)  Isaiah 60:22; 61:10; 62:1–2; (*hafṭarot*)
Hebrew; Aramaic: Targum Jonathan to Prophets. Oriental semi-cursive script; Hebrew with Tiberian vocalisation + accents; Targum with Tiberian vocalisation.
Paper; 1 leaf (minute fragment).  7.3⁺ × 9.1⁺;  10⁺ lines.
Divine name: Hebrew tetragrammaton; Targum יְיָ; Isaiah 60 is *hafṭarah* for *parashat ki tavo'*; heading before Isaiah 61: [נצבים]; this is one fragment of a leaf torn into three parts, separately conserved.
[1137]

**T-S AS 69.54** (= T-S AS 69.33)  Genesis 12:15–20
Hebrew; Aramaic: Onqelos; Judaeo-Arabic. Oriental semi-cursive script (Hebrew broader point); Tiberian vocalisation.
Paper; 1 leaf; very badly mutilated and rubbed. 17.5 × 10.4⁺;  14 lines.
[1138]

**T-S AS 69.60** (= T-S AS 44.3; AS 69.21)  Deuteronomy 33:3–7
Hebrew; Aramaic: Onqelos; Judaeo-Arabic. Oriental(?) script; Hebrew square; Onqelos semi-cursive; unpointed.
Paper; 1 leaf; badly rubbed.  15.2 × 11.1;  15–16 lines.
[1139]

**T-S AS 69.62**  Exodus 32:13–14, 19–20
Aramaic: Onqelos (+ Hebrew lemmata). Spanish(?) square script; unpointed.
Paper; 1 leaf; very badly mutilated.  9.6⁺ × 10.7⁺; 6⁺ lines.
Divine name: יְיָ; Judaeo-Arabic פצל added in margin after 32:14; perhaps = T-S AS 69.96.
[1140]

**T-S AS 69.63**  Genesis 42:34
Hebrew; Aramaic: Onqelos.  Oriental linear square script; Tiberian vocalisation.
Paper; 1 leaf; very badly mutilated.  10.0⁺ × 10.6⁺; 5⁺ lines.
*Verso* mostly blank; Hebrew word עלי perhaps from 42:36.
[1141]

**T-S AS 69.66** (= T-S AS 69.107, 145)  Genesis 31:44–51
Hebrew; Aramaic: Onqelos.  Oriental linear square script; Tiberian vocalisation.
Paper; 1 leaf; mutilated and rubbed.  19.0 × 15.8; 13 lines.
Divine name: Hebrew tetragrammaton; Targum יְיָ.
[1142]

**T-S AS 69.67 (= T-S AS 69.50, 95)** Isaiah 60:19, 21–2; 61:11 – 62:1; (*hafṭarot*)
Hebrew; Aramaic: Targum Jonathan to Prophets. Oriental semi-cursive script; Hebrew with Tiberian vocalisation + accents; Targum with Tiberian vocalisation.
Paper; 1 leaf (minute fragment).  9.7⁺ × 3.9⁺;  11⁺ lines.
Divine name: Targum יֿי.  [1143]

**T-S AS 69.68**  Genesis 11:32 – 12:8
Aramaic: Onqelos (+ Hebrew lemmata). Oriental script; Hebrew large and square; Onqelos semi-cursive; sporadic Tiberian vocalisation.
Paper; 1 leaf; very badly mutilated.  12.8⁺ × 12.5; 12⁺ lines.
Divine name: Hebrew & Targum יֿי.  [1144]

**T-S AS 69.69**  Exodus 12:16, 18–19
Aramaic: Onqelos (+ Hebrew lemmata). Oriental linear square script (untrained); unpointed.
Paper; 1 leaf; mutilated and rubbed.  10.3⁺ × 8.3; 10⁺ lines.  [1145]

**T-S AS 69.70**  Exodus 17:10–12
Hebrew; Aramaic: Onqelos; Judaeo-Arabic. Oriental script; Hebrew square with Tiberian vocalisation + accents; Onqelos semi-cursive with Tiberian vocalisation.
Paper; 1 leaf; very badly mutilated.  13.0 × 7.4⁺; 13 lines.  [1146]

**T-S AS 69.73**  Exodus 27:17 – 28:3 (folio 1); 30:14–23 (folio 2)
Hebrew; Aramaic: Onqelos. Spanish square script; Tiberian vocalisation + accents (Hebrew & Onqelos).
Paper; 2 leaves (1 bifolium); very badly mutilated and rubbed.  19.7⁺ × 14.9;  15⁺ lines.
Divine name: Hebrew tetragrammaton; Targum יְיָ.  [1147]

**T-S AS 69.74**  Exodus 10:6, 9–10
Hebrew; Aramaic: Onqelos; Judaeo-Arabic. Oriental script; Hebrew square with Tiberian vocalisation + accents; Onqelos semi-cursive with Tiberian vocalisation.
Paper; 1 leaf (minute fragment); very badly rubbed.  8.0⁺ × 10.0⁺;  9⁺ lines.  [1148]

**T-S AS 69.75 (= T-S AS 69.4, 141)**  Numbers 12:2–14
Aramaic: Onqelos (+ Hebrew lemmata). Byzantine(?) square script; unpointed.
Paper; 1 leaf; very badly mutilated.  21.9⁺ × 9.4⁺; 14 lines.
Divine name: יֿי; this is part of T-S AS 69.4 folio 1.  [1149]

**T-S AS 69.77**  Leviticus 22:5–12; 22:32 – 23:6
Aramaic: Onqelos. Spanish semi-cursive script; Tiberian vocalisation + accents.
Paper; 1 leaf (minute fragment).  7.0⁺ × 7.4⁺;  9⁺ lines.
Divine name: יְיָ.  [1150]

**T-S AS 69.80**  Deuteronomy 32:49 – 33:2
Aramaic: Onqelos (+ Hebrew lemmata). Oriental square script; Tiberian vocalisation.
Paper; 1 leaf; slightly rubbed.  20.0 × 14.2;  10 lines.
Divine name: יְיָ ; decorative *parashah* notation in margin at 33:1 ❂. Arabic and Hebrew jottings in margins; possibly same manuscript as T-S AS 69.93.  [1151]

**T-S AS 69.84**  Genesis 21:21 – 22:11
Aramaic: Onqelos (+ Hebrew lemmata). Oriental semi-cursive script; sporadic Tiberian vocalisation.
Paper; 1 leaf; very badly mutilated.  13.8⁺ × 12.2; 21⁺ lines.
Divine name: יֿי.  [1152]

**T-S AS 69.85**  Numbers 17:27 – 18:17
Hebrew; Aramaic: Onqelos; Judaeo-Arabic. Oriental script; Hebrew square with Tiberian vocalisation + accents; Onqelos semi-cursive with Tiberian vocalisation.
Paper; 6 leaves (3 bifolia); badly mutilated. 12.5⁺ × 12.6;  11⁺ lines.
Divine name: Hebrew tetragrammaton; Targum יְיָ.  [1153]

**T-S AS 69.87**  Genesis 18:32 – 19:3; 19:9–13
Aramaic: Onqelos. Oriental semi-cursive script; Tiberian vocalisation.
Paper; 1 leaf; very badly mutilated and rubbed. 10.7⁺ × 12.2⁺;  8⁺ lines.
Divine name: יְיָ.  [1154]

**T-S AS 69.89**  Genesis 36:38–42; 37:7–9
Aramaic: Onqelos (+ Hebrew lemmata). Oriental semi-cursive script; unpointed.
Paper; 1 leaf (minute fragment).  5.5⁺ × 4.0⁺;  7⁺ lines.  [1155]

**T-S AS 69.93**  Deuteronomy 32:1–4 (*verso*)
Aramaic: Onqelos (+ Hebrew lemmata). Oriental square script; Tiberian vocalisation.
Paper; 1 leaf; mutilated.  20.0 × 14.0;  10 lines.
Divine name: יְיָ; possibly same manuscript as T-S AS 69.80; *recto* blank except for heading: האזינו חאת הברכה.  [1156]

**T-S AS 69.94**  Exodus 3:15–19; 4:1–6
Aramaic: Onqelos (+ Hebrew lemmata).   Oriental semi-cursive script; Tiberian vocalisation.
Paper; 1 leaf; very badly mutilated.   16.3⁺ × 9.2⁺; 15⁺ lines.
Divine name: tetragrammaton.   [1157]

**T-S AS 69.95** (= T-S AS 69.50, 67)   Isaiah 60:19–22; 61:10 – 62:1; (*haftarot*)
Hebrew; Aramaic: Targum Jonathan to Prophets. Oriental semi-cursive script; Hebrew with Tiberian vocalisation + accents; Targum with Tiberian vocalisation.
Paper; 1 leaf (minute fragment).   7.5⁺ × 8.0⁺;   10⁺ lines.
   [1158]

**T-S AS 69.96**  Exodus 28:4–5, 11–12
Aramaic: Onqelos.   Spanish(?) square script; Tiberian vocalisation.
Paper; 1 leaf (minute fragment).   9.2⁺ × 7.8⁺;   5⁺ lines.
Perhaps = T-S AS 69.62.   [1159]

**T-S AS 69.98**  Exodus 18:12–13, 26–7; 19:1–3
Aramaic: Onqelos.   Oriental semi-cursive script; Tiberian vocalisation.
Paper; 1 leaf; very badly mutilated.   6.3⁺ × 13.4⁺; 6⁺ lines.
Divine name: יי.   [1160]

**T-S AS 69.99**   2 Kings 4:10–11, 19–21
Aramaic: Targum Jonathan to Prophets (+ Hebrew lemmata).   Oriental(?) square script; Tiberian vocalisation + accents.
Paper; 1 leaf (minute fragment).   4.6⁺ × 9.3⁺; 4⁺ lines.
*Hafṭarah* for *parashat wayera'*.   [1161]

**T-S AS 69.102**   Genesis 41:41–3, 46–9
Aramaic: Onqelos (+ Hebrew lemmata).   Oriental semi-cursive script; Tiberian vocalisation.
Paper; 1 leaf; very badly mutilated and rubbed.
9.8⁺ × 10.2⁺;   8⁺ lines.   [1162]

**T-S AS 69.103**   Exodus 32:23–6, 28–9, 31–2, 34–5; 33:1
Hebrew; Aramaic: Onqelos; Judaeo-Arabic. Yemenite square script; Hebrew with Tiberian vocalisation + accents; Onqelos with Babylonian vocalisation.
Paper; 1 leaf; very badly mutilated and stained.
20.8⁺ × [19.0];   2 cols.; 20⁺ lines.
Divine name יי.   [1163]

**T-S AS 69.104**   Leviticus 22:27–32
Aramaic: Onqelos (+ Hebrew lemmata).   Oriental semi-cursive script; Tiberian vocalisation.
Paper; 1 leaf; very badly mutilated.   8.1⁺ × 9.8; 6⁺ lines.
Divine name: יי.   [1164]

**T-S AS 69.105**   Deuteronomy 1:35–7
Hebrew; Aramaic: Onqelos; Judaeo-Arabic. Oriental script; Hebrew square with Tiberian vocalisation + accents; Onqelos semi-cursive and unpointed.
Paper; 1 leaf; badly mutilated and rubbed.
15.0⁺ × 12.5;   12 lines.   [1165]

**T-S AS 69.106**   Genesis 2:1–3
Hebrew; Aramaic: Onqelos (interspersed in a Hebrew poem).   Oriental semi-cursive script; sporadic Tiberian vocalisation.
Paper; 2 leaves (1 bifolium).   16.0 × 12.2;   9–11 lines.
Divine name: יי; heading: בש רח; folio 1r blank.   [1166]

**T-S AS 69.107** (= T-S AS 69.66, 145)
Genesis 36:42–3; 37:2
Hebrew; Aramaic: Onqelos.   Oriental linear square script; Tiberian vocalisation.
Paper; 1 leaf; very badly mutilated.   11.0⁺ × 10.8⁺; 7⁺ lines.   [1167]

**T-S AS 69.108**

Includes Onqelos to Deuteronomy 34:2–3 in a Hebrew poem on the death of Moses, with error זבולון for יהודה.   [1168]

**T-S AS 69.111**   Exodus 15:24–6; 16:12–14
Aramaic: Onqelos.   Oriental semi-cursive script; Tiberian vocalisation.
Paper; 1 leaf (minute fragment).   6.0⁺ × 8.9⁺;  6⁺ lines.
Divine name: יי.   [1169]

**T-S AS 69.112**   Genesis 2:19–20, 22–4
Hebrew; Aramaic: Onqelos.   Oriental script; Hebrew square; Onqelos semi-cursive; unpointed.
Paper; 1 leaf; very badly mutilated and rubbed.
10.3⁺ × 9.2⁺;   9⁺ lines.   [1170]

**T-S AS 69.113**   Genesis 21:15–16, 25–6
Aramaic: Onqelos; Judaeo-Arabic.   Spanish(?) semi-cursive script; unpointed.
Paper; 1 leaf; very badly mutilated.   6.1⁺ × 13.2⁺; 4⁺ lines.   [1171]

**T-S AS 69.114**   Numbers 21:23–5, 28–32 (folio 1); 23:19 – 24:1 (folio 2)
Aramaic: Onqelos (+ Hebrew lemmata).   Oriental semi-cursive script; sporadic Tiberian vocalisation.
Paper; 2 leaves (1 bifolium); very badly mutilated and rubbed.   16.8 × 13.4;   16–17 lines.   [1172]

**T-S AS 69.115** Extract of Onqelos to Exodus 20:15–23; Numbers 28:26–31 (folio 1); Targum Jonathan to Ezekiel 1:1–16 (folio 2) (opening two to three words of each verse)

Aramaic: Onqelos, Targum Jonathan to Prophets. Oriental semi-cursive script; Tiberian vocalisation (folios 1v–2v).

Paper; 2 leaves (1 bifolium); badly mutilated. 8.5⁺ × 7.0⁺; 7⁺ lines.

Divine name: ײ; these are readings (Torah, *maftir* and *haftarah*) for Pentecost; notation חזק after Exodus 20:23. [1173]

**T-S AS 69.117**

Targumic phraseology in part of a liturgical composition (for funeral?), including Hebrew (Job 1:21). [1174]

**T-S AS 69.121** Genesis 22:11–13, 15–18

Aramaic: Onqelos (+ Hebrew lemmata). Oriental square script; Tiberian vocalisation.

Paper; 1 leaf; very badly mutilated. 15.5⁺ × 12.3⁺; 9⁺ lines. [1175]

**T-S AS 69.131** Genesis 42:6–9, 11–14

Hebrew; Aramaic: Onqelos. Oriental linear square script; Tiberian vocalisation.

Paper; 1 leaf; very badly mutilated and rubbed. 14.1⁺ × 15.1; 12⁺ lines. [1176]

**T-S AS 69.132** (= T-S AS 69.45) Exodus 16:31–4; 17:6–9

Aramaic: Onqelos. Oriental semi-cursive script; Tiberian vocalisation.

Paper; 1 leaf (minute fragment). 5.5⁺ × 7.4⁺; 6⁺ lines.

Divine name: ײ. [1177]

**T-S AS 69.133** Exodus 16:8, 12

Hebrew; Aramaic: Onqelos. Oriental semi-cursive script; Tiberian vocalisation.

Paper; 1 leaf (minute fragment). 5.4⁺ × 9.5⁺; 5⁺ lines.

Divine name: ײ. [1178]

**T-S AS 69.134** Exodus 14:10–17 (*recto*); 14:24 – 15:1 (*verso*)

Aramaic: Onqelos. Oriental semi-cursive script; Tiberian vocalisation.

Paper; 1 leaf; very badly mutilated. 10.5⁺ × 7.3⁺; 13⁺ lines.

Divine name: ײ. [1179]

**T-S AS 69.136** Genesis 1:1–2

Aramaic: Onqelos (+ Hebrew lemmata). Oriental semi-cursive script; unpointed.

Paper; 1 leaf; very badly mutilated. 4.9⁺ × 13.9; 3⁺ lines.

Divine name: ײ; scribe seems to have stopped after three lines. [1180]

**T-S AS 69.140** (= T-S AS 69.22) Genesis 27:38–42

Hebrew; Aramaic: Onqelos. Oriental semi-cursive script; Hebrew with Tiberian vocalisation.

Paper; 1 leaf; badly mutilated. 8.4 × 9.6⁺; 8 lines. [1181]

**T-S AS 69.141** (= T-S AS 69.4, 75) Exodus 8:22–4; 8:27 – 9:3

Aramaic: Onqelos (+ Hebrew lemmata). Byzantine(?) square script; unpointed.

Paper; 1 leaf; very badly mutilated. 15.7⁺ × 8.5⁺; 9⁺ lines.

Divine name: ײ. [1182]

**T-S AS 69.144** (= T-S NS 162.13) 2 Samuel 17:21 (folio 1v); 17:28–9; 18:5 (folio 2); 18:11, 17–18 (folio 3); 19:16–17, 22–3 (folio 4); 19:29, 36–7 (folio 5); 19:42–3; 20:3 (folio 6)

Aramaic: Targum Jonathan to Prophets. Oriental semi-cursive script; unpointed.

Paper; 6 leaves (3 bifolia); very badly mutilated. 7.5⁺ × 10.3⁺; 4⁺ lines.

Folio 1r not legible. [1183]

**T-S AS 69.145** (= T-S AS 69.66, 107) Genesis 42:33–6

Hebrew; Aramaic: Onqelos. Oriental linear square script; Tiberian vocalisation.

Paper; 1 leaf; very badly mutilated. 10.5⁺ × 7.7⁺; 9⁺ lines. [1184]

**T-S AS 69.146** Numbers 30:13–17; 31:5–10

Aramaic: Onqelos. Oriental semi-cursive script; unpointed.

Paper; 1 leaf; slightly mutilated, very badly rubbed. 17.9 × 13.5; 15 lines. [1185]

**T-S AS 69.147** Exodus 27:15–20

Hebrew; Aramaic: Onqelos. Oriental semi-cursive script; Hebrew with Tiberian vocalisation + accents; Onqelos with Tiberian vocalisation.

Paper; 1 leaf; very badly mutilated and rubbed. 13.8⁺ × 10.5⁺; 13⁺ lines.

Cipher: צ after 27:19 for number of verses in *parashat terumah*. [1186]

**T-S AS 69.149** Exodus 16:15–16, 20–21

Hebrew; Aramaic: Onqelos. Oriental square script; Onqelos with Tiberian vocalisation.

**[T-S AS 69.149, cont.]**
Paper; 1 leaf (minute fragment).   5.2⁺×9.0⁺;  5⁺ lines.
Two dots above each word of the Hebrew text.   [1187]

**T-S AS 69.151**   Genesis 1:7–16 (folio 1); 2:23 – 3:6 (folio 2)
Hebrew; Aramaic: Onqelos.   Oriental square script; unpointed.
Paper; 2 leaves (1 bifolium); badly mutilated and rubbed (folio 2 very badly).   19.9×14.3; 17 lines.
Divine name: Hebrew אלהים; Targum tetragrammaton.   [1188]

**T-S AS 69.153** (= T-S AS 69.26, 47)   Exodus 31:4–6, 9–10 (folio 1); 31:14–15; 31:18 – 32:1 (folio 2)
Aramaic: Onqelos (+ Hebrew lemmata).   Oriental semi-cursive script; unpointed.
Paper; 2 leaves (1 bifolium); very badly mutilated. 7.1⁺×3.9⁺;  7⁺ lines.   [1189]

**T-S AS 69.154**   Jeremiah 52:18–22 (folio 1); Isaiah 40:23–5; 49:14–15; (*haftarot*)
Hebrew; Aramaic: Targum Jonathan to Prophets. Oriental square script; Hebrew larger with Tiberian vocalisation + accents; Targum with Tiberian vocalisation.
Paper; 2 leaves (1 bifolium); very badly mutilated and rubbed.   17.5×12.8;  13 lines.
These are *haftarot* for *parashot devarim, wa'ethanan* and *'eqev* respectively.   [1190]

**T-S AS 69.155**   Exodus 19:16–17, 24
Aramaic: Onqelos (+ Hebrew lemmata).   Oriental semi-cursive script; sporadic Tiberian vocalisation.
Paper; 1 leaf (minute fragment).   5.1⁺×12.3⁺;  2⁺ lines.
Divine name: יי.   [1191]

**T-S AS 69.160–161**   Leviticus 23:44 – 24:2; 24:7–11 (AS 69.160); 24:16–22; 25:2–7 (AS 69.161)
Aramaic: Onqelos (+ Hebrew lemmata).   Oriental script; lemmata square; Onqelos semi-cursive; Tiberian vocalisation.
Paper; 2 leaves; very badly mutilated and rubbed. 10.2⁺×9.8⁺;  10⁺ lines.
Divine name: יי.   [1192]

**T-S AS 69.162**
Entirely illegible except for ויהי from Onqelos to Deuteronomy 24:5 and a marginal gloss: ומופתיה.   [1193]

**T-S AS 69.165**   Exodus 14:15–17; 14:30 – 15:1
Aramaic: Onqelos.   Oriental semi-cursive script; Tiberian vocalisation.
Paper; 1 leaf (minute fragment).   7.5⁺×5.8⁺;  6⁺ lines.
Divine name: יי.   [1194]

**T-S AS 69.166**   Exodus 28:37–8, 41–2
Aramaic: Onqelos (+ Hebrew lemmata).   Oriental semi-cursive script; sporadic Tiberian vocalisation.
Paper; 1 leaf (minute fragment).   5.3⁺×5.1⁺;  4⁺ lines.   [1195]

**T-S AS 69.168**   Genesis 11:31 – 12:2
Hebrew; Aramaic: Onqelos; Judaeo-Arabic. Oriental script; Hebrew square with Tiberian vocalisation; Onqelos semi-cursive with Tiberian vocalisation; Judaeo-Arabic with Tiberian vocalisation.
Paper; 1 leaf; very badly mutilated and rubbed. 17.4×8.2⁺;  14 lines.
Decorative sign ✿ marks *parashah* at 12:1.   [1196]

**T-S AS 69.169**   2 Kings 12:8–10, 13–17 (folio 1); Habakkuk 3:5–8, 13–14 (folio 2); (*haftarot*)
Aramaic: Targum Jonathan to Prophets (+ Hebrew lemmata).   Oriental linear square script; unpointed.
Paper; 2 leaves (1 bifolium); very badly mutilated. 8.6⁺×8.4⁺;  12⁺ lines.
Divine name: יי; attested as *haftarot* for *parashat sheqalim* (2 Kings) and second day Pentecost (Habakkuk).   [1197]

**T-S AS 69.173**   Jeremiah 11:16 – 12:1 (folio 1); 12:2; 15:15–16 (folio 2); (*haftarah*)
Aramaic: Targum Jonathan to Prophets.   Oriental semi-cursive script; unpointed.
Paper; 2 leaves (1 bifolium); very badly mutilated. 13.5×6.4⁺;  15 lines.
Divine name: ט; this is the triennial *haftarah* for Exodus 27:20 (cf. T-S NS 218.60); folio 2v blank.   [1198]

**T-S AS 69.176**   Ezekiel 1:25–8 (*recto*); Habakkuk 2:20 – 3:3 (*verso*); (*haftarot*)
Aramaic: Targum Jonathan to Prophets.   Oriental semi-cursive script; unpointed.
Paper; 2 leaves (1 bifolium); badly mutilated and rubbed; folio 2 almost entirely missing.   13.8⁺×8.5⁺;  23⁺ lines.
Divine name: יי(?).   [1199]

**T-S AS 69.177** (= T-S AS 69.184)   Exodus 15:17, 19–20; 16:6–8
Aramaic: Onqelos.   Oriental semi-cursive script; Tiberian vocalisation.
Paper; 1 leaf (minute fragment).   6.8⁺×5.9⁺;  5⁺ lines.
Divine name: יי/ײַ.   [1200]

**T-S AS 69.178**   Genesis 6:2–3, 5–7
Aramaic: Onqelos (+ Hebrew lemmata).   Oriental square script; Tiberian vocalisation.
Paper; 1 leaf (minute fragment).   7.3⁺×7.0⁺;  7⁺ lines.
Divine name: יי.   [1201]

**T-S AS 69.179**  Malachi 1:7–8; 3:3–4
Hebrew; Aramaic: Targum Jonathan to Prophets; Judaeo-Arabic.  Oriental linear square script; Hebrew with Tiberian vocalisation + accents; Targum with Tiberian vocalisation.

Paper; 1 leaf (minute fragment).  5.6⁺ × 4.5⁺;  6⁺ lines.

Divine name: Hebrew tetragrammaton.  [1202]

**T-S AS 69.181**  Genesis 12:8–11
Hebrew; Aramaic: Onqelos; Judaeo-Arabic. Oriental semi-cursive script; Targum with Tiberian vocalisation.

Paper; 1 leaf (minute fragment).  8.0⁺ × 4.6⁺;  6⁺ lines.  [1203]

**T-S AS 69.182**

Phrases on *recto* similar to Targum to Leviticus 6:6; *verso* Judaeo-Arabic.  [1204]

**T-S AS 69.184 (= T-S AS 69.177)**
Exodus 16:20–3; 17:5–9
Aramaic: Onqelos.  Oriental semi-cursive script; Tiberian vocalisation.

Paper; 1 leaf (minute fragment).  6.6⁺ × 5.7⁺;  8⁺ lines.

Divine name: יְ.  [1205]

**T-S AS 69.185–194**  Genesis 12:1 (AS 69.185v); 12:2–3 (AS 69.194); 12:4–5 (AS 69.189, 192); 12:7–8 (AS 69.188, 191); 12:20 – 13:3 (AS 69.187); 13:5–7 (AS 69.186); 13:7–9 (AS 69.190, 193)
Hebrew; Aramaic: Onqelos; Judaeo-Arabic. Yemenite square script; Hebrew and Onqelos with Tiberian vocalisation.

Paper; 7 leaves (torn into ten parts, separately conserved); several mutilated.  14.2 × 9.7;  10 lines.

Divine name: Hebrew tetragrammaton; Targum יי; AS 69.185r blank; heading at top of AS 69.185v: פרשה.  [1206]

**T-S AS 69.195**  Genesis 49:12 (folio 1v); 49:24–7 (folio 2)
Aramaic: Onqelos (+ Hebrew lemmata).  Oriental semi-cursive script; unpointed.

Paper; 2 leaves (1 bifolium); very badly mutilated and rubbed.  15.2 × 11.1;  16 lines.

Text ends on third line of folio 2v, followed by a colophon(?) [ ] ברוך[ ] אם[ ] בה[ ] רביס[ ] עריה[ ] שלום.  [1207]

**T-S AS 69.199**  Genesis 41:11–12, 16–17
Aramaic: Onqelos.  Oriental semi-cursive script; Tiberian vocalisation.

Paper; 1 leaf (minute fragment).  3.9⁺ × 6.0⁺;  4⁺ lines.  [1208]

**T-S AS 69.200**  1 Samuel 2:8–11; 3:19–20; (*haftarah*)
Aramaic: Targum Jonathan to Prophets (+ Hebrew lemmata).  Oriental semi-cursive script; Tiberian vocalisation.

Paper; 1 leaf; mutilated.  13.5⁺ × 9.0⁺;  12⁺ lines.

Divine name: יְ/יְ; 2:11 is added in bottom margin of *recto*; Judaeo-Arabic כמל at end of passage; *verso* blank except for ( ה; this is the *haftarah* for New Year.  [1209]

**T-S AS 69.204**  2 Samuel 22:28–32, 39–47
Aramaic: Targum Jonathan to Prophets.  Oriental square script; unpointed.

Vellum; 1 leaf; badly mutilated.  10.3⁺ × 14.2⁺; 9⁺ lines.

Divine name: יי; *haftarah* for *parashat ha'azinu*.  [1210]

**T-S AS 69.206**  Deuteronomy 28:22–3, 29
Aramaic: Onqelos (+ Hebrew lemmata).  Spanish square script; Tiberian vocalisation + accents.

Vellum; 1 leaf; very badly mutilated and rubbed.  6.5⁺ × 10.0⁺;  5⁺ lines.

Divine name: יְיָ.  [1211]

**T-S AS 69.209**  Genesis 1:4–8
Aramaic: Onqelos (+ Hebrew lemmata).  Oriental square script; Tiberian vocalisation.

Vellum; 1 leaf; very badly mutilated.  8.4⁺ × 7.1⁺; 7⁺ lines.

Divine name: יְ.  [1212]

**T-S AS 69.211**  Numbers 14:33–6; 15:3–6
Aramaic: Onqelos.  Oriental square script; unpointed.

Vellum; 1 leaf (minute fragment).  7.2⁺ × 7.4⁺;  7⁺ lines.

Divine name: יי.  [1213]

**T-S AS 69.212 (= T-S AS 69.216)**
Deuteronomy 17:11, 16 (folio 1); 21:5, 13–14 (folio 2)
Hebrew; Aramaic: Onqelos.  Oriental square script; Hebrew with Tiberian vocalisation + accents; Onqelos with Tiberian vocalisation.

Vellum; 2 leaves (1 bifolium); very badly mutilated.  5.7⁺ × 7.8⁺;  4⁺ lines.

Divine name: Hebrew tetragrammaton.  [1214]

**T-S AS 69.213**  Jonah 1:5–10
Hebrew; Aramaic: Targum Jonathan to Prophets. Oriental square script; unpointed.

Vellum; 1 leaf; very badly mutilated.  8.7⁺ × 7.3⁺; 7 lines.

*Haftarah* for Day of Atonement afternoon.  [1215]

**T-S AS 69.215**  Leviticus 15:30–32; 16:4
Hebrew; Aramaic: Onqelos.  Oriental square script; unpointed.

Vellum; 1 leaf; very badly mutilated and rubbed. 7.3⁺ × 14.4⁺;  2 cols.(?);  4⁺ lines. [1216]

**T-S AS 69.216** (= T-S AS 69.212)
Deuteronomy 12:14–15, 20
Hebrew; Aramaic: Onqelos.  Oriental square script; Hebrew with Tiberian vocalisation + accents; Onqelos with Tiberian vocalisation.

Vellum; 1 leaf (minute fragment).  3.6⁺ × 7.5⁺;  2⁺ lines.
Divine name: Hebrew tetragrammaton. [1217]

**T-S AS 69.218**  Numbers 34:9–19
Hebrew; Aramaic: Onqelos.  Oriental square script; unpointed.

Vellum; 1 leaf; very badly mutilated.  18.1 × 11.2⁺; 16–19 lines.
Divine name: Hebrew tetragrammaton. [1218]

**T-S AS 69.220**  Habakkuk 3:7–8, 10–12; (haftarah)
Hebrew; Aramaic: Targum Jonathan to Prophets. Oriental square script; Tiberian vocalisation.

Vellum; 1 leaf; badly mutilated.  7.8⁺ × 13.5⁺;  6⁺ lines.
Divine name: אׁ; haftarah for second day Pentecost or a triennial haftarah for Genesis 8:1 / Deuteronomy 2:31. [1219]

**T-S AS 69.222**  Genesis 32:18–23; 32:26 – 33:1 (folio 1); 33:8–11, 18–20 (folio 2)
Aramaic: Onqelos (+ Hebrew lemmata).  Spanish semi-cursive script; unpointed.

Vellum; 2 leaves (1 bifolium); very badly mutilated; folio 2 almost entirely missing.  13.1 × 20.0;  10 lines. [1220]

**T-S AS 69.223**  Genesis 16:16 – 17:2, 17:14–15
[Hebrew;] Aramaic: Onqelos.  Ashkenazi square script; Tiberian vocalisation + accents.

Vellum; 1 leaf; very badly mutilated.  20.8⁺ × 9.9⁺; [2] cols.;  7⁺ lines.
This fragment preserves only the narrow outer column, with Onqelos. The inner column, which probably contained the Hebrew version, is entirely missing. [1221]

**T-S AS 69.224**  1 Samuel 1:2–8
Hebrew; Aramaic: Targum Jonathan to Prophets. Oriental square script; Hebrew unpointed; Targum with Tiberian vocalisation + accents.

Vellum; 1 leaf; mutilated.  20.9 × 17.3;  12 lines.
Divine name: Hebrew tetragrammaton; Targum ייי. [1222]

**T-S AS 69.225**  Habakkuk 3:15–19; 2 Samuel 21:15–16 (folio 1); Ezekiel 1:12–16, 19 (folio 2); (haftarot)
Hebrew; Aramaic: Targum Jonathan to Prophets. Oriental square script; sporadic Tiberian vocalisation.

Vellum; 2 leaves (1 bifolium); very badly mutilated (folio 2 almost entirely missing).  16.4 × 12.0;  14 lines.
These are haftarot for seventh day Passover (2 Samuel), and Pentecost (Habakkuk and Ezekiel); qere and ketiv are marked in margin of folio 2 (perhaps to Ezekiel 1:8). [1223]

**T-S AS 69.226**  Exodus 12:30–32, 37–40
Hebrew; Aramaic: Onqelos.  Oriental square script; unpointed.

Vellum; 1 leaf; very badly mutilated.  8.7⁺ × 6.2⁺; 13⁺ lines. [1224]

**T-S AS 69.228**  Numbers 18:4–6, 9
Hebrew; Aramaic: Onqelos.  Oriental square script; unpointed.

Vellum; 1 leaf (minute fragment).  7.2⁺ × 8.1⁺;  5⁺ lines.
Gloss in lower margin of recto. [1225]

**T-S AS 69.229**  Isaiah 49:15–18, 22–3
Hebrew; Aramaic: Targum Jonathan to Prophets. Oriental square script; Tiberian vocalisation.

Vellum; 1 leaf; very badly mutilated and rubbed. 6.9⁺ × 10.4⁺;  6⁺ lines.
Divine name: Hebrew tetragrammaton. [1226]

**T-S AS 69.230** (= T-S AS 69.231, 233)
1 Kings 7:43–4, 48; (haftarah)
Hebrew; Aramaic: Targum Jonathan to Prophets. Oriental square script; unpointed.

Vellum; 1 leaf; very badly mutilated.  12.7 × 6.3⁺; [2] cols.;  6⁺ lines.
This is the haftarah for parashat wayaqhel. [1227]

**T-S AS 69.231** (= T-S AS 69.230, 233)
Jeremiah 35:15–17; 1 Kings 5:30–32; (haftarot)
Hebrew; Aramaic: Targum Jonathan to Prophets. Oriental square script; unpointed.

Vellum; 1 leaf; very badly mutilated.  12.3⁺ × 8.0⁺; [2] cols.;  14⁺ lines.
These are the haftarot for parashot mishpatim and terumah. [1228]

**T-S AS 69.233** (= T-S AS 69.230, 231)
1 Kings 7:42–4, 46–8, 50; (haftarah)
Hebrew; Aramaic: Targum Jonathan to Prophets. Oriental square script; unpointed.

**[T-S AS 69.233 (= T-S AS 69.230, 231), cont.]**
Vellum; 1 leaf; very badly mutilated. 9.2⁺ × 8.7⁺;
2 cols.; 9⁺ lines.

Divine name: Hebrew tetragrammaton; this is the *haftarah* for *parashat wayaqhel*; only a trace of column 2 remains.
[1229]

### T-S AS 69.241 (= T-S 20.155; AS 63.24, 51, 72, 85, 95, 96, 117, 129, 153; NS 286.1)
Exodus 22:26–8

Aramaic: Palestinian Targum (+ Hebrew lemmata). Oriental square script; no visible vocalisation.

Vellum; 1 col. of scroll (minute fragment). 2.7⁺ × 7.6⁺; 3⁺ lines.

The rest of this manuscript has Palestinian vocalisation.

Klein *GMPT* I, p.295. See plate 8. [1230]

### T-S AS 69.242   Exodus 19:7, 12, 17, 22/24
Aramaic: Onqelos (+ Hebrew lemmata). Ashkenazi square script; unpointed.

Vellum; 1 leaf; very badly mutilated. 3.0⁺ × 12.5⁺; 2 cols.; 1⁺ lines. [1231]

### T-S AS 69.243
50 minute fragments, not individually numbered, some of which contain targum. [1232]

### T-S AS 70.3   Exodus 17:16 – 18:9; 18:14–23
Aramaic: Onqelos. Oriental semi-cursive script; Tiberian vocalisation.

Paper; 1 leaf; very badly mutilated. 17.5⁺ × 14.8⁺; 21⁺ lines.

Divine name: ייַ. [1233]

### T-S AS 70.8   Leviticus 12:6–7
Hebrew; Aramaic: Onqelos; Judaeo-Arabic. Oriental square script (Hebrew & Onqelos); unpointed.

Paper; 1 leaf; very badly mutilated and rubbed. 19.7 × 9.7⁺; 7 lines. [1234]

### T-S AS 70.10   Leviticus 10:10–19; 11:11–27
Aramaic: Onqelos. Spanish semi-cursive script; Tiberian vocalisation.

Paper; 1 leaf; badly mutilated and rubbed. 16.3⁺ × 21.6; 15⁺ lines.

Divine name: ייָ. [1235]

### T-S AS 70.11   Genesis 49:11–12, 16–17
Hebrew; Aramaic: Onqelos; Judaeo-Arabic. Oriental script; Hebrew larger, square with Tiberian vocalisation + accents; Onqelos semi-cursive with Tiberian vocalisation.

Paper; 1 leaf (minute fragment). 5.7⁺ × 3.2⁺; 6⁺ lines. [1236]

### T-S AS 70.12   Leviticus 23:12–13, 18
Hebrew; Aramaic: Onqelos. Oriental linear square script; Tiberian vocalisation.

Paper; 1 leaf (minute fragment). 4.3⁺ × 7.9⁺; 3⁺ lines. [1237]

### T-S AS 70.13
Minute fragment with Aramaic text; not identified. [1238]

### T-S AS 70.14   Exodus 16:2–5
Hebrew; Aramaic: Onqelos. Oriental square script; unpointed.

Paper; 1 leaf (minute fragment). 5.3⁺ × 6.7⁺; 5⁺ lines. [1239]

### T-S AS 70.15   Exodus 5:22–3; 6:4
Hebrew; Aramaic: Onqelos. Oriental semi-cursive script; unpointed.

Paper; 1 leaf (minute fragment). 5.2⁺ × 8.4⁺; 3⁺ lines.
Order of text confused. [1240]

### T-S AS 70.24 (= T-S AS 70.34)   Genesis 22:7–10, 12–14
Aramaic: Onqelos (+ Hebrew lemmata). Oriental linear square script; Tiberian vocalisation.

Paper; 1 leaf; very badly mutilated. 13.0⁺ × 9.7⁺; 9⁺ lines.

Divine name: ייָ. [1241]

### T-S AS 70.29 (= T-S AS 70.74, 84)   Exodus 21:17–22, 28–33
Aramaic: Onqelos (+ Hebrew lemmata). Oriental semi-cursive script; Tiberian vocalisation.

Paper; 1 leaf (torn into 3 parts). [24.3] × [17.0]; [20] lines. [1242]

### T-S AS 70.33   Genesis 40:1–2, 11–12, 20; 41:24
Hebrew; Aramaic: Onqelos; Judaeo-Arabic. Yemenite square script; Hebrew with Tiberian vocalisation + accents; Onqelos with Babylonian vocalisation.

Paper; 2 leaves (minute fragments, 1 bifolium). 6.9⁺ × 6.3⁺; 4⁺ lines. [1243]

### T-S AS 70.34 (= T-S AS 70.24)   Genesis 22:7–9, 12–13
Aramaic: Onqelos (+ Hebrew lemmata). Oriental linear square script; Tiberian vocalisation.

Paper; 1 leaf (minute fragment). 5.5⁺ × 4.1⁺; 4⁺ lines.
Divine name: ייָ. [1244]

### T-S AS 70.36   Deuteronomy 33:21–8
Aramaic: Onqelos (+ Hebrew lemmata). Oriental square script; Tiberian vocalisation.

[T-S AS 70.36, cont.]
Paper; 1 leaf; slightly mutilated and rubbed.
16.5 × 10.9; 15 lines.
Divine name: ⁜. [1245]

**T-S AS 70.38**   Genesis 5:30 – 6:12
Aramaic: Onqelos (+ Hebrew lemmata).   Oriental semi-cursive script; Tiberian vocalisation.
Paper; 1 leaf; slightly mutilated and badly rubbed.
17.1 × 13.1; 16 lines.
Divine name: ⁜; decorative sign marks *parashah* in margin at 6:9. [1246]

**T-S AS 70.42**   Genesis 9:25 – 10:18
Aramaic: Onqelos (+ Hebrew lemmata).   Oriental semi-cursive script (lemmata in larger square script); Tiberian vocalisation.
Paper; 1 leaf; badly mutilated and rubbed.   17.9 × 9.4⁺; 16 lines.
Divine name: ⁜. [1247]

**T-S AS 70.45**   Genesis 23:2–6, 8–11, 15–16; 23:19 – 24:2
Aramaic: Onqelos (+ Hebrew lemmata).   Oriental square script; Tiberian vocalisation in abbreviations only.
Paper; 2 leaves (1 bifolium); very badly mutilated and rubbed.   12.7⁺ × 16.3;   13⁺ lines. [1248]

**T-S AS 70.46**   Genesis 31:11–13, 16–18
Aramaic: Onqelos (+ Hebrew lemmata).   Oriental semi-cursive script; Tiberian vocalisation.
Paper; 1 leaf; very badly mutilated and rubbed.
10.1⁺ × 7.4⁺; 7⁺ lines. [1249]

**T-S AS 70.47** (= T-S AS 70.107)
Deuteronomy 33:20–23
Hebrew; Aramaic: Onqelos; Judaeo-Arabic.
Oriental script (unusual); Hebrew linear square; Onqelos semi-cursive; unpointed.
Paper; 1 leaf.   15.5 × 10.7;   16 lines.
Divine name: ⁜. [1250]

**T-S AS 70.51**   Deuteronomy 16:18 – 17:8
Aramaic: Onqelos (+ Hebrew lemmata).   Oriental semi-cursive script; unpointed.
Paper; 1 leaf; mutilated, *recto* badly rubbed.
13.0⁺ × 13.2;   14⁺ lines.
Divine name: ⁜. [1251]

**T-S AS 70.52**   Genesis 1:20–30
Aramaic: Onqelos (+ Hebrew lemmata).   Oriental semi-cursive script; Tiberian vocalisation.
Paper; 1 leaf.   18.0 × 12.5;   13 lines.
Divine name: ⁜. [1252]

**T-S AS 70.53**   Genesis 14:9–12
Hebrew; Aramaic: Onqelos; Judaeo-Arabic.
Oriental semi-cursive script; Hebrew with Tiberian vocalisation + accents; Onqelos with Tiberian vocalisation.
Paper; 1 leaf; very badly mutilated and rubbed.
8.8⁺ × 9.8⁺;   10 lines. [1253]

**T-S AS 70.55**   Genesis 6:9–13, 18–21
Aramaic: Onqelos (+ Hebrew lemmata).   Oriental semi-cursive script (lemmata in square script); Tiberian vocalisation.
Paper; 1 leaf; very badly mutilated.   9.8⁺ × 9.8⁺; 8⁺ lines.
Divine name: ⁜. [1254]

**T-S AS 70.57**   Genesis 39:5–7, 14–16
Hebrew; Aramaic: Onqelos; Judaeo-Arabic.
Yemenite square script; Hebrew with Tiberian vocalisation + accents; Onqelos with Babylonian vocalisation.
Paper; 1 leaf; very badly mutilated.   10.4⁺ × 10.8⁺; 9⁺ lines. [1255]

**T-S AS 70.60**   Jonah 1:1–5
Aramaic: Targum Jonathan to Prophets.   Oriental square script (untrained); unpointed.
Paper; 1 leaf.   14.8 × 9.4; 9 lines.
Divine name: tetragrammaton. [1256]

**T-S AS 70.62**   Leviticus 8:25–8, 31–4
Aramaic: Onqelos (+ Hebrew lemmata).   Oriental semi-cursive script; unpointed.
Paper; 1 leaf; very badly mutilated.   12.3⁺ × 7.2⁺; 9⁺ lines.
Divine name: ⁜. [1257]

**T-S AS 70.69**   Genesis 4:11–22
Aramaic: Onqelos.   Oriental semi-cursive script; unpointed.
Paper; 1 leaf; very badly rubbed.   17.0 × 13.2; 14 lines.
Divine name: ⁜. [1258]

**T-S AS 70.70**   Genesis 7:16–21
Hebrew; Aramaic: Onqelos.   Oriental large semi-cursive script; Tiberian vocalisation.
Paper; 1 leaf; mutilated and badly rubbed.   17.2 × 17.2; 11 lines. [1259]

**T-S AS 70.72**   Esther 6:13 – 7:4; 7:9
Aramaic: Targum Esther (+ Hebrew lemmata).
Spanish semi-cursive script (lemmata in square script); unpointed.

[T-S AS 70.72, cont.]
Paper; 1 leaf; very badly mutilated and rubbed.
10.5⁺ × 14.8;  16⁺ lines.
This is different from Targums I, II.
Kasher and Klein *HUCA* LXI, pp. 89–124. [1260]

**T-S AS 70.74 (= T-S AS 70.29, 84)**  Exodus 21:20–28, 31–7
Aramaic: Onqelos (+ Hebrew lemmata).  Oriental semi-cursive script; Tiberian vocalisation.
Paper; 1 leaf (torn in 3 parts).  [24.3] × 17.0; [20] lines. [1261]

**T-S AS 70.75**  Leviticus 23:18–24
Aramaic: Onqelos (+ Hebrew lemmata).  Oriental semi-cursive script (lemmata, linear square); Tiberian vocalisation.
Paper; 1 leaf.  13.5 × 9.1;  12–13 lines.
Divine name: יִי/יִי. [1262]

**T-S AS 70.76 (= T-S AS 70.82)**  Leviticus 19:32–4; 20:2–3
Hebrew; Aramaic: Onqelos.  Oriental(?) square script; unpointed.
Paper; 1 leaf; very badly mutilated and rubbed.
10.6⁺ × 16.3 (margins restored);  8⁺ lines.
Divine name: ג. [1263]

**T-S AS 70.78**  Genesis 4:10–23
Aramaic: Onqelos (+ Hebrew lemmata).  Oriental semi-cursive script; Tiberian vocalisation.
Paper; 1 leaf; slightly mutilated.  16.6 × 12.6;  16 lines.
Divine name: יְ. [1264]

**T-S AS 70.79**  Genesis 38:11–15, 20–24
Hebrew; Aramaic: Onqelos; Judaeo-Arabic. Yemenite square script; Hebrew with Tiberian vocalisation + accents; Onqelos with Babylonian vocalisation.
Paper; 1 leaf; very badly mutilated.  16.0⁺ × 21.0; 14⁺ lines. [1265]

**T-S AS 70.80**  Leviticus 25:3–5
Hebrew; Aramaic: Onqelos; Judaeo-Arabic. Oriental script; Hebrew square; Onqelos semi-cursive.
Paper; 1 leaf; badly mutilated.  10.5⁺ × 9.7;  [11] lines.
Most of *verso* blank after scribal error. [1266]

**T-S AS 70.81**  Leviticus 8:34–5 (folio 1r); Jeremiah 7:21–3 (folio 2v); (*haftarah*)
Aramaic: Onqelos, Targum Jonathan to Prophets (+ Hebrew lemmata).  Oriental semi-cursive scripts; Tiberian vocalisation (Leviticus only).
Paper; 2 leaves (1 bifolium); mutilated.  13.9 × 9.6;  6, 12 lines.
Divine name: יִי (Leviticus); יי (Jeremiah); texts are in different hands and inks; heading before Jeremiah: בשם רח צו׳ בירמיה. [1267]

**T-S AS 70.82 (= T-S AS 70.76)**  Leviticus 21:10–12, 18–20
Hebrew; Aramaic: Onqelos.  Oriental(?) square script (untrained); unpointed.
Paper; 1 leaf; very badly mutilated and rubbed.
7.9⁺ × 15.4;  6⁺ lines.
Margins restored. [1268]

**T-S AS 70.83**  Genesis 27:29–38
Aramaic: Onqelos (+ Hebrew lemmata).  Oriental semi-cursive script; Tiberian vocalisation.
Paper; 1 leaf; slightly mutilated.  17.2 × 13.8;  14 lines. [1269]

**T-S AS 70.84 (= T-S AS 70.29, 74)**
This fragment and those described at T-S AS 70.29 and 74 originally constituted one leaf; see description above. [1270]

**T-S AS 70.85**  Isaiah 33:20–24
Aramaic: Targum Jonathan to Prophets (+ Hebrew lemmata).  Oriental semi-cursive script; very sporadic Tiberian vocalisation.
Paper; 2 leaves (1 bifolium); slightly rubbed.
13.9 × 8.7;  11–12 lines.
Divine name: יי; words omitted in text. [1271]

**T-S AS 70.86**  Genesis 24:10–14, 18–22
Aramaic: Onqelos (+ Hebrew lemmata).  Oriental semi-cursive script; unpointed (except lemmata with Tiberian vocalisation).
Paper; 1 leaf.  14.8 × 12.2;  11–12 lines.
Omission of 24:15–17 unclear; variant to 24:13 גֹא נפקץ/יפקץ. [1272]

**T-S AS 70.90**  Leviticus 27:15–22, 24–32
Aramaic: Onqelos (+ Hebrew lemmata).  Oriental semi-cursive script (lemmata larger than Onqelos); unpointed.
Paper; 1 leaf; very badly mutilated, *recto* very badly rubbed.  15.8⁺ × 8.6⁺;  13⁺ lines.
Divine name: יי. [1273]

**T-S AS 70.91**  Genesis 31:11–13
Hebrew; Aramaic: Onqelos.  Oriental linear square script; Tiberian vocalisation.
Paper; 1 leaf.  19.4 × 12.4;  12 lines.
*Verso* blank. [1274]

**T-S AS 70.93** Genesis 32:13–20
Hebrew; Aramaic: Onqelos. Oriental linear square script; Tiberian vocalisation.
Paper; 1 leaf; mutilated and very badly rubbed. 20.3 × 15.2; 17–18 lines. [1275]

**T-S AS 70.96** Exodus 29:34–9; 29:42 – 30:2
Aramaic: Onqelos (+ Hebrew lemmata). Oriental semi-cursive script; unpointed.
Paper; 1 leaf; very badly mutilated. 14.2⁺ × 9.8⁺; 11⁺ lines.
Divine name: 6יי. [1276]

**T-S AS 70.97** Exodus 20:19/22–20/23
Aramaic: Onqelos (+ Hebrew lemmata). Oriental square script; unpointed.
Paper; 2 leaves; mutilated (folio 2 almost entirely missing). 14.6 × 10.8; 9 lines.
Divine name: יי; heading: בשם יוי; folios 1r and 2 blank. [1277]

**T-S AS 70.99** Genesis 8:17 – 9:2; 9:6–16
Aramaic: Onqelos (+ Hebrew lemmata). Oriental semi-cursive script (lemmata larger square script); unpointed.
Paper; 1 leaf; mutilated and very badly rubbed. 16.8⁺ × 17.2; 17⁺ leaves.
Divine name: יי. [1278]

**T-S AS 70.102** 1 Samuel 17:9–26
Aramaic: Targum Jonathan to Prophets (+ Hebrew lemmata). Oriental semi-cursive script (*recto* larger than *verso*); unpointed.
Paper; 1 leaf; badly mutilated and rubbed. 12.9⁺ × 9.0⁺; 14⁺, 20⁺ lines. [1279]

**T-S AS 70.103** Numbers 28:19–25
Aramaic: Onqelos (+ Hebrew lemmata). Persian(?) square script; Tiberian vocalisation.
Paper; 1 leaf; mutilated. 19.9 × 14.3; 11–12 lines.
Heading on *recto*: [ וחדא מ, illegible. [1280]

**T-S AS 70.104** Genesis 14:17–18
Hebrew; Aramaic: Onqelos. Oriental semi-cursive script; unpointed.
Paper; 1 leaf (mostly cut away). 6.2⁺ × 15.8; 2 lines.
Scribe stopped after two lines on *recto*, remainder blank. [1281]

**T-S AS 70.107 (= T-S AS 70.47)**
Deuteronomy 33:23–7
Hebrew; Aramaic: Onqelos; Judaeo-Arabic. Oriental script; Hebrew linear square; Onqelos semi-cursive.
Paper; 1 leaf. 15.4 × 10.8; 16 lines. [1282]

**T-S AS 70.110** Exodus 6:12
Aramaic: Onqelos. Oriental square script; unpointed.
Paper; 1 leaf; mutilated. 12.5⁺ × 12.1; 5⁺ lines.
Divine name: יי; part of pen exercise(?) in confused order; additional pen exercises in margin; *verso* blank. [1283]

**T-S AS 70.111** Numbers 13:2–4, 18
Aramaic: Onqelos (+ Hebrew lemmata); followed by section of Judaeo-Arabic. Oriental square script; unpointed.
Paper; 1 leaf. 22.9 × 13.1; 18 lines.
Part of pen exercise; *verso* blank except for additional Hebrew pen exercises. [1284]

**T-S AS 70.113** Numbers 16:27–30
Hebrew; Aramaic: Onqelos; Judaeo-Arabic. Oriental script; Hebrew square with Tiberian vocalisation + accents; Onqelos semi-cursive with Tiberian vocalisation.
Paper; 1 leaf; badly mutilated. 13.0⁺ × 12.7; 12⁺ lines. [1285]

**T-S AS 70.114** Joshua 3:5–6; (*haftarah*?)
Aramaic: Targum Jonathan to Prophets (+ Hebrew lemmata). Oriental semi-cursive script; Tiberian vocalisation.
Paper; 1 leaf; badly mutilated. 9.4⁺ × 9.6⁺; 9⁺ lines.
Divine name: יי; heading: בשם רחם; *verso* blank. [1286]

**T-S AS 70.117** Genesis 13:9–10
Hebrew; Aramaic: Onqelos; Judaeo-Arabic. Oriental square script; Tiberian vocalisation.
Paper; 1 leaf; very badly mutilated. 9.4⁺ × 9.4; 8⁺ lines.
Divine name: Onqelos יי. [1287]

**T-S AS 70.118** Leviticus 15:16–30
Hebrew; Aramaic: Onqelos. Oriental semi-cursive script; Tiberian vocalisation + accents.
Paper; 1 leaf; very badly mutilated and rubbed. 20.2⁺ × 13.7⁺; 22⁺ lines. [1288]

**T-S AS 70.121** Genesis 6:5–11
Aramaic: Onqelos (+ Hebrew lemmata). Oriental semi-cursive script; Tiberian vocalisation.
Paper; 1 leaf; mutilated and very badly rubbed. 14.4⁺ × 12.6; 9⁺ lines.
Divine name: יי. [1289]

**T-S AS 70.123** Genesis 38:28 – 39:2; 39:8–11
Hebrew; Aramaic: Onqelos; Judaeo-Arabic. Yemenite square script; Hebrew with Tiberian vocalisation + accents; Onqelos with Babylonian vocalisation.

**[T-S AS 70.123, cont.]**
Paper; 1 leaf; very badly mutilated. 12.5⁺ × 8.4⁺; 12⁺ lines. [1290]

**T-S AS 70.125** Genesis 5:30 – 6:3
Aramaic: Onqelos (+ Hebrew lemmata). Oriental semi-cursive script; Tiberian vocalisation.
Paper; 1 leaf; badly mutilated and rubbed. 10.5⁺ × 12.2; 7⁺ lines.
Divine name: יי. [1291]

**T-S AS 70.126** Genesis 24:52–63
Aramaic: Onqelos (+ Hebrew lemmata). Oriental semi-cursive script; Tiberian vocalisation.
Paper; 1 leaf; badly mutilated. 18.2 × 11.7⁺; 14 lines.
Divine name: יי. [1292]

**T-S AS 70.127** Genesis 44:25–9; 44:32 – 45:1
Aramaic: Onqelos (+ Hebrew lemmata). Oriental semi-cursive script; unpointed.
Paper; 1 leaf; very badly mutilated. 10.8⁺ × 12.3⁺; 10⁺ lines. [1293]

**T-S AS 70.128, 129** Genesis 1:12–15 (AS 70.129), 16–20 (AS 70.128)
Hebrew; Aramaic: Onqelos; Judaeo-Arabic. Oriental script; Hebrew square with Tiberian vocalisation + accents; Onqelos semi-cursive with Tiberian vocalisation.
Paper; 2 leaves; very badly mutilated and rubbed. 9.0⁺ × 10.8⁺; 6⁺ lines.
Divine name: Hebrew אלהים; Onqelos יי. [1294]

**T-S AS 70.130** Isaiah 12:6 – 13:4; 14:32; 2 Samuel 5:13–21; 6:1–2; Isaiah 65:23; (*haftarot*)
Aramaic: Targum Jonathan to Prophets (+ Hebrew lemmata). Oriental square script; unpointed.
Paper; 1 leaf; stained. 13.8 × 9.0; 23 lines.
Divine name: יי; these are triennial *haftarot* for Genesis 24:42; 25:1; 25:19 respectively; headings before 2 Samuel: ויוסף אברהם בשמואל and before Isaiah 65: תולדות יצחק בישעיה. [1295]

**T-S AS 70.131** Leviticus 4:7–13
Hebrew; Aramaic: Onqelos; Judaeo-Arabic. Oriental semi-cursive script; Tiberian vocalisation (Hebrew & Onqelos).
Paper; 1 leaf; mutilated and very badly rubbed. 14.6 × 11.0⁺; 15–16 lines. [1296]

**T-S AS 70.132** Exodus 16:23–31; 17:9–14
Aramaic: Onqelos. Oriental semi-cursive script; Tiberian vocalisation.
Paper; 1 leaf; very badly mutilated. 9.0⁺ × 6.4⁺; 11⁺ lines.
Divine name: יי. [1297]

**T-S AS 70.135** Isaiah 55:7–10; 56:3–6
Aramaic: Targum Jonathan to Prophets (+ Hebrew lemmata). Oriental square script; Tiberian vocalisation.
Paper; 1 leaf; very badly mutilated. 8.5⁺ × 9.5⁺; 8⁺ lines.
Divine name: יי. [1298]

**T-S AS 70.139** Exodus 12:50–51
Aramaic: Onqelos. Oriental square script; unpointed.
Paper; 1 leaf very badly mutilated. 9.8⁺ × 6.0⁺; 4⁺ lines.
Divine name: יי; *verso* blank. [1299]

**T-S AS 70.140–142** Exodus 12:22–7 (AS 70.141), 27–38 (AS 70.140), 38–49 (AS 70.142)
Aramaic: Onqelos. Oriental square script; sporadic Tiberian vocalisation in lighter ink.
Paper; 3 leaves; badly mutilated. 16.6 × 6.4⁺; 13–14 lines.
Divine name: יי. [1300]

**T-S AS 70.145** (= T-S AS 70.152, 160)
Leviticus 5:7–8, 16–17
Aramaic: Onqelos (+ Hebrew lemmata). Oriental semi-cursive script; sporadic Tiberian vocalisation.
Paper; 1 leaf; very badly mutilated. 7.1⁺ × 12.8⁺; 4⁺ lines. [1301]

**T-S AS 70.149** Numbers 35:19–22; 36:1–3
Aramaic: Onqelos (+ Hebrew lemmata). Oriental semi-cursive script; Tiberian vocalisation.
Paper; 1 leaf; very badly mutilated and rubbed. 8.5⁺ × 9.2⁺; 6⁺ lines. [1302]

**T-S AS 70.152** (= T-S AS 70.145, 160)
Leviticus 5:26 – 6:1; 6:10–11
Aramaic: Onqelos (+ Hebrew lemmata). Oriental semi-cursive script.
Paper; 1 leaf; very badly mutilated and rubbed. 7.7⁺ × 12.8⁺; 4⁺ lines.
Divine name: tetragrammaton; trace of decorative *parashah* notation in margin at 6:1. [1303]

**T-S AS 70.160** (= T-S AS 70.145, 152)
Leviticus 5:15–16
Additional minute fragment (6.5⁺ × 6.0⁺) belonging to same manuscript as T-S AS 70.145, 152; see description above; *verso* not identified. [1304]

**T-S AS 70.162** Genesis 12:1–5
Aramaic: Onqelos (+ Hebrew lemmata). Oriental semi-cursive script; Tiberian vocalisation.

[T-S AS 70.162, cont.]
Paper; 1 leaf; mutilated.   14.4⁺ × 11.5⁺;   13⁺ lines.
Divine name: יׁי; cipher in 12:4 זן ט for 75.   [1305]

### T-S AS 70.165 (= T-S AS 70.172)   Genesis 41:8–11, 14–16
Aramaic: Onqelos (+ Hebrew lemmata).   Oriental semi-cursive script (lemmata square); Tiberian vocalisation.
Paper; 1 leaf; very badly mutilated.   10.2⁺ × 13.3; 8⁺ lines.   [1306]

### T-S AS 70.172 (= T-S AS 70.165)   Genesis 38:3–14
Aramaic: Onqelos (+ Hebrew lemmata).   Oriental semi-cursive script (lemmata square); Tiberian vocalisation.
Paper; 1 leaf; mutilated and rubbed.   14.4⁺ × 13.4; 13⁺ lines.
Divine name: יׁי.   [1307]

### T-S AS 70.173   Exodus 31:10–13, 17–18
Hebrew; Aramaic: Onqelos; Judaeo-Arabic. Oriental square script; unpointed.
Paper; 1 leaf; very badly mutilated.   7.2⁺ × 14.3⁺; 8⁺ lines.
Divine name: Hebrew tetragrammaton; Onqelos ייי; Judaeo-Arabic missing for 31:11–12.   [1308]

### T-S AS 70.174   Exodus 28:1–2, 8–9
Aramaic: Onqelos.   Oriental square script; Tiberian vocalisation.
Paper; 1 leaf (minute fragment).   4.5⁺ × 5.5⁺; 3⁺ lines.   [1309]

### T-S AS 70.176 (= T-S AS 70.209–214; AS 71.1–5, 214–217, 281; AS 85.39)
Genesis 44:19–20
Aramaic: Palestinian Targum.   Oriental semi-cursive script; unpointed.
Paper; 1 leaf (minute fragment).   5.9⁺ × 2.9⁺; 5⁺ lines.
Klein *GMPT* I, p.141.   [1310]

### T-S AS 70.178   Ecclesiastes 1:12–16; 2:1–6
Aramaic: Targum Qohelet (+ Hebrew lemmata). Oriental semi-cursive script; unpointed.
Paper; 1 leaf; badly mutilated and rubbed. 13.0⁺ × 14.5;   16⁺ lines.   [1311]

### T-S AS 70.179   Deuteronomy 3:15–18, 20–21
Aramaic: Onqelos (+ Hebrew lemmata).   Oriental semi-cursive script; unpointed.
Paper; 1 leaf; badly mutilated and rubbed. 10.5⁺ × 13.0;   7⁺ lines.
Divine name: יׁי.   [1312]

### T-S AS 70.180   Genesis 41:30–33, 35–9
Aramaic: Onqelos (+ Hebrew lemmata).   Oriental semi-cursive script; Tiberian vocalisation.
Paper; 1 leaf; very badly mutilated.   9.6⁺ × 9.6⁺; 8⁺ lines.   [1313]

### T-S AS 70.182   2 Samuel 17:18–20, 25–7
Aramaic: Targum Jonathan to Prophets (+ Hebrew lemmata).   Oriental semi-cursive script; unpointed.
Paper; 1 leaf; very badly mutilated and rubbed. 5.7⁺ × 9.0⁺;   6⁺ lines.
Decorative *samekh* in margin at 17:20.   [1314]

### T-S AS 70.185   Numbers 21:22–3, 26–8
Aramaic: Onqelos.   Oriental semi-cursive script; sporadic Tiberian vocalisation.
Paper; 1 leaf; very badly mutilated and rubbed. 10.3⁺ × 7.4⁺;   8⁺ lines.   [1315]

### T-S AS 70.186   Poem to Exodus 12:2
Aramaic in part(?).   Oriental semi-cursive script; unpointed.
Paper; 2 leaves (1 bifolium); very badly rubbed. 10.3 × 8.5;   12–13 lines.   [1316]

### T-S AS 70.188   Exodus 25:36–40; 26:3–4
Aramaic: Onqelos (+ Hebrew lemmata).   Oriental semi-cursive script; sporadic Tiberian vocalisation.
Paper; 1 leaf; very badly mutilated.   12.3⁺ × 5.0⁺; 13⁺ lines.   [1317]

### T-S AS 70.192   Exodus 14:19–24; 15:2–10
Aramaic: Onqelos.   Oriental semi-cursive script; Tiberian vocalisation.
Paper; 1 leaf; very badly mutilated.   9.5⁺ × 8.9⁺; 11⁺ lines.
Divine name: יׁי.   [1318]

### T-S AS 70.193   Genesis 22:8–9, 13
Aramaic: Onqelos (+ Hebrew lemmata).   Oriental linear square script; Tiberian vocalisation.
Paper; 1 leaf (minute fragment).   5.0⁺ × 3.0⁺; 4⁺ lines.   [1319]

### T-S AS 70.194   Isaiah 57:17–19; 58:5–7
Aramaic: Targum Jonathan to Prophets (+ Hebrew lemmata).   Oriental semi-cursive script; Tiberian vocalisation.
Paper; 1 leaf; very badly mutilated.   7.5⁺ × 6.7⁺; 7⁺ lines.   [1320]

### T-S AS 70.198   Genesis 49:1–8
Aramaic: Onqelos (+ Hebrew lemmata).   Oriental semi-cursive script; Tiberian vocalisation.
Paper; 1 leaf; mutilated and rubbed.   16.2 × 13.1; 11 lines.   [1321]

**T-S AS 70.199**  Leviticus 2:8 – 3:7
Aramaic: Onqelos (+ Hebrew lemmata).  Oriental square script; Tiberian vocalisation + accents.
Paper; 2 leaves (1 bifolium); badly mutilated. 18.8 × 13.3;  13 lines.
Divine name ׳֯ל֯; Judaeo-Arabic glosses in margins.
[1322]

**T-S AS 70.203**  1 Samuel 20:18–21, 26–7; Isaiah 66:15–17, 20–22;  (*haftarot*)
Aramaic: Targum Jonathan to Prophets (+ Hebrew lemmata).  Oriental square script; unpointed.
Paper; 2 leaves (1 bifolium); badly mutilated. 13.3⁺ × 16.0;  9⁺ lines.
Divine name: ׳׳׳; these are *haftarot* for Mahar Hodesh and Shabbat Rosh Hodesh respectively. [1323]

**T-S AS 70.204**  Ezekiel 45:23 – 46:1; Isaiah 66 1–5 (folio 1); 1 Samuel 20:21–32 (folio 2); (*haftarot*)
Aramaic: Targum Jonathan to Prophets (+ Hebrew lemmata).  Oriental square script; Tiberian vocalisation.
Paper; 2 leaves (1 bifolium); very badly mutilated. 27.8 × 16.0;  19 lines.
Divine name: ״ײ; these are *haftarot* for Shabbat ha-Hodesh, Shabbat Rosh Hodesh and Mahar Hodesh respectively. [1324]

**T-S AS 70.206**  Numbers 28:22–5; Exodus 19:1–10 (folio 1); Numbers 28:26–31; Genesis 21:4–9 (folio 2)
Aramaic: Palestinian Targum (+ Hebrew lemmata).  Oriental square script; unpointed.
Paper; 2 leaves (1 bifolium); very badly mutilated, most of folio 2 missing.  13.9⁺ × 13.9;  16⁺ lines.
Divine name: ״ײ; this is a collection of Torah and *maftir* readings for the festivals.
Klein *GMPT* I, pp. 327, 329. [1325]

**T-S AS 70.208**  Genesis 22:1–7 (folio 1); 22:23 – 23:8 (folio 2)
Hebrew; Aramaic: Onqelos; Judaeo-Arabic. Oriental script; Hebrew square with Tiberian vocalisation + accents; Onqelos semi-cursive with Tiberian vocalisation.
Paper; 2 leaves (1 bifolium); slightly mutilated. 26.0 × 18.5;  18 lines.
Divine name: Hebrew אלהים; Onqelos ״ײ; cipher קמק for number of verses in *parashat wayera'* and decorative *parashah* notation at 23:1 (folio 2) ✿. [1326]

**T-S AS 70.209–214** (= T-S AS 70.176; AS 71.1–5, 214–217, 281; AS 85.39)
Genesis 44:18 (AS 70.209, 210); 48:3–5, 11–13 (AS 70.213); 48:18–20; 49:1 (AS 70.211); 49:4, 8–9 (AS 70.212), 12–13, 18 (AS 70.214)
Aramaic: Palestinian Targum (+ Hebrew lemmata).  Oriental semi-cursive script; sporadic Tiberian vocalisation.
Paper; 5 leaves; very badly mutilated.  7.6⁺ × 12.9⁺ (largest);  6⁺ lines.
*Verso* of T-S AS 70.209, 210 blank.
Klein *GMPT* I, pp. 139, 141, 157–67 (except AS 70.214).
[1327]

**T-S AS 70.218, 219**  Exodus 14:12–13, 27–9 (AS 70.218); Deuteronomy 32:39–40, 51–2 (AS 70.219)
Aramaic: Onqelos (+ Hebrew lemmata).  Spanish semi-cursive script; unpointed.
Paper; 2 leaves; very badly mutilated and rubbed. 5.2⁺ × 13.2;  5⁺ lines.
Divine name: ׳֯ײ. [1328]

**T-S AS 70.220** (= T-S AS 71.101)  Leviticus 17:4
Hebrew; Aramaic: Onqelos.  Oriental square script; unpointed.
1 leaf (minute fragment).  4.1⁺ × 7.3⁺;  4⁺ lines.
Divine name: Hebrew tetragrammaton; *verso* not identified, mostly rubbed. [1329]

**T-S AS 70.221**  Exodus 35:35 – 36:3; 36:12–17
Hebrew; Aramaic: Onqelos; Judaeo-Arabic. Oriental script; Hebrew linear square with Tiberian vocalisation + accents; Onqelos semi-cursive with Tiberian vocalisation.
Paper; 2 leaves (1 bifolium); badly mutilated and rubbed.  17.7 × 13.3;  17–18 lines.
Divine name: Hebrew tetragrammaton; Onqelos י֯ײ. [1330]

**T-S AS 70.222**  Joshua 2:2–4, 6–10; Micah 5:13 – 6:2; 6:4 + *Tosefta*; (*haftarot*)
Aramaic: Targum Jonathan to Prophets (+ Hebrew lemmata).  Oriental square script; Tiberian vocalisation.
Vellum; 2 leaves (1 bifolium); badly mutilated and rubbed.  14.4 × 10.5;  15 lines.
Divine name: י֯; these are *haftarot* for *parashot shelah* and *balaq* respectively. [1331]

**T-S AS 70.225**  Exodus 12:23–6, 46–8
Hebrew; Aramaic: Onqelos.  Oriental square script; unpointed.

[T-S AS 70.225, cont.]
Vellum; 1 leaf; very badly mutilated. 8.3⁺×9.9⁺; 2(?) cols.; 12⁺ lines.
Divine name: Hebrew tetragrammaton; Onqelos ״׳. [1332]

**T-S AS 70.229** *Tosefta* to Genesis 44:18
Aramaic: Palestinian Targum. Oriental square script; Tiberian vocalisation.
Vellum; 1 leaf; very badly mutilated. 10.2⁺×5.7⁺; 18⁺ lines.
Divine name: יֽ; *verso* unidentified.
Klein *GMPT* I, p.135. [1333]

**T-S AS 70.230** Genesis 21:20 – 22:5
Hebrew; Aramaic: Onqelos. Oriental square script; unpointed.
Vellum; 1 leaf; mutilated. 19.1×17.0⁺; 15–19 lines.
Divine name: ״׳. [1334]

**T-S AS 70.233** 2 Samuel 21:20 – 22:1
Hebrew; Aramaic: Targum Jonathan to Prophets. Oriental square script; Hebrew with Tiberian vocalisation + accents; Targum unpointed.
Vellum; 1 leaf; mutilated. 8.8×7.8; 10–11 lines.
Divine name: Hebrew tetragrammaton; Targum ״׳. [1335]

**T-S AS 70.237** Ezekiel 1:6–7, 10
Hebrew; Aramaic: Targum Jonathan to Prophets. Oriental square script; Tiberian vocalisation.
Vellum; 1 leaf (minute fragment). 9.8⁺×5.3⁺; 8⁺ lines. [1336]

**T-S AS 70.238** (= T-S AS 70.240) 2 Samuel 22:13–16, 23–6
Hebrew; Aramaic: Targum Jonathan to Prophets. Spanish square script in poetic format; Tiberian vocalisation.
Vellum; 1 leaf; very badly mutilated. 9.7⁺×13.9⁺; 8⁺ lines.
Divine name: Hebrew tetragrammaton; Targum ⟨יֽ⟩. [1337]

**T-S AS 70.239** Deuteronomy 7:25 – 8:6; 8:13–19
Aramaic: Onqelos (+ Hebrew lemmata). Oriental square script; sporadic Tiberian vocalisation in darker ink.
Vellum; 1 leaf; very badly mutilated. 10.5⁺×8.6⁺; 13⁺ lines.
Divine name: ״׳/״׳. [1338]

**T-S AS 70.240** (= T-S AS 70.238) 2 Samuel 22:9–10, 16–17
Part of same leaf as T-S AS 70.238; see description above. [1339]

**T-S AS 70.242** (= T-S AS 70.250) Genesis 11:15–19
Aramaic: Onqelos (+ Hebrew lemmata). Oriental square script; unpointed.
Vellum; 1 leaf; slightly mutilated. 10.5⁺×10.4; 7 lines. [1340]

**T-S AS 70.245** Numbers 3:45–8; 3:51 – 4:5; 4:7–10, 14–15
Hebrew; Aramaic: Onqelos. Oriental square script; unpointed.
Vellum; 1 leaf; badly mutilated. 17.0⁺×[23.0]; 2 cols.; 14⁺ lines.
Divine name: Hebrew tetragrammaton. [1341]

**T-S AS 70.247 and AS 70.267** Joshua 5:6–7, 9–10, 14–15; (*hafṭarah*)
Hebrew; Aramaic: Targum Jonathan to Prophets. Oriental square script; unpointed.
Vellum; 1 leaf; very badly mutilated (+ minute fragment, AS 70.267). 14.4⁺×[23.0]; 2 cols.; 9⁺ lines.
This is the *hafṭarah* for first day Passover. [1342]

**T-S AS 70.250** (= T-S AS 70.242) Genesis 12:8–12
Aramaic: Onqelos (+ Hebrew lemmata). Oriental square script; unpointed.
Vellum; 1 leaf; mutilated. 12.2×10.5; 7 lines.
Divine name: יֽ. [1343]

**T-S AS 70.252** 2 Kings 4:1, 3–4, 6–10; (*hafṭarah*)
Hebrew; Aramaic: Targum Jonathan to Prophets. Oriental square script; Hebrew with Tiberian vocalisation + accents; Targum with Tiberian vocalisation.
Vellum; 1 leaf; very badly mutilated and rubbed. 6.5⁺×16.5⁺; 2 cols.; 6⁺ lines.
Vocalisation and accents of Hebrew in darker ink; this is the *hafṭarah* for *parashat wayera'*. [1344]

**T-S AS 70.258 and AS 70.263** Isaiah 49:10–15, 18–21
Hebrew; Aramaic: Targum Jonathan to Prophets. Oriental square script; Hebrew with Tiberian vocalisation + accents; Targum with Tiberian vocalisation.
Vellum; 1 leaf; very badly mutilated. 9.0⁺×9.5⁺; 10⁺ lines. [1345]

**T-S AS 70.260**
Minute fragment; probably targum, not identified. [1346]

**T-S AS 70.262** Ezekiel 28:26 – 29:1; 29:4–5; (*haftarah*)
Aramaic: Targum Jonathan to Prophets. Oriental square script; unpointed.
Vellum; 1 leaf; very badly mutilated. 6.3⁺ × 7.2⁺; 6⁺ lines.
This is the *haftarah* for *parashat wa'era'*. [1347]

**T-S AS 70.263**
See T-S AS 70.258 above. [1348]

**T-S AS 70.264**
Minute fragment; possibly targum, not identified. [1349]

**T-S AS 70.267**
See T-S AS 70.247 above. [1350]

**T-S AS 70.268**
Minute fragment; possibly targum, not identified. [1351]

**T-S AS 70.269** Jeremiah 31:8–9, 15; (*haftarah*)
Hebrew; Aramaic: Targum Jonathan to Prophets. Oriental square script; unpointed.
Vellum; 2 leaves (or 2 sheets of a scroll, sewn together). 8.3⁺ × 17.5⁺; 2 cols. (per sheet); 6⁺ lines.
Divine name: Targum ייי; *verso* of both sheets blank; this is the *haftarah* for second day New Year. [1352]

**T-S AS 70.272** Genesis 2:16–21
Aramaic: Onqelos (+ Hebrew lemmata). Oriental square script; unpointed.
Vellum; 1 leaf; badly mutilated. 13.8 × 6.2⁺; 9 lines.
Divine name: יי; variant in 2:18 אינשא for אדם. [1353]

**T-S AS 70.275** Deuteronomy 16:2–3(?), 16
Aramaic: Onqelos. Oriental square script; Tiberian vocalisation.
Paper; 1 leaf (minute fragment). 3.6⁺ × 5.0⁺; 4⁺ lines.
Divine name: יְיָ; part of 16:2–3 unclear לדרי דריא(?). [1354]

**T-S AS 70.276**
37 minute fragments without individual classmarks, a number of which are targumic. The first and third pieces in the upper row contain Onqelos to Exodus 20:22–3, and a small vellum piece in Italian (perhaps early Oriental) script in the third row contains Onqelos to Exodus 20:5, with a heading in majusculae on the *verso*; probably the beginning of *parashat mishpatim* (Exodus 21:1). [1355]

**T-S AS 71.1–5** (= T-S AS 70.176, 209–214; AS 71.214–217, 281; AS 85.39) Genesis 44:16–18; 47:26–7 (AS 71.1,2); 47:28 – 49:7 (AS 71.3–5)
Aramaic: Palestinian Targum (+ Hebrew lemmata). Oriental semi-cursive script; sporadic Tiberian vocalisation.
Paper; 5 leaves; very badly mutilated. 7.2⁺ × 13.0 (largest); 8⁺ lines.
Divine name: אדני; *verso* of T-S AS 71.1,2 blank; 47:26–7 out of place.
Klein *GMPT* I, pp. 139–41, 157–67. [1356]

**T-S AS 71.6** Exodus 12:21–5
Aramaic: Onqelos (+ Hebrew lemmata, some missing). Oriental semi-cursive script; Tiberian vocalisation.
Paper; 1 leaf; slightly mutilated. 21.0 × 12.0; 16 lines.
Divine name: א; heading: בשם רחמ; *verso* blank except for one line of Arabic. [1357]

**T-S AS 71.9** Genesis 26:28, 31–3
Hebrew; Aramaic: Onqelos; Judaeo-Arabic. Oriental script; Hebrew square with Tiberian vocalisation + accents; Onqelos semi-cursive with Tiberian vocalisation.
Paper; 1 leaf; very badly mutilated. 9.4⁺ × 13.0⁺; 10⁺ lines. [1358]

**T-S AS 71.10** Genesis 46:20–29
Hebrew; Aramaic: Onqelos. Oriental linear square script; Tiberian vocalisation.
Paper; 1 leaf; badly rubbed. 19.8 × 14.1; 15–16 lines. [1359]

**T-S AS 71.11** Jeremiah 31:6–8, 15–16
Aramaic: Targum Jonathan to Prophets (+ Hebrew lemmata). Oriental semi-cursive script; Tiberian vocalisation.
Paper; 1 leaf; very badly mutilated. 8.5⁺ × 9.8⁺; 9⁺ lines.
Divine name: יְיָ. [1360]

**T-S AS 71.12** Leviticus 1:2–3
Aramaic: Onqelos. Oriental semi-cursive script; unpointed.
Paper; 1 leaf; badly mutilated. 12.8⁺ × 7.3⁺; 6⁺ lines.
Divine name: יְיָ; text ends in the middle of 1:3, followed by Hebrew and Arabic jottings on remainder of *recto* and *verso*, including two copies of the opening phrase of Mishnah *Berakhot* 1:1. [1361]

**T-S AS 71.13** Exodus 15:4–10 (folio 1); Numbers 28:10, 16–17 (folio 2)
Aramaic: Onqelos (+ Hebrew lemmata). Oriental linear square script; Tiberian vocalisation.

[T-S AS 71.13, cont.]
Paper; 2 leaves (1 bifolium); slightly mutilated.
10.5 × 7.3; 9–11 lines.
Divine name: יְ֔יָ; heading before Numbers 28:16: תֻּנ֗ום
מֹ֗וסף פֹּסֹ֗ח בחודש הרא' (folio 2v). [1362]

**T-S AS 71.20**  Genesis 11:15–26
Hebrew; Aramaic: Onqelos.  Oriental(?) square script; Tiberian vocalisation + accents (Hebrew & Onqelos) in lighter ink.
Paper; 1 leaf; badly mutilated.  15.6⁺ × 18.6;  14⁺ lines. [1363]

**T-S AS 71.26**  Genesis 5:10–28
Aramaic: Onqelos (+ Hebrew lemmata).  Oriental semi-cursive script; unpointed.
Paper; 1 leaf; very badly mutilated.  11.2⁺ × 10.5⁺; 15⁺ lines.
Verso blank. [1364]

**T-S AS 71.28**  Genesis 32:7–8
Hebrew; Aramaic: Onqelos.  Oriental linear square script; unpointed.
Paper; 1 leaf; lower half cut away.  7.7⁺ × 12.6; 3 lines.
Text ends abruptly after Hebrew of 32:8; verso blank. [1365]

**T-S AS 71.29**  Genesis 11:13–17, 21–5
Aramaic: Onqelos; Judaeo-Arabic (+ Hebrew lemmata).  Oriental semi-cursive script; unpointed.
Paper; 1 leaf; badly mutilated and rubbed. 12.5⁺ × 16.5;  9⁺ lines. [1366]

**T-S AS 71.31**  Jeremiah 2:22–7; (haftarah)
Aramaic: Targum Jonathan to Prophets.  Oriental square script; unpointed (except for sporadic Tiberian vocalisation in 2:23).
Paper; 1 leaf; slightly mutilated and rubbed. 14.4 × 10.0;  15 lines.
This is the haftarah for parashat mas'ei. [1367]

**T-S AS 71.32**  Numbers 28:28–31
Aramaic: Onqelos.  Oriental square script; unpointed.
Paper; 1 leaf; very badly mutilated and rubbed. 12.5⁺ × 5.6⁺;  9⁺ lines.
Verso illegible. [1368]

**T-S AS 71.34**  Genesis 7:19–21 (folio 1); 8:9–11 (folio 2)
Hebrew; Aramaic: Onqelos; Judaeo-Arabic. Oriental semi-cursive script; Tiberian vocalisation.
Paper; 2 leaves (1 bifolium); very badly mutilated. 13.2⁺ × 9.3⁺;  10⁺ lines. [1369]

**T-S AS 71.35**  Ezekiel 20:3–8; (haftarah)
Hebrew; Aramaic: Targum Jonathan to Prophets. Oriental script; Hebrew square with Tiberian vocalisation; Targum semi-cursive with sporadic Tiberian vocalisation.
Paper; 1 leaf; badly mutilated.  12.7⁺ × 12.7;  10⁺ lines.
Divine name: Hebrew tetragrammaton; Targum יי; this is the haftarah for parashat qedoshim. [1370]

**T-S AS 71.40**  Genesis 41:13–16, 22–6
Hebrew; Aramaic: Onqelos; Judaeo-Arabic. Yemenite square script; Hebrew with Tiberian vocalisation + accents; Onqelos with Babylonian vocalisation.
Paper; 1 leaf; very badly mutilated.  10.5⁺ × 4.8⁺; 12⁺ lines.
Divine name: Hebrew אלהים. [1371]

**T-S AS 71.43**  Leviticus 17:13–14; 18:3–5
Aramaic: Onqelos (+ Hebrew lemmata).  Oriental semi-cursive script; unpointed.
Paper; 1 leaf (minute fragment).  6.9⁺ × 4.7⁺;  6⁺ lines. [1372]

**T-S AS 71.54**
Minute paper fragment, possibly with a targum or an Aramaic poem to Esther 5–6. [1373]

**T-S AS 71.55–57**  Genesis 7:18, 21 (AS 71.56); 7:23; 8:1 (AS 71.55, 57)
Hebrew; Aramaic: Onqelos.  Oriental semi-cursive script; Hebrew with Tiberian vocalisation + accents; Onqelos unpointed.
Paper; 3 minute fragments of 2 leaves.  5.3⁺ × 6.9⁺; 4⁺ lines. [1374]

**T-S AS 71.59**  Exodus 19:1–7 (folio 1)
Aramaic: Palestinian Targum (+ Hebrew lemmata).  Oriental semi-cursive script; unpointed except for sporadic dagesh.
Paper; 2 leaves (1 bifolium); slightly mutilated and badly rubbed.  13.4 × 9.0;  11–13 lines.
Klein GMPT I, p.259. [1375]

**T-S AS 71.64**  Exodus 12:21–31 (folio 1); Aramaic introductory poem to haftarot (folio 2v)
Aramaic: Onqelos (+ Hebrew lemmata).  Oriental semi-cursive script; Tiberian vocalisation.
Paper; 2 leaves (1 bifolium).  16.2 × 12.0;  13–15 lines.
Divine name: יי; folio 2r contains a Hebrew poem and folio 2v an introductory reshut to the haftarot containing a legend about the miraculous effects of Jonathan b. 'Uzziel's study of the Torah (cf. T-S B11.17). See plate 21. [1376]

**T-S AS 71.71**  Genesis 44:11–20
Hebrew; Aramaic: Onqelos.  Oriental semi-cursive script; Hebrew with Tiberian vocalisation + accents; Onqelos with Tiberian vocalisation.
Paper; 1 leaf; mutilated.  15.7⁺×14.4; 15⁺ lines.
[1377]

**T-S AS 71.75**  Deuteronomy 29:6–7, 9–10
Hebrew; Aramaic: Onqelos.  Oriental linear square script; Tiberian vocalisation (*recto* only).
Paper; 1 leaf; very badly mutilated.  11.4⁺×12.7; 7⁺ lines.
Divine name: Onqelos יׄ.  [1378]

**T-S AS 71.82**  Genesis 3:22 – 4:3; 4:9–14
Aramaic: Onqelos (+ Hebrew lemmata).  Oriental semi-cursive script; Tiberian vocalisation.
Paper; 1 leaf; badly mutilated and rubbed. 12.0⁺×11.1⁺; 10⁺ lines.
Divine name: יׄ.  [1379]

**T-S AS 71.88**  Numbers 29:38 – 30:9 (folio 1); 31:29–35, 41–7 (folio 2)
Aramaic: Onqelos (+ Hebrew lemmata).  Oriental semi-cursive script; Tiberian vocalisation.
Paper; 2 leaves (1 bifolium); badly mutilated and very badly rubbed.  17.0×13.1; 18 lines.
Divine name: יי; heading for beginning of *parashah* at 31:2 (folio 1r); folio 1 almost entirely illegible.  [1380]

**T-S AS 71.92**  Genesis 22:8–10, 13–14
Aramaic: Onqelos.  Oriental linear square script; Tiberian vocalisation.
Paper; 1 leaf (minute fragment).  8.9⁺×4.7⁺; 7⁺ lines.
[1381]

**T-S AS 71.96**  Deuteronomy 7:12–18, 20–24
Aramaic: Onqelos (+ Hebrew lemmata).  Oriental semi-cursive script; Tiberian vocalisation.
Paper; 1 leaf; very badly mutilated and rubbed. 15.0⁺×10.1⁺; 13⁺ lines.
Divine name: יׄ.  [1382]

**T-S AS 71.98 (= T-S AS 71.108, 117)**
Genesis 39:8, 10
Hebrew; Aramaic: Onqelos; Judaeo-Arabic. Oriental script; Hebrew square with Tiberian vocalisation + accents; Onqelos semi-cursive with Tiberian vocalisation.
Paper; 1 leaf (minute fragment).  5.2⁺×6.9⁺; 5⁺ lines.
[1383]

**T-S AS 71.99**  Genesis 6:13–17
Hebrew; Aramaic: Onqelos.  Oriental script; Hebrew square; Onqelos semi-cursive; unpointed.
Paper; 1 leaf; slightly mutilated and rubbed. 17.4×12.8;  11 lines.
[1384]

**T-S AS 71.101 (= T-S AS 70.220)**  Leviticus 17:4–5, 9
Hebrew; Aramaic: Onqelos.  Oriental square script; unpointed.
Paper; 1 leaf (minute fragment).  3.5⁺×9.1⁺; 4⁺ lines.
[1385]

**T-S AS 71.105**  Genesis 38:25–7
Hebrew; Aramaic: Onqelos; Judaeo-Arabic. Oriental script; Hebrew square with Tiberian vocalisation + accents; Onqelos semi-cursive with Tiberian vocalisation.
Paper; 1 leaf.  13.8×9.5;  11 lines.  [1386]

**T-S AS 71.108 (= T-S AS 71.98, 117)**
Genesis 39:7, 9
Hebrew; Aramaic: Onqelos; Judaeo-Arabic. Oriental script; Hebrew square with Tiberian vocalisation + accents; Onqelos semi-cursive with Tiberian vocalisation.
Paper; 1 leaf (minute fragment).  5.0⁺×4.8⁺; 3⁺ lines.
[1387]

**T-S AS 71.111**
Minute paper fragment with single Aramaic word in margin: וניערוק.  [1388]

**T-S AS 71.114**  Exodus 6:3–4, 6
Hebrew; Aramaic: Onqelos.  Oriental semi-cursive script; unpointed(?).
Paper; 1 leaf (minute fragment).  4.1⁺×8.0⁺; 2⁺ lines.
[1389]

**T-S AS 71.117 (= T-S AS 71.98, 108)**
Genesis 39:8–11
Minute paper fragment, 6.0⁺×7.4⁺; see description at T-S AS 71.98 above.  [1390]

**T-S AS 71.119–121**  1 Kings 1:7–9, 14–17, 25; (*haftarah*)
Aramaic: Targum Jonathan to Prophets (+ Hebrew lemmata).  Oriental square script; Tiberian vocalisation + accents (in darker ink).
Paper; 3 minute fragments.  4.8⁺×11.1⁺; 5⁺ lines.
These are fragments of two or three leaves; this is the *haftarah* for *parashat ḥayye sarah*.  [1391]

**T-S AS 71.122, 125**  Genesis 8:9–11
Hebrew; Aramaic: Onqelos; Judaeo-Arabic. Oriental script; Hebrew linear square with Tiberian vocalisation + accents; Onqelos semi-cursive with Tiberian vocalisation.

[T-S AS 71.122, 125, cont.]
Paper; 1 leaf (torn into two parts, separately conserved); very badly mutilated. [15.2⁺] × 8.3⁺; [11⁺] lines.
[1392]

### T-S AS 71.123, 126(?), 128, 129, 132(?) (= T-S AS 71.167, 168, 170, 175, 190)
Isaiah 54:12; 55:2 (AS 71.129); 40:31; 41:8 (AS 71.128, folio 1); 41:15–16 (AS 71.128, folio 2; AS 71.123); 2 Kings 4:1–3, 5–8, 11–12, 17 (AS 71.128, folio 2); (*haftarot*)
Hebrew; Aramaic: Targum Jonathan to Prophets. Oriental square script; Hebrew with Tiberian vocalisation + accents; Targum with Tiberian vocalisation.

Paper; 3⁺ leaves (1 bifolium); very badly mutilated. 13.3⁺ × 18.5 (largest); 10⁺ lines.

These are *haftarot* for *parashot noah*, *lekh lekha* and *wayera'* respectively; fragments T-S AS 71.126, 132 not identified, but they belong to the same manuscript.
[1393]

### T-S AS 71.124   Leviticus 3:14 – 4:1; 4:5–8 (folio 1); 4:11–12, 17 (folio 2)
Aramaic: Onqelos (+ Hebrew lemmata). Oriental semi-cursive script; unpointed.

Paper; 2 leaves (1 bifolium); very badly mutilated. 10.5⁺ × 5.8⁺; 9⁺ lines.

Divine name: ייּ; part of 3:15 seems to have been omitted.
[1394]

### T-S AS 71.125
See T-S AS 71.122 above. [1395]

### T-S AS 71.126
See T-S AS 71.123 above. [1396]

### T-S AS 71.127   Deuteronomy 32:20–21, 31–2
Aramaic: Onqelos (+ Hebrew lemmata). Oriental semi-cursive script; unpointed.

Paper; 1 leaf; very badly mutilated and rubbed. 4.7⁺ × 9.1⁺; 3⁺ lines.
[1397]

### T-S AS 71.128, 129
See T-S AS 71.123 above. [1398]

### T-S AS 71.131   Genesis 38:16–17, 19–21
Hebrew; Aramaic: Onqelos; Judaeo-Arabic. Oriental script; Hebrew square with Tiberian vocalisation + accents; Onqelos semi-cursive with Tiberian vocalisation.

Paper; 1 leaf; very badly mutilated. 13.4⁺ × 12.1⁺; 10⁺ lines.
[1399]

### T-S AS 71.132
See T-S AS 71.123 above. [1400]

### T-S AS 71.142   Numbers 1:30–32, 34–6
Hebrew; Aramaic: Onqelos; Judaeo-Arabic. Oriental script; Hebrew square with Tiberian vocalisation + accents; Onqelos semi-cursive with Tiberian vocalisation.

Paper; 1 leaf; very badly mutilated. 13.5⁺ × 11.2⁺; 13⁺ lines.
[1401]

### T-S AS 71.145   Leviticus 2:6 – 3:6 (folio 1); 4:21–5, 28–33, 35 (folio 2)
Aramaic: Onqelos (+ Hebrew lemmata). Oriental semi-cursive script (lemmata larger square script); Tiberian vocalisation.

Paper; 2 leaves (1 bifolium); badly mutilated. 18.6 × 14.0; 15 lines.

Divine name: יי.
[1402]

### T-S AS 71.148   Exodus 5:7–19
Aramaic: Onqelos (+ Hebrew lemmata). Oriental semi-cursive script; unpointed.

Paper; 1 leaf; badly mutilated and rubbed. 17.0⁺ × 14.0; 14⁺ lines.

Divine name: יי.
[1403]

### T-S AS 71.150   Genesis 3:16–24
Hebrew; Aramaic: Onqelos. Oriental square script; unpointed.

Paper; 1 leaf; slightly mutilated and rubbed. 20.2 × 14.1; 17 lines.

Divine name: Hebrew and Onqelos tetragrammaton.
[1404]

### T-S AS 71.152   Genesis 11:19–21, 26–9
Aramaic: Onqelos; Judaeo-Arabic (+ Hebrew lemmata). Oriental semi-cursive script (lemmata square); unpointed.

Paper; 1 leaf; very badly mutilated. 9.4⁺ × 10.3⁺; 9⁺ lines.
[1405]

### T-S AS 71.158   Genesis 3:12–15
Hebrew; Aramaic: Onqelos; Judaeo-Arabic. Oriental script; Hebrew square; Onqelos semi-cursive; Tiberian vocalisation.

Paper; 1 leaf; mutilated and badly rubbed. 14.6⁺ × 13.5; 14⁺ lines.

Divine name: Hebrew tetragrammaton; Onqelos יי.
[1406]

### T-S AS 71.161   Genesis 41:49–51
Aramaic: Onqelos (+ Hebrew lemmata). Oriental semi-cursive script (lemmata square); Tiberian vocalisation.

Paper; 1 leaf; very badly mutilated and rubbed. 9.5⁺ × 7.7⁺; 7⁺ lines.

*Verso* illegible.
[1407]

**T-S AS 71.162**  Genesis 36:17, 20–21 (folio 1); 37:13–21 (folio 2)
Hebrew; Aramaic: Onqelos. Oriental semi-cursive script; Hebrew with Tiberian vocalisation + accents; Onqelos with Tiberian vocalisation.

Paper; 2 leaves (1 bifolium); badly mutilated and rubbed.  19.8 × 13.5; 15 lines.  [1408]

**T-S AS 71.164**  Numbers 29:20–22, 24–7
Aramaic: Onqelos (+ Hebrew lemmata). Oriental semi-cursive script; Tiberian vocalisation.

Paper; 1 leaf (minute fragment); badly rubbed. 9.8⁺ × 3.9⁺; 7⁺ lines.  [1409]

**T-S AS 71.167** (= T-S AS 71.123 et al.)
Isaiah 42:13–14; 54:3–4; (*haftarot*)

Minute fragment, 7.0⁺ × 5.8⁺; *haftarot* for *parashot bere'shit* and *noah*; see description at T-S AS 71.123 above.  [1410]

**T-S AS 71.168** (= T-S AS 71.123 et al.)
Isaiah 54:11–12; 55:1–2; (*haftarah*)

Minute fragment, 8.2⁺ × 4.7⁺; *haftarah* for *parashat noah*; see description at T-S AS 71.123 above.  [1411]

**T-S AS 71.169**  Joshua 1:3–5; 1 Kings 8:63–4; (*haftarot*)
Hebrew; Aramaic: Targum Jonathan to Prophets. Oriental square script; unpointed.

Paper; 1 leaf (minute fragment).  4.0⁺ × 6.2⁺; 5⁺ lines.

Divine name: Hebrew tetragrammaton; Targum ײ; these are triennial *haftarot* for Deuteronomy 9:1 and 10:1 respectively.  [1412]

**T-S AS 71.170** (= T-S AS 71.123 et al.)
2 Kings 4:12, 21; (*haftarah*)

Minute fragment, 3.4⁺ × 14.4⁺; *haftarah* for *parashat wayera'*; see description at T-S AS 71.123 above.  [1413]

**T-S AS 71.171**  Genesis 49:12–13, 15–16
Hebrew; Aramaic: Onqelos; Judaeo-Arabic. Oriental script; Hebrew square with Tiberian vocalisation + accents; Onqelos semi-cursive with Tiberian vocalisation.

Paper; 1 leaf; very badly mutilated.  7.7⁺ × 6.0⁺; 8⁺ lines.  [1414]

**T-S AS 71.175** (= T-S AS 71.123 et al.)
Isaiah 40:31; 41:5–8; (*haftarah*)

Minute fragment, 10.4⁺ × 5.0⁺; *haftarah* for *parashat lekh lekha*; see description at T-S AS 71.123 above.  [1415]

**T-S AS 71.176**  Exodus 19:1
Hebrew; Aramaic: Onqelos. Oriental script; Hebrew large, square; Onqelos semi-cursive; Tiberian vocalisation.

Paper; 1 leaf; mutilated.  14.2 × 10.0; 9 lines.
Heading: בשמ׳ ר׳ת׳ס תרגום אלעצרה; reading for Pentecost; *verso* blank.  [1416]

**T-S AS 71.179**  Numbers 35:14–18, 31–4
Aramaic: Onqelos (+ Hebrew lemmata). Oriental semi-cursive script; Tiberian vocalisation.

Paper; 1 leaf; very badly mutilated and rubbed. 7.0⁺ × 10.3⁺; 6⁺ lines.  [1417]

**T-S AS 71.180**  Genesis 1:10–27
Aramaic: Onqelos (+ Hebrew lemmata). Oriental semi-cursive script; unpointed.

Paper; 1 leaf; badly mutilated and rubbed. 18.0 × 10.1⁺; 17 lines.
Divine name: ײ/ ײי.  [1418]

**T-S AS 71.184**  Genesis 12:7–11, 14–18
Aramaic: Onqelos. Oriental semi-cursive script; unpointed.

Paper; 1 leaf; badly mutilated.  8.3⁺ × 12.1; 9 lines.
Divine name: ײי. Decorative *custodes* ❂.  [1419]

**T-S AS 71.190** (= T-S AS 71.123 et al.)
Isaiah 40:30 – 41:1; 41:7–8; (*haftarah*)

Minute fragment, 9.1⁺ × 9.7⁺; *haftarah* for *parashat lekh lekha*; see description at T-S AS 71.123 above.  [1420]

**T-S AS 71.191**

Unidentified; Aramaic composition with Tiberian vocalisation; possibly targum to Prophets; very badly rubbed.  [1421]

**T-S AS 71.194**  Ezekiel 20:3–6; (*haftarah*)
Hebrew; Aramaic: Targum Jonathan to Prophets. Oriental script; Hebrew square; Targum semi-cursive; Tiberian vocalisation.

Paper; 1 leaf (minute fragment).  6.3⁺ × 8.5⁺; 4⁺ lines.

Divine name: Hebrew tetragrammaton; Targum ײי; this is the *haftarah* for *parashat qedoshim*.  [1422]

**T-S AS 71.197**  Genesis 31:43–6 (+ 47–8?)
Hebrew; Aramaic: Onqelos. Oriental script; Hebrew square with Tiberian vocalisation + accents; Onqelos semi-cursive with Tiberian vocalisation.

Paper; 1 leaf; mutilated and very badly rubbed. 13.0⁺ × 13.1; 14⁺ lines.

Almost entirely illegible. Targum of 31:46 follows that of 31:47, 48(?).  [1423]

**T-S AS 71.198**  Numbers 29:14–26
Aramaic: Onqelos (+ Hebrew lemmata).  Oriental semi-cursive script; Tiberian vocalisation.
Paper; 1 leaf; badly mutilated and rubbed.  17.0 × 13.5; 14 lines.  [1424]

**T-S AS 71.201**  Unidentified targum(?)
Aramaic.  Spanish square script; unpointed.
Paper; 1 leaf (minute fragment).  6.5⁺ × 4.2⁺;  8⁺ lines.  [1425]

**T-S AS 71.204**  Genesis 21:15–21
Aramaic: Onqelos.  Oriental linear square script; Tiberian vocalisation.
Paper; 1 leaf; badly mutilated.  16.3 × 12.6;  14 lines.
Divine name: יי֒; text ends on line 5 of *verso*, lower half blank.  [1426]

**T-S AS 71.208, 210**  Genesis 3:7–11
Hebrew; Aramaic: Onqelos; Judaeo-Arabic. Oriental script; Hebrew larger, square; Onqelos semi-cursive; Tiberian vocalisation.
Paper; 1 leaf (torn into two parts, separately conserved).  8.8⁺, 5.5⁺ × 13.7;  7⁺, 5⁺ lines.
Divine name: Hebrew tetragrammaton; Onqelos יי֒.  [1427]

**T-S AS 71.211, 212**  Genesis 21:11–19
Aramaic: Onqelos (+ Hebrew lemmata).  Oriental square script; unpointed.
Paper; 1 leaf (torn into two parts, separately conserved); very badly mutilated.  20.3⁺ × 13.5⁺;  14⁺ lines.
Divine name: יי֒.  [1428]

**T-S AS 71.214–217** (= T-S AS 70.176, 209–214; AS 71.1–5; AS 85.39)  Genesis 47:29 – 48:1; 48:6–10, 15–17; 48:21 – 49:3; 49:6–7, 11–12, 16–17
Aramaic: Palestinian Targum (+ Hebrew lemmata).  Oriental semi-cursive script; sporadic Tiberian vocalisation.
Paper; 4 leaves; very badly mutilated.  7.0⁺ × 10.2⁺; 9⁺ lines.
Divine name: יי֒.
Klein *GMPT* I, pp.157–69.  [1429]

**T-S AS 71.218**  Genesis 41:25–40
Aramaic: Onqelos (+ Hebrew lemmata).  Oriental semi-cursive script; Tiberian vocalisation.
Paper; 1 leaf; mutilated.  15.6 × 10.5;  15 lines.
Divine name: יי֒.  [1430]

**T-S AS 71.220**  Zechariah 13:9 – 14:7; (*hafṭarah*)
Hebrew; Aramaic: Targum Jonathan to Prophets. Oriental square script; Hebrew with Tiberian vocalisation + accents; Targum with Tiberian vocalisation.
Paper; 1 leaf; very badly mutilated.  16.7⁺ × 15.8; 17⁺ lines.
Divine name: Hebrew tetragrammaton; Targum יי֒; this is the *hafṭarah* for first day Tabernacles.  [1431]

**T-S AS 71.222**  Genesis 19:5–8, 10–12
Aramaic: Onqelos (+ Hebrew lemmata).  Oriental semi-cursive script; Tiberian vocalisation.
Paper; 1 leaf; very badly mutilated and rubbed. 9.0⁺ × 13.2;  7⁺ lines.  [1432]

**T-S AS 71.225**  Exodus 5:23 – 6:6
Hebrew; Aramaic: Onqelos.  Oriental semi-cursive script; unpointed.
Paper; 1 leaf; very badly mutilated.  8.2⁺ × 10.5⁺; 9 lines.
Divine name: Hebrew tetragrammaton; Onqelos יי֒; cipher כבד for number of verses in *parashat shemot* after 6:1.  [1433]

**T-S AS 71.227**  Genesis 4:9–12, 14–16
Aramaic: Onqelos (+ Hebrew lemmata).  Oriental square script; Tiberian vocalisation.
Paper; 1 leaf; very badly mutilated.  7.7⁺ × 7.3⁺; 8⁺ lines.
Divine name: יי֒.  [1434]

**T-S AS 71.229**  Exodus 40:17–33
Aramaic: Onqelos.  Oriental linear square script; unpointed.
Paper; 2 leaves (1 bifolium); slightly mutilated and rubbed.  13.5 × 8.7;  15–16 lines.
Repeated phrase [כמא] דפקיד יוי ית משה was intentionally omitted by the scribe in 40:19, 21, 23, 25, 27, 29, 32; but 40:28 was unintentionally omitted; folio 1r and lower half of folio 2v blank (except for small Arabic jotting).  [1435]

**T-S AS 71.240**  Genesis 5:9–10, 24–5
Hebrew; Aramaic: Palestinian Targum(?).  Oriental square script; Tiberian vocalisation + accents.
Vellum; 1 leaf (minute fragment).  10.6⁺ × 6.5⁺; [3] cols.;  4⁺ lines.
Divine name: Targum אדני; probably belongs to Kahle *MdW* II and Klein *GMPT* MS B.  [1436]

**T-S AS 71.242**  Exodus 30:12–16
Aramaic: Onqelos.  Oriental semi-cursive script; Tiberian vocalisation + accents.
Vellum; 1 leaf (small scrap).  4.4⁺ × 18.7;  3 lines.
Divine name: יי֒; *mafṭir* of *parashat sheqalim*.  [1437]

### T-S AS 71.243

Hebrew and Aramaic; probably liturgical, not targum. [1438]

### T-S AS 71.244  Exodus 12:27–9

Hebrew; Aramaic: Onqelos. Oriental square script; Tiberian vocalisation.

Vellum; 1 leaf; slightly mutilated. 12.6 × 10.7; 10 lines.

Divine name: Hebrew tetragrammaton (with unusual vocalisation); Onqelos יְיָ/יְיָ. [1439]

### T-S AS 71.245 (= T-S AS 71.257, 267)

1 Kings 1:11–13, 20–21; (*haftarah*)

Hebrew; Aramaic: Targum Jonathan to Prophets. Oriental square script; Tiberian vocalisation.

Vellum; 1 leaf; very badly mutilated. 9.9⁺ × 10.6⁺; [2] cols.; 7⁺ lines.

Divine name: יְיָ; this is the *haftarah* for *parashat ḥayye sarah*. [1440]

### T-S AS 71.246  Malachi 3:6–10; Isaiah 57:16–19; 40:17–21, 25–6, 31; (*haftarot*)

Hebrew; Aramaic: Targum Jonathan to Prophets. Oriental square script; Hebrew with Tiberian vocalisation; Targum unpointed.

Vellum; 2 leaves (1 bifolium); very badly mutilated. 16.0⁺ × 9.2⁺; 15⁺ lines.

Divine name: Hebrew tetragrammaton; Targum יְיָ; these are triennial *haftarot* for Numbers 25:10; 26:52 and 27:15 respectively. [1441]

### T-S AS 71.248  *Tosefta* to Genesis 49:1

Aramaic: Palestinian Targum. Oriental square script (small); Tiberian vocalisation.

Vellum; 1 leaf (2 scraps sewn together); mutilated and rubbed. 12.5⁺ × 7.8⁺; 20⁺ lines.

*Verso* contains part of a Hebrew liturgical composition with mention of the ingathering of exiles to Jerusalem. [1442]

### T-S AS 71.249  Deuteronomy 15:10–12, 15–17

Hebrew; Aramaic: Onqelos. Spanish(?) square script; unpointed.

Vellum; 1 leaf; badly mutilated and rubbed. 13.2⁺ × 10.5⁺; 1⁺ col.; 12⁺ lines.

Divine name: Onqelos יְיָ. [1443]

### T-S AS 71.250

Partly in Aramaic but probably not targum. [1444]

### T-S AS 71.251  Isaiah 49:21–2; Zephaniah 3:16; Joshua 24:4–6; (*haftarot*)

Hebrew; Aramaic: Targum Jonathan to Prophets. Oriental square script; Hebrew with Tiberian vocalisation + accents (in darker ink); Targum with sporadic Tiberian vocalisation.

Vellum; 1 leaf; very badly mutilated. 15.3⁺ × 14.1⁺; 2 cols.; 11⁺ lines.

Divine name: Targum יְיָ; these are triennial *haftarot* for Genesis 9:18, 11:1 and 12:1 respectively; *verso* overwritten in darker ink. [1445]

### T-S AS 71.252  Isaiah 2:3; Judges 11:30–31; 35–7; (*haftarot*)

Hebrew; Aramaic: Targum Jonathan to Prophets. Oriental square script; sporadic Tiberian vocalisation.

Vellum; 1 leaf; very badly mutilated. 17.3⁺ × 12.2⁺; 12⁺ lines.

Divine name: Targum יְיָ; these are triennial *haftarot* for Leviticus 26:3 and 27:2 respectively; trace of heading: שפטים[ ] before Judges 11. [1446]

### T-S AS 71.253  Isaiah 11:9–11; 62:9–10; 63:3–5; Obadiah 1:3–6; (*haftarot*)

Hebrew; Aramaic: Targum Jonathan to Prophets. Oriental square script; Tiberian vocalisation (Hebrew).

Vellum; 1 leaf; very badly mutilated. 12.2⁺ × 12.1⁺; 2 cols.; 14⁺ lines.

These are triennial *haftarot* for Numbers 17:16, 18:25 and 20:14 respectively. [1447]

### T-S AS 71.256  Isaiah 49:19–20; Jeremiah 23:19–20; (*haftarot*)

Hebrew; Aramaic: Targum Jonathan to Prophets. Oriental square script; Hebrew with Tiberian vocalisation + accents; Targum unpointed.

Vellum; 1 leaf; very badly mutilated. 6.6⁺ × 8.9⁺; 7⁺ lines.

Divine name: Targum יְיָ. [1448]

### T-S AS 71.257 (= T-S AS 71.245, 267)

1 Kings 1:14–15, 17–18; (*haftarah*)

Hebrew; Aramaic: Targum Jonathan to Prophets. Oriental square script; Tiberian vocalisation.

Vellum; 1 leaf; very badly mutilated. 9.9⁺ × 8.5⁺; [2] cols.; 8⁺ lines.

Divine name: יְיָ; this is the *haftarah* for *parashat ḥayye sarah*. [1449]

### T-S AS 71.258, 259  Isaiah 41:2–8; (*haftarah*)

Hebrew; Aramaic: Targum Jonathan to Prophets. Oriental square script; Tiberian vocalisation.

[T-S AS 71.258, 259, cont.]
Vellum; 1 leaf (torn into two parts, separately conserved); very badly mutilated.   18.6 × 8.2⁺;   13 lines.

Divine name: Hebrew tetragrammaton; Targum ⟨⟩ (in margin); this is the *haftarah* for *parashat lekh lekha*. T-S AS 71.259, the minute fragment, has not been identified.
[1450]

**T-S AS 71.261**   Isaiah 12:3 – 13:4; 14:32; 2 Samuel 5:13–17; (*haftarot*)
Hebrew; Aramaic: Targum Jonathan to Prophets. Oriental square script; Hebrew with Tiberian vocalisation + accents; Targum with sporadic Tiberian vocalisation.

Vellum; 1 leaf; very badly mutilated and shrunken. 26.0⁺ × 13.1⁺;   30⁺ lines.

Divine name: Hebrew tetragrammaton; Targum ייי; notation ס in margin and heading: ויוסף אברהם בש[מואל] at 2 Samuel; these are triennial *haftarot* for Genesis 24:42 and 25:1 respectively.
[1451]

**T-S AS 71.262**   Deuteronomy 1:28–9, 31–4
Hebrew; Aramaic: Onqelos.   Oriental square script; Tiberian vocalisation + accents (Hebrew & Onqelos); Massorah Magna.

Vellum; 1 leaf; very badly mutilated.   8.1⁺ × [18.8]; 2 cols.;   6⁺ lines.

Divine name: Hebrew tetragrammaton; Onqelos ײ.
[1452]

**T-S AS 71.263**   Leviticus 15:26–9; 15:32 – 16:2
Hebrew; Aramaic: Onqelos.   Oriental square script; unpointed.

Vellum; 1 leaf; badly mutilated.   14.0⁺ × 10.6⁺; [2] cols.;   14⁺ lines.

Divine name: Hebrew tetragrammaton; blank space before 16:1 to indicate *parashah*.
[1453]

**T-S AS 71.265**   Isaiah 43:11–12; 2 Samuel 22:13–14; (*haftarot*)
Hebrew; Aramaic: Targum Jonathan to Prophets. Oriental square script; Hebrew with Tiberian vocalisation + accents; Targum with Tiberian vocalisation.

Vellum; 1 leaf; very badly mutilated.   9.1⁺ × 7.3⁺; 4⁺ lines.

These are triennial *haftarot* for Exodus 31:1 and 32:15 respectively.
[1454]

**T-S AS 71.267** (= T-S AS 71.245, 257)
1 Kings 1:9–10, 13–19; (*haftarah*)
Hebrew; Aramaic: Targum Jonathan to Prophets. Oriental square script; Tiberian vocalisation.

Vellum; 1 leaf; very badly mutilated.   12.5⁺ × 13.0⁺; 2 cols.;   11⁺ lines.

This is the *haftarah* for *parashat hayye sarah*.
[1455]

**T-S AS 71.270**   Isaiah 41:8–9, 17; (*haftarah*)
Hebrew; Aramaic: Targum Jonathan to Prophets. Oriental square script; Tiberian vocalisation + accents (in darker ink on *recto*).

Vellum; 1 leaf; very badly mutilated.   8.8⁺ × 8.6⁺; [2] cols.;   7⁺ lines.

This is the *haftarah* for *parashat lekh lekha*; followed by heading: [    ] דוירא אליו.
[1456]

**T-S AS 71.281**

Several of these unnumbered minute fragments contain targum; the first four pieces in the third row are Palestinian Targum to Genesis 48–49 and are part of T-S AS 71.1–5 *et al.*.

Klein *GMPT* I, pp.157–63, 169.
[1457]

**T-S AS 72.2**   Genesis 12:2–3
Hebrew; Aramaic: Onqelos; Judaeo-Arabic. Oriental square script; Tiberian vocalisation (Hebrew & Onqelos).

Paper; 1 leaf (minute fragment).   7.2⁺ × 8.3⁺;   7⁺ lines.
[1458]

**T-S AS 72.3**   Numbers 35:34 – 36:1; 36:4–6
Hebrew; Aramaic: Onqelos; Judaeo-Arabic. Oriental semi-cursive script; sporadic Tiberian vocalisation.

Paper; 1 leaf; very badly mutilated and rubbed. 13.8⁺ × 10.3⁺;   17⁺ lines.
[1459]

**T-S AS 72.6**   Jeremiah 2:2, 4–5
Hebrew; Aramaic: Targum Jonathan to Prophets; Judaeo-Arabic.   Oriental(?) square script; unpointed.

Paper; 1 leaf (minute fragment).   6.6⁺ × 7.3⁺;   5⁺ lines.

Divine name: Hebrew tetragrammaton.
[1460]

**T-S AS 72.7**   Genesis 34:21–3, 26–8
Aramaic: Onqelos (+ Hebrew lemmata).   Oriental semi-cursive script; sporadic Tiberian vocalisation.

Paper; 1 leaf (minute fragment).   7.0⁺ × 6.1⁺;   8⁺ lines.
[1461]

**T-S AS 72.8**   Genesis 3:19–20; 4:6–8
Aramaic: Onqelos (+ Hebrew lemmata).   Oriental semi-cursive script; Tiberian vocalisation.

Paper; 1 leaf (minute fragment).   5.6⁺ × 6.0⁺;   6⁺ lines.
[1462]

**T-S AS 72.9**   Genesis 22:9–10, 14
Aramaic: Onqelos (+ Hebrew lemmata).   Oriental square script; Tiberian vocalisation.

Paper; 1 leaf (minute fragment).   4.1⁺ × 6.7⁺;   3⁺ lines.

Divine name: ײ.
[1463]

**T-S AS 72.11**  Numbers 28:16–18, 23–5
Aramaic: Onqelos (+ Hebrew lemmata).  Oriental semi-cursive script; unpointed.
Paper; 1 leaf; very badly mutilated and rubbed. 9.1⁺ × 11.0⁺;  7⁺ lines.  [1464]

**T-S AS 72.12**  Numbers 18:20–21
Aramaic: Onqelos (+ Hebrew lemmata).  Oriental semi-cursive script; unpointed.
Paper; 1 leaf; very badly mutilated.  7.6⁺ × 6.9⁺; 4⁺ lines.
Penultimate line of *recto* contains intrusive (Hebrew?) phrase in square script; *verso* contains Psalm 105 (Hebrew) in larger North African linear semi-cursive script.  [1465]

**T-S AS 72.13**  Leviticus 15:15–18
Hebrew; Aramaic: Onqelos; Judaeo-Arabic. Oriental script; Hebrew square with Tiberian vocalisation + accents; Onqelos semi-cursive with Tiberian vocalisation.
Paper; 1 leaf; very badly mutilated and rubbed. 13.3 × 8.1⁺;  12 lines.
Error in 15:15 קדם כדנא! Targum and Judaeo-Arabic to 15:18 added in bottom margin of *verso* in brown ink.  [1466]

**T-S AS 72.14**  Genesis 43:9–10, 13–14
Hebrew; Aramaic: Onqelos.  Oriental linear square script; Tiberian vocalisation.
Paper; 1 leaf; very badly mutilated.  7.0⁺ × 12.6⁺; 4⁺ lines.  [1467]

**T-S AS 72.17 (= T-S AS 72.25, 105)**  Exodus 9:4–5, 8
Hebrew; Aramaic: Onqelos; Judaeo-Arabic. Yemenite square script; Hebrew with Tiberian vocalisation + accents; Onqelos with Babylonian vocalisation.
Paper; 1 leaf (minute fragment).  5.5⁺ × 6.6⁺;  5⁺ lines.
Divine name: Hebrew tetragrammaton; this is part of the same leaf as T-S AS 72.105.  [1468]

**T-S AS 72.18**  Ezekiel 38:4; 1 Kings 8:11; (*haftarot*)
Hebrew; Aramaic: Targum Jonathan to Prophets. Oriental square script; Hebrew with Tiberian vocalisation + accents; Targum with Tiberian vocalisation.
Paper; 1 leaf (minute fragment).  8.2⁺ × 5.3⁺;  4⁺ lines.
Divine name: Hebrew tetragrammaton; these are *haftarot* for the intermediate Sabbath of Tabernacles and Shemini 'Aseret respectively.  [1469]

**T-S AS 72.19**  Numbers 21:35; 22:2–3
Hebrew; Aramaic: Onqelos; Judaeo-Arabic. Oriental script; Hebrew large, square with Tiberian vocalisation + accents; Onqelos semi-cursive, unpointed.
Paper; 1 leaf (minute fragment).  7.0⁺ × 5.2⁺;  4⁺ lines.  [1470]

**T-S AS 72.20**  Exodus 14:20–22
Hebrew; Aramaic: Onqelos.  Oriental semi-cursive script; Tiberian vocalisation + accents.
Paper; 1 leaf; mutilated and badly rubbed.  10.9⁺ × 8.2; 9⁺ lines.  [1471]

**T-S AS 72.23**  1 Kings 8:59–62, 66; Joshua 1:1–2; (*haftarot*)
Hebrew; Aramaic: Targum Jonathan to Prophets. Oriental square script; unpointed.
Paper; 1 leaf; very badly mutilated.  4.7⁺ × 13.1⁺; 6⁺ lines.
Divine name: Hebrew tetragrammaton; Targum ײַ; these are *haftarot* for *Shemini 'Aseret* and *parashat wezot haberakhah* respectively; heading before Joshua 1: חאת הברכה ביהושע קארו לה(?)[ ] אורייתא.  [1472]

**T-S AS 72.25 (= T-S AS 72.17, 105)**  Exodus 3:7–8, 10–11
Hebrew; Aramaic: Onqelos; Judaeo-Arabic. Yemenite square script; Hebrew with Tiberian vocalisation + accents; Onqelos with Babylonian vocalisation.
Paper; 1 leaf (minute fragment).  6.2⁺ × 7.0⁺;  6⁺ lines.  [1473]

**T-S AS 72.26**  Genesis 5:26; 6:5–6
Aramaic: Onqelos (+ Hebrew lemmata).  Oriental semi-cursive script; Tiberian vocalisation.
Paper; 1 leaf (minute fragment).  5.4⁺ × 6.6⁺;  2⁺ lines.
Divine name: יְ.  [1474]

**T-S AS 72.28**  Exodus 12:41–2; Numbers 28:20–22
Aramaic: Onqelos (+ Hebrew lemmata in Numbers).  Oriental semi-cursive script; Tiberian vocalisation.
Paper; 1 leaf; very badly mutilated.  6.0⁺ × 6.3⁺; 5⁺ lines.
Divine name: ײַ/ 𐡋. Reading and *maftir* for Passover.  [1475]

**T-S AS 72.34**  Exodus 20:14/17–16/19
Aramaic: Palestinian Targum (expansive). Oriental semi-cursive script; Tiberian vocalisation + accents (in very faint ink).
Paper; 1 leaf very badly mutilated.  10.7⁺ × 8.3⁺; 8⁺ lines.  [1476]

**T-S AS 72.35** (= T-S AS 72.37–40)  Genesis 24:30–35
Aramaic: Onqelos (+ Hebrew lemmata). Oriental semi-cursive script; Tiberian vocalisation.
Paper; 1 leaf; very badly mutilated. 5.5⁺ × 10.7⁺; 4⁺ lines.
Divine name: ייי. [1477]

**T-S AS 72.36**  Exodus 12:29–31
Aramaic: Onqelos (+ Hebrew lemmata). Oriental linear square script; very sporadic Tiberian vocalisation.
Paper; 1 leaf; very badly mutilated. 8.6⁺ × 7.5⁺; 7⁺ lines.
Abbreviation: 'ה at the end of the lemma to 12:29. [1478]

**T-S AS 72.37–40** (= T-S AS 72.35)  Genesis 24:27–30, 32–3
Aramaic: Onqelos (+ Hebrew lemmata). Oriental semi-cursive script; Tiberian vocalisation.
Paper; 1 leaf (torn into five parts, separately conserved). [16.0⁺] × [10.7⁺]; [13⁺] lines. [1479]

**T-S AS 72.43**
Aramaic, probably part of a liturgical composition and not targum (*selihah*? or *qinnah*). [1480]

**T-S AS 72.45**  Exodus 25:12–13, 22–3
Aramaic: Onqelos (+ Hebrew lemmata). Oriental semi-cursive script; Tiberian vocalisation.
Paper; 1 leaf (minute fragment). 5.0⁺ × 5.0⁺; 4⁺ lines. [1481]

**T-S AS 72.47** (= T-S AS 72.72, 73)  Numbers 7:18–19; abridged version of 7:42–54
Aramaic: Onqelos (+ Hebrew lemmata). Oriental semi-cursive script; Tiberian vocalisation.
Paper; 1 leaf (minute fragment). 4.4⁺ × 5.8⁺; 4⁺ lines.
Abbreviation: 'ה follows lemma to 7:48. [1482]

**T-S AS 72.55**  Genesis 35:14–18, 20–26
Aramaic: Onqelos (+ Hebrew lemmata). Oriental square script; unpointed.
Vellum; 1 leaf; very badly mutilated. 13.3⁺ × 7.0⁺; 11⁺ lines.
Blank line and medial lemma in 35:22, which according to the Massorah is a פסקא באמצע פסוק. [1483]

**T-S AS 72.57**  Isaiah 54:10–13; 55:1–2 (folio 1); 2 Kings 4:9–12, 19–21 (folio 2); (*haftarot*)
Hebrew; Aramaic: Targum Jonathan to Prophets. Oriental square script; Tiberian vocalisation.
Paper; 2 leaves (1 bifolium); very badly mutilated. 12.2⁺ × 5.9⁺; 10⁺ lines. [1484]

**T-S AS 72.59**  Leviticus 17:13 – 18:9
Aramaic: Onqelos (+ Hebrew lemmata). Oriental semi-cursive script; Tiberian vocalisation (very faint, in lighter ink).
Paper; 1 leaf; badly mutilated. 14.7⁺ × 10.3⁺; 14⁺ lines.
Divine name: ייי. [1485]

**T-S AS 72.61–64**  Numbers 3:15, 18 (AS 72.62); 3:25 (AS 72.61); 3:32–6 (AS 72.63); 3:38–9, 41–2, 45–6, 50 (AS 72.64); 4:3–4, 7–8 (AS 72.63); 4:10–11 (AS 72.61); 4:16 (AS 72.62)
Aramaic: Onqelos (+ Hebrew lemmata). Oriental square script; unpointed.
Paper; 8 leaves (4 bifolia); very badly mutilated. 12.2⁺ × 5.5⁺; 4⁺ lines. [1486]

**T-S AS 72.65**  Genesis 36:40–42; 37:1–2
Hebrew; Aramaic: Onqelos. Oriental linear square script; Tiberian vocalisation.
Paper; 1 leaf; badly mutilated and rubbed. 11.9⁺ × 12.1⁺; 7⁺ lines. [1487]

**T-S AS 72.69**
Targum Onqelos(?) of Exodus 15:18 inserted in a Hebrew text of Exodus 15:18–26. [1488]

**T-S AS 72.71**  Numbers 13:26–32
Aramaic: Onqelos (+ Hebrew lemmata). Oriental linear square script; sporadic Tiberian vocalisation.
Paper; 1 leaf; slightly mutilated and rubbed. 16.2⁺ × 9.2⁺; 17 lines. [1489]

**T-S AS 72.72, 73** (= T-S AS 72.47)  Numbers 7:42–66 (abridged)
Aramaic: Onqelos (+ Hebrew lemmata). Oriental semi-cursive script; Tiberian vocalisation.
Paper; 1 leaf (torn into three parts, separately conserved). [12.8] × 8.4; [12] lines.
Abbreviation 'ה after each lemma and in each repetitive section. [1490]

**T-S AS 72.75–77**  Deuteronomy 23:15 – 28:7 (folio 1, AS 72.75–76); 32:34 – 33:9 (folio 2, AS 72.77)
Aramaic: Palestinian Fragment-targum (+ Hebrew lemmata). Oriental square script; unpointed.
Paper; 2 leaves (1 bifolium) (torn into three parts, separately conserved); mutilated and rubbed. 9.2⁺ × 14.0; 19⁺ lines.
Divine name: ייי.
Klein *GMPT* I, pp.339–41, 357–59. See plate 10. [1491]

**T-S AS 72.81** (= T-S AS 72.101)   1 Kings 3:26 – 4:1; Ezekiel 37:15–16, 19–23; (*haftarot*)
Hebrew; Aramaic: Targum Jonathan to Prophets. Yemenite square script; Babylonian vocalisation + sporadic Tiberian accents.

Paper; 1 leaf; very badly mutilated.   19.0⁺ × 7.8⁺; 17⁺ lines.

Divine name: יי; these are *haftarot* for *parashot miqqeṣ* and *wayiggash* respectively; heading at Ezekiel 37: [ שמיגד.   [1492]

**T-S AS 72.86**   Jeremiah 52:20, 22
Hebrew; Aramaic: Targum Jonathan to Prophets. Oriental square script; Tiberian vocalisation.

Paper; 1 leaf; very badly mutilated and rubbed. 12.1⁺ × 12.6⁺; 7⁺ lines.   [1493]

**T-S AS 72.87**   Leviticus 18:30 – 19:1
Hebrew; Aramaic: Onqelos.   Oriental square script; unpointed.

Paper; 1 leaf; mutilated.   10.0⁺ × 12.3;  7 lines.

Divine name: Hebrew tetragrammaton; lines are irregular and Onqelos of 18:30 incomplete; this may be a pen exercise; missing portion of *recto* and entire *verso* seem to have been blank.   [1494]

**T-S AS 72.88**   Genesis 1:1–3 (*recto*)
Hebrew; Aramaic: Onqelos.   Oriental(?) square script; unpointed.

Paper; 1 leaf; slightly mutilated and rubbed. 15.8 × 12.4;  11 lines.

Divine name: Hebrew אלהים; Onqelos יי; Onqelos to 1:1,2 follows Hebrew 1:2; *verso* contains Hebrew text of Deuteronomy 33:29, 8.   [1495]

**T-S AS 72.89**   Numbers 7:13–17
Hebrew; Aramaic: Onqelos.   Oriental square script; Hebrew much larger, with Tiberian vocalisation + accents; Onqelos inserted in spaces at ends of lines as well as on separate lines, with Tiberian vocalisation.

Paper; 1 leaf; mutilated.   10.9⁺ × 9.8;  9–11⁺ lines.
[1496]

**T-S AS 72.95**   Genesis 12:18 – 13:4; 13:8–12
Aramaic: Onqelos (+ Hebrew lemmata).   Oriental semi-cursive script; unpointed.

Paper; 1 leaf; badly mutilated.   10.2⁺ × 11.3⁺;  10⁺ lines.
Divine name: יי.   [1497]

**T-S AS 72.96**   Exodus 7:26–28
Aramaic: Onqelos.   Oriental square script; Tiberian vocalisation.

Paper; 1 leaf; very badly mutilated and rubbed. 11.2⁺ × 11.9⁺;  6⁺ lines.

*Verso* blank.   [1498]

**T-S AS 72.99, 100**   Leviticus 16:10–11, 14–15 (AS 72.99); 18–20, 23–4 (AS 72.100)
Hebrew; Aramaic: Onqelos.   Oriental(?) square script; Tiberian vocalisation (except 72.100 (*verso*), unpointed).

Paper; 2 leaves; badly mutilated.   10.5⁺ × 16.3; 7⁺ lines.

Divine name: יי.   [1499]

**T-S AS 72.101** (= T-S AS 72.81)   1 Kings 2:1–3, 6–8; (*haftarah*)
Hebrew; Aramaic: Targum Jonathan to Prophets. Yemenite square script; Hebrew with Babylonian vocalisation + Tiberian accents; Targum with Babylonian vocalisation.

Paper; 1 leaf; very badly mutilated.   10.9⁺ × 9.2⁺; 9⁺ lines.

Divine name: יי; this is the *haftarah* for *parashat wayeḥi*; heading: במלכים א׳ ב׳ [  ].   [1500]

**T-S AS 72.102**   Exodus 28:3–5, 9–12
Aramaic: Onqelos (+ Hebrew lemmata). Persian(?) square script; Tiberian vocalisation (in very faint ink).

Paper; 1 leaf; very badly mutilated.   12.5⁺ × 8.7⁺; 7⁺ lines.   [1501]

**T-S AS 72.103**   Leviticus 22:27–31 (*recto*)
Aramaic: Onqelos.   Oriental semi-cursive script; Tiberian vocalisation (in darker ink).

Paper; 1 leaf; very badly mutilated and rubbed. 13.3⁺ × 7.9⁺;  9⁺ lines.

*Verso* faded and illegible.   [1502]

**T-S AS 72.104**   Exodus 19:1–3
Hebrew; Aramaic: Onqelos.   Oriental square script; unpointed.

Paper; 1 leaf; very badly mutilated.   14.5⁺ × 4.5⁺; 11⁺ lines.

*Verso* blank.   [1503]

**T-S AS 72.105** (= T-S AS 72.17, 25)   Exodus 8:28 – 9:14
Hebrew; Aramaic: Onqelos; Judaeo-Arabic. Yemenite square script; Hebrew with Tiberian vocalisation + accents; Onqelos with Babylonian vocalisation.

Paper; 1 leaf; mutilated.   27.6 × 18.8;  2 cols.; 26 lines.

Divine name: Hebrew tetragrammaton; Onqelos יי.
[1504]

**T-S AS 72.106**   Numbers 19:8–18 (folio 1); 21:7–20 (folio 2)
Aramaic: Onqelos (+ Hebrew lemmata).   Oriental square script; unpointed.

**[T-S AS 72.106, cont.]**
Paper; 2 leaves (1 bifolium); badly rubbed.
16.3 × 12.5; 14 lines. [1505]

**T-S AS 72.107** Ezekiel 43:22–3; 1 Kings 18:1, 5–6, 11; (*haftarot*)
Hebrew; Aramaic: Targum Jonathan to Prophets. Oriental square script; Tiberian vocalisation + accents (Hebrew only).
Vellum; 1 leaf; very badly mutilated. 4.3⁺ × 19.1; 2 cols.; 4⁺ lines.
Divine name: Hebrew tetragrammaton; Targum ייי; these are *haftarot* for *parashot teṣaweh* and *ki tisa'* respectively. [1506]

**T-S AS 72.108** Deuteronomy 14:24–6, 28–9
Hebrew; Aramaic: Onqelos. Oriental square script; unpointed.
Vellum; 1 leaf; very badly mutilated. 13.7⁺ × 12.7⁺; 11⁺ lines.
Divine name: Hebrew tetragrammaton; Onqelos יְיָ; error at end of 14:25 בידך for ביה. [1507]

**T-S AS 72.110 (= T-S AS 72.127)** Isaiah 1:31 – 2:5; 22:1–10; (*haftarot*)
Aramaic: Targum Jonathan to Prophets (+ Hebrew lemmata). Oriental square script; unpointed.
Vellum; 1 leaf; very badly mutilated. 15.7 × 6.8⁺; 16 lines.
Divine name: יי; these are unattested (perhaps triennial *haftarot* for Deuteronomy 23:10, 22). [1508]

**T-S AS 72.112** Isaiah 11:6–9, 10–11
Hebrew; Aramaic: Targum Jonathan to Prophets. Oriental square script; unpointed.
Vellum; 1 leaf; very badly mutilated. 9.3⁺ × 10.3⁺; 8⁺ lines. [1509]

**T-S AS 72.113** Numbers 14:43 – 15:2; 15:13–16
Aramaic: Onqelos. Oriental square script; sporadic Tiberian vocalisation (in darker ink).
Vellum; 1 leaf; very badly mutilated. 8.3⁺ × 10.1⁺; 5⁺ lines.
Divine name: יי. [1510]

**T-S AS 72.114** Zephaniah 3:17, 20; Joshua 24:3, 7–10, 14; (*haftarot*)
Aramaic: Targum Jonathan to Prophets (+ Hebrew lemmata). Oriental square script; Tiberian vocalisation (in darker ink).
Vellum; 1 leaf; very badly mutilated and rubbed. 9.8⁺ × 8.5⁺; 10⁺ lines.
Divine name: ייי; these are triennial *haftarot* for Genesis 11:1 and 12:1 respectively. [1511]

**T-S AS 72.115 (= T-S AS 72.116, 119, 130)**
Exodus 10:16–17; 11:4–5
Aramaic: Onqelos (+ Hebrew lemmata). Ashkenazi/Italian square script; Tiberian vocalisation (very faint).
Vellum; 1 leaf (minute fragment). 4.5⁺ × 6.1⁺; [2] cols.; 5⁺ lines.
Divine name: יְ. [1512]

**T-S AS 72.116 (= T-S AS 72.115, 119, 130)**
Exodus 10:13–14; 11:1–2
Minute fragment, 6.0⁺ × 5.0⁺; see description at T-S AS 72.115 above. [1513]

**T-S AS 72.119 (= T-S AS 72.115, 116, 130)**
Exodus 8:26; 10:24
Minute fragment, 4.3⁺ × [16.8]; see description at T-S AS 72.115 above. [1514]

**T-S AS 72.120** Numbers 17:28 – 18:8
Hebrew; Aramaic: Onqelos. Oriental square script; unpointed.
Vellum; 1 leaf; badly mutilated. 20.1⁺ × 13.5⁺; 21⁺ lines.
Divine name: Hebrew tetragrammaton; Onqelos יי. [1515]

**T-S AS 72.126** Genesis 1:1–2, 3–5
Aramaic: Onqelos (+ Hebrew lemmata, 1:3–5 only). Oriental square script; Tiberian vocalisation (1:3–5 only).
Vellum; 1 leaf; mutilated, bottom cut away. 9.9⁺ × 10.1; 7⁺ lines.
Divine name: יְ; 1:1–2 (on *verso*?) seems to be a pen exercise. [1516]

**T-S AS 72.127 (= T-S AS 72.110)** Isaiah 1:31–2; 22:1–3
Minute fragment, 5.7⁺ × 4.8⁺; see description at T-S AS 72.110 above. [1517]

**T-S AS 72.130 (= T-S AS 72.115, 116, 119)**
Exodus 10:22–4, 28–9
Minute fragment, 4.8⁺ × 7.1⁺; see description at T-S AS 72.115 above. [1518]

**T-S AS 72.135** Malachi 1:8–11; Hosea 11:7–9; (*haftarot*)
Hebrew; Aramaic: Targum Jonathan to Prophets. Oriental square script; unpointed.
Vellum; 1 leaf; very badly mutilated. 10.4⁺ × 5.7⁺; 11⁺ lines.
Divine name: Targum יי. [1519]

**T-S AS 72.136**  Ezekiel 1:28 – 2:2 (folio 2r)
Hebrew; Aramaic: Targum Jonathan to Prophets.
Oriental square script; Tiberian vocalisation.

Vellum; 2 leaves (1 bifolium); very badly mutilated.
7.7⁺ × 16.0;  6⁺ lines.

Folio 1 contains only a few unidentified letters; folio 2v blank. [1520]

**T-S AS 72.137**

Several of the unnumbered minute fragments contain targum. [1521]

**T-S AS 85.39 (= T-S AS 71.1 et al.)**  Genesis 44:18

Aramaic: Palestinian Targum (expansive).
Oriental semi-cursive script; sporadic Tiberian vocalisation.

Paper; 1 leaf; very badly mutilated.  5.9⁺ × 8.5⁺; 6⁺ lines.

This is part of the same leaf as T-S AS 71.2. [1522]

**T-S AS 85.147**  Exodus
Hebrew and Aramaic, Massorah to Onqelos.
Oriental semi-cursive script; unpointed.

Paper; 1 leaf (minute fragment).  4.0⁺ × 3.2⁺; 6⁺ lines.
Sign ⊙ to separate entries. [1523]

**T-S AS 89.95**  Genesis 7:7–21
Aramaic: Onqelos (+ Hebrew lemmata).  Oriental semi-cursive script; unpointed.

Paper; 1 leaf; very badly mutilated and rubbed.
13.5⁺ × 7.8⁺;  14⁺ lines. [1524]

**T-S AS 95.261**  Judges 5:8, 10
Hebrew; Aramaic: Targum Jonathan to Prophets.
Oriental square script; unpointed.

Vellum; 1 leaf; very badly mutilated.  5.7⁺ × 8.4⁺;
3⁺ lines (and 4 lines added in margin).

Basic text contains variants and margin contains variant version to 5:8 (*tosefta*?). [1525]

**T-S AS 116.453**  Exodus 12:2
Aramaic: Targumic poem.  Oriental linear square script; sporadic Tiberian vocalisation.

Paper; 1 leaf; mutilated and rubbed.  16.6 × 13.7; 14–16 lines.

The first three lines of the same poem are preserved in T-S H12.11. [1526]

**T-S AS 124.105**

Aramaic text, possibly targumic; unidentified. [1527]

**T-S AS 133.174**  Exodus 24:2–18 (*recto*)
Aramaic: Onqelos (+ Hebrew lemmata).  Oriental semi-cursive script; unpointed.

Paper; 1 leaf; slightly mutilated and rubbed.
15.6 × 12.9;  20 lines.

Divine name: ⟨⟩; notation פרש after 24:18 to indicate end of *parashat mishpaṭim*; *verso* very badly rubbed and barely legible, but definitely a different hand and different but unidentified composition. [1528]

**T-S AS 135.285**

Contains Onqelos to Deuteronomy 34:1 embedded in part of a poetic composition of mixed Hebrew and Aramaic. [1529]

**T-S AS 137.174**  2 Samuel 22:7–11; 23:3–5
Hebrew; Aramaic: Targum Jonathan to Prophets.
Oriental square script; unpointed.

Paper; 1 leaf; very badly mutilated.  11.1⁺ × 13.2⁺;
11⁺ lines.

Variant in 22:8 ואתנגרפת for ואיזדעזעו/ואתרכינו; margin of *verso* contains Hebrew for 22:16–17, 20–26 in semi-cursive script in margin. [1530]

**T-S AS 143.291**  Genesis 22
Aramaic: Targumic(?) poem.  Oriental linear square script; unpointed.

Paper; 1 leaf; slightly mutilated and rubbed.
16.4 × 12.7;  15 lines.

Contains several Hebrew biblical quotations. [1531]

**T-S AS 151.56**  Habakkuk 3:1 (*tosefta*)
Aramaic: Targum Jonathan to Prophets.  Oriental semi-cursive script; Tiberian vocalisation.

Paper; 1 leaf; mutilated.  14.0 × 10.9;  7 lines.

Text ends in the middle of the *recto*, due to scribal error; *verso* contains fragment of a Judaeo-Arabic medical composition. [1532]

**T-S AS 160.229**  Genesis 8:21 – 9:3
Hebrew; Aramaic: Onqelos.  Oriental square script; unpointed.

Vellum; 1 leaf; very badly mutilated and rubbed.
14.6 × 7.3⁺;  1 col. (originally 2?);  14 lines. [1533]

**T-S AS 166.167**  Ezekiel 43:11–17
Aramaic: Targum Jonathan to Prophets (+ Hebrew lemmata).  Oriental semi-cursive script; Tiberian vocalisation.

Paper; 1 leaf; very badly mutilated and rubbed.
9.5⁺ × 9.2⁺;  2 cols.;  8⁺ lines. [1534]

**T-S AS 167.170**  1 Samuel 15:35 – 16:1;
Ezekiel 36:16–17; (*hafṭarot*)
Aramaic: Targum Jonathan to Prophets (+ Hebrew lemmata).  Oriental semi-cursive script; Tiberian vocalisation.

[T-S AS 167.170, cont.]
Paper; 1 leaf; very badly mutilated.   5.9⁺ × 8.0⁺;
2⁺ lines.

Divine name: יְ; these are *haftarot* for *parashot zakhor*
and *parah*.   [1535]

## T-S AS 186.140

Paper leaf containing pen exercises, including Onqelos to
Genesis 1:1–2 (also Hebrew and Judaeo-Arabic).   [1536]

## T-S AS 199.67   Jonah 1:8–10

Aramaic: Targum Jonathan to Prophets.   Oriental
semi-cursive script; Tiberian vocalisation.

Paper; 1 leaf; very badly mutilated and rubbed.
14.7⁺ × 12.7;   12⁺ lines.

*Verso* blank; several fragments have been pasted together,
one incorrectly.   [1537]

## T-S AS 201.388   Exodus 14:28–9 (*recto*)

Hebrew; Aramaic: Onqelos.   Oriental semi-cursive
script; Tiberian vocalisation.

Paper; 1 leaf; very badly mutilated and rubbed.
6.3⁺ × 8.0⁺;   5⁺ lines.

*Verso* rubbed and illegible; *recto* barely legible.   [1538]

## T-S AS 202.225   Isaiah 62:5; Malachi 1:11;
2:2–4; (*haftarot*)

Aramaic: Targum Jonathan to Prophets (+ Hebrew
lemmata).   Oriental semi-cursive script; unpointed.

Paper; 1 leaf (minute fragment).   4.1⁺ × 5.0⁺;   7⁺ lines.

Heading (*recto*) before Malachi 1:11 [מפ]טר בתרי עשרה;
these are triennial *haftarot* for Exodus 29:1 and 30:1
respectively.   [1539]

## T-S AS 202.428   Genesis 16:2–5

Aramaic: Onqelos (+ Hebrew lemmata).   Oriental
semi-cursive script; Tiberian vocalisation.

Paper; 1 leaf; very badly mutilated.   7.2⁺ × 5.3⁺;
4⁺ lines.   [1540]

## T-S AS 203.266–269   Genesis 11:21–2, 29–32
(AS 203.266); 12:3–6, 8–13 (AS 203.269);
12:14–20; 13:2–7 (AS 203.267); 13:9–13;
13:16 – 14:1 (AS 203.268)

Hebrew; Aramaic: Onqelos; Judaeo-Arabic.
Oriental square script; sporadic Tiberian
vocalisation.

Paper; 4 leaves; badly mutilated and rubbed.
18.0⁺ × 14.5⁺ (largest);   21⁺ lines.

Divine name: Hebrew tetragrammaton; Onqelos יְיְ.   [1541]

## T-S AS 208.321, 322, 327, 334, 335, 369,
372   Genesis 9:15–16 (AS 208.372); 9:13–16,
18–22 (AS 208.369); 21:24–6, 32–3 (AS 208.322);
21:27–30; 22:1–3; 23:16–18; 24:3–5 (AS 208.334);
23:19 – 24:2; 24:5–8 (AS 208.327); 24:2–3, 7–8
(AS 208.321)

Hebrew; Aramaic: Onqelos; Judaeo-Arabic.
Oriental semi-cursive script; unpointed.

Paper; 5 leaves (torn into seven parts, separately
conserved); very badly mutilated.   12.7⁺ × 15.3⁺
(largest);   1 col. (+ filled margin);   14⁺ lines (main text).

Divine name: Hebrew and Onqelos יי; originally a
bilingual text; Judaeo-Arabic added in margins.   [1542]

## Or.1080 2.31   Jeremiah 34:13–16; 35:18–19;
1 Kings 5:26–8; (*haftarot*)

Hebrew; Aramaic: Targum Jonathan to Prophets.
Oriental semi-cursive script; unpointed.

Vellum; 1 leaf.   16.6 × 10.5 (irregular);   18 lines.

Divine name: יְיְ; scribal omission of Jeremiah 34:15
(Targum), 16 (Hebrew); these are *haftarot* for *parashot
mishpatim* and *terumah*; heading on *verso*: ויקח לי תרומה
בהלכי.   [1543]

## Or.1080 2.47   Genesis 1:1–30 (folios 1–2);
3:3 – 4:7 (folios 3–4)

Hebrew; Aramaic: Onqelos.   Spanish semi-cursive
script; Tiberian vocalisation + accents (Hebrew &
Targum).

Vellum; 4 leaves (2 bifolia).   21.4 × 16.4;   20 lines.

Divine name: יְ/ קְ; variants to Onqelos in margins under
נ״א.   [1544]

## Or.1080 3.31

Aramaic (targumic?) poem with many biblical allusions:
flood, Joshua, Gideon, etc..   [1545]

## Or.1080 B1.1   Deuteronomy 4:43 – 5:29

Hebrew; Aramaic: Onqelos; Judaeo-Arabic.
Oriental square script; Hebrew with Tiberian
vocalisation + accents; Onqelos slightly smaller,
with Tiberian vocalisation.

Paper; 6 leaves (3 bifolia).   17.6 × 12.5;   18 lines.

Divine name: Hebrew יְיָ; Onqelos יְיְ; the word סתום is
written in the spaces of *parashot setumot*.   [1546]

## Or.1080 B2.1   Exodus 12:7–33

Hebrew; Aramaic: Onqelos.   Oriental square
script; Babylonian vocalisation + accents; sporadic
Tiberian vocalisation + accents in darker ink.

Vellum; 1 leaf.   28.9 × 25.4;   2 cols.;   29 lines.

Letter ס in margin at 12:29 denotes triennial *sidra*;
massoretic notes to Onqelos 12:26 in bottom margin: הזאת
דם הדין...   [1547]

**Or.1080 B2.2(a)** Genesis 29:32 – 30:16 (folio 1, marked 37); Leviticus 19:4–25 (folio 2, marked 39); Deuteronomy 2:16 – 3:2 (folio 3, marked 36); 12:11–30 (folio 4, marked 38); 28:50–67 (folio 5, marked 35)

Hebrew; Aramaic: Onqelos. Yemenite square script; Babylonian vocalisation.

Vellum; 5 leaves (parts of some columns vertically incised). 31.2 × 20.6+; 2 cols.; 23–6 lines.

Divine name: Hebrew tetragrammaton; Targum יי; some folios display mirror writing adhered from adjoining leaves. [1548]

**Or.1080 B2.2(b)** Ezekiel 22:15–16; 20:1–11; (*haftarot*)

Hebrew; Aramaic: Targum Jonathan to Prophets. Yemenite square script; Hebrew with Tiberian vocalisation + accents; Targum with Babylonian vocalisation.

Paper; 1 large and 4 small fragments + 6 minute pieces (all from 1 leaf). 17.2+ × 14.5+; 2 cols.; 14+ lines.

Divine name: Hebrew tetragrammaton; Targum יי; decorative heading painted in colours ❁ before 20:1 קדשים ביחזקאל; these are the *haftarot* for *parashot aharei mot* and *qedoshim*. [1549]

**Or.1080 B6.1** 2 Kings 4:12–27; (*haftarah*)

Hebrew; Aramaic: Targum Jonathan to Prophets. Oriental square script; Hebrew with Tiberian vocalisation + accents; Targum unpointed.

Vellum; 1 leaf. 21.7 × 20.5; 2 cols.; 19 lines.

Divine name: Hebrew אלהים; Targum יְיָ; this is the *haftarah* for *parashat wayera'*. [1550]

**Or.1080 B6.2** Leviticus 14:52 – 15:18

Hebrew; Aramaic: Onqelos. Oriental square script; Babylonian vocalisation + accents + דקמל, דק (Hebrew & Targum); Tiberian vocalisation + accents added to Hebrew in darker ink.

Vellum; 1 leaf. 35.0 × 28.4; 2 cols.; 24 lines.

Divine name: Hebrew tetragrammaton; Targum יײ. [1551]

**Or.1080 B10.1** Genesis 7:18 – 8:16

Aramaic: Onqelos (+ Hebrew lemmata). Oriental semi-cursive script; Tiberian vocalisation.

Vellum; 1 leaf. 15.9 × 11.4; 20–21 lines.

Divine name: יְיָ; variants of definite article and *dalet* particle between lines at 7:22. [1552]

**Or.1080 B18.1** (= T-S B13.4; NS 218.61) Exodus 12:1–42 (folios 4v–6v); 17:8–16 (folios 3v–4v); Numbers 19:1 – 20:13 (folios 1v–3v); Deuteronomy 26:15 – 27:8 (folio 1)

Aramaic: Palestinian Targum (+ Hebrew lemmata). Oriental square script; very sporadic Tiberian vocalisation.

Vellum; 6 leaves (3 bifolia). 15.0 × 15.2; 16–19 lines.

Divine name: Hebrew and Targum יי; these are the readings for the four sabbaths preceding Passover and for Purim; Hebrew and Judaeo-Arabic headings: תרגום פרה (folio 1v); תרגום אלפוריים (folio 3v); תרגום החדש (folio 4v). Klein *GMPT* I, pp.209–19, 253, 321–25, 345–47. [1553]

**Or.1080 B18.4** Jonah 2:10 – 4:10 (folios 1–2); Isaiah 55:6 – 56:7 (folios 3r–4r); 57:14–19 (folio 4v); (*haftarot*)

Hebrew; Aramaic: Targum Jonathan to Prophets. Oriental square script; Hebrew with Tiberian vocalisation + accents; Targum with sporadic Tiberian vocalisation; Massorah Parva.

Vellum; 4 leaves (1 bifolium). 20.0 × 18.0; 18 lines.

Divine name: Hebrew tetragrammaton; Targum יי; liturgical note after Jonah 2:11: ואמר מי אל כמוך ישב ירחמו; note תתן אמת בסופה דאפטרתא וכד קימין וקרן בספרא מן יונה שנית: before Isaiah 55: שבתא דשובה דבין ריש שתה לצומא; note following Isaiah 56:7 (folio 4r), but actually a heading for Isaiah 57 (folio 4v): דצומא דיומא דכיפורי בישעיה. [1554]

**Or.1080 B18.5** Obadiah 1:19–21; Amos 2:6–13; (*haftarot*)

Hebrew; Aramaic: Targum Jonathan to Prophets. Oriental semi-cursive script; unpointed.

Vellum; 1 leaf. 16.9 × 13.2; 20–21 lines.

Divine name: Hebrew יי; Targum יי; these are *haftarot* for *parashot wayishlah* and *wayeshev*; heading before Amos: וישב בתרי עסרא. [1555]

**Or.1081 B12.1** Proverbs 17:1 – 18:5

Hebrew; Aramaic: Targum Proverbs (+ Yalqut Shim'oni and Rashi). Late Sephardi (but probably not from Spain) square script; commentaries in cursive script; Hebrew with Tiberian vocalisation + accents; Targum smaller, unpointed.

Paper; 1 leaf (Hebrew partially damaged). 21.7 × 14.7; 2 cols. (Rabbinic Bible layout with 4 sections); Hebrew 14–16 lines; Targum 19–20 lines.

Chapters and verses are numbered in Hebrew with יי for 16; heading of Targum column is ינתן. See plate 24. [1556]

**West. Coll. Bib.I.3** Genesis 1:10–25

Hebrew; Aramaic: Onqelos. Oriental square script; Hebrew with Tiberian vocalisation + accents; Targum with Tiberian vocalisation added in darker ink; Massorah Parva.

[West. Coll. Bib.I.3, cont.]
Vellum; 1 leaf; badly mutilated, *verso* very badly rubbed. 20.1 × 16.8; 2 cols.; 25 lines.
Divine name: Hebrew אלהים; Targum יְ.  [1557]

### West. Coll. Bib.I.11a   Genesis 2:1–38
Hebrew; Aramaic: Onqelos.   Spanish(?) square script; Tiberian vocalisation + accents.
Vellum; 1 leaf (conjoined with I.11b); very badly mutilated. 37.8 × [31.0]; 2 cols.; 31 lines.
Divine name: Hebrew אלהים; Targum יְ; this leaf was conjoined with I.11b but they are originally from two distinct manuscripts; margins contain corrections to the text, Hebrew liturgy (*qiddush*) and names [of owners?] אני הצעיר שלמה בני and שלמה בנימין יוסף מרחבך רחן אברהם (?)פרנאלה ער] [ גדניה.  [1558]

### West. Coll. Bib.I.11b   Genesis 5:15 – 6:13
Hebrew; Aramaic: Onqelos.   Ashkenazi/Italian square script; Tiberian vocalisation + accents.
Vellum; 1 leaf (conjoined with I.11a).   38.1 × 30.5; 2 cols.; 31 lines.
Divine name: Hebrew אלהים; Targum יְ; blank line and פ in margin to indicate beginning of *parashah* at 6:9; converse translation: ואיתוהי ארי לא אמית יתיה in 5:24.  [1559]

### West. Coll. Bib.I.21   Genesis 7:2–13
Hebrew; Aramaic: Onqelos.   Oriental semi-cursive script; Hebrew with Tiberian vocalisation + accents; Targum unpointed; Massorah Parva.
Paper; 2 leaves (1 bifolium). 20.0 × 14.3; 15 lines.
Divine name: Hebrew tetragrammaton; Targum 6י.  [1560]

### West. Coll. Bib.I.37   Genesis 14:8–16
Hebrew; Aramaic: Onqelos.   Oriental script; Hebrew square; Targum semi-cursive; unpointed.
Paper; 1 leaf; slightly mutilated and rubbed. 18.9 × 12.7⁺; 19 lines.
The scribe abandoned the text in the middle of the *verso* after a false start on 14:17; pen exercises in margin of *recto*.  [1561]

### West. Coll. Bib.I.50   Genesis 20:15 – 21:20
Aramaic: Onqelos (+ Hebrew lemmata).   Oriental semi-cursive script; Tiberian vocalisation (lemmata unpointed).
Paper; 2 leaves (1 bifolium). 18.0 × 13.6; 14–15 lines.
Divine name: יְ/ 6.  [1562]

### West. Coll. Bib.II.66   Leviticus 8:11–26
Hebrew; Aramaic: Onqelos.   Oriental square script; Babylonian vocalisation + accents (Hebrew & Targum); Hebrew with Tiberian vocalisation + accents added in darker ink.
Vellum; 1 leaf; badly mutilated and rubbed. 33.7 × 29.0⁺; 2 cols.; 24 lines.
Divine name: Hebrew tetragrammaton; Targum ייי.
Pencilled note identifies fragment as Kittel-Kahle MS Ea 11.  [1563]

### West. Coll. Bib.II.84   Leviticus 11:35–47; 12:2–6
Hebrew; Aramaic: Onqelos.   Oriental square script; Tiberian vocalisation + accents; Massorah Parva.
Vellum; 1 leaf; badly mutilated and rubbed. 32.6 × 26.4; 2 cols.; 26 lines.
Divine name: Hebrew tetragrammaton; Targum יְ.  [1564]

### West. Coll. Bib.III.88   Deuteronomy 27:2–6, 17–21
Hebrew; Aramaic: Onqelos.   Oriental square script; sporadic Babylonian vocalisation.
Vellum; 1 leaf; very badly mutilated. 17.2⁺ × 10.2⁺; 2 cols.; 18⁺ lines.
Divine name: Hebrew tetragrammaton; Targum יְ.  [1565]

### West. Coll. Bib.IV.36   1 Samuel 23:19–20, 25–6; 24:2–3/3–4, 8/9 (folio 1); 24:12–14/13–15, 19–20/20–21; 25:3–4, 9–10 (folio 2)
Hebrew; Aramaic: Targum Jonathan to Prophets. Oriental square script; sporadic Babylonian vocalisation + Babylonian accents; Massorah Parva(?).
Vellum; 2 leaves (1 bifolium); very badly mutilated and rubbed; upper three-quarters of leaves cut away and missing. 6.0⁺ × 19.4; 2 cols.; 5⁺ lines.
Divine name: Targum ייי.
Pencilled note identifies fragment as Kittel-Kahle MS Eb 12.  [1566]

### West. Coll. Bib.IV.64   Jeremiah 51:50–51; 2 Kings 24:18 – 25:4 (folio 1); Jeremiah 8:23 – 9:6 (folio 2); (*haftarot*)
Hebrew; Aramaic: Targum Jonathan to Prophets. Oriental square script (folios in different hands); Tiberian vocalisation (folio 1); unpointed (folio 2).
Vellum; 2 leaves (1 bifolium). 21.3 × 18.0; 15 lines.
Divine name: Hebrew tetragrammaton; Targum יְ (folio 1) / יְ (folio 2); *haftarot* not attested in this order.  [1567]

### West. Coll. Bib.V.20   Isaiah 55:11 – 56:7; 57:14 – 58:2; (*haftarot*)
Hebrew; Aramaic: Targum Jonathan to Prophets. Oriental square script; Hebrew with Tiberian vocalisation + accents (some reinforced in darker ink); Targum unpointed; Massorah Parva.

**[West. Coll. Bib.V.20, cont.]**
Vellum; 1 leaf; slightly mutilated. 26.3 × 22.9⁺; 24 lines.

Divine name: Hebrew tetragrammaton; Targum ייי; these are *hafṭarot* for Fast of Gedaliah and Day of Atonement; heading to Isaiah 57: דצומא דיומא דכיפורי בישעיה. [1568]

## West. Coll. Tal.II.75   Genesis 2:13 – 3:20

Aramaic: Onqelos (+ Hebrew lemmata). Oriental semi-cursive script (lemmata to 3:16, 17 in square script); unpointed.

Paper; 2 leaves (1 bifolium); slightly rubbed. 18.6 × 14.0; 17 lines.

Divine name: ייי; pen exercises in the margins. [1569]

## West. Coll. Ar.I.73   Joshua 1:6–11

Hebrew; Aramaic: Targum Jonathan to Prophets. Oriental square script; unpointed.

Vellum; 1 leaf; slightly mutilated. 11.8 × 12.0; 13 lines.

Divine name: Hebrew tetragrammaton; Targum ייי. [1570]

## West. Coll. Ar.I.95, 137   Numbers 15:26–32 (Ar.I.95); 16:13–18 (Ar.I.137)

Hebrew; Aramaic: Onqelos; Judaeo-Arabic. Oriental script; Hebrew square; Targum semi-cursive; unpointed (except one word with Tiberian vocalisation in 15:27).

Paper; 2 leaves (in the same binding but not consecutively placed). 23.6 × 15.8; 16–17 lines.

Divine name: Hebrew tetragrammaton; Targum ייי. [1571]

## West. Coll. Misc.69   1 Samuel 12:9–10; 13:6–8

Hebrew; Aramaic: Targum Jonathan to Prophets. Oriental square script; Hebrew with Tiberian vocalisation + accents; Targum with Babylonian vocalisation (and possibly sporadic Palestinian vocalisation).

Vellum; 1 leaf; very badly mutilated and rubbed. 9.8⁺ × 9.6⁺; 10⁺ lines.

Divine name: Hebrew tetragrammaton; Targum ייי. [1572]

## West. Coll. Misc.70   1 Samuel 8:20–22; 17:1–2; (*hafṭarot*)

Hebrew; Aramaic: Targum Jonathan to Prophets. Oriental square script; Tiberian vocalisation.

Vellum; 1 leaf; slightly mutilated. 19.5 × 17.7; 13 lines.

Divine name: Hebrew tetragrammaton; Targum ייי / tetragrammaton; these are *hafṭarot* for *parashot shofṭim* and *ki teṣe'*; decorative פרש ❈ and heading: כי תצא למלחמה בשמואל before 1 Samuel 17. [1573]

## West. Coll. Misc.71   Leviticus 4:24 – 6:10

Aramaic: Onqelos (+ Hebrew lemmata). Oriental semi-cursive script; Tiberian vocalisation.

Paper; 2 leaves (1 bifolium); slightly rubbed. 23.7 × 16.3; 21 lines.

Divine name: ייי. [1574]

## West. Coll. Misc.94   Psalms 33:5 – 35:4

Aramaic: Targum Psalms (+ Hebrew lemmata). Oriental semi-cursive script; unpointed; supralinear lines above lemmata.

Paper; 1 leaf; mutilated and rubbed. 20.4 × 14.2; 24 lines.

Divine name: ייי. [1575]

## West. Coll. Misc.95   Genesis 8:7–11

Aramaic: Onqelos (+ Hebrew lemmata). Oriental semi-cursive script; Tiberian vocalisation.

Paper; 1 leaf; badly mutilated. 8.6⁺ × 12.5; 5⁺ lines. [1576]

## West. Coll. Misc.96   Leviticus 23:4–16

Aramaic: Onqelos (+ Hebrew lemmata). Oriental semi-cursive script; sporadic Tiberian vocalisation.

Paper; 1 leaf. 16.3 × 12.8; 14 lines.

Divine name: ייי. [1577]

## West. Coll. Misc.97   Numbers 33:44 – 34:8

Aramaic: Onqelos (+ Hebrew lemmata, several missing). Oriental semi-cursive script; Tiberian vocalisation.

Paper; 1 leaf; slightly mutilated and rubbed. 17.0⁺ × 13.5; 15 lines.

Divine name: ייי. [1578]

## West. Coll. Glass 36 (= T-S B2.5(?); NS 115.71)   Massorah to Onqelos (alphabetic, letter *hê*)

Hebrew; Aramaic. Oriental square script; sporadic Babylonian vocalisation.

Vellum; 1 leaf; mutilated. 19.8 × 14.3; 27 lines (including bottom margin).

Weil *ALUOS* V, pp. 114–31. [1579]

## West. Coll. Glass 41 (recto)   Isaiah 42:1–5

Hebrew; Aramaic: Targum Jonathan to Prophets. Oriental square script; Babylonian vocalisation (Hebrew & Targum); Tiberian vocalisation (added to Hebrew only).

Vellum; 1 leaf; very badly mutilated. 16.8⁺ × 11.1⁺; 13⁺ lines.

Divine name: Hebrew tetragrammaton; *verso* blank. [1580]

## DECORATIONS IN MANUSCRIPTS

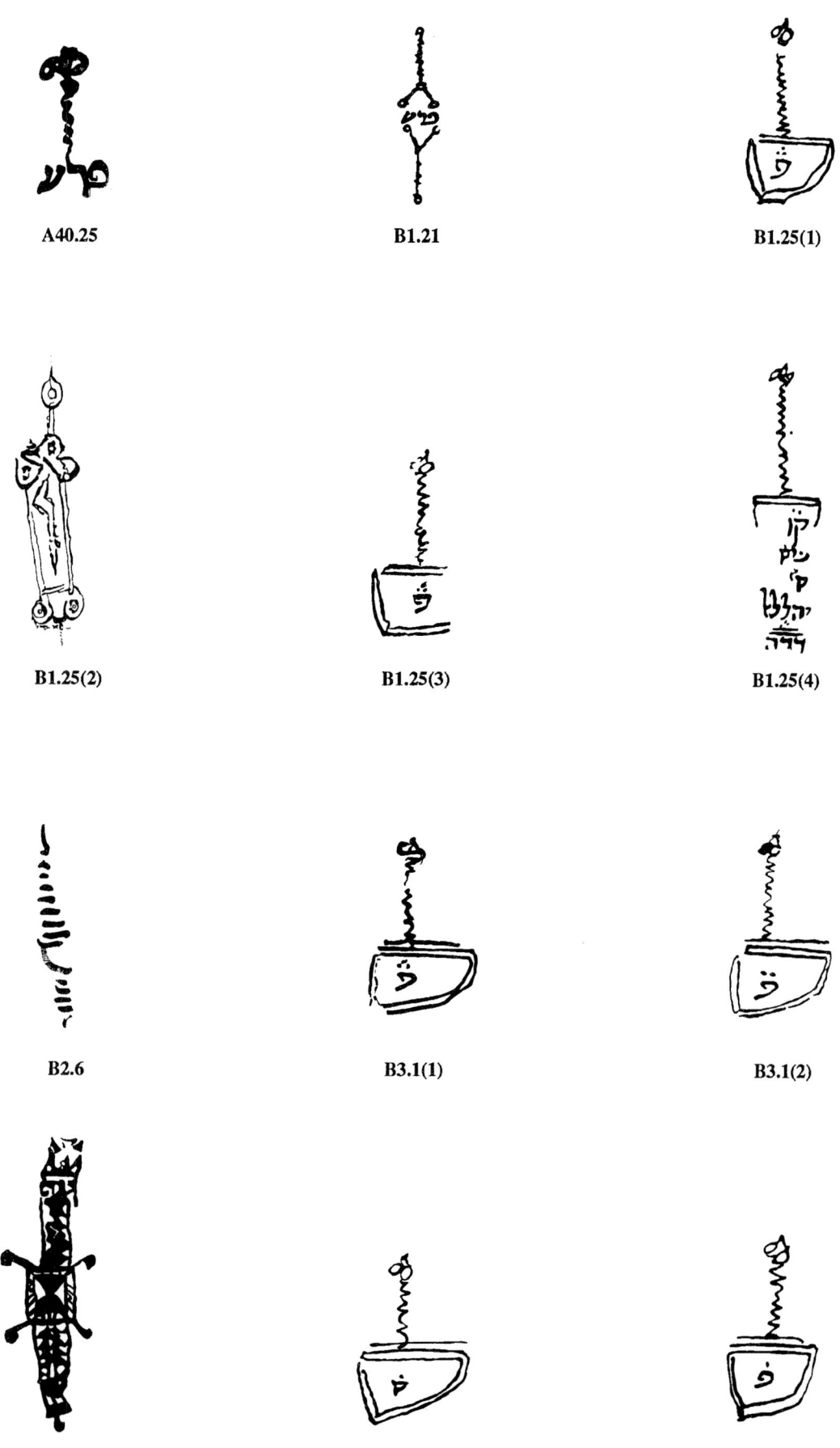

A40.25    B1.21    B1.25(1)

B1.25(2)    B1.25(3)    B1.25(4)

B2.6    B3.1(1)    B3.1(2)

B3.1(3)    B3.1(4)    B3.1(5)

## DECORATIONS

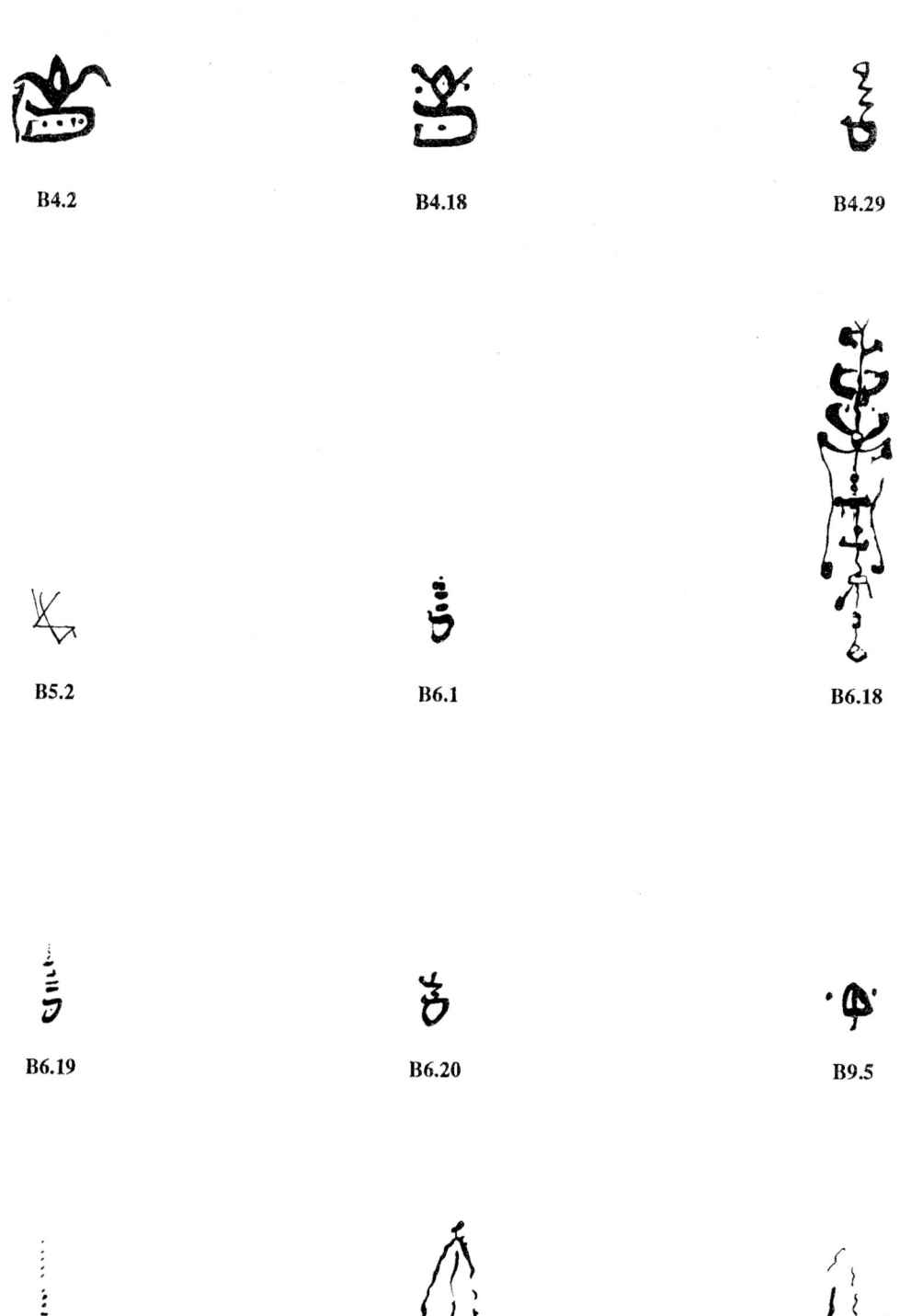

## DECORATIONS

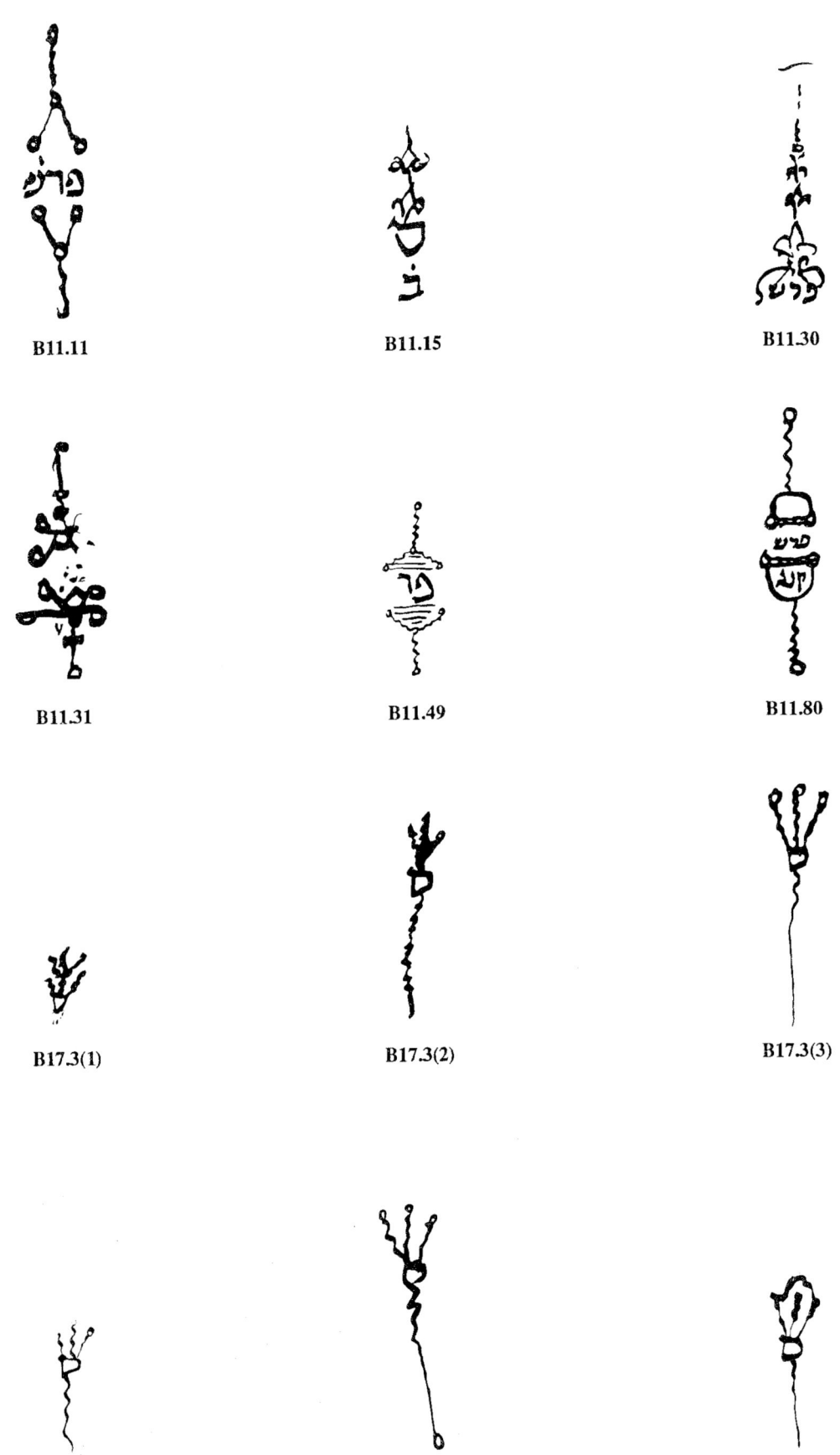

## DECORATIONS

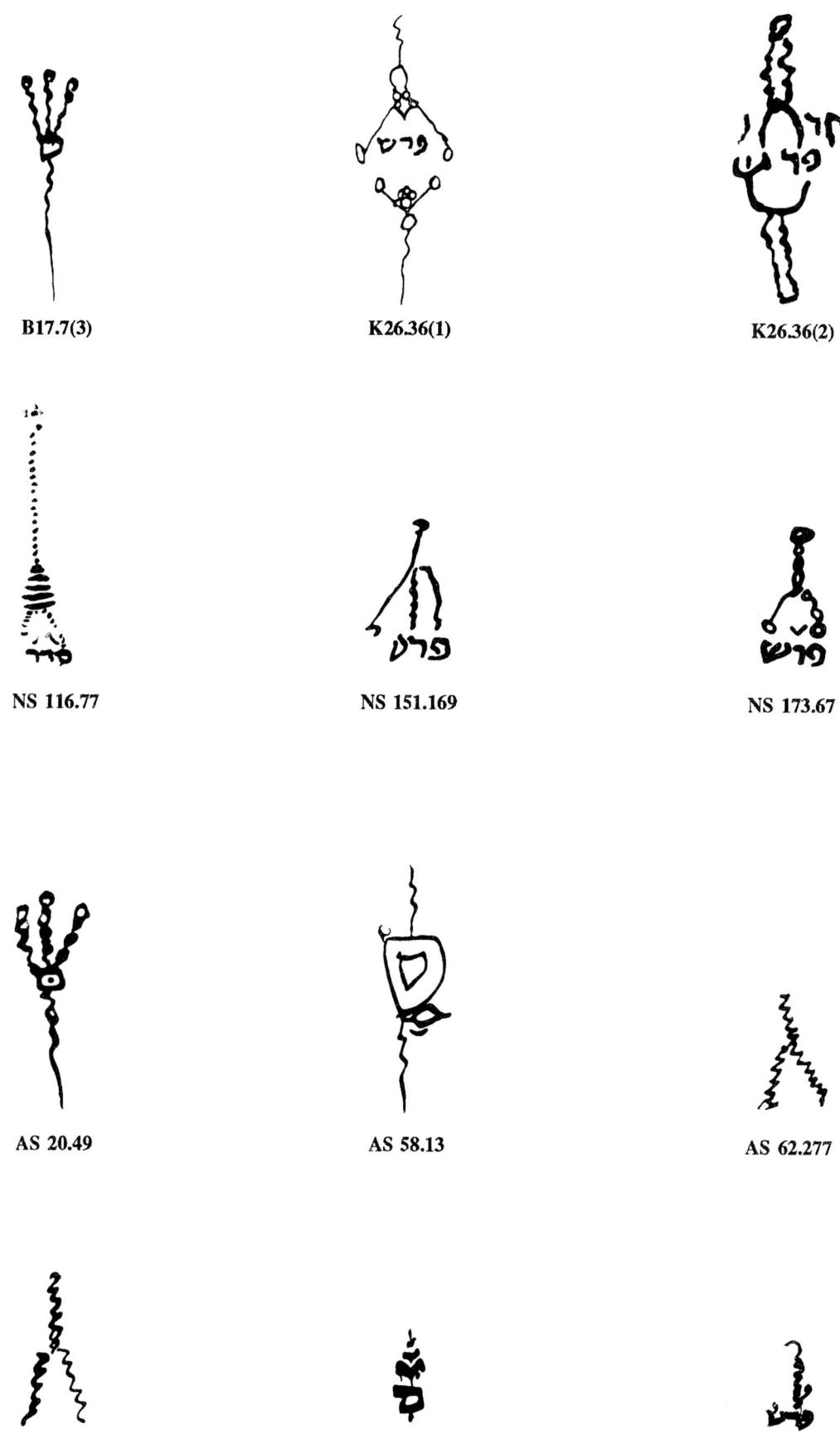

DECORATIONS

AS 69.80

AS 69.168

AS 70.208

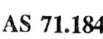
AS 71.184

Or.1080 B2.2(b)

West. Coll. Misc. 70

# CANONICAL INDEX

## Genesis

1: 21, 27, 105, 150, 200, 210, 254, 266, 281, 287, 308, 310, 311, 323, 344, 442, 486, 502, 534, 560, 561, 562, 569, 586, 604, 622, 637, 663, 670, 681, 714, 742, 756, 760, 767, 850, 868, 873, 912, 921, 1111, 1180, 1188, 1212, 1252, 1294, 1418, 1495, 1516, 1544, 1557

2: 131, 291, 308, 310, 311, 324, 534, 562, 637, 675, 744, 803, 912, 914, 934, 1166, 1170, 1188, 1353, 1558, 1569

3: 3, 131, 194, 308, 322, 324, 444, 464, 505, 566, 572, 644, 689, 744, 914, 992, 1188, 1379, 1404, 1406, 1427, 1462, 1544, 1569

4: 193, 194, 291, 308, 322, 419, 444, 464, 566, 674, 689, 691, 744, 982, 992, 1258, 1264, 1379, 1434, 1462, 1544

5: 3, 26, 194, 245, 254, 265, 308, 419, 566, 674, 986, 1056, 1246, 1291, 1364, 1436, 1474, 1559

6: 15, 26, 119, 193, 194, 245, 254, 265, 275, 310, 424, 528, 664, 695, 719, 753, 932, 953, 986, 1056, 1118, 1201, 1246, 1254, 1289, 1291, 1384, 1474, 1559

7: 15, 26, 119, 168, 193, 194, 275, 310, 424, 516, 545, 719, 720, 739, 753, 932, 953, 985, 1259, 1369, 1374, 1524, 1552, 1560

8: 168, 199, 212, 311, 465, 497, 545, 720, 739, 897, 932, 947, 1045, 1278, 1369, 1374, 1392, 1533, 1552, 1576

9: 197, 212, 292, 311, 497, 589, 720, 739, 753, 947, 1045, 1247, 1278, 1533, 1542

10: 197, 212, 280, 292, 753, 1247

11: 212, 262, 280, 285, 362, 470, 555, 831, 871, 1133, 1144, 1196, 1340, 1363, 1366, 1405, 1541

12: 285, 470, 589, 708, 1128, 1138, 1144, 1196, 1203, 1206, 1305, 1343, 1419, 1458, 1497, 1541

13: 249, 275, 470, 589, 831, 1113, 1206, 1287, 1497, 1541

14: 127, 249, 275, 305, 831, 869, 935, 1253, 1281, 1541, 1561

15: 127, 180, 255, 305, 353, 368, 587, 859, 942, 945

16: 127, 138, 180, 353, 368, 506, 587, 859, 945, 1061, 1221, 1540

17: 26, 61, 127, 138, 305, 506, 587, 859, 860, 1017, 1061, 1115, 1221

18: 28, 29, 61, 119, 138, 263, 305, 570, 860, 955, 1017, 1059, 1154

19: 28, 29, 119, 259, 570, 699, 929, 1059, 1154, 1432

20: 219, 259, 288, 692, 699, 857, 1562

21: 62, 106, 175, 181, 219, 237, 247, 259, 268, 270, 295, 471, 521, 552, 599, 643, 645, 692, 707, 740, 832, 857, 1115, 1152, 1171, 1325, 1334, 1426, 1428, 1542, 1562

22: 13, 62, 166, 182, 237, 259, 317, 489, 521, 621, 677, 798, 971, 1042, 1152, 1175, 1241, 1244, 1319, 1326, 1334, 1381, 1463, 1531, 1542

23: 182, 272, 296, 563, 939, 1248, 1326, 1542

24: 30, 176, 290, 296, 300, 563, 684, 725, 793, 820, 965, 1248, 1272, 1292, 1477, 1479, 1542

25: 30, 182, 290, 300, 303, 679, 910, 1130

26: 30, 303, 312, 472, 605, 679, 1130, 1358

27: 217, 312, 605, 746, 794, 1181, 1269

28: 161, 182, 217, 312, 673, 1136

29: 161, 229, 312, 319, 673, 1121, 1548

30: 182, 319, 673, 1548

31: 4, 31, 161, 229, 490, 617, 1142, 1249, 1274, 1423

32: 4, 218, 235, 314, 315, 474, 1220, 1275, 1365

33: 235, 314, 315, 1220

34: 314, 315, 478, 597, 1461

35: 243, 315, 318, 1483

36: 132, 160, 235, 243, 315, 498, 597, 1155, 1167, 1408, 1487

37: 32, 132, 167, 235, 315, 529, 551, 597, 839a, 1104, 1155, 1167, 1408, 1487

38: 32, 48, 160, 183, 315, 529, 549, 671, 691, 839a, 892, 927, 1122, 1265, 1290, 1307, 1386, 1399

39: 48, 183, 191, 315, 839a, 916, 927, 1122, 1255, 1290, 1383, 1387, 1390

40: 33, 48, 183, 191, 315, 839a, 1114, 1243

41: 17, 48, 119, 151, 191, 585, 762, 839a, 892, 1114, 1162, 1208, 1243, 1306, 1313, 1371, 1407, 1430

42: 48, 149, 152, 335, 839a, 877, 1037, 1141, 1176, 1184

43: 48, 149, 152, 157, 163, 839a, 937, 1037, 1055, 1075, 1467

44: 48, 163, 217, 327, 639, 671, 687, 839a, 843, 895, 1071, 1075, 1084, 1127, 1293, 1310, 1327, 1333, 1356, 1377, 1522

45: 48, 217, 495, 839a, 1083, 1084, 1293

46: 48, 386, 495, 532, 839a, 1054, 1083, 1359

47: 48, 495, 532, 571, 660, 699, 839a, 1057, 1356, 1429

48: 48, 164, 253, 532, 571, 660, 839a, 1073, 1327, 1356, 1429

49: 48, 63, 184, 253, 359, 445, 461, 514, 687, 797, 839a, 840, 862, 1207, 1236, 1321, 1327, 1356, 1414, 1429, 1442

50: 687, 709, 779

## Exodus

–: 1523

1: 41, 238, 321, 779, 823

2: 62, 134, 190, 258, 264, 319, 321, 537, 741, 823, 952, 1018

3: 7, 40, 62, 134, 190, 233, 319, 321, 823, 952, 1047, 1117, 1157, 1473

[Exodus]
- 4: 7, 26, 40, 233, 246, 321, 517, 665, 687, 780, 1067, 1117, 1157
- 5: 133, 169, 190, 321, 531, 1085, 1240, 1403, 1433
- 6: 133, 169, 190, 253, 321, 530, 531, 600, 1015, 1240, 1283, 1389, 1433
- 7: 162, 321, 530, 775, 1015, 1097, 1498
- 8: 321, 530, 775, 1182, 1504, 1514
- 9: 162, 201, 449, 614, 765, 830, 1182, 1468, 1504
- 10: 39, 293, 830, 1005, 1011, 1016, 1148, 1512, 1513, 1514, 1518
- 11: 64, 65, 459, 959, 1005, 1011, 1016, 1041, 1050, 1512, 1513
- 12: 20, 64, 65, 66, 177, 223, 240, 302, 314, 329, 338, 349, 358, 366, 431, 434, 438, 459, 472, 522, 687, 693, 706, 713, 959, 990, 1001, 1004, 1011, 1016, 1041, 1050, 1131, 1145, 1224, 1299, 1300, 1316, 1332, 1357, 1376, 1439, 1475, 1478, 1526, 1547, 1553
- 13: 66, 293, 314, 338, 426, 449, 452, 472, 526, 648, 680, 887, 1019, 1131
- 14: 40, 66, 148, 223, 252, 354, 363, 370, 431, 449, 452, 522, 523, 584, 603, 680, 687, 837, 990, 993, 1021, 1027, 1131, 1179, 1194, 1318, 1328, 1471, 1538
- 15: 8, 9, 40, 64, 135, 252, 301, 363, 370, 452, 523, 584, 687, 697, 736, 789, 791, 801, 837, 842, 861, 1169, 1179, 1194, 1200, 1318, 1362
- 16: 134, 135, 185, 301, 363, 533, 758, 787, 789, 791, 1134, 1169, 1177, 1178, 1187, 1200, 1205, 1239, 1297
- 17: 58, 134, 185, 301, 501, 668, 687, 758, 787, 855, 858, 925, 1116, 1134, 1146, 1177, 1205, 1233, 1297, 1553
- 18: 16, 178, 301, 696, 853, 866, 1109, 1123, 1160, 1233
- 19: 178, 185, 189, 201, 256, 269, 316, 427, 428, 441, 483, 602, 619, 685, 696, 750, 784, 1098, 1105, 1123, 1160, 1191, 1231, 1325, 1375, 1416, 1503
- 20: 5, 36, 148, 189, 201, 256, 269, 304, 307, 316, 340, 427, 483, 488, 509, 520, 536, 606, 611, 612, 613, 614, 619, 623, 668, 700, 711, 784, 804, 870, 1088, 1093, 1098, 1105, 1173, 1277, 1476
- 21: 536, 598, 749, 1066, 1068, 1070, 1093, 1242, 1261
- 22: 19, 422, 536, 749, 1065, 1069, 1230
- 23: 19, 422, 536, 827
- 24: 422, 1528
- 25: 179, 422, 764, 1317, 1481
- 26: 171, 179, 203, 422, 598, 764, 941, 1317
- 27: 171, 179, 422, 511, 904, 1147, 1186
- 28: 141, 179, 319, 422, 511, 578, 1124, 1135, 1147, 1159, 1195, 1309, 1501
- 29: 37, 141, 234, 319, 422, 468, 477, 902, 969, 1124, 1276
- 30: 37, 136, 141, 234, 319, 422, 459, 468, 487, 654, 676, 902, 1077, 1092, 1147, 1276, 1437
- 31: 119, 136, 319, 422, 654, 1092, 1189, 1308
- 32: 1, 69, 108, 119, 136, 142, 171, 319, 422, 668, 905, 938, 1140, 1163, 1189
- 33: 69, 108, 171, 319, 422, 635, 1163
- 34: 1, 67, 69, 142, 302, 319, 422, 610, 635, 848, 881
- 35: 34, 67, 68, 69, 141, 142, 319, 350, 422, 610, 881, 1103, 1330
- 36: 34, 69, 141, 142, 319, 350, 422, 457, 1081, 1103, 1107, 1330
- 37: 70, 145, 350, 422, 457, 579, 581, 1078
- 38: 70, 142, 350, 422, 457, 579, 849, 1078
- 39: 6, 40, 71, 119, 120, 143, 422, 447, 668, 747, 849, 1106
- 40: 71, 422, 447, 538, 1009, 1044, 1052, 1106, 1435

## Leviticus
- 1: 35, 239, 342, 355, 422, 668, 687, 906, 972, 1049, 1361
- 2: 214, 251, 355, 422, 805, 919, 972, 1049, 1322, 1402
- 3: 214, 251, 422, 659, 824, 1322, 1394, 1402
- 4: 35, 72, 119, 232, 251, 422, 527, 539, 659, 704, 824, 826, 839, 926, 1064, 1296, 1394, 1402, 1574
- 5: 35, 72, 73, 119, 216, 232, 251, 313, 422, 527, 539, 547, 922, 1080, 1126, 1301, 1303, 1304, 1574
- 6: 216, 313, 422, 1303, 1574
- 7: 119, 313, 422
- 8: 119, 186, 313, 422, 556, 1257, 1267, 1563
- 9: 186, 422, 519, 556, 653, 936, 1119
- 10: 186, 350, 422, 519, 653, 669, 687, 743, 1119, 1235
- 11: 75, 350, 422, 519, 653, 722, 743, 782, 978, 1235, 1564
- 12: 422, 519, 978, 1234, 1564
- 13: 119, 422, 519, 544, 978
- 14: 74, 118, 137, 278, 422, 544, 567, 924, 1072, 1551
- 15: 137, 284, 422, 544, 1216, 1288, 1453, 1466, 1551
- 16: 102, 283, 284, 422, 1216, 1453, 1499
- 17: 284, 365, 422, 785, 880, 1329, 1372, 1385, 1485
- 18: 18, 284, 365, 422, 816, 880, 1372, 1485, 1494, 1499
- 19: 365, 422, 601, 816, 1125, 1263, 1494, 1499, 1548
- 20: 282, 422, 1263, 1499
- 21: 422, 1268
- 22: 298, 422, 627, 669, 687, 706, 933, 1150, 1164, 1502
- 23: 73, 107, 117, 215, 227, 276, 298, 422, 425, 548, 583, 638, 737, 899, 920, 966, 1150, 1192, 1237, 1262, 1577
- 24: 117, 422, 917, 1192
- 25: 38, 117, 320, 422, 492, 917, 1192, 1266
- 26: 38, 77, 117, 186, 319, 320, 365, 422, 662, 950, 967, 1076
- 27: 144, 365, 422, 1273

## Numbers

**1:** 77, 146, 301, 319, 748, 752, 763, 1401
**2:** 77, 301, 328, 575, 748, 821
**3:** 46, 248, 301, 328, 821, 940, 978, 1341, 1486
**4:** 25, 46, 141, 248, 301, 978, 1341, 1486
**5:** 10, 25, 301, 717, 751, 788, 796, 978
**6:** 51, 195, 361, 513, 649, 751, 759, 788, 796, 978
**7:** 51, 141, 195, 274, 580, 590, 649, 856, 1482, 1490, 1496
**8:** 195, 274, 361, 513, 580, 1020
**9:** 49, 274, 294, 482, 513, 582, 1020
**10:** 297, 565, 903, 951, 960
**11:** 54, 226, 230, 297, 299, 683, 745, 903
**12:** 54, 76, 230, 683, 1110, 1149
**13:** 54, 76, 154, 230, 683, 1110, 1284, 1489
**14:** 154, 694, 811, 970, 1095, 1101, 1213, 1510
**15:** 24, 211, 694, 811, 907, 970, 1101, 1213, 1510, 1571
**16:** 24, 154, 202, 211, 345, 907, 1285, 1571
**17:** 24, 202, 289, 345, 493, 845, 918, 1153, 1515
**18:** 24, 196, 211, 345, 493, 507, 694, 918, 1153, 1225, 1465, 1515
**19:** 196, 202, 414, 459, 507, 1038, 1058, 1505, 1553
**20:** 202, 319, 1058, 1553
**21:** 11, 319, 507, 576, 813, 913, 931, 1172, 1315, 1470, 1505
**22:** 241, 813, 913, 1014, 1470
**23:** 11, 116, 228, 241, 1172
**24:** 59, 155, 228, 241, 1079, 1172
**25:** 47, 59, 155, 1079
**26:** 47, 59, 155, 672, 773, 1079
**27:** 59, 231, 485
**28:** 59, 231, 358, 426, 510, 608, 614, 655, 799, 800, 825, 870, 1131, 1173, 1280, 1325, 1362, 1368, 1464, 1475
**29:** 59, 86, 242, 267, 298, 341, 425, 429, 500, 607, 629, 799, 802, 1380, 1409, 1424
**30:** 59, 86, 224, 298, 1185, 1380
**31:** 59, 78, 224, 456, 494, 812, 1053, 1185, 1380
**32:** 59, 86, 456, 666, 1053
**33:** 59, 666, 889, 1578
**34:** 59, 1218, 1578
**35:** 59, 79, 778, 958, 1302, 1417, 1459
**36:** 79, 778, 958, 1302, 1459

## Deuteronomy

**1:** 59, 90, 422, 814, 874, 1165, 1452
**2:** 59, 73, 153, 225, 422, 874, 1548
**3:** 59, 336, 422, 469, 481, 1112, 1312, 1548
**4:** 59, 87, 336, 422, 469, 473, 874, 1546
**5:** 59, 73, 87, 88, 158, 422, 473, 1546
**6:** 59, 87, 88, 422, 625
**7:** 59, 87, 88, 422, 625, 815, 1338, 1382
**8:** 59, 87, 422, 815, 995, 1338
**9:** 59, 87, 89, 116, 422, 815, 995, 996
**10:** 59, 87, 89, 422
**11:** 89, 236, 422
**12:** 89, 123, 236, 422, 574, 956, 957, 989, 1217, 1548
**13:** 87, 123, 236, 422, 886, 957, 961, 989
**14:** 87, 123, 726, 961, 1023, 1507
**15:** 87, 123, 252, 425, 726, 898, 1023, 1443
**16:** 115, 123, 156, 425, 451, 864, 898, 1251, 1354
**17:** 111, 115, 451, 499, 678, 864, 1214, 1251
**18:** 111, 451
**19:** 451, 476, 1013, 1043
**20:** 451, 476
**21:** 42, 91, 114, 451, 455, 852, 1214
**22:** 42, 91, 114, 455, 727, 1039
**23:** 455, 727, 1039, 1491
**24:** 170, 455, 727, 1039, 1491
**25:** 43, 170, 455, 459, 487, 727, 1039, 1491
**26:** 43, 91, 165, 366, 455, 636, 1074, 1491, 1553
**27:** 80, 91, 165, 455, 636, 833, 944, 974, 1074, 1491, 1553, 1565
**28:** 80, 165, 187, 455, 650, 833, 1035, 1211, 1491, 1548
**29:** 187, 455, 628, 733, 1108, 1378
**30:** 92, 273, 455, 728, 755
**31:** 44, 92, 147, 453, 455, 459, 535, 728, 755, 833, 949, 984, 1082
**32:** 44, 92, 121, 250, 337, 359, 445, 453, 459, 728, 729, 755, 761, 833, 949, 1010, 1082, 1087, 1151, 1156, 1328, 1397, 1491
**33:** 53, 81, 110, 277, 279, 359, 445, 455, 459, 710, 729, 755, 834, 911, 1087, 1120, 1139, 1151, 1245, 1250, 1282, 1491
**34:** 45, 53, 57, 81, 110, 244, 279, 455, 524, 702, 946

## Joshua

**1:** 375, 394, 413, 459, 512, 867, 1412, 1472, 1570
**2:** 1331
**3:** 390, 1286
**5:** 173, 369, 372, 377, 390, 901, 1342
**6:** 12, 173, 369, 372, 394, 512
**7:** 12
**8:** 458
**9:** 979
**10:** 633, 979
**17:** 954, 963, 968, 1012
**18:** 93, 988
**19:** 93, 988
**20:** 93
**22:** 82
**23:** 795
**24:** 388, 454, 795, 964, 979, 1051, 1445, 1511

## Judges

**1:** 82
**2:** 82
**4:** 126, 415, 458

[Judges]
- **5:** 23, 126, 174, 192, 376, 398, 415, 458, 640, 688, 701, 771, 991, 1525
- **6:** 94
- **7:** 94, 730
- **8:** 93, 94, 730
- **9:** 93
- **10:** 409
- **11:** 352, 381, 409, 458, 546, 1446
- **13:** 141, 376, 397, 554

## 1 Samuel
- **1:** 125, 331, 375, 377, 378, 387, 541, 577, 656, 703, 908, 1222
- **2:** 125, 375, 377, 446, 615, 656, 658, 703, 1209
- **3:** 375, 615, 1209
- **4:** 375
- **5:** 375
- **6:** 375, 891
- **7:** 375
- **8:** 309, 375, 458, 1573
- **9:** 309, 375
- **10:** 309, 375
- **11:** 309, 375
- **12:** 309, 375, 409, 1008, 1572
- **13:** 95, 309, 983, 1008, 1062, 1572
- **14:** 95, 309, 1046, 1062
- **15:** 95, 395, 414, 458, 459, 987, 1046, 1062, 1535
- **16:** 95, 395, 1046, 1062, 1535
- **17:** 95, 140, 458, 646, 651, 894, 1046, 1060, 1062, 1279, 1573
- **18:** 95, 458, 1060
- **19:** 95, 1026, 1062
- **20:** 95, 943, 997, 1008, 1025, 1323, 1324
- **21:** 407, 997, 1008, 1025
- **22:** 128, 407
- **23:** 407, 1566
- **24:** 1566
- **25:** 1566

## 2 Samuel
- **1:** 923
- **5:** 261, 387, 440, 1295, 1451
- **6:** 261, 387, 393, 440, 558, 1295
- **7:** 261
- **8:** 261
- **9:** 261
- **17:** 652, 1183, 1314
- **18:** 652, 1183
- **19:** 652, 1183
- **20:** 652, 1183
- **21:** 124, 454, 593, 647, 1223, 1335
- **22:** 122, 124, 204, 206, 325, 351, 460, 463, 559, 593, 698, 770, 828, 875, 1210, 1335, 1337, 1339, 1454, 1530
- **23:** 60, 159, 460, 1530
- **24:** 83, 389

## 1 Kings
- **1:** 83, 330, 396, 409, 415, 416, 418, 630, 822, 1391, 1440, 1449, 1455
- **2:** 326, 377, 392, 847, 1500
- **3:** 83, 376, 377, 1492
- **4:** 377, 1492
- **5:** 458, 771, 1228, 1543
- **6:** 109, 343, 377, 458, 771, 807, 900
- **7:** 52, 376, 406, 407, 446, 542, 1227, 1229
- **8:** 14, 112, 389, 407, 413, 446, 542, 564, 819, 1412, 1469, 1472
- **10:** 357
- **11:** 357
- **18:** 141, 343, 406, 546, 1506
- **19:** 352, 546, 809
- **21:** 591
- **22:** 591

## 2 Kings
- **2:** 459
- **4:** 334, 374, 376, 415, 416, 774, 829, 1089, 1094, 1096, 1161, 1344, 1393, 1413, 1484, 1550
- **5:** 260
- **7:** 410, 863
- **8:** 491, 735, 806, 890
- **9:** 491, 806, 890
- **12:** 1197
- **13:** 882
- **16:** 890
- **17:** 890, 1100, 1102
- **22:** 22, 372, 403, 404
- **23:** 22, 372, 407
- **24:** 1567
- **25:** 22, 1567

## Isaiah
- **1:** 381, 459, 460, 626, 661, 682, 690, 896, 1508, 1517
- **2:** 381, 460, 626, 661, 1446, 1508
- **4:** 385, 423
- **5:** 222, 382, 385, 401, 417, 423, 588
- **6:** 222, 347, 398, 401, 415, 417, 588, 872, 976
- **7:** 347, 382
- **8:** 382
- **9:** 221, 398, 401, 415, 976
- **10:** 390, 393, 525
- **11:** 371, 382, 384, 390, 393, 525, 550, 1447, 1509
- **12:** 172, 371, 390, 393, 405, 1295, 1451
- **13:** 387, 1295, 1451
- **14:** 1295, 1451
- **17:** 387
- **18:** 387
- **19:** 126, 415, 458, 496, 573

[Isaiah]
21: 356
22: 356, 364, 896, 1508, 1517
23: 808, 962
24: 356, 421
27: 383, 882
29: 380, 661
30: 661, 1036
31: 568, 1036
32: 568, 661
33: 379, 387, 817, 1086, 1271
34: 624
35: 381, 387, 624
37: 1003
40: 374, 377, 386, 412, 616, 769, 876, 1132, 1190, 1393, 1415, 1420, 1441
41: 139, 374, 377, 416, 459, 1096, 1132, 1393, 1415, 1420, 1450, 1456
42: 103, 113, 376, 388, 409, 416, 458, 459, 504, 541, 772, 829, 1099, 1410
43: 382, 406, 412, 698, 705, 879, 1454
44: 382, 406, 558, 786
46: 356, 661
48: 382, 385, 624, 1086
49: 377, 385, 388, 624, 772, 1190, 1226, 1345, 1445, 1448
51: 45, 379, 380, 382, 387, 440
54: 113, 374, 376, 412, 416, 458, 769, 838, 1099, 1393, 1410, 1411, 1484
55: 306, 332, 390, 395, 416, 596, 769, 776, 876, 1132, 1298, 1393, 1411, 1484, 1554, 1568
56: 332, 384, 390, 504, 776, 923, 1298, 1554, 1568
57: 306, 375, 384, 390, 504, 553, 1320, 1441, 1554, 1568
58: 306, 319, 553, 1320, 1568
59: 553, 930
60: 56, 205, 373, 389, 391, 402, 458, 543, 735, 1137, 1143, 1158
61: 45, 56, 180, 373, 394, 402, 616, 705, 923, 1137, 1143, 1158
62: 56, 180, 373, 394, 402, 448, 458, 543, 616, 705, 999, 1028, 1030, 1033, 1137, 1143, 1158, 1447, 1539
63: 373, 394, 402, 854, 1447
65: 379, 385, 387, 402, 1295
66: 385, 402, 568, 1323, 1324

## Jeremiah
1: 98, 480, 682, 686, 690
2: 98, 129, 339, 458, 734, 980, 1367, 1460
3: 220, 734
5: 85, 98, 1029
6: 85, 98, 690, 757, 1029, 1091
7: 558, 690, 757, 1267
8: 96, 690, 723, 757, 1091, 1567
9: 96, 207, 377, 508, 558, 723, 757, 1091, 1567
10: 385
11: 1198
12: 705, 781, 1198
13: 781
15: 705, 1198
16: 397, 768
17: 376, 397, 766, 768, 783
18: 84
23: 84, 1002, 1086, 1448
24: 84
28: 411, 998
30: 129, 356, 387, 724
31: 306, 332, 375, 383, 395, 446, 458, 724, 738, 846, 1352, 1360
32: 50, 418, 475, 980
33: 50, 817
34: 333, 379, 387, 398, 458, 817, 976, 1543
35: 771, 1228, 1543
37: 1000
41: 718
42: 382, 718
47: 50
48: 50
51: 1567
52: 460, 1190, 1493

## Ezekiel
1: 348, 390, 399, 405, 446, 667, 836, 1173, 1199, 1223, 1336, 1520
2: 348, 667, 1520
16: 209, 213, 377, 392, 595
18: 385, 624
20: 410, 642, 928, 1370, 1422, 1549
22: 376, 377, 1549
23: 360
24: 360
26: 450, 977
27: 450, 977
28: 208, 380, 1347
29: 208, 377, 458, 835, 1007, 1347
32: 360
33: 97, 360
34: 97, 376, 460, 766, 777, 1022
36: 97, 209, 390, 395, 414, 458, 459, 1535
37: 209, 376, 377, 390, 404, 407, 459, 731, 754, 883, 1492
38: 1469
39: 97
40: 50, 97
41: 97
42: 97
43: 52, 109, 141, 209, 377, 406, 458, 557, 878, 1506, 1534
44: 766, 768, 783
45: 371, 390, 395, 458, 557, 633, 1324

[Ezekiel]
- **46:** 130, 458, 1324
- **47:** 130, 390, 557

## Hosea
- **1:** 104
- **2:** 46, 55, 104, 381, 459, 766
- **4:** 382
- **5:** 104
- **6:** 104, 595
- **10:** 384, 595, 973, 1024
- **11:** 377, 415, 973, 1090, 1519
- **12:** 377, 391, 396
- **13:** 391
- **14:** 373, 391, 596, 776

## Joel
- **2:** 776
- **4:** 891

## Amos
- **2:** 377, 415, 1555
- **3:** 415, 1000

## Obadiah
- **1:** 356, 377, 387, 415, 1447, 1555

## Jonah
- **1:** 271, 402, 633, 893, 1215, 1256, 1537
- **2:** 271, 1554
- **3:** 271, 400, 1554
- **4:** 400, 429, 1554

## Micah
- **5:** 1331
- **6:** 391, 546, 1331
- **7:** 400, 429

## Nahum
- **2:** 99
- **3:** 99

## Habakkuk
- **2:** 348, 1199
- **3:** 188, 348, 388, 433, 594, 772, 790, 865, 1091, 1197, 1199, 1219, 1223, 1532
- **15:** 594
- **16:** 594
- **17:** 594

## Zephaniah
- **1:** 188
- **2:** 188
- **3:** 188, 388, 1445, 1511

## Haggai
- **2:** 99, 356, 459

## Zechariah
- **1:** 1040
- **2:** 554, 975, 1034, 1040
- **3:** 100, 467, 554, 975
- **4:** 383, 467, 515, 716
- **5:** 385, 624, 716
- **6:** 383, 385
- **8:** 100
- **9:** 100
- **10:** 100
- **11:** 100
- **13:** 188, 429, 1431
- **14:** 14, 112, 188, 319, 400, 407, 446, 631, 1431

## Malachi
- **1:** 188, 415, 418, 630, 698, 705, 909, 1090, 1202, 1519, 1539
- **2:** 377, 411, 415, 698, 705, 770, 879, 888, 998, 1539
- **3:** 377, 385, 411, 415, 721, 888, 909, 998, 1090, 1202, 1441

## Psalms
- **33:** 1575
- **34:** 1575
- **35:** 1575

## Proverbs
- **17:** 1556
- **18:** 1556
- **31:** 2

## Job
- **1:** 1174
- **5:** 884

## Song of Solomon
- **2:** 286
- **4:** 286
- **5:** 286, 851
- **6:** 851

## Ecclesiastes
- **1:** 1311
- **2:** 1311

## Esther
- **–:** 367
- **1:** 357
- **5:** 257
- **6:** 257, 346, 1260
- **7:** 257, 1260

## Daniel
- **–:** 435

## 1 Chronicles
- **1–9:** 839a

# GENERAL INDEX

abbreviation, abridgement and extract
40, 50, 53, 54, 80, 178, 179, 196, 249, 266, 267, 290, 303, 350, 451, 453, 455, 580, 590, 610, 702, 888, 1020, 1098, 1103, 1173, 1248, 1478, 1482, 1490

Abraham
801

account
141

acrostic
369, 431, 432, 437, 438, 509, 612, 697, 711

African
110, 166, 1465

alphabetic
200, 369, 431, 432, 437, 438, 509, 609, 612, 697, 711, 732, 1579

*'amidah*
402

Arabic
134, 141, 206, 215, 244, 281, 316, 359, 364, 452, 459, 477, 480, 505, 510, 520, 526, 540, 588, 655, 906, 1151, 1357, 1361, 1435

Ashkenazi
138, 419, 497, 566, 696, 699, 1221, 1231

Ashkenazi/Italian
393, 889, 1071, 1075, 1077, 1083, 1092, 1512, 1559

Atonement, Day of
267, 306, 319, 400, 402, 425, 429, 553, 738, 930, 1215, 1568

Av, Ninth of
332, 377, 776, 1091

*'Avot* (tractate)
423, 681

Babylonian
12, 13, 17, 19, 40, 48, 49, 50, 51, 52, 53, 54, 55, 56, 57, 58, 59, 60, 61, 62, 63, 64, 65, 66, 67, 68, 69, 70, 71, 72, 73, 74, 75, 76, 77, 78, 79, 80, 81, 82, 83, 84, 85, 86, 87, 88, 89, 90, 91, 92, 93, 94, 95, 96, 97, 98, 99, 100, 130, 194, 205, 342, 349, 356, 360, 361, 364, 368, 372, 373, 374, 375, 376, 377, 382, 389, 411, 444, 447, 448, 450, 451, 533, 535, 568, 595, 609, 642, 662, 716, 717, 718, 719, 720, 721, 722, 723, 724, 725, 726, 727, 728, 729, 730, 731, 732, 733, 734, 735, 768, 777, 778, 779, 780, 781, 788, 795, 807, 808, 811, 812, 814, 816, 887, 898, 905, 927, 928, 941, 942, 944, 945, 946, 947, 949, 950, 951, 952, 953, 954, 955, 956, 957, 958, 959, 960, 961, 962, 963, 964, 965, 966, 967, 968, 969, 970, 971, 972, 973, 974, 975, 976, 977, 979, 980, 982, 983, 984, 985, 986, 987, 988, 989, 990, 991, 992, 993, 995, 996, 997, 998, 999, 1000, 1001, 1002, 1003, 1004, 1005, 1007, 1008, 1009, 1010, 1011, 1012, 1013, 1014, 1015, 1016, 1017, 1018, 1019, 1020, 1021, 1022, 1023, 1024, 1025, 1026, 1028, 1029, 1031, 1032, 1033, 1034, 1035, 1036, 1037, 1038, 1039, 1040, 1041, 1042, 1043, 1044, 1045, 1046, 1047, 1049, 1050, 1051, 1052, 1053, 1054, 1055, 1056, 1057, 1058, 1059, 1060, 1061, 1062, 1122, 1163, 1243, 1255, 1265, 1290, 1371, 1468, 1473, 1492, 1500, 1504, 1547, 1548, 1549, 1551, 1563, 1565, 1566, 1572, 1579, 1580

Baghdad
210

Ben Naftali
114

*Berakhot* (tractate)
1361

blessings
51, 369, 403, 445, 786

bridegroom
443, 500, 712, 843

Byzantine
1110, 1149, 1182

calendar
20, 274

catchword
135, 280, 291, 350, 602, 910

chancery
244

children
8, 445, 459

Christian
346

cipher
15, 48, 54, 59, 61, 67, 76, 87, 115, 121, 132, 133, 163, 169, 230, 285, 305, 310, 312, 313, 315, 449, 459, 468, 470, 536, 580, 628, 664, 1017, 1186, 1305, 1326, 1433

code
401

colophon
20, 21, 22, 23, 41, 307, 394, 459, 526, 594, 613, 709, 790, 866, 1207

commandments
401, 427, 612, 1045

commentary
420, 466, 497

communities on rivers
210

composition/s
433, 443, 503, 518, 584, 615, 618, 619, 640, 738, 805, 915, 1115, 1174, 1421, 1442, 1480, 1528, 1529, 1532

condolence
584

confessional
433

conversion
346

Coptic
141

Creation
430, 612, 801

cross
346

cursive
1117, 1556

*custos/odes*
115, 129, 291

Darius
1112

dated manuscript
341, 526

death
584, 805, 1168

decoration
15, 59, 77, 88, 215, 220, 380, 381, 382, 385, 388, 458, 468, 569, 610, 628, 664, 868, 891, 932, 1000, 1061, 1106, 1151, 1196, 1246, 1303, 1314, 1326, 1549, 1573

## GENERAL INDEX

design
  48, 61, 316, 998
dignitary
  322, 480
document
  244, 341, 455, 674
dots
  79, 246, 282, 1187
draft
  655
drawing
  48, 102, 132
enemies
  479
ethics
  618
eulogy
  805
extract (of Onqelos)
  *see* abbreviation
fasting
  306, 776, 923, 1568
Faṭimid
  655
festival/s
  298, 348, 390, 706, 1325
flood
  1545
Fragment-targum
  180, 345, 350, 1103, 1491
funeral
  1174
Galilean Aramaic
  367, 693, 697; *see also* Palestinian Targum
Gideon
  1545
Greek
  367
*haftarah/rot*
  14, 23, 45, 46, 50, 52, 55, 56, 109, 112, 113, 126,
  129, 130, 141, 163, 169, 173, 180, 205, 206, 207,
  208, 209, 213, 221, 306, 319, 332, 339, 343, 348,
  352, 356, 369, 371, 372, 373, 374, 375, 376, 377,
  379, 380, 381, 382, 383, 384, 385, 386, 387, 388,
  389, 390, 391, 392, 393, 394, 395, 396, 397, 398,
  399, 400, 401, 402, 403, 404, 405, 406, 407, 408,
  409, 410, 411, 412, 413, 414, 415, 416, 417, 418,
  423, 429, 433, 440, 446, 454, 458, 459, 460, 467,
  496, 504, 512, 515, 525, 536, 540, 541, 542, 543,
  546, 550, 553, 554, 557, 558, 564, 568, 585, 594,
  595, 596, 616, 624, 630, 633, 661, 682, 686, 690,
  698, 705, 735, 738, 766, 768, 769, 770, 771, 772,
  776, 783, 817, 829, 835, 838, 876, 879, 882, 891,
  896, 901, 909, 923, 928, 930, 976, 979, 980, 998,
  999, 1000, 1065, 1086, 1089, 1090, 1091, 1094, 1096,
  1099, 1112, 1132, 1137, 1143, 1158, 1161, 1173,
  1190, 1197, 1198, 1199, 1209, 1210, 1215, 1219,
  1223, 1227, 1228, 1229, 1267, 1286, 1295, 1323,
  1324, 1331, 1342, 1344, 1347, 1352, 1367, 1370,
  1376, 1391, 1393, 1410, 1411, 1412, 1413, 1415,
  1420, 1422, 1431, 1440, 1441, 1445, 1446, 1447,
  1448, 1449, 1450, 1451, 1454, 1455, 1456, 1469,
  1472, 1484, 1492, 1500, 1506, 1508, 1511, 1519,
  1535, 1539, 1543, 1549, 1550, 1554, 1555, 1567,
  1568, 1573; *see also* triennial

Haggadah (Passover)
  482
halakhah
  505
Ḥanukkah
  467, 590
Hebraism
  110, 512
High Holydays
  402
history
  592
Ḥodesh (Maḥar)
  1323
Ḥodesh (Shabbat)
  1324
holidays
  274
instructions
  206, 210, 322, 461, 697
intermediate (days of festivals)
  302, 404, 407, 482, 1469
Italian
  393, 889, 1071, 1075, 1077, 1083, 1092, 1355, 1512,
  1559
Italy
  419
Jerusalem
  846, 1442
Jonathan b. 'Uzziel
  222, 1376
Joshua
  1545
jottings
  281, 452, 505, 540, 588, 906, 1151, 1361, 1435
Judaeo-Arabic
  7, 10, 17, 18, 20, 24, 25, 26, 27, 28, 29, 30, 31,
  32, 33, 34, 35, 36, 37, 38, 39, 40, 41, 42, 43, 44,
  45, 46, 47, 48, 59, 134, 189, 210, 213, 304, 306,
  318, 319, 321, 322, 338, 345, 347, 366, 370, 373,
  374, 375, 417, 418, 423, 425, 426, 452, 455, 458,
  460, 461, 464, 465, 466, 468, 469, 472, 473, 474,
  475, 482, 485, 486, 487, 488, 490, 494, 495, 498,
  499, 502, 503, 505, 527, 533, 537, 539, 540, 545,
  547, 549, 560, 571, 575, 588, 602, 615, 624, 663,
  672, 673, 674, 697, 708, 709, 710, 751, 752, 763,
  793, 794, 820, 821, 822, 825, 826, 842, 845, 850,
  852, 853, 856, 859, 865, 905, 911, 912, 916, 918,
  921, 923, 926, 927, 936, 1120, 1122, 1126, 1127,
  1128, 1133, 1136, 1138, 1139, 1140, 1146, 1148,
  1153, 1163, 1165, 1171, 1196, 1202, 1203, 1204,
  1206, 1209, 1234, 1236, 1243, 1250, 1253, 1255,
  1265, 1266, 1282, 1284, 1285, 1287, 1290, 1294,
  1296, 1308, 1322, 1326, 1330, 1358, 1366, 1369,
  1371, 1383, 1386, 1387, 1392, 1399, 1401, 1405,
  1406, 1414, 1427, 1458, 1459, 1460, 1466, 1468,
  1470, 1473, 1504, 1532, 1536, 1541, 1542, 1546,
  1553, 1571
lectionary
  356, 536, 827, 1065, 1112
legend
  222, 1376
letters
  322, 480
lists
  274, 316, 370, 477, 626, 752, 1045, 1112

## GENERAL INDEX

liturgy
166, 210, 322, 361, 402, 433, 515, 590, 607, 615, 619, 634, 667, 713, 715, 738, 843, 1115, 1174, 1438, 1442, 1480, 1554, 1558

*maftir*
242, 267, 298, 341, 414, 429, 459, 607, 629, 802, 870, 1131, 1173, 1325, 1437

Maimonides
401

majuscule
59, 148, 182, 186, 191, 216, 230, 253, 304, 319, 580, 597, 1110, 1355

marriage
341

Massorah to Hebrew
1, 2, 35, 53, 59, 62, 64, 72, 73, 79, 80, 83, 87, 95, 114, 117, 119, 125, 133, 137, 141, 158, 160, 162, 163, 164, 165, 167, 350, 393, 395, 444, 491, 527, 532, 574, 585, 586, 699, 722, 729, 743, 752, 788, 808, 868, 890, 932, 964, 966, 978, 984, 985, 1009, 1014, 1029, 1044, 1045, 1053, 1056, 1059, 1073, 1074, 1082, 1087, 1091, 1104, 1452, 1483, 1554, 1557, 1560, 1564, 1566, 1568

Massorah to Onqelos
72, 86, 89, 179, 365, 422, 451, 453, 455, 609, 732, 818, 839a, 941, 978, 1045, 1523, 1547, 1579

medicine
1133, 1532

*Megillah*
51, 108, 649

menorah
443

midrash
167, 321, 339, 1017, 1041, 1058, 1104

mirror texts
356, 495, 767, 1548

Mishnah
51, 108, 341, 649, 681, 1361

*miṣwot*
626, 640

morning service
8

mourning
443, 923

mysticism
329

Nehardea, Neharda'ei
230, 422, 662, 726, 1017

New Year
166, 306, 332, 341, 377, 395, 446, 458, 521, 541, 607, 634, 738, 1115, 1209, 1352

Ninth of Av
332, 776, 1091

Nisan
437, 697

North African
110, 166, 1465

notes
15, 20, 21, 24, 26, 30, 43, 44, 45, 46, 48, 52, 53, 54, 59, 72, 75, 79, 80, 83, 89, 114, 126, 141, 148, 158, 179, 182, 186, 187, 189, 190, 191, 206, 209, 215, 227, 230, 235, 236, 244, 253, 254, 274, 285, 301, 303, 310, 315, 347, 350, 371, 373, 374, 375, 377, 386, 393, 405, 425, 426, 434, 441, 458, 459, 487, 524, 526, 561, 610, 624, 628, 664, 690, 722, 743, 830, 833, 842, 910, 923, 1044, 1059, 1114, 1151, 1173, 1303, 1326, 1451, 1528, 1547, 1554, 1563, 1566

novellae
198

Oriental/Spanish
529

ownership, notation of
148, 434, 441, 867, 1558

Palestinian (Targum)
120, 158, 160, 161, 162, 163, 164, 165, 167, 168, 169, 180, 188, 307, 366, 383, 401, 420, 428, 434, 488, 509, 523, 532, 536, 538, 585, 611, 613, 619, 639, 645, 650, 668, 669, 671, 687, 700, 706, 711, 736, 804, 827, 842, 844, 881, 1066, 1067, 1068, 1069, 1070, 1073, 1085, 1097, 1104, 1106, 1107, 1108, 1230, 1310, 1325, 1327, 1333, 1356, 1375, 1429, 1436, 1442, 1457, 1476, 1491, 1522, 1553

Palestinian (triennial *sidra* and vocalisation)
40, 48, 74, 77, 88, 89, 92, 134, 163, 168, 169, 188, 536, 1064, 1065, 1230, 1572

paraphrase
369

*parashah*
15, 24, 26, 30, 43, 44, 45, 46, 48, 52, 54, 55, 56, 59, 61, 67, 76, 87, 109, 113, 115, 126, 130, 132, 133, 136, 141, 169, 182, 186, 187, 190, 191, 206, 207, 211, 213, 221, 230, 235, 236, 253, 254, 274, 285, 301, 303, 305, 310, 312, 313, 315, 319, 320, 321, 339, 343, 352, 370, 374, 377, 392, 395, 396, 397, 398, 406, 409, 410, 412, 414, 422, 454, 458, 459, 468, 470, 507, 530, 541, 546, 554, 557, 558, 580, 597, 628, 630, 664, 766, 768, 769, 783, 829, 835, 876, 882, 896, 909, 928, 976, 999, 1000, 1017, 1089, 1090, 1094, 1096, 1099, 1110, 1114, 1132, 1137, 1151, 1161, 1186, 1190, 1196, 1197, 1210, 1227, 1228, 1229, 1246, 1303, 1326, 1331, 1344, 1347, 1355, 1367, 1370, 1380, 1391, 1410, 1411, 1413, 1415, 1420, 1422, 1433, 1437, 1440, 1449, 1450, 1453, 1455, 1456, 1472, 1492, 1500, 1506, 1528, 1535, 1543, 1546, 1549, 1550, 1555, 1559, 1573

Passover
148, 173, 252, 302, 372, 377, 393, 403, 404, 405, 407, 459, 482, 525, 550, 901, 1131, 1223, 1342, 1553

Patriarchs
1045

pen-exercises
145, 150, 200, 273, 280, 316, 323, 341, 362, 401, 477, 502, 510, 512, 520, 534, 604, 613, 622, 663, 810, 838, 848, 984, 1283, 1284, 1494, 1516, 1536, 1561, 1569

Pentecost
148, 256, 304, 348, 405, 433, 446, 483, 594, 612, 619, 620, 870, 1091, 1173, 1197, 1219, 1223, 1416

Persian
16, 27, 125, 211, 323, 573, 701, 921, 936, 1280, 1501

petition
364, 655

*piyyuṭ*
425, 443, 462, 463, 484, 623, 629

poetry
2, 128, 166, 304, 344, 349, 361, 367, 369, 394, 427, 430, 431, 432, 434, 435, 436, 437, 438, 496, 500, 509, 523, 592, 607, 608, 612, 613, 620, 630, 640, 667, 693, 697, 702, 711, 713, 800, 801, 803, 841, 843, 875, 1010, 1082, 1166, 1168, 1316, 1337, 1373, 1376, 1526, 1529, 1531, 1545

praise
  213, 430, 433, 500, 843
prayer
  479, 632, 712
Purim
  134, 858, 925, 1116, 1553
*qiddush*
  461, 1558
*qinnah*
  1480
rabbinic
  198, 921, 1556
Radaq
  421
Rashi
  419, 421, 497, 1556
red (ink)
  181, 200, 283, 321, 405, 451, 569, 572
*reshut*
  428, 439, 592, 620, 802, 1376
responsum
  452
rubric
  569
Sabbath
  404, 407, 459, 461, 467, 923, 1469, 1553
Safar
  526
scribblings
  134
scroll
  364, 370, 378, 536, 827, 1053, 1054, 1055, 1065, 1066, 1067, 1068, 1069, 1070, 1230, 1352
*selihah*
  166, 607, 629, 632, 641, 1480
Sephardi
  1556
*Shabbat*
  222
*Shemini 'Aseret*
  298, 564, 620, 1469, 1472
shorthand
  1088, 1098
sign
  48, 54, 56, 89, 174, 1000, 1196, 1246, 1523
signature
  602
*Simhat Torah*
  413
slaughter (ritual)
  401, 505
song
  40, 433, 445
Spanish
  11, 47, 127, 137, 142, 155, 186, 190, 191, 203, 253, 319, 363, 392, 421, 529, 530, 531, 534, 548, 563, 576, 583, 591, 670, 681, 684, 689, 744, 748, 817, 834, 875, 892, 913, 931, 1133, 1140, 1147, 1150, 1159, 1171, 1211, 1220, 1235, 1260, 1328, 1337, 1425, 1443, 1544, 1556, 1558
*Sukkah*
  222
supralinear
  79, 129, 249, 251, 282, 565, 818, 1575
Syriac
  291
Tabernacles
  112, 242, 319, 400, 407, 413, 423, 425, 429, 446, 620, 629, 802, 1431, 1469
Ten Commandments
  427, 612
ten utterances
  430
*tosefta/tot*
  166, 174, 192, 327, 330, 357, 369, 372, 393, 433, 461, 467, 621, 639, 668, 669, 671, 687, 691, 715, 798, 843, 895, 1071, 1115, 1331, 1333, 1442, 1525, 1532
triennial cycle
  14, 40, 48, 59, 74, 77, 88, 89, 92, 134, 163, 168, 169, 274, 356, 371, 379, 380, 381, 382, 383, 384, 385, 386, 387, 388, 389, 391, 440, 459, 496, 504, 532, 536, 568, 585, 595, 624, 661, 698, 705, 743, 772, 817, 879, 891, 932, 1061, 1106, 1198, 1219, 1295, 1412, 1441, 1445, 1446, 1447, 1451, 1454, 1508, 1511, 1539, 1547
unidentified
  442, 450, 518, 646, 657, 716, 885, 901, 915, 948, 1031, 1032, 1129, 1333, 1421, 1425, 1520, 1527, 1528
untrained (hand)
  148, 159, 173, 178, 359, 428, 445, 459, 467, 477, 511, 512, 526, 627, 1145, 1256, 1268
vizier
  655
watermark
  28
wedding (*haftarah*)
  923
Yalqut Shim'oni
  1556
Yemenite
  17, 19, 40, 48, 59, 87, 93, 94, 97, 113, 205, 302, 306, 372, 377, 390, 416, 533, 642, 661, 723, 785, 887, 905, 927, 928, 988, 991, 1119, 1122, 1132, 1163, 1206, 1243, 1255, 1265, 1290, 1371, 1468, 1473, 1492, 1500, 1504, 1548, 1549
*zikhronot*
  402
*zulat*
  619

# PLATES

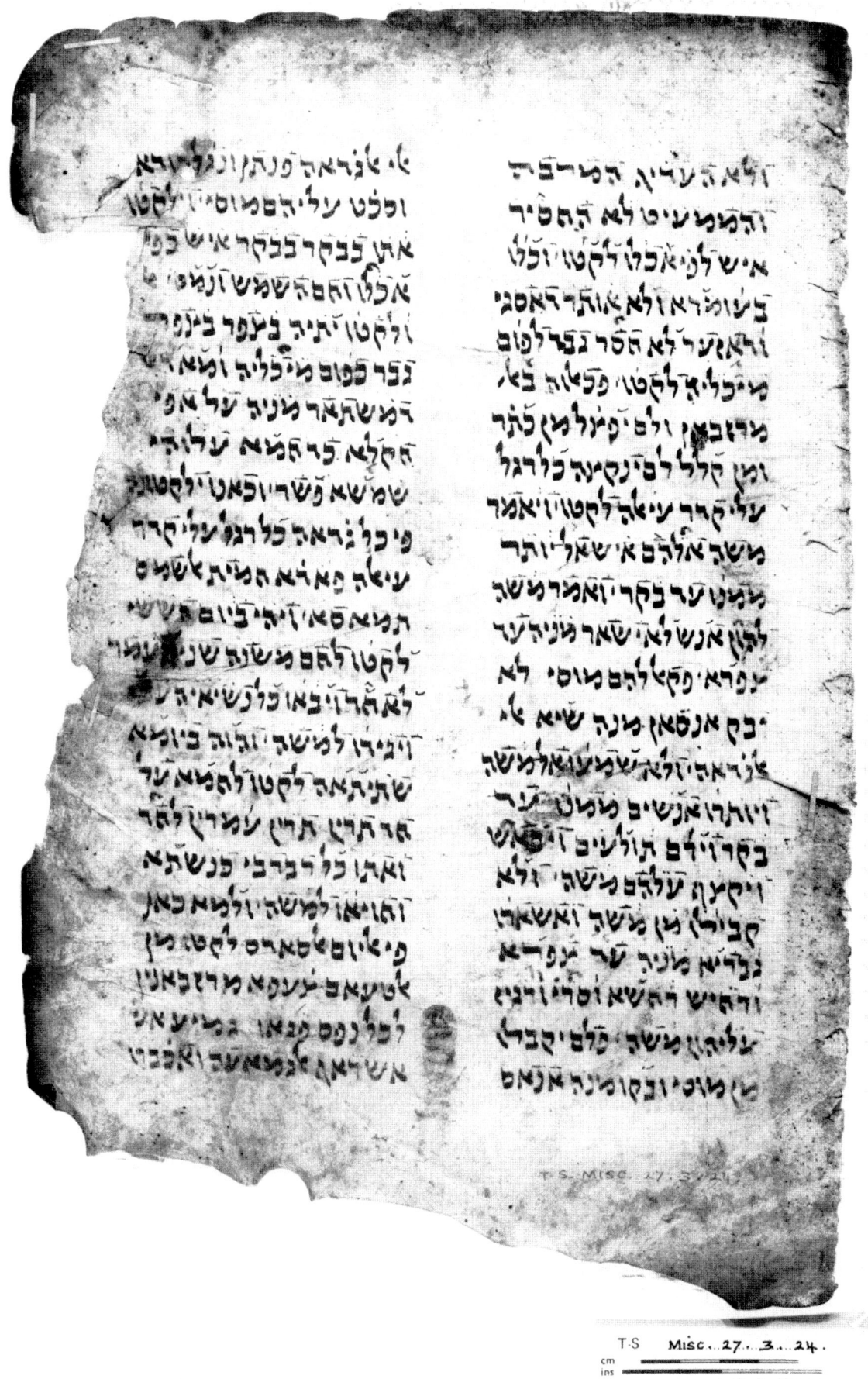

Plate 1: T-S Misc.27.3.24 recto, including Onqelos to Exodus 16:18–22; see entry no. [533]

עֲטָרֹת וְאֵת עֲרֹעֵר: וּבְנוּ בְנֵי גָד יָת דִיבוֹן וְיָת עֲטָרוֹת וְיָת עֲרֹעֵר: וְאֵת עַטְרֹת
שׁוֹפָן וְאֵת יַעְזֵר וְיָגְבֳּהָה: וְיָת עַטְרוֹת שׁוֹפָן וְיָת יַעְזֵר וְלִמְדָא: וְאֵת בֵּית נִמְרָה
וְאֵת בֵּית הָרָן עָרֵי מִבְצָר וְגִדְרֹת צֹאן: וְיָת בֵּית נִמְרָה וְיָת בֵּית הָרָן קִרְוִין
כְּרִיכָן וְחַטְרִין דְעָן: וּבְנֵי רְאוּבֵן בָּנוּ אֶת חֶשְׁבּוֹן וְאֶת אֶלְעָלֵא וְאֵת קִרְיָתָיִם:
וּבְנֵי רְאוּבֵן בְּנוֹ יָת חֶשְׁבּוֹן וְיָת אֶלְעָלֵא וְיָת קִרְיָתַיִם: וְאֶת נְבוֹ וְאֶת בַּעַל מְעוֹן
מוּסַבֹּת שֵׁם וְאֶת שִׂבְמָה וַיִּקְרְאוּ בְשֵׁמֹת אֶת שְׁמוֹת הֶעָרִים אֲשֶׁר בָּנוּ: וְיָת נְבוֹ
וְיָת בַּעַל מְעוֹן מַקְפָן שְׁמָהָן וְיָת כְּבָמָה וּקְרוֹ בִשְׁמָהָן יָת שְׁמָהַת קִרְוַיָא דִבְנוֹ:
וַיֵּלְכוּ בְּנֵי מָכִיר בֶּן מְנַשֶּׁה גִּלְעָדָה וַיִּלְכְּדֻהָ וַיּוֹרֶשׁ אֶת הָאֱמֹרִי אֲשֶׁר בָּהּ:
וַאֲזָלוּ בְּנֵי מָכִיר בַּר מְנַשֶּׁה לְגִלְעָד וּכְבַשׁוּהָא וְתָרִיךְ יָת אֱמוֹרָאָה דְבָהּ: וַיִּתֵּן
מֹשֶׁה אֶת הַגִּלְעָד לְמָכִיר בֶּן מְנַשֶּׁה וַיֵּשֶׁב בָּהּ: וִיהַב מֹשֶׁה יָת גִלְעָד לְמָכִיר
בַּר מְנַשֶּׁה וִיתִיב בַּהּ: וְיָאִיר בֶּן מְנַשֶּׁה הָלַךְ וַיִּלְכֹּד אֶת חַוֹּתֵיהֶם וַיִּקְרָא אֶתְהֶן
חַוֹּת יָאִיר: וְיָאִיר בַּר מְנַשֶּׁה אֲזַל וּכְבַשׁ יָת כַּפְרָנֵיהוֹן וּקְרָא יָתְהוֹן כַּפְרָנֵי יָאִיר:
וְנֹבַח הָלַךְ וַיִּלְכֹּד אֶת קְנָת וְאֶת בְּנֹתֶיהָ וַיִּקְרָא לָה נֹבַח בִּשְׁמוֹ: וְנֹבַח אֲזַל
וּכְבַשׁ יָת קְנָת וְיָת כַּפְרָנָהָא וּקְרָא לַהּ נֹבַח בִּשְׁמֵיהּ:

קוֹף עִם שְׁמַן עִיבַּל

אֵלֶּה מַסְעֵי בְנֵי יִשְׂרָאֵל אֲשֶׁר יָצְאוּ מֵאֶרֶץ מִצְרַיִם לְצִבְאֹתָם בְּיַד מֹשֶׁה
וְאַהֲרֹן: אִלֵּין מַטְלָנֵי בְנֵי יִשְׂרָאֵל דִּנְפָקוּ מֵאַרְעָא דְמִצְרַיִם לְחֵילֵיהוֹן בִּידָא דְמֹשֶׁה
וְאַהֲרֹן: וַיִּכְתֹּב מֹשֶׁה אֶת מוֹצָאֵיהֶם לְמַסְעֵיהֶם עַל פִּי יְהוָה וְאֵלֶּה מַסְעֵיהֶם
לְמוֹצָאֵיהֶם: וּכְתַב מֹשֶׁה יָת מַפְּקָנֵיהוֹן לְמַטְלָנֵיהוֹן עַל מֵימְרָא דַיְיָ וְאִלֵּין
מַטְלָנֵיהוֹן לְמַפְּקָנֵיהוֹן: וַיִּסְעוּ מֵרַעְמְסֵס בַּחֹדֶשׁ הָרִאשׁוֹן בַּחֲמִשָּׁה עָשָׂר יוֹם
לַחֹדֶשׁ הָרִאשׁוֹן מִמָּחֳרַת הַפֶּסַח יָצְאוּ בְנֵי יִשְׂרָאֵל בְּיָד רָמָה לְעֵינֵי כָּל מִצְרָיִם:
וּנְטָלוּ מֵרַעְמְסֵס בְּיַרְחָא קַדְמָאָה בְּחַמְשַׁת עַסְרָא יוֹמָא לְיַרְחָא קַדְמָאָה
מִבָּתַר פִּסְחָא נְפָקוּ בְנֵי יִשְׂרָאֵל בְּרֵישׁ גְּלֵי לְעֵינֵי כָּל מִצְרָאֵי: וּמִצְרַיִם מְקַבְּרִים
אֵת אֲשֶׁר הִכָּה יְהוָה בָּהֶם כָּל בְּכוֹר וּבֵאלֹהֵיהֶם עָשָׂה יְהוָה שְׁפָטִים: וּמִצְרָאֵי
מְקַבְּרִין יָת דִּקְטוֹל יְיָ בְּהוֹן כָּל בּוּכְרָא וּבְטָעֲוָתְהוֹן עֲבַד יְיָ דִינִין: וַיִּסְעוּ בְנֵי
יִשְׂרָאֵל מֵרַעְמְסֵס וַיַּחֲנוּ בְּסֻכֹּת: וּנְטָלוּ בְנֵי יִשְׂרָאֵל מֵרַעְמְסֵס וּשְׁרוֹ בְּסֻכּוֹת:
וַיִּסְעוּ מִסֻּכֹּת וַיַּחֲנוּ בְאֵתָם אֲשֶׁר בִּקְצֵה הַמִּדְבָּר: וּנְטָלוּ מִסֻּכּוֹת וּשְׁרוֹ בְּאֵתָם
דִּבִסְטַר מַדְבְּרָא: וַיִּסְעוּ מֵאֵתָם וַיָּשָׁב עַל פִּי הַחִירֹת אֲשֶׁר עַל פְּנֵי בַּעַל צְפוֹן
וַיַּחֲנוּ לִפְנֵי מִגְדֹּל: וּנְטָלוּ מֵאֵתָם וְתָב עַל פּוּם חִירָתָא דְקֳדָם בְּעֵיל צְפוֹן וּשְׁרוֹ
קֳדָם מִגְדוֹל: וַיִּסְעוּ מִפְּנֵי הַחִירֹת וַיַּעַבְרוּ בְתוֹךְ הַיָּם הַמִּדְבָּרָה וַיֵּלְכוּ דֶּרֶךְ
שְׁלֹשֶׁת יָמִים בְּמִדְבַּר אֵתָם וַיַּחֲנוּ בְּמָרָה: וּנְטָלוּ מִן קֳדָם חִירָתָא וַעֲבָרוּ בְּגוֹ יַמָּא

Plate 3: T-S B6.24, folio 2r, including Onqelos to Genesis 17:22–27, 18:4–6; see entry no. [138]

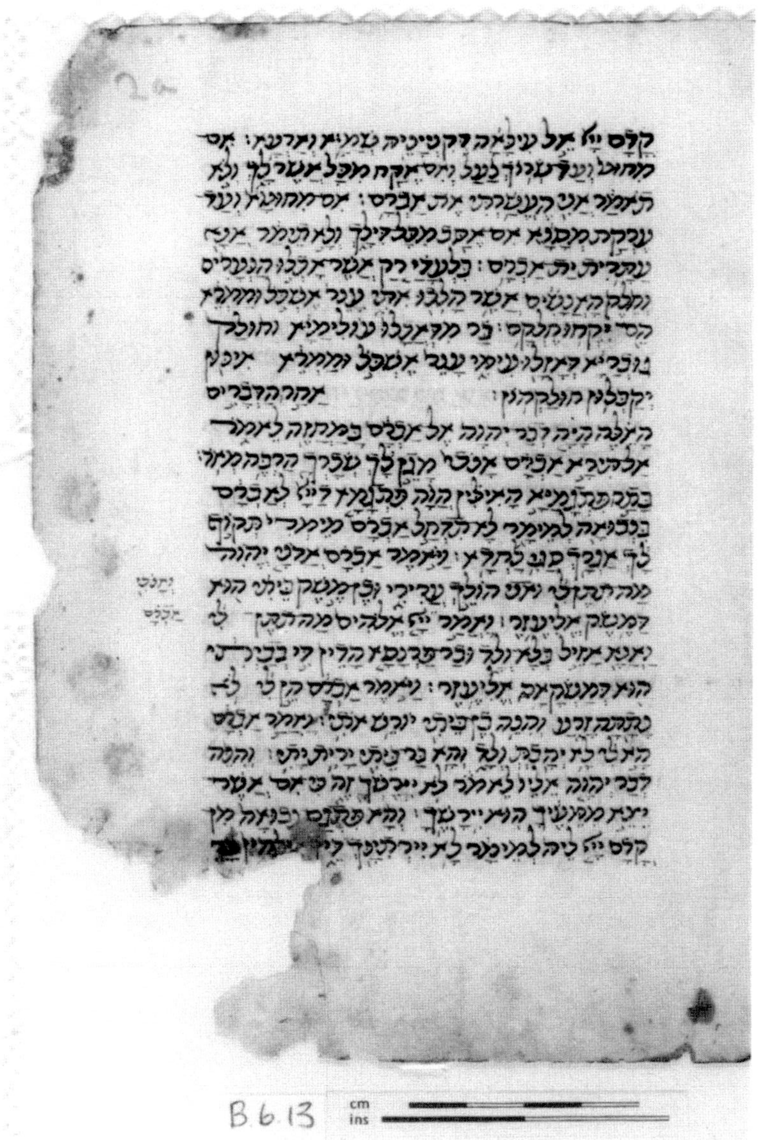

Plate 5: T-S B6.13, folio 2r,
including Onqelos to Genesis 14:19 – 15:4;
see entry no. [127]

Plate 4: T-S B11.114,
Onqelos to Exodus 30:7–13;
see entry no. [319]

Plate 7: T-S B15.4,
including Targum Jonathan to Judges 13:6–8;
see entry no. [376]

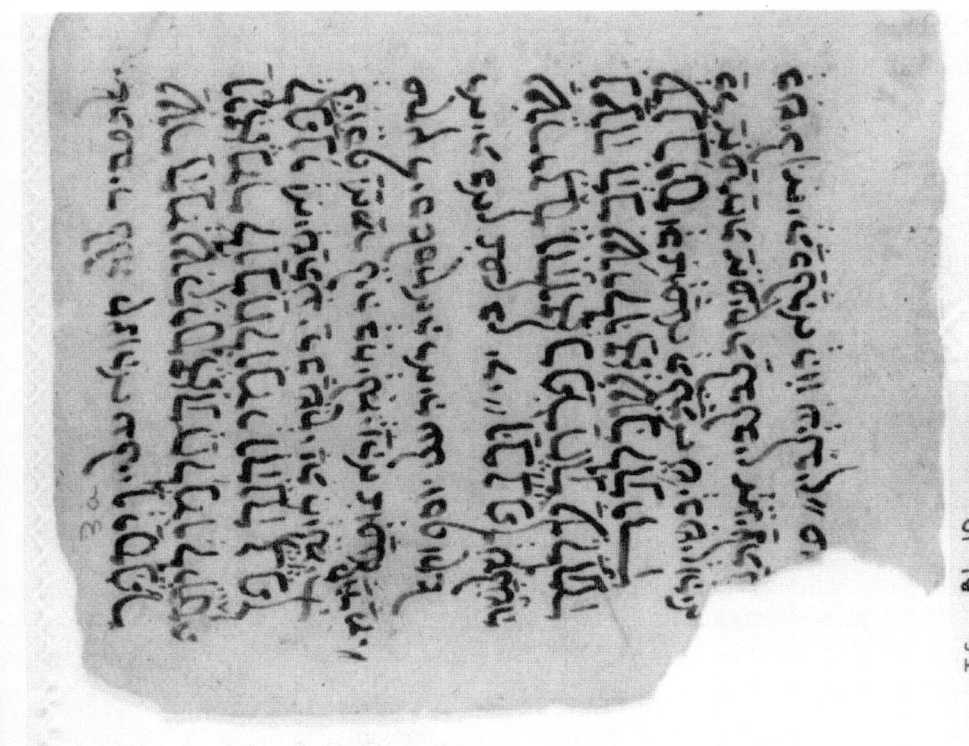

Plate 6: T-S B1.10, folio 3r,
including Onqelos to Genesis 40:8–10;
see entry no. [33]

Plate 8: T-S 20.155 recto, AS 63.24,117,129 recto, AS 69.241 recto, scroll,
Palestinian Targum to Exodus 21:36 – 22:27;
see entries nos. [536], [1065], [1069], [1230]

Plate 9: T-S Misc.27.1.4, folio 1r, including Palestinian Targum to Genesis 46:26–33; see entry no. [532]

Plate 10: T-S AS 72.77, folio 2r, Palestinian Fragment–targum to Deuteronomy 32:34–42; see entry no. [1491]

Plate 11: T-S NS 182.69, folio 3v, Palestinian targumic toseftot to Exodus 4:25,26, 12:42; see entry no. [687]

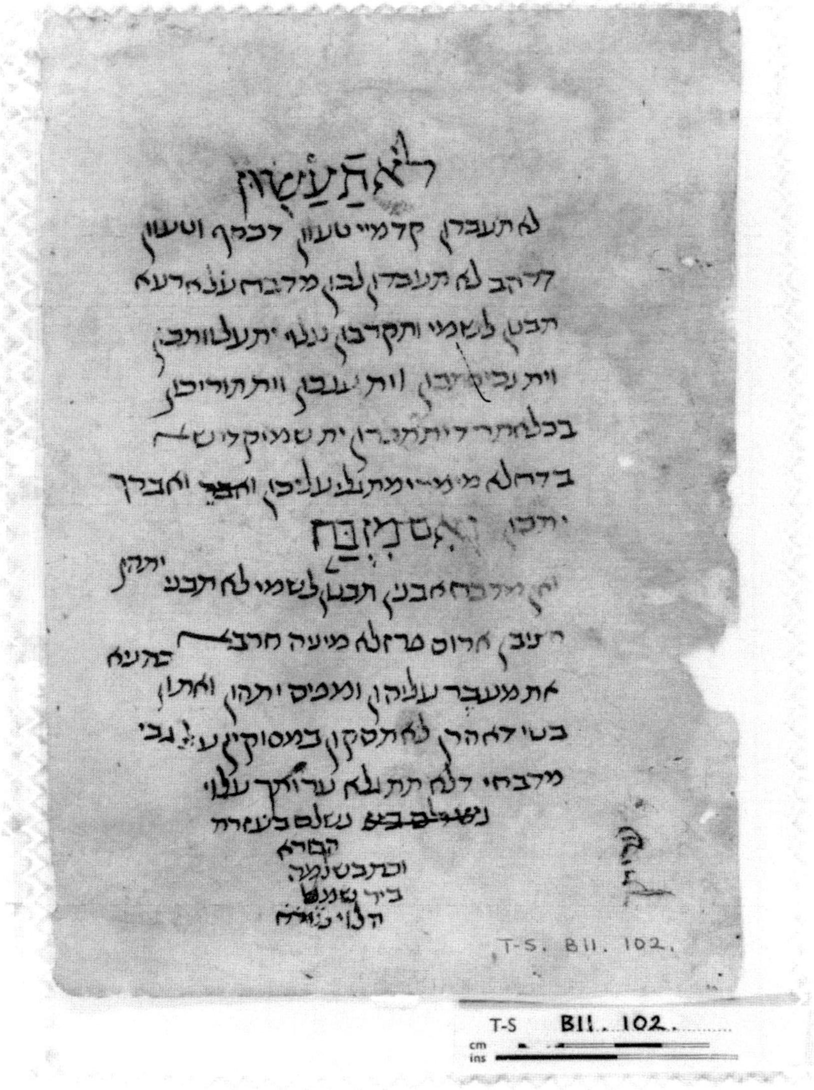

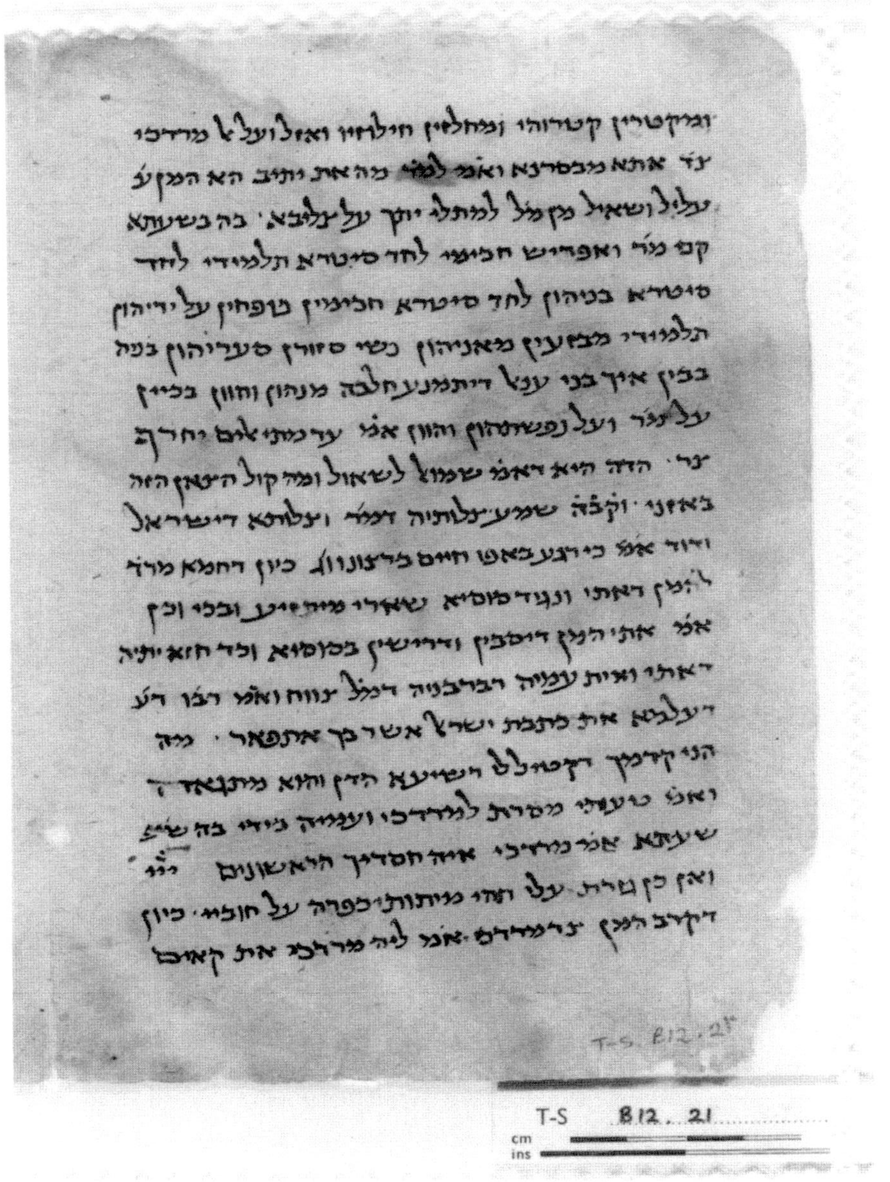

Plate 13: T-S B12.21, folio 2v,
Targum to Esther 6:11;
see entry no. [346]

Plate 12: T-S B11.102 verso,
Palestinian Targum to Exodus 20:20/23–23/26;
see entry no. [307]

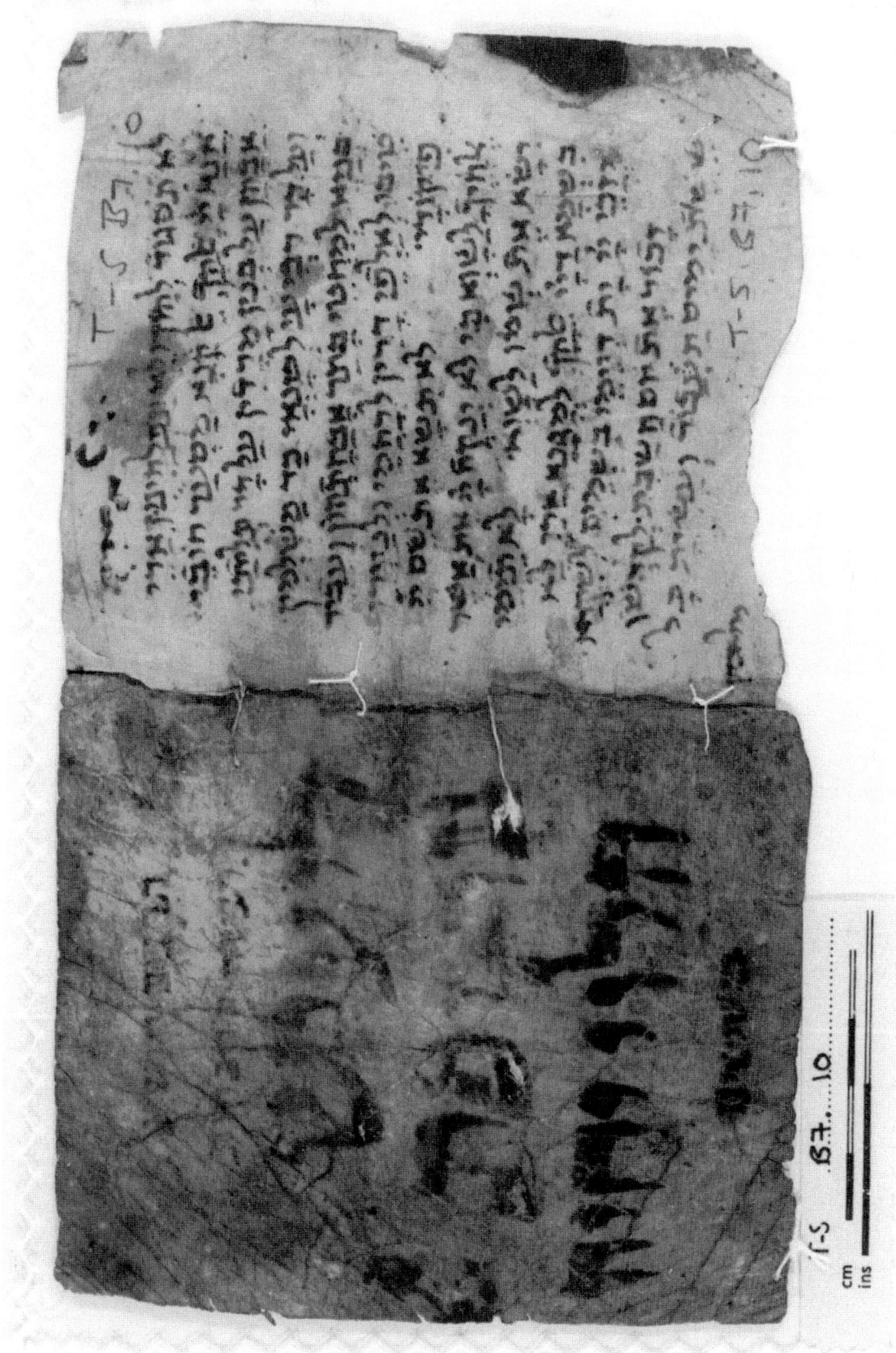

Plate 14: T-S B7.10, folios 1r, 2v, including Onqelos to Exodus 20:5–8; see entry no. [148]

Plate 16: T-S B9.10, folio 2v, Onqelos extract to Exodus 27:7 – 28:7; see entry no. [179]

Plate 15: T-S B2.5 recto, Onqelos extract to Deuteronomy 33:10–19; see entry no. [53]

Plate 18: T-S C7.112 recto,
including Onqelos to Genesis 4:24 – 5:8;
see entry no. [419]

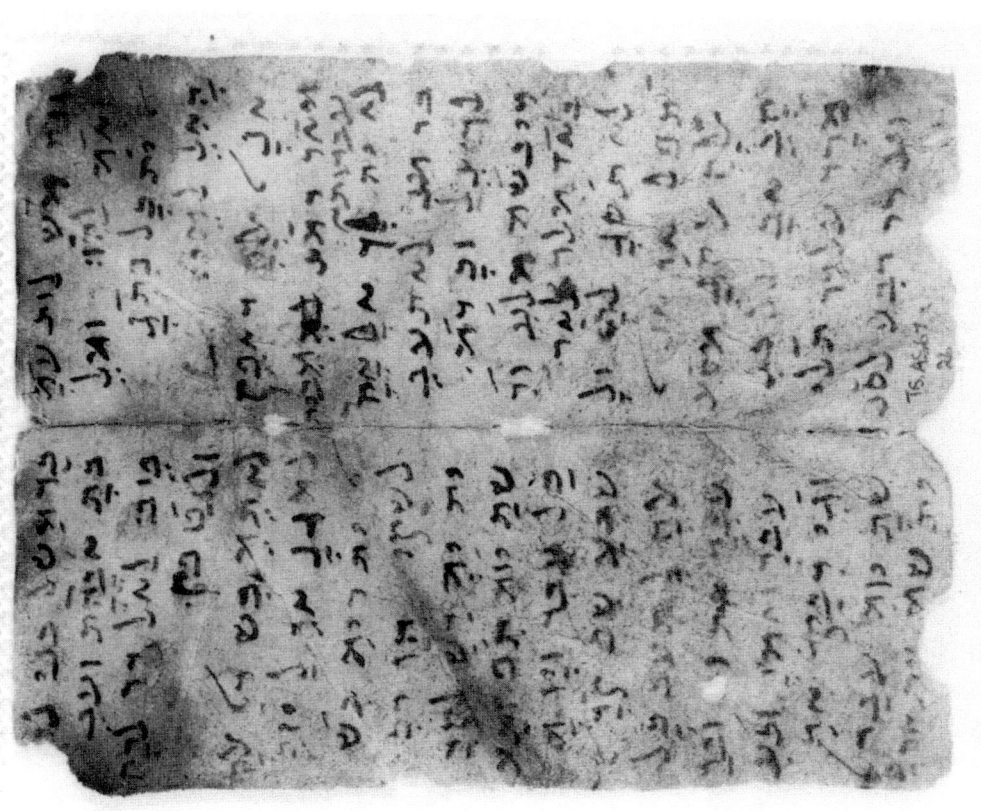

Plate 17: T-S AS 67.26, folios 1v, 2r,
shorthand of Onqelos to Exodus 19:25 – 20:11;
see entry no. [1098]

Plate 19: T-S NS 172.169 verso, including Targum Jonathan to Isaiah 30:18, 1:26 – 2:3, 32:1–5;
see entry no. [661]

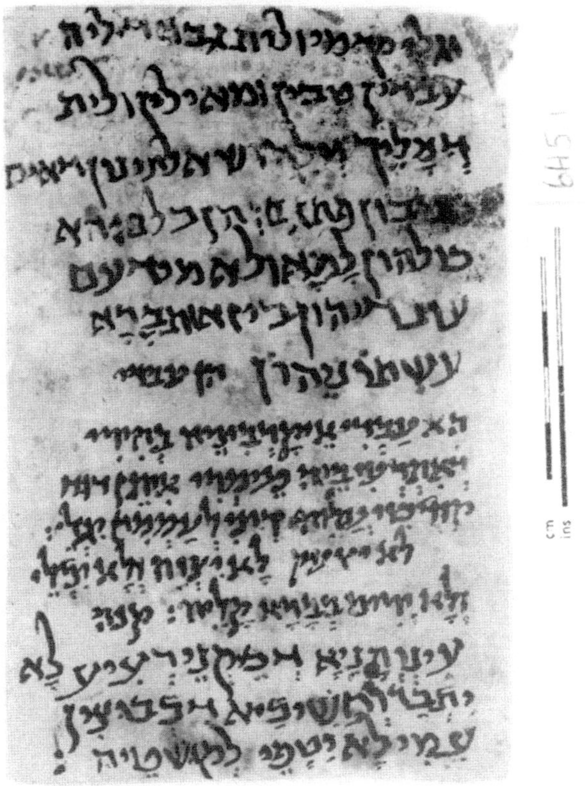

Plate 21: T-S AS 71.64, folio 2v,
Aramaic introductory poem (reshut) to the haftarot;
see entry no. [1376]

Plate 20: T-S 6H5.1, folio 12v,
Targum Jonathan to Isaiah 41:28 – 42:3;
see entry no. [459]

Plate 22: T-S NS 57.1 verso, Targum Jonathan to Isaiah 19:14–18;
see entry no. [573]

Plate 23: T-S C7.132 verso, including Targum Jonathan to Isaiah 24:8–11;
see entry no. [421]

Plate 24: Or.1081 B12.1 verso,
including Targum to Proverbs 17:17 – 18:5;
see entry no. [1556]